Clinical psychology

Psychopathology through the lifespan

Clinical psychology
Psychopathology through the lifespan

Paul Bennett

McGraw Hill Education
Open University Press

Open University Press
McGraw-Hill Education
McGraw-Hill House
Shoppenhangers Road
Maidenhead
Berkshire
England
SL6 2QL

email: enquiries@openup.co.uk
world wide web: www.openup.co.uk

and Two Penn Plaza, New York, NY 10121-2289, USA

First published 2015

Copyright © Paul Bennett, 2015

All rights reserved. Except for the quotation of short passages for the purposes of criticism and review, no part of this publication may be reproduced, stored in a retrieval system, or transmitted, in any form or by any means, electronic, mechanical, photocopying, recording or otherwise, without the prior written permission of the publisher or a licence from the Copyright Licensing Agency Limited. Details of such licences (for reprographic reproduction) may be obtained from the Copyright Licensing Agency Ltd of Saffron House, 6–10 Kirby Street, London, EC1N 8TS.

A catalogue record of this book is available from the British Library

ISBN-13: 978-0-335-24769-1
ISBN-10: 0-335-24769-5
eISBN: 978-0-335-24770-7

Library of Congress Cataloging-in-Publication Data
CIP data applied for

Typeset by Aptara, Inc.

Fictitious names of companies, products, people, characters and/or data that may be used herein (in case studies or in examples) are not intended to represent any real individual, company, product or event.

Praise for this book

"This is a comprehensive, well-structured and highly readable account of the application of biopsychosocial approaches across the lifespan for people with mental health concerns. Its integrative format provides informed explanations of problems, theoretical frameworks and evidence based treatments. It will be of interest to all clinical psychologists and will be very useful for all those considering a career in clinical psychology."

Professor Paul Kennedy, Oxford Institute of Clinical Psychology Training, University of Oxford

"Clinical psychology is probably one of the most frequently taught subjects within UK universities given the overall popularity of the discipline. It is ironic therefore that many of the recommended texts are written by US authors and project a very North American perspective to understanding psychopathology.

This most recent text by Paul Bennett is a refreshing challenge to this orthodoxy. It draws very much on a UK tradition towards understanding mental health and the provision of psychological therapy services. Its strength is that it adopts a life-span approach and contrasts the impact of early influences, childhood experiences and psychosocial factors in adult life on psychopathology. It seeks equipoise between biological and psychological approaches to therapy, and provides a comprehensive overview of psychopathology. As well as contrasting different causative models, it evaluates different treatment approaches and documents different childhood and adult psychological disorders.

I would certainly recommend it as an undergraduate text to support clinical psychology and psychopathology courses. It is comprehensive, balanced and rich in detail."

Graham Turpin, Emeritus Professor of Clinical Psychology, University of Sheffield

"This is an excellent book, comprehensive and well-informed. Its breadth of coverage is remarkable, and it manages to be extremely readable without being in any way superficial. I expect it to be of value not only to undergraduate students and clinical psychology trainees, but also to be a welcome addition to the bookshelves of many professionals. The inclusion in an appendix of a list of DSM criteria is a welcome bonus. It is up-to-date, clearly written, and gives a well-balanced perspective on issues which might be contentious or controversial. I shall be recommending it widely."

R Glynn Owens, Professor of Psychology, University of Auckland

Contents

Introduction to the book — xv

1 Developmental models of mental health — 1
  The psychoanalytic approach — 1
    Sigmund Freud — 1
    Freud and mental health — 4
    Freud analysed — 5
  Attachment theory — 6
  Social mentalities — 8
  Cognitive models — 9
    Schema models — 10
  The humanistic approach — 11
    Carl Rogers — 12
  A neurochemical model — 13
    A trauma model of schizophrenia — 16
  Chapter summary — 17
  Further reading — 19

2 Childhood influences on mental health — 20
  Developing emotions and emotional regulation — 20
  Genetic influences on childhood mental health — 21
  The biopsychosocial model — 22
  Parental and family influences — 23
    Family factors — 23
    Parental or family dynamics — 25
    Child sexual abuse — 26
    Single-parent families — 27
    Family conflict and divorce — 27
  Beyond the family — 29
    Socio-economic factors — 29
    Peer influences — 29
    Risky behaviours — 30
    Looked-after children — 30
  Chapter summary — 31
  Further reading — 32

3 Influences on mental health during adulthood — 33
  Socio-economic status — 33
  Gender — 35

Minority status	36
Ethnicity	36
Sexuality	38
Family dynamics	39
High negative emotional expression	39
Living alone	39
Caring	40
Old age doesn't come alone	41
Social context	41
Cognitive functioning	42
End of life	42
Chapter summary	43
Further reading	44
4 Biological processes and interventions	**45**
The brain	46
The regulation of mood	46
The regulation of planned behaviour	47
Neurons and neurotransmitters	48
The neurotransmitters	49
Serotonin	*49*
Norepinephrine	*49*
Dopamine	*49*
The autonomic nervous system	49
Norepinephrine and epinephrine	*50*
Acetylcholine	*50*
Gamma-aminobutyric acid	*50*
Pharmacotherapy	50
Treating depression	51
Drugs that increase norepinephrine: MAOIs	*51*
Drugs that increase serotonin: tricyclics, SSRIs, and SNRIs	*52*
Treating anxiety	53
Drugs that enhance the action of GABA: benzodiazepines	*53*
Drugs that increase norepinephrine and serotonin: SSRIs and SNRIs	*53*
Treating schizophrenia	53
Drugs that reduce dopamine levels: phenothiazines	*53*
Increasing NMDA activity	*54*
Adherence to drug treatments	54
Medication: a cost-effective treatment?	55
Drugs come with a caveat	56
Neurological treatments	57
Electroconvulsive therapy	57
Transcranial magnetic stimulation	58
Psychosurgery	58
Chapter summary	59
Further reading	60

5 A psychotherapy primer — 61
- Psychoanalysis — 62
  - Psychoanalysis beyond Freud — 63
- Humanistic therapy — 63
- Behaviour therapy — 65
  - Behavioural explanations of anxiety — 65
  - Behaviour therapy for anxiety — 66
- The cognitive shift — 67
  - Cognitive therapy for mood disorders — 67
    - *Changing cognitions* — 68
    - *Changing behaviour* — 69
  - Cognitive behaviour therapy for anxiety disorders — 70
    - *Mindfulness* — 70
- Back to basics? The third wave — 72
  - Acceptance and commitment therapy — 72
- A systems approach — 74
  - Structural family therapy — 74
  - Strategic family therapy — 76
- Applied behaviour analysis — 77
  - Teaching simple behaviours — 77
  - Teaching complex behaviours — 78
  - Discouraging inappropriate behaviours — 78
    - *Functional analysis* — 78
    - *The token economy* — 79
- Chapter summary — 79
- Further reading — 80

6 Behavioural disorders in childhood and adolescence — 81
- A word of warning — 81
- Attention-deficit/hyperactivity disorder — 82
  - Biological explanations — 83
  - Psychosocial explanations — 84
  - Treatment — 85
- Conduct disorder — 86
  - Biological explanations — 87
  - Psychosocial explanations — 88
  - Treatment — 88
- School refusal — 90
  - Psychosocial explanations — 91
  - Treatment — 92
- Eating disorders — 92
  - Anorexia nervosa — 92
  - Bulimia nervosa — 93
  - Biological explanations — 94
  - Psychosocial explanations — 95

Treatment	96
Anorexia	96
Bulimia	97
Chapter summary	99
Further reading	100

7 Life-long problems? — **101**

Autistic spectrum disorder	101
Psychosocial explanations	102
Biological explanations	103
Treatment	104
Personality disorders	105
Borderline personality disorder	106
Psychosocial explanations	107
Biological explanations	108
Treatment	109
Antisocial personality and psychopathy	111
Biological explanations	112
Psychosocial explanations	113
Treatment	113
Chapter summary	115
Further reading	116

8 Anxiety disorders — **117**

Neurological factors	117
A trans-diagnostic model of anxiety	118
Childhood origins of anxiety	119
Treatment consequences	120
Separation anxiety disorder	121
Psychosocial explanations	122
Treatment	122
Specific phobias	122
Biological explanations	123
Psychosocial explanations	123
Treatment	124
Generalized anxiety disorder	125
Biological explanations	125
Psychosocial explanations	126
Treatment	127
Panic disorder	127
Biological explanations	128
Psychosocial explanations	128
Treatment	129
Obsessive-compulsive disorder	129
Biological explanations	131
Psychosocial explanations	131
Treatment	134

Chapter summary 136
Further reading 137

9 Disorders of mood 138
Depression 138
    Biological explanations 139
    Psychological explanations 140
    Psychosocial explanations 141
    Treatment 142
Suicide 145
    Psychosocial explanations 146
    Treatment 147
Bipolar disorder 148
    Biological explanations 148
    Psychosocial explanations 149
    Treatment 149
Seasonal affective disorder 150
    Biological explanations 151
    Treatment 152
Chapter summary 153
Further reading 153

10 Trauma 154
Post-traumatic stress disorder 154
    Biological explanations 155
    Psychosocial explanations 155
        Repeated trauma in children 157
    Treatment 157
Dissociative identity disorder 161
    Psychosocial explanations 162
    Treatment 164
Chapter summary 165
Further reading 165

11 Psychosis 166
Introduction 166
Challenging the diagnosis 167
Psychosocial explanations 168
Explaining hallucinations and delusions 169
    Explaining persecutory delusions 170
Treatment 172
    Antipsychotic medication 172
    Early signs 173
    Family interventions 174
    Cognitive behaviour therapy 174
Chapter summary 177
Further reading 178

12 The problem with pleasure — 179

- Drug use and addiction — 179
- Common pathways to addiction — 180
- Alcohol — 180
    - Biological explanations — 181
    - Psychosocial explanations — 181
    - Treatment — 182
- Cannabis — 183
    - Biological explanations — 184
    - Treatment — 184
- Heroin — 185
    - Biological explanations — 185
    - Psychosocial explanations — 185
    - Treatment — 186
- Gambling disorder — 187
    - Biological explanations — 187
    - Psychosocial explanations — 187
    - Treatment — 188
- Transvestic disorder — 189
    - Psychosocial explanations — 190
    - Treatment — 191
- Gender dysphoria — 191
    - Biological explanations — 192
    - Psychosocial explanations — 192
    - Treatment — 192
- Paedophilic disorder — 193
    - Psychosocial explanations — 195
    - Treatment — 196
- Chapter summary — 197
- Further reading — 199

13 Mind and body — 200

- Somatic symptom disorder — 200
    - Psychosocial explanations — 202
    - Treatment — 203
- Illness anxiety disorder — 205
    - Psychosocial explanations — 205
    - Treatment — 206
- Body dysmorphic disorder — 207
    - Psychosocial explanations — 208
    - Biological explanations — 208
    - Treatment — 208
- Conversion disorder — 209
    - Psychological explanations — 210
    - Biological explanations — 210
    - Treatment — 211

Alzheimer's disease	212
Biological explanations	213
Treatment	214
Caring for the carers	216
Chapter summary	217
Further reading	218
Glossary	219
Appendix: DSM-5 diagnostic criteria	222
References	232
Index	267

Introduction to the book

The basic philosophy of this book

The book adopts a psychosocial-biological perspective, in that it considers risk for many disorders to be a consequence of an interaction between biological, social, and psychological risk factors. For this reason, the first chapters of the book explore this issue in considerable detail.

The chapters in the second part of the book, which consider the various mental health problems separately, usually introduce biological risk factors and processes before psychological and social ones. This does *not* imply primacy of the biological factors.

- Biological risk factors interact with social and psychological factors to determine risk for a range of disorders. The stress-diathesis model is a general statement of this relationship. This suggests an individual's genetic make-up may increase risk for a disorder but does not predetermine it. Unless an individual experiences stressful circumstances, they may never experience the disorder. Both are required. Importantly, also, the model suggests that even if an individual does not have a strong genetic risk for a particular disorder, if they experience sufficiently high levels of relevant social and psychological risk factors, they may nevertheless develop the disorder. The level of risk factors required to trigger a disorder in an individual at low genetic risk may be considerably higher than that required for someone at high risk. But they are not immune from the disorder.
- Biological and psychological models explain the same phenomena, but at a different level. A biological process associated with anxiety, for example, involves two neural networks called the behavioural inhibition system (BIS). Activity of these networks involves differing neurotransmitters. However, activity of the BIS is also explainable in terms of behaviour and underlying cognitive states. All these descriptors are of the same processes, but at different levels, and none is 'more true' or 'better' than the others. They are merely different.
- Finally, psychological processes affect neurological processes, and neurological changes can be evident in psychological measures. Depression, for example, has been associated with low levels of the neurotransmitter serotonin. It would be foolish to imagine that psychological therapies work independently of this neurotransmitter, that somehow people get better following cognitive behaviour therapy while maintaining low levels of serotonin. Effective therapies change levels of serotonin, through different mechanisms to pharmacological therapies, but nevertheless with the same outcome. Similarly, it is possible to track changes in cognitions and other psychological markers of various disorders following the use of pharmacological treatments.

Issues of diagnosis and formulation

A second issue within this book is that of diagnosis. The bible of psychiatric diagnosis is known as the 'Diagnostic and Statistical Manual', now in its fifth edition. This manual is crucial for psychiatrists, as a diagnosis leads to a clear treatment path. Someone with depression is treated with antidepressants, schizophrenia with antipsychotics, and so on. However, the system has a number of unhelpful philosophical implications, including:

- An assumption of a dichotomy between normal and abnormal mental states. An individual either is 'mentally ill' or is not. This dichotomy has become increasingly difficult to sustain. Many 'abnormal' states ascribed to the 'mentally ill' have now been found to occur in many members of the 'normal' population – people who live normal lives and who have never been considered in any way 'abnormal'. Many people, for example, report having heard voices in their head, but are not impaired or troubled by this experience.
- When an individual is ill, they behave or experience mental events that are in some way abnormal and different from those of 'normal' people. Again, this is an argument rejected by the findings of cognitive psychology. There is increasing evidence that while the thought content and behaviour of people with and without mental health problems may differ, the cognitive processes underlying them are essentially the same.

A further issue for those involved in psychological therapies is that a diagnosis provides little useful information to guide the progress of therapy. Knowing someone is diagnosed with schizophrenia or anorexia provides little information of value to a psychotherapist. They need to understand much more about the experience of the individual: what led to their problems, their thoughts, worries, behaviour, and so on. They need a *formulation*: an explanation of how and why the individual is experiencing the problems they are.

Although the content of a formulation will necessarily differ according to the orientation of the therapist, a typical cognitive behavioural formulation would consider:

- The presenting problem(s): what is troubling the individual?
- Predisposing factors: what factors have left them vulnerable to any problems they are experiencing?
- Precipitating factors: why have they developed problems *now*?
- Perpetuating cognitions and consequences: what thoughts are they experiencing and behaviours are they engaged in that are maintaining their problems?

Together, these lead to a formulation of the problem and a treatment plan that would be acceptable to the individual and within the resources available to them.

A formulation is an explanatory hypothesis about the nature of the clinical problem. It has two main functions: to guide the therapist in what to do and to help establish criteria for evaluating the effectiveness of the intervention. Formulations are not static, and may change in the light of information emerging over time, as will the focus and form of any intervention. They are necessarily guided by the theoretical perspective of the therapist, which will focus on the questions asked and the formulation established. These may be quite different for, say, a psychoanalyst and a cognitive behaviour therapist. This is, of course, both a strength and a weakness: a strength because it allows the therapist to select in a relatively parsimonious way from the myriad of potential contributors to a problem those most likely to be relevant; a weakness because these theoretical blinkers may focus the therapist too exclusively on what they consider to be important aspects of a client's experience, and too little on what may actually be important. On this basis, some have argued that good therapists are aware of several aetiological models and can either integrate them into a meaningful synthesis or identify which are relevant to particular clients.

So central is formulation to clinical psychology, and therapy in general, that each chapter in the final part of the book considers a formulation for one of the mental health problems described therein. In addition, it examines in some detail one or more decision points in the process of therapy. By contrast, the book does not provide a list of the diagnostic criteria for each condition, as this adds little to our psychological understanding of them (they are available at the end of the book). Rather, it focuses on trying to understand the experiences of people with various mental health problems, and the biological, social, and psychological processes underpinning them.

A transdiagnostic approach

It has been estimated that the average individual diagnosed with a mental health disorder will have not just one disorder: their symptoms will lead them to be diagnosed with an average of 2.1 disorders. Of course, just like the family with 2.4 children, such an individual cannot actually exist; but the key issue is that many people have co-existing disorders. Of note also is that improvements in one disorder seem to be matched by improvements in others that are not the focus of any intervention. In some ways, therefore, to consider each condition separately may well underestimate the extent of the psychological problems individuals diagnosed with any one disorder are likely to be experiencing. From a more theoretical perspective, it is also important to consider similarities as well as differences between the conditions. Factors common to a range of disorders include:

- *Errors of attention* may maintain a disorder as an individual selectively attends to information that is consistent with their concerns, or fails to attend to information that is inconsistent with their concerns and which would change their understanding of the situation or help them cope better with it.
- *Errors of memory* may occur in the encoding or retrieval stages of memory. We tend to preferentially attend to stimuli pertinent to our survival. As a consequence, people who experience severe life-threatening trauma tend to attend to and remember threatening aspects of the situation. By contrast, a bias in retrieval of memories occurs as a result of 'mood-dependent memory'. We tend to recall memories from the past that are consistent with our present mood. If we are feeling depressed, for example, we are more likely to recall depressive memories, which in turn may exacerbate our mood.
- A number of *reasoning errors* may also result in disorder. These errors include errors of interpretive reasoning (why things happen), expectancy reasoning (what

will happen in the future), and hypothesis testing (attempts to assess the validity or invalidity of worrisome or depressed thoughts).
- *Thought processes* involved in mood disorders include intrusive thoughts, worry, and rumination. The more frequent the negative thoughts, the more impact they are likely to have on mood.
- A number of *behaviours* are also implicated in the initiation and continuation of emotional disorders. Avoidance of feared situations is a consistent factor that maintains long-term anxiety. This may involve behavioural avoidance or cognitive avoidance strategies such as distraction from distressing thoughts. Although this may reduce distress in the short term, in the longer term it maintains anxiety, as the individual fails to habituate to worrying thoughts or learn they are exaggerated fears.

In reading this book, then, while noting that each of the conditions described has its own defining features, it is important to remember they also have many common features, and causal factors whether they be psychological, neurological or genetic.

Finally...

The first chapters in the book deal in detail with a number of factors associated with mental health problems: their childhood origins, how adult stresses can influence risk for emotional problems, and the fundamentals of pharmacological and psychological therapy approaches. Each of the later chapters, which deal with individual types of mental health problems, can be read separately. But these early chapters may both prepare you for issues that will be encountered in the later ones and/or provide a more in-depth review of issues discussed there. So, the book is best read as a sort of interaction between early and later chapters.

Enough! Enjoy!

Paul Bennett

Chapter 1

Developmental models of mental health

This chapter considers why there are clear individual differences in how we respond and the extent to which we experience any stress. Some people are resilient in the face of significant stressors; others struggle to cope with apparently much less stressful circumstances and go on to develop mental health problems. The chapter examines a number of theories that attempt to explain risk for psychopathology through the life course from a number of perspectives, including the psychoanalytic, cognitive, humanistic, and neurological approaches.

By the end of this chapter, you should have an understanding of differing theoretical models of vulnerability to mental health problems. These will consider vulnerability from the following perspectives:

- Psychoanalytic models and attachment theory
- Gilbert's mentalities approach
- Cognitive and behavioural models
- Humanistic approaches
- Neurobiological models

The psychoanalytic approach

Sigmund Freud

This first section considers the theory lying at the heart of psychoanalytic thinking, that of Sigmund Freud. It was developed early in the twentieth century, and while psychoanalytic theory has progressed since that time, psychoanalysts continue to pay respect and to draw linkages to Freudian theory. The Centre for Modern Psychoanalytic Studies of the New York

State, for example, states that: 'Modern psychoanalysis rests upon the theoretical framework and clinical approach of Sigmund Freud' [http://www.cmps.edu; accessed 15 October 2013]. The continuing importance of Freud means this section is not just here for historical interest: it still has resonance in modern psychoanalytic thinking.

Freud may be considered the first modern psychotherapist. He certainly developed the first psychological theory of psychopathology – and it adopted a developmental perspective. His theory explained how childhood factors contribute to the development of mental health problems in adulthood. He identified five stages through which a child matures, and how problems at each stage may block appropriate development and lead to long-term personality disorders (Freud 1922). In addition, he examined how stresses in adulthood may cause the individual to revert to behave in ways associated with previous developmental stages.

Freud considered the adult personality to have three competing elements: the id, ego, and superego, which emerge during different developmental stages. Although these can be considered as metaphors or descriptions of hypothetical constructs, Freud himself considered them to be biological entities within the brain. In order of development, the three elements are:

- *The id*: seeks to gain immediate gratification. It does not know boundaries and self-control. It is driven by what Freud considered to be the basic instincts of sex and aggression, and motivated by the 'pleasure principle'.
- *The ego:* operates under the 'reality principle'. Its goal is still to maximize sexual or aggressive gratification, but it does so by responding to the demands of external influences including the child's mother and father. It learns to conform to their expectations, but does so in order to maximize its own gratification.
- *The superego*: the individual's internal controller of behaviour. The ego internalizes what were initially external constraints on behaviour to become the individual's morals. It controls behaviour by acting as a 'conscience', leading to feelings of guilt if societal norms are violated.

These three elements of personality emerge during five developmental stages:

1. The oral stage

In the oral stage, a child only has the id. Evident between birth and around 18 months, this stage is characterized by the child obtaining gratification through oral manipulation: sucking, licking, placing objects in its mouth, and so on. The child demands immediate attention and is unable to delay gratification. Its response to frustration is to protest until its demands are met. It is selfish, and unable to accommodate to the wishes of others.

2. The anal stage

In this stage, between 18 and 36 months, the child develops its ego as a consequence of learning the relationship between its behaviour and external outcomes: both good and bad. It begins to respond to factors beyond itself. This process is exemplified through the process of toilet training. Through this, the child learns that it can gain approval from other people (primarily the mother) by learning to control when and where it goes to the toilet. The child learns how its actions result in rewards or punishment, and begins to adapt its behaviour accordingly. This awareness generalizes to other responses over time.

3. The phallic stage

In this stage, the superego develops as a result of the child's experiences and resolution of sexual conflict. The process differs for boys and girls, and occurs between the ages of 3 and 5 years.

- *The Oedipal conflict*: Boys in the phallic stage develop a sexual interest in their mother, driven by the id: a process known as the Oedipal complex. While pleasurable, the child believes that this places him in conflict with his father and he would lose any open conflict with him. Indeed, he becomes afraid his father may actually castrate him in order to prevent his rivalry: a phenomenon known as castration anxiety. The boy's way of resolving this conflict between the sexual attraction to his mother and fear of the consequences of conflict with his father is to align himself with his father: to adopt his beliefs and values. Identification with his father allows him to, symbolically, make love to his mother, while at the same time presenting no threat to his father. He also establishes beliefs concerning morals and behaviour based on those of his father: a superego.
- *The Electra complex*: Freud believed that as girls enter the phallic stage they notice they are different from boys in one significant way: they have no penis. As a consequence they feel incomplete and inadequate, and experience 'penis envy'. They also believe that if they were to become their father's lover, they would 'possess' their father's penis; at least for a short time. In addition, if they became pregnant, they may bring a penis into the world if they had a male baby. This places them in a situation analogous to that of a boy, competing with their mother for sexual gratification from their father. And they behave in the same way. By identifying with their mother, and adopting her beliefs and values, they hope to symbolically make love to their father while reducing the threat from their mother. In doing so, they begin to develop their superego.

4. The latency stage

The fourth stage of development is the latency stage, which continues until puberty. During this stage, the individual channels their sexual and aggressive urges through age-appropriate interests and activities such as sports and hobbies.

5. The genital stage

This stage begins in puberty and continues throughout life. During this stage, individuals are driven by two basic motivating forces: sex and aggression. Healthy individuals discharge the energy associated with these instincts through socially appropriate channels: sexual intercourse with age-appropriate adults, career, and so on. If, however, people fail to find such outlets, energy builds until it can no longer be contained and is released in an uncontrolled fashion, guided by unconscious influences and potentially involving behaviours including violence and rape.

As an adult, the id, ego, and superego are in constant competition with each other, largely within our unconscious. They have a common goal to maximize their gains in relation to sexual or aggressive instincts. However, they compete to control how we achieve those goals. The id, which seeks immediate and uncontrolled gratification, may want sexual intercourse regardless of outcome or its effect on others. The ego may seek sexual gratification but be more controlled in its ways of achieving this so it can achieve its sexual goals without societal sanctions. The superego controls our behaviour, by acting as an internal brake to any inappropriate behaviour. The dominance of these elements, and how they control the basic instincts of sexual and aggressive gratification, determines our behaviour. Over-control by any one element may lead to inappropriate behaviour: from rape if the id becomes dominant, to obsessive-compulsive behaviour if the ego becomes too controlling.

Freud and mental health

According to Freud, the adult ego experiences a number of types of anxiety:

- *Ego-based anxiety*: the most basic form of anxiety, rooted in reality, includes fear of 'realistically' negative consequences: break up of a relationship, an accident, and so on.
- *Neurotic anxiety*: arises from an unconscious fear that the libidinal impulses of the id will take control at an inopportune time and result in punishment.
- *Moral anxiety*: results from fear of violating moral or societal codes.

Anxiety is clearly unpleasant, and the ego attempts to reduce it using various types of unconscious defence mechanisms (see Table 1.1). These are intended to prevent the individual being overwhelmed by any distress they would otherwise experience. The most basic

Table 1.1 Some Freudian defence mechanisms

Defence	Definition	Example
Repression	Blocking threatening material from consciousness	An adult unable to recall being abused as a child
Denial	Preventing threatening material from entering consciousness	A parent who cannot accept the death of their child
Projection	Attributing one's own unacceptable impulse or action to another	Someone who denies their homosexuality, and considers homosexuals are constantly making sexual approaches
Displacement	Changing the target of an unacceptable impulse	'Kicking the cat' instead of whoever caused anger or upset
Reaction formation	Expressing the exact opposite of an unacceptable desire	A person who is considering ending a relationship, but continues to show strong affection for their partner
Sublimation	Expressing an unacceptable impulse in a symbolic manner	An individual with a strong drive for unattainable sexual relationships focuses their attention on achievement in their career or sport
Conversion	Expressing painful psychic material through symbolic physiological symptoms	A soldier who finds it unacceptable to shoot others, develops paralysis in his hands
Undoing	A repetitive action that symbolically atones for an unacceptable impulse or behaviour	Repeated washing of hands following an extramarital affair

defence mechanism is 'repression'. Through this process, the individual actively prevents the disturbing issue becoming conscious: keeping the distress within their unconscious. This repression may not always prove successful, and the causes of anxiety may become evident through symbolism within dreams. An example of this can be found in Freud's (1914) interpretation of the dream reported by a rather reserved woman who had indefinitely postponed her wedding ceremony. The dream included images of flowers as table decorations for a party. When asked to freely associate to the elements in her dream, she associated the word violet with violate, a word carrying sexual connotations. Freud interpreted the flowers as symbols of fertility and the birthday as a symbol of an impending birth or pregnancy. Accordingly, her dreams symbolized her desire to become impregnated by her fiancé.

A second type of defence is known as 'displacement'. Here, the cause of anxiety is displaced from its true cause to a less distressing object. Perhaps the most famous example of this can be found in the case of Little Hans, who had a fear of horses. According to Freud, this reflected his castration anxiety. Freud noted that as a consequence of being in the phallic phase, Hans was frightened of his father. Rather than acknowledge this fear, however, Hans displaced his fear onto another strong object: horses became a symbolic representation of his father. A simpler explanation for the cause of his fear – that a horse had nearly trampled him immediately before his symptoms began – was not taken into account.

As well as the ego-based anxieties that may be experienced as an adult, Freud believed that adult mental health problems could arise as a consequence of ego anxieties experienced during childhood. These prevent the individual progressing through all developmental stages: they remain stuck in an immature stage. An individual who experiences difficulties during the phallic stage, for example, may develop problems of gender identity, sexuality or more general anxiety as castration anxiety generalizes to other threatening contexts. Behaviour forms a defence against the anxiety experienced during that stage. Obsessive-compulsive behaviour, for example, results from being fixated in the anal phase, and involves attempts to control a threatening environment. On occasion, individuals may experience difficulties during a certain stage, but still manage to progress to the next. However, if they experience similar difficulties in adulthood, they may regress to a previous stage and begin to behave in ways that reflect its characteristics. The stage to which they regress is influenced by the severity of the stress and the similarity of the current stressor to problems experienced in it.

Freud analysed

Freud broke new ground to develop a complex model of human development. His contribution to the development of theories of personality and psychopathology is without question. Indeed, if we disregard the biological base of psychoanalytic theory, it provides a coherent model of how the individual shifts from the highly internally focused child to one who responds to external conditioning, and eventually develops their own internal monitoring and reward/punishment system. As such, this is compatible with a number of more recent developmental models.

What has proven more difficult to accept has been the notion of the driving forces behind our behaviour – the concept that our behaviour is driven by sexual and death instincts. Even Freud's close follower and one-time adherent, Carl Jung, considered Freud's emphasis on sex as the major motivator of human behaviour to be too simplistic and reductionist. Freud's theory was based largely on his interpretations of the experiences of relatively few middle-class Viennese women, who may or may not have been representative of the wider population of both women and men. Perhaps even more problematic, in the present age where the testability of theories is crucial to their viability, it is almost impossible to assess the accuracy of his conclusions and theory based on these data. Although a number of researchers (e.g. Dollard and Miller 1950) have tried to use experimental studies to assess Freud's theory, they have gained little evidence to either prove or disprove Freud's theories. Because processes such as id drives, ego defences, and so on operate at an unconscious level, they cannot be measured directly, and it is unclear how they may be measured indirectly. In addition, Freud's theory provides few, if any, testable hypotheses. If, for example, a person is considered to be fixated within the anal phase, they may be expected to behave in an 'anal' way: compulsively tidy, and so on. However, if that individual is engaging their defence mechanisms, they could potentially behave in exactly the opposite way: untidy, haphazard, and so forth. Both outcomes are consistent with the theory (at least from a *post hoc* perspective), making hypothesis testing almost impossible.

Attachment theory

The central tenet of psychoanalytic theory, that adult mental health problems are rooted in childhood trauma or disruptions, lies at the heart of John Bowlby's (1969) attachment theory, developed some 60 years after Freud. Bowlby believed that children are biologically pre-programmed to form a strong emotional attachment with one other person and that disruption of this bond during childhood contributes to mental health problems in adulthood. Initially, he believed that this attachment was almost uniquely with the child's mother (a process he called 'monotropy'), although over time he conceded that hierarchies of attachment can develop and may include male caregivers and others.

These attachments do not form in the first 6 months of life. Nevertheless, even at this time, the child engages in behaviours that draw the attention of potential caregivers: smiling, babbling, and so on. By around 6 months of age the child begins to discriminate between familiar and unfamiliar adults, and soon develops clear attachments with one or more caregivers. The child's behaviour is driven by the need to maintain proximity to their caregiver. They protest when they move away, greet them on return, and so on. Paradoxically, the secure proximity of the caregiver allows the infant to explore its surroundings without anxiety. As the child matures, they develop what Bowlby termed an 'internal working model of social relationships'. This enables the child to interpret the behaviour of their attachment figure and to respond in ways that facilitate their attachment. The model matures over time. By the age of 4, the child is no longer uncompromisingly demanding, and has learned to negotiate a relationship with their caregiver. They may no longer be frightened when separated if they are aware the caregiver will return after a certain period of time. By the ages of 7–11 years, attachment shifts from a need for proximity to a need for availability. Relatively long separations may be tolerated as long as the child knows contact can be made should this be necessary. By adolescence, peers may also become attachment figures, although these will not replace the parental attachment role. In adulthood, an individual's interaction with others is guided by memories and expectations based on their internal model, which are used to evaluate the nature of relationships with important others. Adults with experience of strong and consistent attachments are likely to consider others as trustworthy, the self as valuable and as effective in interacting with others. These beliefs may be less strong where an attachment history has been less positive.

According to Bowlby, if attachments are not initiated and maintained within the first two years of life, the child will experience significant long-term psychological problems. If they are disrupted in the subsequent three years, this may also be damaging, although less so. The failure to form an attachment – or its disruption – is known as 'maternal deprivation', and its consequences potentially include delinquency, poor anger control and aggression, depression, and psychopathy. More recently, the notion of a critical period has been considered to be too absolute, and there is now believed to be a 'sensitive period' during which it is highly desirable that selective attachments develop. Its timeframe is broader and the effect less fixed and irreversible than first proposed. Indeed, the long-term impact of poor early attachment may be moderated by subsequent positive relationships and family contexts. Evidence of this protective effect can be found in the outcomes of children from Romanian orphanages who experienced horrific circumstances in their early years with minimal adult contact. After being moved to a more emotionally supportive environment, 70 per cent of these children showed little or no evidence of disordered attachment in adulthood (Pearce and Pezzot-Pearce 2007).

Ainsworth and Bowlby (1991) developed attachment theory further by identifying four attachment patterns that emerge as a consequence of differing caregiver–child interactions:

- *Secure*: Achieved by around 65 per cent of children, this is a consequence of the caregiver responding consistently and appropriately to the child's needs. The young child protests if the caregiver moves away, but is comforted on their return. They may be comforted by a stranger, but prefer their caregiver.
- *Anxious-avoidant*: The child shows little or no distress when the caregiver is away, and is equally comforted by strangers. They feel little attachment, and may be rebellious, have a poor self-image and low self-esteem.
- *Anxious-ambivalent*: The child is highly dependent on the attachment figure. They are preoccupied with the caregiver's availability, seek contact, but once this is achieved they feel angry and resentful. This attachment style occurs as a result of inconsistent, inappropriate, and apparently uncaring caregiver responses to the child's needs.
- *Disorganized/disoriented*: This forms an extreme response often associated with abuse or maltreatment of the child. The child may be frightened, engage in stereotypic behaviour such as freezing or rocking, and show disorientation by approaching a caregiver but with their back turned.

These attachment styles map on to similar patterns in adulthood: secure, anxious-preoccupied, dismissive-avoidant, and fearful-avoidant (Bartholomew and Horowitz 1991). Securely attached adults tend to have high self-esteem, and to have positive views of their partners and other relationships. They achieve both intimacy with their partners, and retain independence within a strong relationship. Anxious-preoccupied individuals are dependent within their adult relationships, seeking intimacy, approval, and high levels of responsiveness from their partners. They worry about their relationships and have lower self-esteem than those who are securely attached. As the name suggests, dismissive-avoidant individuals avoid attachment with others, and consider themselves to be invulnerable to attachment needs. Within any relationship, they tend to deny strong emotional attachments especially when rejected by partners. Finally, fearful-avoidant adults struggle with emotional closeness, both wanting it while at the same time finding it uncomfortable. They have low self-esteem and as a consequence do not trust their partners within any relationship. They tend to suppress their emotions. An early secure attachment appears to have a lasting protective function. The worst prognosis is for children with disorganized attachment. Around 80 per cent of neglected or abused children show this pattern of attachment, and show highly disturbed relationships with others. They have been characterized as alternating between aggression and withdrawal, and have a high rate of psychopathology in adulthood, although no one diagnosis is predicted (Pearce and Pezzot-Pearce 2007).

Social mentalities

A more recent theoretical approach has further developed the importance of attachment. According to Gilbert (2010), our emotional well-being is derived from the interplay of evolutionarily derived competencies or 'mentalities' that shape the relationship between self and others. Gilbert (2010) noted that what he termed 'biosocial goals', such as the desire to form attachments, sexual relationships, or achieve dominance over others, are driven by different systems of 'mentalization'. Each system is a cluster of related processes, or organizing patterns, that include motivations to form certain types of social relationship, direct attention, recruit relevant cognitive processing, and guide emotional and behavioural outputs. Liotti and Gilbert (2011) noted, for example, that the mentality involving a desire to seek status and compete with others may motivate the individual to seek relevant information about potential competitors, make a judgement about whether competing with them would be advantageous, consider an action plan of how to compete with them, and then monitor the success or failure of any plan. Achieving dominance, or seeing them do badly, will result in positive affect. By contrast, a caring mentality system involves motivation to reduce another's distress, focus attention on their distress, and develop strategies by which this can be reduced. We experience sympathy and concern, and 'turn off' aggression.

Gilbert considers a number of mentalities to be central to our sense of self and behaviour. They include:

- *Care-giving*: involves motivation to understand the motives and feelings of the cared-for person (i.e. to empathize with them), make responsive actions to their needs, and experience pleasure at success.
- *Care-eliciting and attachment*: the motivation to seek attachment with early and then later attachment figures, and engaging in behaviours that achieve and sustain this outcome. The ability to identify signs that signal attachment and those that indicate less positive outcomes.
- *Mating*: the sexual motivation and its related behaviours and emotions.
- *Cooperative* mentalities involve developing shared goals and a commitment to their achievement. This may involve complex and prolonged commitment or a simple one-off shared agenda.

- *Competitive* mentalities are triggered by concerns with our social standing, what people think of us, and so on. These concerns drive efforts to work out how to manipulate the impression we make on others. Success in developing appropriate strategies to outsmart others in a struggle for social power or to simply 'look good' increases pleasure and positive affect

The sense of self is derived from the totality of these mentalities. It is a superordinate system incorporating these various mentality systems, and as they change so does the sense of self. The greater the level of coherence across the systems, the more 'robust' the sense of self. In addition, individuals may vary considerably in their mentalization abilities in each system, and deficits in mentalization may occur early and as a consequence of childhood experiences. Hill et al. (2008), for example, found that young children with insecure attachments were less able than those with secure attachments to evaluate the psychological processes underlying the behaviour of a character in a high threat story. This attachment-related deficiency in mentalization may translate into problems in adulthood, and has been associated with a range of disorders, including difficulties in regulation of mood, attention, and self-control typical of people diagnosed with borderline personality disorder. It has also been linked to a wider range of disorders, including **schizophrenia**, eating disorders, obsessive-compulsive disorders, and depression (Fonagy et al. 2011).

The link to attachment theory is obvious in relation to the care eliciting and attachment mentality. But it can also be found in Gilbert's argument that cooperative motives also involve feelings of safeness. In order to collaborate, individuals must feel safe enough to be in the proximity of others, to share, and feel they will not be cheated or exploited. This reciprocity occurs both in childhood and adulthood and requires those involved to have secure attachments. Even more strongly, Hrdy (2009) argued that both attachment and cooperative motives underpin the evolution of mentalization in the human species. She noted that humans are the only primate to share child care to a significant degree. This cooperative, shared caring of infants put an evolutionary pressure on the development of the child's attentional and cognitive abilities to determine strangers' likely response to them. Infants needed to be good at detecting who is likely to be more safe and soothing and who is less so: to develop a strong care-seeking mentality. Gilbert considered a similar evolutionary model and argued that the various mentalities have been developed and refined as a consequence of evolutionary pressures.

Cognitive models

Mentalization involves a range of processes, including motivation, attention, cognitive processing, and emotions. As such, theories of mentalization reflect both past theories, such as attachment theory, and newer theories, including those focusing on the cognitive processing associated with a range of mental health disorders. The most influential of the latter, known as 'schema models', begin their explanation in childhood, and identify common processes underpinning most mental health disorders: irrational or faulty beliefs (schemata) about the world and ourselves within it.

Schema models

Schema models of psychopathology are based on the assumption that our thoughts influence our mood, behaviour, and physiological state. Early models (e.g. Beck 1977) suggested depression and other negative mood states resulted from 'irrational' or 'faulty cognitions'. Beck referred to these thoughts as negative automatic thoughts (NATS). They come to mind automatically as the individual's first response to a situation and are without apparent logic or grounding in reality. Despite this, their very automaticity means they are unchallenged and taken as true. Those associated with depression, for example, include:

- *Absolutistic thinking*: thinking in 'all-or-nothing' terms: 'If I don't succeed in achieving my goals, I am a total failure.'
- *Over-generalization*: drawing a general (negative) conclusion on the basis of a single incident: 'That's it – this always happens to me. I'm always a failure…'
- *Arbitrary inference*: drawing a conclusion without sufficient evidence to support it: 'They don't like me…I could tell from the moment we met…'

Beck called these types of thought 'surface cognitions'. The individual is conscious of them, and able to articulate them if asked. However, he also identified a more complex, unconscious, set of beliefs about ourselves and the world. These are usually inaccessible to the individual and cannot easily be reported by them, although they may be accessed during the process of therapy. These cognitive schemata (singular, schema) drive our accessible thoughts, our interpretations of the world. We can develop a number of schemata about ourselves and our relationships with others. A person with a 'self-blame schema', for example, may blame themself for all the things that 'go wrong' in their life. Schemata that an individual needs someone strong in their life and cannot function well without them may lead to a high dependence on others, and so on.

Reflecting his own psychoanalytic background, Beck believed our cognitive schemata develop in childhood as a consequence of learning experiences within the home and beyond. Negative schemata, for example, may develop as a consequence of experiencing frequent criticism, neglect or conditional positive regard. Some negative schemata, including those associated with episodic disorders such as depression, may not be activated all the time. However, when a vulnerable individual encounters stressful circumstances in adulthood, in particular circumstances that echo previous childhood experiences (e.g. divorce or separation reflecting earlier experiences of parental rejection), their low mood may trigger activation of their underlying negative schemata, and they become depressed.

For others, negative childhood experiences translate into long-term difficulties in adulthood. Beck contended we are all 'hardwired' to a greater or lesser extent to behave in ways that at some point have benefited our species' survival. In our evolutionary history, there have been times when it was advantageous to be particularly fearful of other people or unknown situations, narcissistic, aggressive, and so on. However, these biologically determined traits may no longer be useful, or even actively deleterious. According to Beck, most people have childhood experiences that moderate these behavioural or emotional tendencies and we remain unaffected by them. However, some may have childhood experiences that maintain or even exacerbate unadaptive behaviours. The aggressive child who gains rewards for its aggression or the shy child who is protected from social encounters by its parents, for example, are more likely to continue with their behaviour than if they are challenged in some way. Many of these extreme responses to the environment become so maladaptive they cause the individual significant distress and are frequently labelled as various types of personality disorders.

This is a cognitive theory, thus Beck argued that these behavioural modes are driven by specific schemata about the individual and others around them. Someone who is shy and fearful of others, for example, may believe that they are a bad person, unworthy of love or positive regard. An aggressive individual may believe that it is not a just world, and that the only way to survive is through force or aggression. According to Young and Lindemann (1992), the child and then the adult typically engage in behaviours or cognitive processes that maintain their dysfunctional schemata and behaviour through the life course by a variety of means, including:

- *Schema maintenance*: resisting evidence or information that may disconfirm schema through cognitive distortions and self-defeating behavioural patterns.
- *Avoidance*: avoiding situations that may test or provide information counter to the schema
- *Schema compensation*: over-compensating for a negative schema by acting in the direction opposite to the schema's content

These cognitive models were the first developmental models of mental health problems to receive strong empirical testing, and have generally been supported – although the relationship between childhood schema and subsequent beliefs and actions is yet to be explored longitudinally. However, we know there is a strong reciprocity between mood and cognition: negative cognitions lower mood, and low mood increases the salience of negative cognitions. Depressive thoughts, for example, can be triggered in non-depressed individuals following mood induction techniques in which they read aloud a series of adjectives describing negative mood states. There has been some debate as to whether cognitive distortions contribute to the *initiation* of episodes of depression or simply *maintain* periods of low mood. Beck contended that schemata maintain depression triggered by low mood in response to negative events, but do not trigger the initial low mood. However, work by researchers such as Abela and D'Allesandro (2002) has suggested that activation of negative schemata may also act as a direct trigger to low mood following adverse events.

The humanistic approach

Arising in the late 1950s, the major early figures of the humanistic movement, including Carl Rogers and Abraham Maslow, drew on a number of philosophical influences including existentialism, Buddhism, phenomenology, and psychoanalysis. Their approach had two central tenets:

1. Individuals can provide valid reports of their own experiences, thoughts, motivations, and so on. These subjective understandings of the world drive our behaviour and emotions. Although consistent with modern cognitive models, these views contrasted markedly with the dominant theories at the time: psychoanalysis, which considered behaviour to be driven by unconscious instincts and ego-related process, and behavioural theory (see Chapter 5), which denied the relevance of internal 'events'.

2. The individual has 'free will' and can make behavioural choices independently of past learning history or the unconscious influence of innate drives. Again, this tenet provided a stark contrast to the prevailing psychoanalytic and behavioural theories of the time.

The humanists focused on mental health, the positive, rational aspects of our mental functioning and higher motivations. That said, Rogers also provided a model of mental health problems, and his work is the focus of the rest of this section.

Carl Rogers

Rogers (1961) believed all individuals have an innate need to grow, develop and enhance their abilities in ways they choose – a process known as self-actualization. According to Rogers, this is rarely, if ever, a transcendental, peak, experience. Rather, it occurs when a person's 'ideal self' (who they would like to be) is consistent with their perception of who they actually are. Rogers described the self-actualized person as a 'fully functioning' individual, while also acknowledging that this is frequently a state we work towards but may never actually achieve. In his view, the five characteristics of the fully functioning person were:

- *Open to experience*: they experience and acknowledge both positive and negative emotions.
- *Existentially involved*: they are in touch with different experiences as they occur, avoiding prejudging and preconceptions. They live in and fully appreciate the present, and are not always looking back to the past or forward to the future.
- *Trusting in feelings*: they pay attention and respond to their 'instinctive' responses and trust themselves to make the right decision.
- *Creative*: they freely engage in creative thinking and risk-taking.
- *Fulfilled in their life*: they are happy and satisfied with life, and open to new challenges and experiences

Rogers believed we live in a subjective world of our own creation: the phenomenal field. In many ways, this maps onto reality, but it may also be distorted and inaccurate. Nevertheless, our reaction to events, whether behavioural or emotional, is based on our perception of the world, not an external 'objective' reality: in other language, a cognitive model of understanding the world.

According to Rogers, the perception of our self, 'who we are', is core to our mental health. In fact, Rogers believed we experience two 'selfs': who we believe ourselves to be (the actual self) and who we would like to be (the ideal self). According to Rogers, a process known as the **actualizing tendency** naturally drives us towards the ideal self, and that any discrepancy between our actual and ideal selves that may develop over time has a profound influence on our emotions. When the two are relatively similar (what Rogers termed 'congruent'), we experience positive emotions. When the two are incongruent, we experience sadness and other negative emotions, and the actualizing process is inhibited. The beginnings of incongruence lie in childhood. Rogers believed the way parental love and approval are given can either facilitate or interfere with the process of actualization. Through a process known as conditional positive regard, some parents link their disapproval of bad behaviour with disapproval or negative feelings towards their child ('Your behaviour is bad. I don't love you when you behave this way'). Love and approval are granted only if the child behaves in a way consistent with the parents' values and expectations. As a result, the child begins to adopt the parents' 'conditions of worth', and begins to behave in ways that are valued by them. Over time, the child internalizes the goals of the parents into their ideal self, and work towards achieving them rather than their own goals and aspirations. The child and the subsequent adult they become fail to follow the path towards self-actualization. This separation of the actual and ideal self becomes a cause of distress, depression, anxiety, and other negative emotions – and the greater the separation, the greater the distress.

According to Rogers, three elements of the individual's interactions with others can facilitate their move towards self-actualization:

- *Unconditional positive regard*: the opposite of conditional positive regard – experiencing love and acceptance without having to behave in a way that is favoured by the observer ('I do not approve of your behaviour...but I love you nonetheless').
- *Genuineness*: an environment in which the individual can express their own sense of self with no constraints, rather than playing a role or hiding behind a façade.
- *Empathy*: an environment in which the individual is involved with people who understand their perspective of the world; who share their phenomenal field.

As with psychoanalytic theory, the humanistic approach to personality has been criticized for being difficult to operationalize: how do we know, for example, when an individual is experiencing self-actualization or moving towards it (or, indeed, how close they are to it)? The theory has been criticized for being too individualistic. Roger's belief that we are driven by our biologically determined needs, with no consideration of how these needs may be shaped and influenced by others, does not fit with the more flexible and responsive individuals we now consider ourselves to be. He has also been accused of assuming human growth is always good and not recognizing the 'human capacity for evil'. His belief that children should not be trammelled and have goals and values imposed upon them, has also resulted in a number of experimental educational approaches that have not always proved successful. Conversely, his belief that we create our own view of the world that is subjective and that we benefit emotionally from living in the present (being existentially involved) are central to cognitive theory discussed earlier in the chapter and acceptance and commitment therapy considered in Chapter 5.

A neurochemical model

Most biological models of psychiatric disorders involve a link between neurotransmitter activity or neurological deficits and disordered emotions or behaviour. These models are usually described in 'real time': low levels of serotonin cause depression, and so on. One exception to this rule involves biological explanations for the development of schizophrenia, which adopt a clear developmental model.

To understand the need for such a model, it is necessary to describe some of the symptoms of the disorder and how they develop. There are various ways the symptoms can be described. However, one of the most useful identified three clusters of symptoms, known as disorganized, **positive**, and **negative symptoms**:

- *The disorganized cluster* is characterized by chaotic speech, behaviour and flat or inappropriate mood.
- *Positive symptoms* include **hallucinations** and **delusions**.
- *Negative symptoms* involve an absence of activation: apathy, lack of motivation, or **poverty of speech**.

Symptoms within each cluster appear to co-exist, but do so in the absence of symptoms from the other clusters.

The most successful biological model of these symptoms involves a neurotransmitter called dopamine. The original dopamine hypothesis stated they were a consequence of excess dopamine activity or dopamine receptors at key neuronal synapses being supersensitive to normal amounts of dopamine in key brain systems. The brain systems involved included the limbic system, a brain area known as A10, with links to the thalamus, hippocampus and frontal cortex, and the substantia nigra. Evidence for the model came from a number of domains (Lieberman et al. 1990):

- Amphetamine has been shown to increase dopamine levels and can produce schizophrenic-like symptoms (mostly paranoia) in at least some naïve individuals.
- Some of the most effective drugs for treating schizophrenia, known as **phenothiazines** (see Chapter 4), reduce dopamine activity.
- Post-mortem evidence has shown high levels of dopamine receptor sites in the brains of people with schizophrenia, suggesting a 'supersensitivity' to dopamine (although this may have been a result of long-term medication more than the natural history of the condition).

Importantly, the model was unable to explain how or why any increases in dopamine occurred and why they were not evident to any significant degree in children. It also only provided an explanation of the positive symptoms of schizophrenia. Negative symptoms and disorganized symptoms were unexplained. Thus, the original model provided only a partial explanation of the symptoms of schizophrenia. Subsequent additions, in the extended dopamine hypothesis (Lieberman et al. 1990), however, were able to account for both its developmental process and the emergence of negative and disorganized symptoms.

According to this model, dopamine levels of the young child are generally unexceptional. However, as a consequence of the normal levels of stress associated with adolescence or young adulthood, and possibly heightened social stress as a consequence of their odd and a social behaviour (Pagano et al. 2004), vulnerable individuals may experience excess dopamine release within the relevant neurological systems. As a consequence, they experience a number of the positive symptoms, which may last many years. However, as excessive dopaminergic activity is neurotoxic, this eventually causes degeneration of the dopaminergic neurons, reduces dopamine activity, and allows the emergence of disorganized and negative symptoms.

Evidence for this neuronal degeneration can be found in consistent findings of enlarged cerebral **ventricles** and decreased cortical volume, especially in the temporal and frontal lobes of people diagnosed with schizophrenia (Basso et al. 1998). The various affected brain areas include systems that influence attention, memory and mood (limbic system), planning and coordination (frontal and prefrontal lobe), and acoustic and verbal memory (temporal lobes). Technologies such as **functional magnetic resonance imaging** (fMRI) allow us to examine the relationship between these neural deficits and specific cognitive processes. Bleich-Cohen et al. (2009), for example, found reduced functional processing in the amygdala and prefrontal cortex to be associated with a lack of sensitivity to bizarre facial expressions presented on a computer screen. On a more cautionary note, while the evidence of this neural degeneration is consistent and unequivocal, critics of the model question whether this degeneration is a result of this developmental process, or the outcome of the powerful medication that people diagnosed with schizophrenia take over extended periods of time.

It is now possible to identify factors that contribute to the vulnerability of some individuals to the influence of dopamine. Exploration of the genetic basis of the disorder now largely involves examination of the genome of individuals with and without the disorder. But before this approach, studies had a simpler goal: to identify the relative risk for the disorder among family members of an affected individual. Unfortunately, this apparently simple goal often proved elusive, difficult, and dogged with methodological and interpretive problems. One early study (Kety 1988), for example, compared rates of schizophrenia among the biological relatives of 34 adopted children who later developed schizophrenia and 34 control cases with no evidence of schizophrenia. They found no differences in the number of relatives in either group with a confirmed diagnosis of schizophrenia, but did find differences when they included diagnoses of 'borderline state', 'inadequate personality', and 'uncertain schizophrenia' (and one subsequent diagnosis of bipolar disorder). Using these diagnoses, they found nine affected relatives in the families of the cases and two among the controls. Controversy raged at the time in response to these findings. Advocates of a strong genetic basis for schizophrenia argued the diagnoses were valid and represented a spectrum of schizophrenia-like disorders, each associated with a common underlying genetic disorder. Others contended that expressing a range of disorders was a desperate, and inappropriate, attempt to find a common genetic basis that was not really there.

More recent studies have resulted in less challengeable and more interesting findings. Tienari et al. (2000), for example, found risk for schizophrenia to be four times higher among the children of women diagnosed as having schizophrenia than among the children of the comparison mothers: a total **incidence** of 8.1 per cent versus 2.3 per cent. These data suggest a genetic route to schizophrenia but that other factors are clearly involved. Using data from the same study, Wahlberg et al. (2000) reported an interaction between genetic and environmental factors. Children of women diagnosed with schizophrenia who lived in households with good communication between the family members were not at increased risk of schizophrenia; rates in households with poor communication deviance were significantly raised. That is, the development of schizophrenia seemed to depend on both genetic risk and communication deviance within the adoptive family.

Finding the genes involved has also proved elusive, so much so that as recently as 2008, Sanders et al. expressed their frustration in the title of their paper: 'No significant association of 14 candidate genes with schizophrenia in a large European ancestry sample.' Since then, a number of candidate genes conferring risk for schizophrenia have emerged, including the ERBB4 gene, responsible for dopamine regulation, and the 5-HTR2A gene, which is involved in serotonin regulation. However, the gene that has received most attention is the DISC1 (Disrupted in Schizophrenia 1) gene. Originally linked to schizophrenia in a Scottish family (Millar et al. 2000), **alleles** of the DISC 1 gene appear to influence neural growth and proliferation, and a number of processes including mitochondrial transport and cell-to-cell adhesion. They are expressed in brain regions known to be involved in schizophrenia, including the cerebral cortex and hippocampus, and are involved in neural development and brain maturation. They are highly expressed during critical periods of brain development, particularly in the prenatal period and the onset of puberty, although they are active throughout life. Although their mechanism is not fully understood, it appears that when some gene alleles fail to work effectively, maturation of the brain, and key areas relevant to schizophrenia are disrupted. Variants of the DISC1 gene have been linked to reduced grey matter density and volume, abnormal hippocampal structure/function, and impaired memory (see Weiner and Lubow 2010).

A second set of risk factors involves insult to the developing foetus. One route through which this may occur involves maternal viral infection. Brown et al. (2004) found maternal exposure to the flu virus during the first trimester of pregnancy was associated with a sevenfold increase in risk of a child subsequently being diagnosed with schizophrenia. Other viruses associated with increased risk of schizophrenia include rubella and herpes simplex. Stress during pregnancy may also increase risk, evident among children of mothers who have experienced a family death while pregnant (Khashan et al. 2008), or more extended stressors such as occupation during the Second World War and the Israeli Six-Day War (e.g. Malaspina et al. 2008). The factor common to all these processes appears to involve immune function activation. An excess of **pro-inflammatory cytokines** associated with inflammation can result in brain cell abnormalities associated with schizophrenia, and (in animal studies) a wide spectrum of behavioural abnormalities including impaired social interaction, increased (and occasionally decreased) anxiety, and increased impulsivity (Watanabe et al. 2010). These abnormalities may be a result of impaired neural development similar to that associated with the DISC1 gene.

A trauma model of schizophrenia

The model outlined above suggests that children have an innate risk for developing schizophrenia as a consequence of genetic or early-life, but essentially normal, mediated abnormalities of dopamine function. Trauma models also consider schizophrenia to be a consequence of the dysregulation of dopamine in adulthood. However, they suggest that this dysregulation is a consequence of childhood traumas such as sexual abuse or neglect. Read et al. (2014) drew on both observational and biochemical studies to support this contention. The first line of evidence they consider is the strong association between childhood abuse, either physical or sexual, and a number of disorders of adulthood, including schizophrenia. The prevalence of childhood sexual abuse among women and men diagnosed with schizophrenia or similar disorders lies between 22 and 46 per cent and between 22 and 39 per cent respectively: both rates are roughly double those in the wider population. The trauma is also likely to have begun at a relatively early age. Children diagnosed as schizophrenic are more likely to have experienced parental hostility, to have run away from home, and to have been placed in children's homes (e.g. Rodnick et al. 1984). Men who experienced parental abstinence and institutionalization during childhood are at higher than average risk of experiencing a range of symptoms, including thought disorder, hallucinations, and delusions (Walker et al. 1981).

There is also evidence of dopamine dysregulation both in children and adults who experienced childhood trauma. Functional MRI, for example, has identified relatively high levels of dopamine activity in adults exposed to significant chronic stress as a child (Pruessner et al. 2004). In addition, the degree of damage to areas of adult brains, including to the hippocampus and prefrontal cortex, associated with excess dopamine activity appears to be related to the occurrence and severity of childhood sexual abuse (Sheffield et al. 2013).

Less traumatic family interactions have also been implicated in risk for schizophrenia. An early psychoanalytic theory suggested that schizophrenia is a consequence of being raised by an apparently warm and engaging mother, who in reality is cold, domineering, and self-centred: the schizophrenogenic mother. According to Fromm-Reichman (1948), these confusing signals make the child's world difficult to interpret, and lead to similarly chaotic or confusing behaviour and cognitions. In their double-bind model, Bateson et al. (1956) proposed a similar process. They believed that parents often respond to their children in contradictory ways: they may say one thing, but their behaviour betrays a different set of beliefs – telling the child they are loved in a dismissive and cold manner, and so on. They may also place contradictory demands on the child: 'Go and play with your friends; I miss you when you are not around.' These contradictory demands confuse the child, and eventually trigger schizophrenia. There is little or no evidence in favour of either theory.

Current affairs

The models described in this chapter have a somewhat exclusive focus. They provide a psychological model or a biological model. They do not provide a psychobiological model. But how useful is this absolute dichotomy? There are some advantages to these models: or else they would not exist. But do they also have significant disadvantages? Is it important to understand the nature of the stress that may trigger neurological changes in young people at risk of schizophrenia? Can we benefit from understanding the biological impact of experiencing abuse as a child? Are we too cautious and constrained in our theories of psychopathology, or does the focus on one aspect of a disorder have strength and utility that would be lost in more complex and multi-modal theories?

Chapter summary

1. Freud considered the human psyche to be composed of three biological systems: the ego, superego, and id.
2. These emerge at different developmental stages. The id is present in the oral stage, the ego emerges during the anal stage, and the superego during the phallic stage.
3. Freud identified three types of anxiety: ego-based, neurotic, and moral. The ego defends itself against these anxieties through unconscious defence mechanisms, including repression, projection, and displacement.

4. A second cause of mental health problems involves the individual becoming 'stuck' in an early developmental stage or regressing to it as a consequence of the experience of some degree of trauma.
5. Bowlby considered poor attachment as a child to be a risk factor for later psychopathology.
6. Attachment begins after 6 months, requiring complete and immediate access to a caregiver. Over time, attachment needs shift from one of proximity to availability.
7. Although Bowlby initially considered the mother to be the attachment figure (monotropy), he later acknowledged that others could also fulfil this role.
8. Ainsworth subsequently identified four attachment patterns found among children: secure, anxious-avoidant, anxious-ambivalent, and disorganized/disoriented.
9. Negative attachment patterns can lead to difficulties in attachment and distinctive attachment styles in adulthood: anxious-preoccupied, dismissive-avoidant, and fearful-avoidant.
10. Early life experiences may also be involved in establishing mentalization systems that govern our key responses to environmental events as adults.
11. Gilbert argued our responses to the world and our sense of self are linked to mentalities (clusters of characteristics including motivation, attentional processes, cognitive processing, and behaviour).
12. Beck believed our emotions are governed by surface cognitions and underlying schemata.
13. Schemata are established during childhood and negative schemata may influence emotions and behaviour consistently in personality disorders or intermittently in episodic conditions such as depression.
14. Schemata are maintained in the long term by processes that include schema maintenance, avoidance, and schema compensation.
15. Rogers believed all individuals view the world through their own phenomenological framework, and the individual has free will to make behavioural choices.
16. The healthy individual is one who has achieved or is progressing towards self-actualization.
17. This movement is facilitated by unconditional positive regard and a social environment in which the individual can express their own sense of self and is with others who can understand their view of the world.
18. Self-actualization is blocked by the experience of conditional positive regard.
19. Biological theories of schizophrenia assume dopamine to be the key neurotransmitter associated with the disorder.
20. The extended dopamine hypothesis explains why high levels of dopamine contribute to the positive symptoms of schizophrenia in the early stages of the disorder, while neuronal damage explains the subsequent development of negative or disorganized symptoms.
21. These processes may occur as a response to early-life trauma.

Further reading

Beck, A. (1997) Cognitive therapy: reflections, in J. Zeig (ed.) *The Evolution of Psychotherapy: The third conference*. New York: Brunner/Mazel.

Gilbert, P. (2009) *The Compassionate Mind*. London: Constable.

Howes, O.D. and Kapur, S. (2009) The dopamine hypothesis of schizophrenia: version III – the final common pathway, *Schizophrenia Bulletin*, 35: 549–62.

Rogers, C. (1980) *A Way of Being*. Chicago, IL: Mariner Books.

Storr, A. (2001) *Freud: A very short introduction*. Oxford: Oxford Paperbacks.

Chapter 2

Childhood influences on mental health

Risk for mental health problems both as a child and adult is significantly influenced by experiences during childhood, and even experiences that occur before we are born. This chapter provides an introduction to these factors. It examines how the developing child may be more or less vulnerable to emotional and behavioural problems, before considering how external factors, including family, peers, social and economic factors, may also exert an influence.

By the end of this introductory chapter, you will have an understanding of:

- The development of childhood emotional regulation
- Pre-natal influences on child and adult mental health
- The influence of parents and the family
- The impact of social and economic factors

Developing emotions and emotional regulation

Children's experiences of emotions and their ability to regulate them develop over time. Young babies appear to experience core emotions including happiness, sadness, and anger in immediate response to events. By the age of 6–10 weeks, they show pleasure through smiling in response to social interactions. Around the ages of 8–12 months, they begin to show emotional reactions to expected events, including perceived threats. They show distress when separated from people with whom they are attached, and respond with anxiety or distress when approached by strangers. By this time, they evidence a wider range of emotions, including anger, sadness, enjoyment, fear, interest, and surprise. By the age of 24 months, additional emotions including guilt, shame, embarrassment, and pride become evident.

As the child develops these emotions, they also develop rudimentary strategies for regulating any negative emotions they may experience. In the first 6 months of life, emotional regulation involves looking away from the source of emotional arousal. Over the next 6 months, the child learns to self-sooth, through the use of simple strategies such as hair twirling, thumb sucking or rocking. Parents play a significant role through the use of distraction or soothing. By the age of 2 years, these strategies have been augmented or replaced by the use of transitional objects (soft toys, comfort blankets, and so on) and the use of physical avoidance starts to emerge.

By the age of 2–3 years, the child is able to express emotions and experience their regulation through the use of make-believe play, and they begin to talk about their feelings and discuss ways to resolve difficult emotions. They may also make direct attempts to avoid challenging or threatening circumstances, sometimes involving physical acts such as covering their eyes or ears. They are able to switch their thoughts away from troubling sources of distress. From around the age of 5 years, the child is able to reflect on their emotional experiences and verbalize issues that are distressing them. They show conscious awareness and planning in emotional regulation and are beginning to be able to influence emotions in others in order to reduce their impact on the child: calming a friend to reduce their anger, and so on.

The level of 'emotional competence' held by developing children is a function of a range of factors, including biological influences and the environment in which the child is raised. This includes both the immediate environment of the family and the wider environment of school, peers, and the social and economic context in which the two are situated. Children have different temperaments. Some are calmer or more emotionally labile than others. Children who are brought up in families high in conflict may witness poor emotional control and as a consequence never learn to manage their emotions or be encouraged to do so. Poverty and economic disadvantage may impact on family dynamics as well as peer behaviour and its influences. Highly adverse circumstances significantly increase risk for so-called externalizing conditions such as antisocial behaviour. Nevertheless, risk for a range of emotional problems is a consequence of an interaction between the child's temperament and the social circumstances in which they are raised.

The root of these emotional and behavioural disorders appears to be very similar to those in adults. Bishop et al. (2004), for example, concluded that both childhood and adolescent emotional disorders are characterized by cognitive biases very similar to those found in adult disorders. They found that depressive symptoms, for example, were associated with attending to and remembering negative memories and emotional content in social interactions. Depressed young people are also less likely to use effective strategies such as problem-solving and positive reappraisal or to have confidence in their ability to manage their negative emotions as others (Garnefski et al. 2007).

Genetic influences on childhood mental health

Even before we are born, we are subject to a variety of factors that influence our risk of developing mental health problems. Some may be evident at birth; some will develop over time. Perhaps the most obvious candidate for this type of influence is our genetic inheritance. Some developmental disorders are evident from an early age and may be strongly influenced by pre-natal factors. A number of syndromes associated with learning difficulties, for example, have a clear genetic origin.

Fragile X syndrome is the most common inherited cause of learning difficulties, affecting approximately 1 in 1000 male and 1 in 2500 female births. Its impact on intellect varies considerably. Some children may have profound learning disabilities, whereas others will have normal intelligence. It is also associated with high levels of social anxiety, poor attention span, and hyperactivity. Perseveration is common: the child may repeat the same behaviour, including stereotypical behaviours such as hand flapping, time and time again. They may be hypersensitive to a variety of sensory stimuli, and find even the different textures of materials to be irritating. The condition is thought to result from abnormal brain cell development, impaired plasticity, and dysregulation of a neurotransmitter called glutamate as well as the dopamine pathways – both of which may impact on learning and mood.

The syndrome is caused by a defect within the FMR-1 (Fragile X Mental Retardation) gene located on the X chromosome. In Fragile X syndrome, a small region of the gene undergoes repeated, unnecessary duplications of a number of amino acids that result in a 'longer' gene sequence. When the number of repeats is small (fewer than 200), the individual may have no signs of the disorder. Where there are a larger number of repeats, the learning difficulties associated with Fragile X syndrome are observed. Because of the X-linkage, the frequency of the syndrome is greater in males than in females. This is because females typically have two X chromosomes, and males have one X and one Y chromosome. A female who inherits a chromosome carrying the Fragile X gene from either parent is likely to inherit a normal X chromosome from the other parent, which masks the presence of the Fragile X gene. However, she may carry the gene and be capable of passing it on to her children. By contrast, because a male has only one X chromosome, if he inherits an affected X chromosome, he will inevitably inherit the condition.

A second common condition, Down syndrome, involves genetic processes, but is not inherited. Rather, it is a consequence of disruptions in cell division in the growing foetus, resulting in it having three chromosome-21s instead of the normal two. For this reason, it is often called trisomy-21. As this process may result from ageing of the female egg cells (oocytes), the risk of having a child with Down syndrome increases with the age of the mother. One in 1250 births of women aged 25 will result in the birth of a child with Down syndrome; by the age of 40, however, the chances are 1 in 106 births. People affected by Down syndrome are short and stocky in stature, and have characteristic facial characteristics, including upward-slanting eyes, sparse, fine straight hair, and a large furrowed tongue that protrudes as the result of a small mouth. They may also have a number of other less obvious characteristics, including serious heart malformations. All people with this condition have some degree of learning difficulty. Autopsy reveals brain tissue very similar to that found in Alzheimer's disease.

The biopsychosocial model

Risk for Down and Fragile X syndromes is entirely determined by genetic factors. Risk for many other mental health problems is also influenced by genetic and pre-natal factors. Risk for schizophrenia, for example, appears to be mediated by alleles of the DISC1, ERBB4, and 5-HTR2A genes. However, it is important to frame this concept carefully. Genes influence *risk* for mental health problems, but the expression of this risk is influenced by environmental factors, as has already been identified in the context of schizophrenia. This biopsychosocial approach is premised on the belief that what determines whether each of us will develop any mental health disorder is a function of our genetic inheritance *and* the experiences we have through the life course. Individuals at high genetic risk for a particular disorder may develop it after experiencing relatively small amounts of stress. Those at low genetic risk may only succumb after significant stress. However, *both* genetics *and* stress (as a consequence of life events, the social or economic situation in which the person lives, and so on) contribute to the final expression of the disorder. The next section of the chapter focuses on the second half of this equation, considering some of the most important childhood psychosocial influences that impact on well-being and mental health.

Parental and family influences

One of the most obvious psychosocial influences on children's mental health is the family in which they live. This may impact on both concurrent mental health and their well-being as an adult.

Family factors

Challenging family environments are not only associated with childhood mental health problems, they also contribute to risk for longer-term problems. Adversity at this time can include both active adversity such as sexual or physical assault, or more passive adversity including neglect, parental mental health problems, parental separation, or living with drug-addicted parents. Both types appear to impact negatively on the child.

In the short term, Schilling et al. (2007) found that childhood adversity increased risk for depression and drug use equally for girls and boys. Boys who experienced difficult parental relationships were more likely to engage in antisocial behaviour, while girls were more likely to experience sexual abuse or assault and to experience significant negative emotional responses to it. Similarly, Henry et al. (2001) found that lack of emotional closeness within the family and poor parenting at the age of 12 years was predictive of both violence and delinquency at the age of 17 years.

These and similar findings clearly show the impact of the family on children's mental health is important. However, its effects appear to be less significant than one might expect. In a **meta-analysis** of more than 150 published and unpublished manuscripts, Hoeve et al. (2009) concluded that parent factors accounted for only 11 per cent of the variance in childhood delinquent behaviour. High levels of rejection and hostility towards the child were especially predictive. High levels of parental control were also associated with delinquency, although this may well have been a response rather than a cause. In a similar meta-analysis, McLeod et al. (2007) concluded that parenting accounted for less than 6 per cent of the variance in what they termed child externalizing problems (such as aggression, delinquency, and hyperactivity) and less than 4 per cent of the variance in childhood anxiety. Parental factors accounted for 8 per cent of the variance in child depression, with depression linked to parental hostility and parental rejection more than parental control.

While the impact of adverse parental relationships may be modest, it is long lasting. Data from a Finnish study of over 4000 adults (Pirkola et al. 2005), for example, found that 60 per cent of adults aged between 30 and 64 years retrospectively reported at least one childhood adversity, including maternal problems with alcohol, paternal mental health problems, family discord or being bullied at school. Of those who reported such experiences, 17 per cent had been given a psychiatric diagnosis while an adult. This compared to 10 per cent of those who did not experience such adversity. Men whose father experienced mental health problems were over four times more likely to develop depression than those without this experience. Women whose mother experienced mental health problems were three times more likely to develop depression.

These findings are not isolated. In a study involving 34,000 community-dwelling adults, Harrington et al. (2011) found childhood adversity was consistently associated with alcohol and drug problems. There is evidence from Bangkok that family violence experienced as a child increases risk for illicit drug use, problem drinking, and **suicidal ideation** (Jirapramukpitak et al. 2011). Finally, a Dutch study by Spinhoven et al. (2010) teased out the relative effects of childhood and adulthood factors, concluding that childhood adversity was a stronger contributor to risk of anxiety or depression than negative life events occurring in adulthood.

The mechanism through which early adversity influences subsequent mental health is complex, and may extend over considerable time. Difficulties associated with poor or neglectful parenting, for example, may result in association with deviant peers, poor school attendance, and poor academic performance, all of which may combine to maintain risk of longer-term behavioural problems and a diagnosis of antisocial personality disorder (Farrington 2000). In other contexts, even if a child shows no evidence of mental health problems at the time of family stress, this may result in sensitivity to stressors, which can trigger later episodes of disorder should these be re-encountered in adulthood.

In a test of this 'sensitivity hypothesis', McLaughlin et al. (2010) used data from a large population cohort to explore how early life experiences and subsequent negative life experiences combined to influence risk for disorder. They found the more adverse childhood circumstances an individual experienced, the more likely they were to experience later problems. In addition, they found that among people who had experienced significant stressors in the year prior to the survey, those who had also experienced early adversity were almost twice as likely to develop a mental health disorder, including depression, post-traumatic stress, and anxiety disorders. This sensitivity to adult stresses may be influenced by long-term beliefs about the self. Swannell et al. (2012), for example, found incidents of **self-harm** among both men and women were associated with previous neglect or physical abuse, and partly driven by beliefs of self-blame. Similarly, Glassman et al. (2007) found the relationships between early adversity and low mood were mediated by self-criticism. Accordingly, it seems that one mechanism through which childhood adversity may influence later psychopathology is through the establishment of negative self-schemas that form an enduring risk for a number of negative mood states. Finally, difficulties as a child may prevent the development of personal skills that could mitigate against later difficulties.

This section has addressed a number of familial risk factors for mental health problems. By default, therefore, one may assume that the absence of any risk factors will result in positive mental health outcomes. This seems a reasonable conclusion, but there have also been studies of factors that actively promote positive mental health in young people. The (British)

Children's Society (2013), for example, conducted interviews with children and young people of all ages to identify factors associated with positive health. Their top ten factors were: family, friends, health, appearance, time use, future, home, money and possessions, school, and choice. In more detail, the top three factors were:

- *Choice and autonomy*: having a loving and supporting family that supported a 'reasonable level' of choice or autonomy. Having friends and peers that support choice in terms of appearance and self-expression.
- *Family harmony and parental support*: although these factors are associated with the degree of choice and autonomy given to the interviewees, these factors were also an independent factor associated with well-being.
- *Money and possessions*: having money and cherished possessions were protective. By contrast, direct experience of deprivation was more strongly related to well-being than household indicators of poverty. Some parents would protect children from at least some individual impacts of poverty.

Parental or family dynamics

One very specific mechanism through which adults may influence children is by teaching them appropriate or inappropriate ways of responding to stress or thinking about the world. One simple example of this process involves the inter-generational transmission of specific phobias: many young children learn to be frightened of the same things as their phobic parents (or siblings). A more complex process can be observed in the way adults teach children to regulate their emotional state. In the first few years of life, caregivers unconsciously engage with, or disengage from, infants' attention in order to alter their arousal levels. During any social interaction, too much attention may result in excess arousal and distress, too little may result in a lack of social engagement. Appropriate parenting involves being sensitive to children's levels of arousal in any interaction and either attending to or disengaging from the child in order to provide the optimal level of attention. This cyclical process of attention engagement and disengagement is one way through which infants learn how to regulate their own emotions and behaviour, and inappropriate levels of attention can result in anxiety problems. Disruption of this learning process may result in both short- and longer-term difficulties in emotional regulation.

As the child gets older, other factors may contribute to emotional disorders. Authoritarian, intrusive, over-protective or controlling parenting, for example, increases risk for anxiety disorders both in children and the adults they become (e.g. Varela et al. 2009). By contrast, parental acceptance, warmth, sensitivity, and responsiveness are associated with lower levels of anxiety (Hane et al. 2008). Walsh (1998) identified three sets of factors that promote parental or family resilience and which promote good mental health: (1) a family orientation of making meaning out of adversity, maintaining a positive outlook on life, and have 'transcendent' or spiritual beliefs; (2) being organized in ways that are flexible, connected, and able to use support from extended family or community resources; and (3) having communications with others that are generally clear, consistent, and truthful.

There may be multiple pathways to child anxiety, including parental modelling of anxious responses to events and reinforcement of the child's own anxieties and the development of insecure attachments. Low levels of responsiveness, and modelling of high levels of anxiety and modelling inappropriate coping strategies are particularly prevalent among parents who are anxious themselves, and may contribute to the high levels of psychological disorders among their children. In a similarly subtle process, Craig et al. (2004) demonstrated the way in which parents may create health-related anxiety. They observed women playing with their 4- to 8-year-old children in a structured play setting and found that mothers with health anxiety gave their children less attention than other mothers during normal play. However, they were more responsive to their child when they played with a medical box.

Complex family dynamics have also been explored in the context of anorexia. Girls who experience this problem are likely to come from families with high levels of negative affect and discord and have mothers who are perfectionists (Woodside et al. 2002). Successful dieting may be one way of gaining acceptance from parents with high aspirations, particularly where the child has not 'succeeded' in other life domains. Not eating may make an individual important within the family, and give them some degree of control over other family members ('I'll eat if you…'). It may also provide a means of punishing them ('I'm not eating because you…'). A second consequence of anorexia is that it can lead the individual to be treated as a child, and allow them to avoid the responsibilities they would otherwise have to face; again, this may be most influential in families where there is a high emphasis on achievement.

Some family therapists have developed an even more complex model of family dynamics in anorexia. Here, the person with anorexia is viewed as a symptom of a dysfunctional family rather than an individual with problems in the absence of context. Minuchin et al. (1978) defined the characteristics of 'anorexic families' as being enmeshed, over-protective, rigid, and conflict-avoidant. That is, there is conflict between parents that is controlled and hidden. According to Minuchin et al., adolescence is a stressful time for such families, as the adolescent's push for their independence within the family increases the risk of the parental conflict being exposed. The development of anorexia prevents total dissension within the family, and may even hold it together as the family unites around the 'identified patient'. The presentation of the young person as weak and in need of family support ensures that they become the focus of family attention, which is deflected away from parental conflict. Evidence for this theory is mainly based on the clinical experience of the Minuchin group of family therapists.

Child sexual abuse

One form of childhood adversity that has received particular attention involves sexual abuse. Although a range of people are known to abuse children, the majority of abuse occurs within families or extended families, and may last for several years. Although it is difficult to know the exact **prevalence** of this problem, around 20 per cent of women and up to 10 per cent of men report having experienced some form of sexual abuse as a child in surveys across the world (WHO 2014). Key indicators among younger children include age-inappropriate knowledge of sexual acts, sexual interactions with others, excessive masturbation or acting out sexual acts using toys. They may also experience a number of emotional and behavioural problems, including bed-wetting or soiling, hyperactivity or crying spells. Among older children, behavioural and emotional problems may be more common and include excessive nervousness, **flashback memories** of the events, guilt and shame, substance abuse, and memory problems.

Over the longer term, these experiences can result in increased risk of mental health problems. Spataro et al. (2004), for example, found that children known to have been sexually abused followed up at adulthood were four times more likely to have developed significant mental health problems than children not exposed to this abuse. Not surprisingly, perhaps, higher levels of abuse result in higher risk of problems. Cheasty et al. (1998), for example, found that women who had been sexually abused as children had higher levels of mental health problems than those who had not been. However, only those women who had experienced abuse that involved penetration or attempted penetration considered themselves to have negative mental health problems as a consequence of their experiences. Similarly, Molnar et al. (2001) found that having been raped, knowing the perpetrator, and the duration of abuse were each associated with higher risk for mental health problems, even among a group of women who had all been sexually abused.

Unexpectedly, perhaps, other forms of childhood abuse may have equally or more serious long-term impacts than sexual abuse. Coid et al. (2003) found that childhood physical, but not sexual, abuse was associated with poor mental health, in a cross-sectional survey of over 1000 North London women. By comparison, sexual abuse as an adult was associated with a number of negative outcomes. Using a more restricted outcome, Swannell et al. (2012) found that adults who reported being physically abused or neglected were around two and half times more likely to report self-harming than those without these experiences. Sexual abuse was not associated with self-harm. Accordingly, while childhood sexual abuse clearly increases risk for mental health problems, it may not play a unique and greater role than other forms of childhood adversity.

Single-parent families

In the UK alone, there are around two million one-parent families, the mental health consequences of which are therefore extremely important. Reassuringly, perhaps, there is little to suggest that being raised in a single-parent household has any adverse effect, although many of the social and economic factors associated with this state, such as low income and living in poor housing, may. Tobias et al. (2010), for example, found that the 5- to 14-year-old children of single mothers were 25 per cent more likely to have poor mental health than those in two-parent families. However, this effect was largely attributable to the lower income and poorer maternal health of the single parent. Similarly, Black et al. (2002) found that 5-year-olds who experienced maltreatment or who had mothers with depressive symptoms had more behavioural and emotional problems than others. Being in a one- or two-parent household was not a predictive factor. Finally, Fergusson et al. (2007), in a **longitudinal study**, reported that being in a single-parent family was associated with risk for adult anxiety disorder, welfare dependence, and violent and property offences. However, again, these relationships disappeared after taking account of other social factors. Access to grandparents appears to be a beneficial or protective factor for all children, but especially those from one-parent households.

Family conflict and divorce

Divorce brings with it not just the stresses of single parenthood, but also risk of significant distress as a consequence of disrupted relationships and high levels of parental distress. However, although there is a modest association between short-term child maladjustment and divorce, a poor outcome is not inevitable. Young children typically experience 2–3 years of readjustment following divorce. During this time, they may show aggression, depression, non-compliance, acting out, and problems in peer relationships. This period of disruption, however, is likely to be followed by a process of adjustment and improvement. Older children may also experience emotional distress associated with acting out, difficulties in school, and disconnection from the family. Even so, most children recover and experience minimal long-term problems extending into adulthood (Angarne-Lindberg and Wadsby 2012). But not all outcomes are so positive. Many women from divorced families report more psychological and relationship problems than those from non-divorced families. They may also have poorer relationships with their parents during adolescence, and lower self-esteem and social support in adulthood than women from intact families (Mustonen et al. 2011).

These differing outcomes may be a consequence of factors related to the nature of the divorce and its precursors. Divorce is usually the end-point of significant parental distress that may be apparent to the child. In addition, divorce is more likely to occur in families that are already adversely affected by a variety of economic stresses and parental mental health problems. Parents in high-conflict marriages are typically less warm towards their children, more rejecting, harsher in their discipline, more depressed, and fathers in particular are likely to withdraw from the parenting role. Unsurprisingly, these factors impact on the child. Children in high-conflict marriages are more likely to experience emotional and behavioural problems, including poor academic performance, aggression, delinquency, poor self-esteem, and depression. This marital discord rather than divorce itself may be the primary predictor of poor outcomes. Divorce is also likely to be more disruptive of long-term mental health if it is acrimonious and relationships with parents are disrupted (Gilman et al. 2003). Children may be protected from these effects if they maintain a good relationship with at least one parent, and/or have good emotional support from friends and siblings.

The mechanisms through which the experience of divorce may adversely impact on later life are not clear. One mechanism may involve the loss of a close attachment figure, with consequent difficulties in adult attachment – an explanation consistent with findings that maintaining a good relationship with at least one parent is protective against mental health problems. Another mechanism seems to be the impact on children's beliefs about themselves. Particularly important may be its impact on self-esteem (Palosaari et al. 1996).

Current affairs

If the family, its situated context, and individuals within it have a significant effect on the present and future well-being of the children within it, should these become the focus of interventions even if there is no evidence of present problems? Should we, for example, work with families to help them develop appropriate care of their children, work with neighbourhoods to improve the environment, work with schools to maximize the mental well-being of all students: addressing bullying policy, supportive relationships between teachers and at-risk children, and so on. This could either improve the mental well-being of a generation of children and save millions in the treatment of mental health problems throughout their lifespan, or a colossal waste of money. But which is it?

Beyond the family

This chapter has already hinted that social factors wider than those of the family will impact on childhood mental health – and this certainly is the case. All-pervasive factors, including the economic circumstances in which a child is brought up, their physical environment, and the wider social environment, will impact on mental health. The impact of peers and levels of engagement in risky behaviours will also make their mark.

Socio-economic factors

Being brought up and living in a position of economic disadvantage has a clear and negative impact on mental health throughout the life course. In one study of its impact on children, for example, Meltzer et al. (2000) found that 5- to 15-year-olds from low-income families were nearly three times more likely to experience some form of mental health problem than those from better-off families. Among the findings were some concerning statistics: one in 40 children in low-income households aged 5–10 years engaged in self-harming behaviour versus fewer than one in 100 from high-income households; and young men from low-income families are at twice the risk of suicide than those who are better off.

Low socio-economic status may impact on a child through a variety of means: poor housing and pressure of space within housing, stressed parents potentially having multiple jobs, lack of social opportunities due to restricted finances, and so on. The wider environment may also contribute to poor mental health. Poor neighbourhoods and neighbourhood adversity, such as high levels of crime, drug use, neglect of neighbourhood resources, and lack of social cohesion, can also negatively impact on levels of well-being and depression. However, a positive home environment may help to significantly moderate their effects (Wickrama and Noh 2010).

Peer influences

Young people spend as much time with their peers as they do with their family. Not surprisingly, therefore, these interactions have implications for their mental health. Some peer interactions may result from choice on the part of the young person. There is evidence, for example, that young people diagnosed with conduct disorder may choose to associate with others with the same behavioural problems: a synergy that may exacerbate their behaviour. At an even more extreme level, Coid et al. (2013) found that individual antisocial behaviour or membership of UK urban gangs had its cost. Both violent men not in gangs and gang members evidenced significantly higher levels of **psychosis** and anxiety and used mental health services more than comparison groups. Fear of recrimination and having been victimized themselves contributed significantly to this pathology.

Other influences may be less voluntary. Around 25 per cent of children report being bullied by their peers: a negative interaction associated with a range of emotional and behavioural problems, including **self-harm**, borderline personality disorder, and suicide. Fisher et al. (2012), for example, found children aged 5–12 years who were bullied were more than twice as likely to report self-harming than those without this experience. In another UK study, Schreier et al. (2009) found children aged 13 who were bullied between the ages of 8 and 10 years were twice as likely to develop 'psychosis-like symptoms' than their non-bullied peers by the age of 13. Wolke et al. (2012) highlighted the impact of both physical and social bullying. They found that children who were chronically physically bullied were around five times more likely to develop symptoms of borderline personality disorder than their peers. The risk for those who experienced both physical and social bullying such as exclusion from social groups was seven times greater. Cyber-bullying is now emerging as a significant problem, with both recipients and bullies appearing to be at greater risk of depression and suicide than those not involved (Bonanno and Hymel 2013). Being bullied as a child has also been associated with a range of adult disorders, including anxiety, antisocial personality disorder, as well as suicide and suicide attempts (Sourander et al. 2009).

Not surprisingly, perhaps, the child's response to bullying has implications for both the amount of bullying they experience and its emotional impact. Agoston and Rudolph (2011) found that what they termed adaptive stress responses, involving 'effortful engagement', reduced the negative emotional effects of peer stresses associated with bullying, teasing, and social isolation. Disengagement tended to increase isolation and low mood.

Risky behaviours

Risk for mental health problems may be associated with a number of risky behaviours, the most obvious of which is the use of intoxicants such as alcohol and street drugs. Many young people drink alcohol and use drugs – and most experience no negative effects. However, a minority do experience problems, some of which may be acute, some of which may be longer term. Moderate cannabis use appears to have few negative effects in the short term, although heavy short-term use has been associated with manic symptoms. Longer-term use potentially doubles the risk for psychosis compared with not smoking cannabis, although much of the risk is to a small group of individuals with particular alleles of the catecholamine-*O*-methyl transferase (COMT) gene, which increases the release of dopamine into the prefrontal lobe synapses and markedly increases risk of subsequent schizophreniform disorder (Caspi et al. 2005).

Alcohol consumption is also higher among young people with mental health problems. However, the direction of causality may be bidirectional and it is often a consequence rather than cause of mental health problems. Conduct problems, anxiety, and depression are predictive of subsequent alcohol (and cannabis) consumption. By contrast, high alcohol consumption may result in episodes of deliberate self-harm possibly due to its disinhibitory effects (Loh et al. 2013). Interestingly, a relatively benign beverage also appears to be associated with anxiety in young people. Trapp et al. (2014) found consumption of energy drinks to increase anxiety in young men, but not women.

Looked-after children

A final group of young people considered here are those without a family, who are brought up under the care of the state. This situation has clear mental health consequences for the children involved. McCann et al. (1996), for example, found that nearly 70 per cent of young people aged 13–17 years who were looked after by Oxfordshire Council evidenced some form of 'psychiatric disorder', although not all may have experienced the severity required for a psychiatric diagnosis. This compared to 15 per cent of a comparison group raised in their family of origin. The most common problem was conduct disorder, evident in 28 per cent of the group. However, mood disorders were also highly prevalent: 26 per cent were diagnosed with 'overanxious' disorder, while 23 per cent experienced clinically significant levels of depression. According to the UK Social Exclusion Unit (1998), around 30 per cent are excluded from school as a result of behavioural problems or truancy. Things do not significantly improve when young adults leave care. Saunders and Broad (1997), for example, noted that 17 per cent of leavers experienced long-term mental health problems, including depression, eating disorders, and phobias. Thirty-five per cent had deliberately harmed themselves since the age of 15 years, 60 per cent had thought of taking their own life, while 25–30 per cent of female leavers went on to become teenage parents. Relatively few go on to further education, and have poor job or career opportunities.

One explanation for this high prevalence of mental health problems is that it results from the high levels of risk factors experienced *before* entering care. Most children in care come from 'broken families', from poor neighbourhoods, and overcrowded homes. Many children experience maternal mental health problems and/or paternal criminality. Many have poor relationships and attachment to their parents or carers. Unfortunately, the lack of close relationships with adults in care homes means that the latter cannot be remedied. Behavioural difficulties perhaps already established before entering the home frequently continue and further reduce positive adult associations. School is disrupted due to poor concentration, behavioural difficulties, prejudice, and bullying by peers.

Children who go to stable foster homes or who are adopted, and achieve stable relationships with caring adults may benefit from them. Nevertheless, Dumaret et al. (1997) found that 68 per cent of the adults with this experience they interviewed were rated as well integrated socially or 'average'. Clearly many were not, although the figure is much less positive for those whose placements break down or have multiple placements.

Chapter summary

1. The developing emotional life of the child is influenced by gross factors such as the social environment in which they are raised, and more micro factors including the strategies parents use to calm the young child.
2. There are a number of pre-natal influences on childhood mental health:
   a) Genetic factors responsible for disorders such as Fragile X syndrome and Down syndrome.
   b) Genetic factors that contribute to risk, together with environmental factors, for such disorders as schizophrenia.
   c) Foetal exposure to viral infections.
   d) Maternal stress.
3. Biological and psychosocial factors influence risk in a model known as the biopsychosocial model.
4. A number of parental and family influences influence risk for both childhood and adult mental health problems. These include:
   a) Family adversity.
   b) Parental or family dynamics.

c) Child sexual abuse.
   d) Single parenthood (or co-existing factors such as parental stress, economic disadvantage).
   e) Family conflict and divorce.
5. Factors beyond the family may also be important, including:
   a) Socio-economic factors.
   b) Negative peer influences such as bullying and gang membership.
   c) Risky personal behaviours, including drug and alcohol use.
   d) Being raised in care.

Further reading

McPherson, K.M., Kerr, S., McGee, E. et al. (2013) *The Role and Impact of Social Capital on the Health and Wellbeing of Children and Adolescents: A systematic review*. Glasgow: Glasgow Centre for Population Health.

Meltzer, H., Gatward, R., Goodman, R. and Ford, T. (2000) *The Mental Health of Children and Adolescents in Great Britain*. London: The Stationery Office.

Ogden, T. and Amlund Hagen, K. (2013) *Adolescent Mental Health: Prevention and intervention*. London: Routledge.

Repetti, R.L., Taylor, S.E. and Seeman, T.E. (2002) Risky families: family social environments and the mental and physical health of offspring, *Psychological Bulletin*, 128: 330–66.

Chapter 3

Influences on mental health during adulthood

Just as external forces influence risk for mental health problems in children, the same is true for adults. This chapter considers a number of factors that moderate this risk, beginning with overarching factors such as socio-economic status, gender and minority status, before moving to more circumscribed factors including family dynamics and problems particularly associated with older adults.

By the end of this chapter, you will have an understanding of how the following factors may influence mental health:

- Socio-economic status
- Gender
- Minority status, including ethnicity and sexual minorities
- Family dynamics
- Ageing and adjustment to life changes

Socio-economic status

With the notable exception of anorexia, almost all mental health problems are most prevalent among the economically less well off. Explanations for this phenomenon have drawn on two opposing arguments. The first suggests that low socio-economic status (SES) somehow causes or contributes to poor mental health; the second suggests that poor mental health results in low SES. The first of these explanations is often referred to as the social causation model. The second is known as social drift: individuals drift down the SES gradient as a consequence of their poor mental health.

To tease these explanations out, longitudinal studies that allow us to determine which factors precede which outcomes are necessary. There is much evidence of social causation. Corcoran et al. (2009), for example, found the prevalence of schizophrenia was highest among individuals whose parents had been unemployed, had received social welfare, or were single parents. That is, social deprivation appeared to increase risk for subsequent development of the disorder. Similarly, use of antidepressant medication is higher among both men and women who have experienced economic difficulties in childhood than those who have not (Mauramo et al. 2012). These effects may even be intergenerational. Ritsher et al. (2001) followed a cohort of people from various socio-economic groups whose parents had either experienced an episode of major depression or were depression-free. They hypothesized that if the social causation model held, the children of blue-collar parents were at increased risk of developing depression. If the social drift model held, having depressed parents placed participants at risk of low SES. Their data supported the social causation hypothesis. The children of blue-collar workers were more than three times as likely to develop a major depressive disorder than children of white-collar workers. Parental depression did not predict the socio-economic status of their offspring. Nor was there any evidence of drift following the onset of depression.

These findings should not be surprising. The lower the individual is within the social structure, the greater the likelihood of their exposure to stressful life events, hassles and problems, and the greater the emotional impact they have. They may experience poor and crowded housing, multiple jobs, economic instability, difficulties paying bills, lack of resources to finance holidays, and so on (e.g. Ahnquist and Wamala 2011). They may also lack social capital: a feeling of safety in the community in which one lives. This may interact with other problems associated with low SES to increase risk further. Taylor et al. (2012), for example, found that women with the highest levels of mental health problems included those who were single parents, unable to work or unemployed, had poor finances, and felt unsafe in their home and lacking in control over their life. People in higher socio-economic groups also have more social and psychological resources known to be protective against mental health problems than the less well off (Grzywacz et al. 2004). Higher levels of social support and 'reserve capacity' (a combination of optimism, self-esteem, and social support) are also found among the better off (Matthews et al. 2008).

Evidence of the opposite process, social drift, can also be found, although perhaps less consistently than evidence of social causation. One good example of this is a Finnish study (Aro et al. 1995) that followed people discharged from hospital with a diagnosis of schizophrenia over a 17-year period. Although these individuals typically started at the same economic status as their parents, many experienced a progressive decline in SES over the course of the study. Most became unemployed. This effect was stronger in men than women, perhaps because fewer women than men were primary wage earners so their families were less vulnerable to their fluctuating mental health. It should be noted that of all mental health problems, schizophrenia has one of the worst prognoses, and is associated with long-term and repeated difficulties. Such an effect is therefore much less likely to be found in the context of other, less debilitating disorders. Of course, the opposite process may also occur. Zivin et al. (2012), for example, found that depressed US military veterans who responded to treatment were more likely to gain employment, and to continue their employment over an 18-month period than those who remained depressed.

Gender

According to the World Health Organization, gender is an important determinant of mental health (WHO undated). Some mental health disorders may be directly associated with being female. Disorders such as pre-menstrual **dysphoric** disorder, post-partum depression and psychosis, and emotional difficulties associated with the menopause are uniquely gender-related, and mechanisms underpinning these conditions may be largely biological. They each involve disruption of oestrogen levels, which have been associated with reduced levels of serotonin, a **neurosteroid** with strong anti-anxiety effects called allopregnanolon, and increases in dopamine levels (e.g. Lokuge et al. 2011).

There are also gender differences in the prevalence of several more common mental disorders, including depression, anxiety, and somatic complaints, and these may have a more social explanation. According to the WHO, depression is twice as common in women than men, and is more difficult to treat. A similar differential has been found for the prevalence of a variety of anxiety disorders (McLean et al. 2011). By contrast, men are at twice the risk of experiencing alcohol dependence, and are more than three times as likely to be diagnosed with antisocial personality disorder. The WHO found no evidence of gender differences in the rates of disorders such as schizophrenia and bipolar disorder.

A number of explanations have been proposed for these findings, and in particular the higher rate of **neurotic-type disorders** among women. One suggestion is that the differences may be more apparent than real, and are a consequence of women being more willing to report psychological distress than men. However, while this may be true in day-to-day medical consultations, it is not true of research addressing this question, and a number of well-conducted prevalence studies involving detailed clinical interviews have consistently found gender differences in rates of mental health problems between men and women (Weich et al. 1998).

Other theories have suggested mechanisms already used to explain socio-economic differences in health: differential exposure and vulnerability to stressors. According to the WHO, many disparities in mental health arise from women's more frequent experience of poverty, discrimination, and socio-economic disadvantage than men. Women comprise 75 per cent of the world's poor and earn significantly less than men even when they are in paid work. In addition, they are more likely than men to occupy insecure, low-status jobs. These, in turn, are associated with the experience of higher levels of negative life events and chronic stressors, insecure housing tenure, and low levels of social support; all of which, as noted earlier in the chapter, are associated with risk for mental health problems. These may be further augmented by the role of caring (for partners, parents or children) often taken by women in society.

Of particular note is that even when working full-time, women still tend to do more work around the home than their male partners. This process, known as work–home spill-over, is now widely recognized as contributing to high levels of stress, although it may not result in sufficient distress to warrant a diagnosis of a formal mental health disorder. The more children there are in a family, the more likely their mothers are to experience the negative effects of work–home spill-over: an effect not found in men. In addition, women who work overtime typically experience more stress than women who do not work overtime – again, an effect not found in men. Indeed, the opposite effect may be found (Krantz and Lundberg 2006), probably because men are protected against housework if they work overtime.

Even more problematic for some is the issue of violence towards women. Women are more subject to physical assault within the family, rape, and other traumatizing events than men. Although these events may be relatively uncommon, they may profoundly affect those involved and contribute to the high rates of anxiety or depression among women. Cloutier et al. (2002), for example, found that 19 per cent of their sample of women in North Carolina had been subjected to a sexual assault at some time in their life. These women were two and a half times more likely to report 'poor mental health' than those without this experience. Such is the impact of physical violence that it can overwhelm other, even highly negative, life events. Al-Modallal et al. (2012), for example, found evidence of relatively high levels of depression and anxiety among victims of partner violence among women living in refugee camps in Jordan.

An alternative approach to this issue suggests that women may be more vulnerable to some types of stress than men. Elliott (2000), for example, suggested that women are more dependent on the support provided by social networks than men, and may be differentially affected by events that disrupt them. Related to this may be problems associated with the loss of attachment to the extended family, as children are more mobile and increasingly move from the family home as they mature.

Minority status

Ethnicity

Minority status can be conferred by a number of factors: ethnicity, sexual choices, appearance, and so on. However, it is usually taken to mean obvious differences as a result of ethnicity. Thankfully, being part of a minority ethnic group appears to have relatively little impact on mental health. It may even be protective. In a large study of over 3500 US citizens, for example, Williams et al. (2007) found the lifetime prevalence of depression was highest for whites (17.9%), followed by Caribbean blacks (12.9%) and African-Americans (10.4%). Similarly, Asnaani et al. (2010) found that white Americans were more likely to be diagnosed with social anxiety disorder, generalized anxiety disorder, and panic disorder than African-, Hispanic-, and Asian-Americans.

The one diagnosis that does seem to be more prevalent among people from ethnic minorities is schizophrenia. In a systematic review and meta-analysis of over 83 relevant studies conducted in the UK, Kirkbride et al. (2012) found that rates were elevated in several ethnic minority groups compared with the white (British) population. Black Caribbean and African people were five times more likely to be diagnosed as schizophrenia than whites: people from South Asian groups were at double the risk. In the USA also, Eack et al. (2012) found African-Americans to be three times more likely to be diagnosed with schizophrenia than whites.

This very specific finding clearly requires explanation. In order to explore the issue, the first thing to ask is whether these differences are real, or whether they are more apparent than real. Worryingly, the evidence seems to support the latter contention. Barnes (2007), for example, found systematic differences in the diagnosis of schizophrenia across different ethnic groups in all the psychiatric hospitals in one US state. African-Americans with similar symptoms were less likely to be diagnosed with bipolar and major depressive disorders, and more likely to be diagnosed with schizophrenia than white patients.

The causes of any bias are unclear, although Eack et al. (2012) provided some insight into this issue. They examined diagnoses given to both white and African-American people receiving in-patient care in US hospitals and found, as predicted, African-Americans were three times more likely to be diagnosed with schizophrenia than the white patients. Detailed discussion with patients and clinicians led the authors to conclude that these differences were due to the perceived honesty of the patients: the clinicians did not appear to trust African-Americans' responses to questions about their symptoms and made diagnostic inferences based on a suspicion of symptom denial, poor insight, or uncooperativeness. Accordingly, one must conclude that at least some, if not all, the differences in these diagnostic differences may be a function of clinician factors rather than true differences in prevalence rates.

If this is the case, then people in minority groups may experience no higher levels of mental health problems in general than the majority population. Nevertheless, within these groups some individuals may be more at risk than others. Some may be vulnerable as a consequence of the association between being a member of an ethnic minority and being in a lower socio-economic group. Two other groups may also be vulnerable to mental health problems: people who experience high levels of discrimination, or expect to do so, and new immigrants.

Disentangling cause and effect in research into the effects of discrimination is not easy. Hammond et al. (2010) found that health care workers who experienced more racial discrimination were more likely to be depressed than those who experienced little or no discrimination. Similarly, Lindström (2008) found that young people from an ethnic minority background who believed that employers would discriminate according to race, colour of skin, religion or cultural background reported higher levels of poor psychological health than those without this expectation. Unfortunately, in studies inevitably based on self-report, it is not clear whether depression resulted from discrimination, or whether people who were depressed were more attentive or biased towards seeing discrimination or even behaved in ways that rendered negative reactions from others they interpreted as racial discrimination. Nevertheless, it is plausible that exposure to repeated discrimination can lead to increased risk of mental health problems. A strong ethnic identity may protect against the effects of such discrimination, as may a strong social network (Chou 2012).

Immigration also harbours a number of stresses that place individuals at risk of mental health problems. Some stresses may be economic. Lindert et al. (2009), for example, found prevalence rates for depression of 20 per cent among economic migrants who had jobs in their new country and 44 per cent among refugees who did not. However, other factors are clearly at work. Within refugee populations, for example, a key predictor of poor mental health is the experience of difficulties prior to leaving their country of origin. Torture, experience of conflict or 'local terror' are all significant predictors of poor mental health. In addition, once in their new country, all immigrants face the challenge of coping with a set of new cultural demands and norms, and the decision whether to embrace or resist integration into this new culture. The outcome of this process may vary across cultures. Amer and Hovey (2007), for example, found Arab Christians benefited from integration into a broader US culture, while Arab Muslims experienced no benefits in terms of mental health from such integration. For them, maintaining strong religious beliefs and strong family ties were preventive of mental health problems.

Perhaps the people who are most challenged in terms of integration are the children of immigrants, who may experience demands from parents to continue in the culture of their origin, and demands from friends and others to adopt that of their new country. According to Pumariega et al. (2005), this can result in a number of outcomes, including 'ethnic self-hate', the development of an adversarial identity against the majority culture that may involve joining gangs or groups of youths with similar views, and depression or substance abuse. A third response, known as biculturalism, involves validation and affirmation of both cultures, and may be the most mental health protective.

Sexuality

Minority status is not just conferred by visible differences. Sexual minorities also experience prejudice that may impact on their mental health. A large survey conducted among the Australian gay, lesbian, and transgender population (Leonard et al. 2012) found that the most common health conditions among their participants were depression and anxiety/nervous disorders, with depression rates ranging from a high of 50 per cent among transsexual males to a low of 24.5 per cent in gay men. Nearly 80 per cent of the sample had experienced at least one episode of intense anxiety in the 12 months prior to the survey, and over a quarter had been diagnosed with, or treated for, an anxiety disorder in the same period. These rates were markedly higher than population norms, and were attributed to the high levels of discrimination and abuse these people experienced. They may also reflect the internalization of dysfunctional beliefs about their sexuality as a consequence of this discrimination.

Unfortunately, avoiding such abuse may also take a toll. Cole et al. (1996) found that healthy gay men who concealed their sexual identity were more likely to experience poor mental and physical health than those who were able to express their sexuality. According to the authors, there is an interaction between stigma and discrimination evident through other people's actions and some individuals' responses to these actions. They argued that sexual minorities experience higher exposure to stressors than the majority. Over time, this results in poor emotional regulation and possibly poor health.

Current affairs

Mental health is clearly associated with a range of social, economic, and environmental factors. It should come as no surprise that living on a deprived inner-city estate (and all that that implies) places people more at risk of mental health problems than living in more economically viable and advantageous surroundings. So, how should we set about reducing levels of mental health problems? The UK government's response to this problem has been to institute a programme of increased access to varying levels of cognitive behaviour therapy for the treatment of anxiety and depression. But are there better, albeit more complex, alternatives? Should we as a nation consider more fundamental ways of increasing the nation's health: economic, social or environmental changes that may affect whole populations?

Family dynamics

High negative emotional expression

One of the most understood links between family dynamics and mental health problems involves people diagnosed with schizophrenia. The key factor appears to be a hostile, critical, family atmosphere, now known as high negative expressed emotion (NEE). When exposed to this environment, people who have recovered from an episode of schizophrenia are significantly more likely to experience a relapse than if they live in a low NEE environment, particularly if they experience it for 35 hours or more a week (Miklowitz 2004).

Because high NEE triggers relapse, but not first episodes of schizophrenia, clinicians consider it to be a consequence of the family struggling to cope with an individual whose behaviour may be at odds with family values and day-to-day activities rather than a cause of this dysfunctional behaviour. High NEE lies within a circle of causality, being both a response to 'difficult' or inexplicable behaviour and a contributor to its development. Accordingly, levels of NEE tend to be higher in families where odd behaviour is seen as wilful and under the control of the individual, and lower where it is attributed to an illness or an uncontrollable cause (Yang et al. 2004). Also of note is that the impact of family processes may be moderated by a number of individual, cognitive factors. Kéri and Kelemen (2009), for example, found that individuals with particularly poor attention and immediate memory experienced more 'unusual thoughts' while they were the subject of family criticism than those who had better attention and memory. Since its early link to schizophrenia, high NEE has been identified as a common factor affecting outcomes in a range of disorders, including borderline personality disorder, bipolar disorder, and depression (e.g. Fruzzetti et al. 2005; Proudfoot et al. 2010)

Living alone

Being a single parent brings a number of stresses and acts as a risk factor for mental health problems. Cooper et al. (2008), for example, found that the prevalence of 'common mental disorders' (anxiety, depression, etc.) was twice as high among single mothers than mothers who had partners. Among male single parents, the prevalence was four times higher. According to Cooper et al., the primary contributor to risk of mental health problems in women appeared to be economic hardship and lack of social support. Indeed, single mothers in low socio-economic groups often had multiple jobs and experienced more employment, housing, finance, and social problems than those who were better off; each of which contributed to poor mental health. In men, financial factors appear to be less important than for women; lack of social support may be a key factor for them (Wade et al. 2011).

Much of the stress associated with being a single parent stems from the time and economic pressures that such people experience. However, any distress may be further added to by factors associated with this living situation; in particular, the dissolution of marriages or partnerships. Breslau et al. (2011) found that people who had mental health disorders were less likely to marry or establish a long-term partnership, and the dissolution of either form of relationship increased risk of specific phobias, major depression, and alcohol abuse. The nature of the relationship prior to separation may also impact on mental health outcomes. Overbeek et al. (2006) found that getting divorced increased risk for alcohol abuse, **dysthymia**, and social phobia but only among those people who considered their pre-divorce marriage to be of a high quality. Those who considered their marital relationship to be poor experienced no ill-effects. Also of interest are the findings of Richards et al. (1997), who found no protective effect of re-marrying or establishing subsequent long-term relationships. Finally, many older people live alone as a consequence of separation or divorce from partners, or bereavement. Levels of psychological **morbidity** are particularly high in this group. In a sample of 80- to 90-year-olds, for example, Wilson et al. (2007) found those who were living alone and geographically separated from friends or family were two and half times more likely to be depressed than those with closer family.

Caring

Adulthood potentially brings a number of responsibilities within families, often beyond those expected or hoped for. One key demand placed on some individuals within families is that of caring for another family member who has a long-term mental or physical health problem.

Caring for people within the family that experience ill-health can occur at any time. Younger adults may experience the negative consequences of caring for a child with serious illness. Raina et al. (2005), for example, explored factors associated with well-being among carers of children with cerebral palsy. Key predictors of distress were lower levels of child mental and physical health, higher levels of behavioural problems, and poor family function. The impact of these was moderated by caregivers' higher self-esteem and sense of mastery over the caregiving situation.

Many adults may also find themselves caring for adults of the same age. This, too, brings a degree of stress and increased risk for mental health problems. Mazzotti et al. (2013), for example, found that 63 per cent of women and 38 per cent of men caring for someone with cancer showed evidence of at least moderate levels of anxiety or depression, while Chung et al. (2010) found 27 per cent of carers for people with heart failure experienced significant depressive symptoms. A number of factors have been found to moderate the extent to which mental health problems are experienced in this context, including how capable patients are at looking after themselves, how much control they feel they have over the condition, the complexity of the caregiving tasks, and how much time carers have to devote to the caregiving role. Beyond these immediate disease-related factors, others are also important, including the carer's own health, the quality of the relationship between carer and patient, and the degree of support available to the carer.

Another disease that carers are increasingly having to confront is Alzheimer's, the most common form of dementia. The confused and disinhibited behaviour of people with this disorder (see Chapter 13) makes caring for them extremely challenging both physically and mentally. As a consequence, Mahoney et al. (2005) found 23.5 per cent per cent of caregivers showed clinical levels of anxiety, and 10.5 per cent could be diagnosed with depression. Ferrara et al. (2008) provided an insightful view of carers of Alzheimer's sufferers in their Italian sample of carers. They were predominantly female, and 70 per cent were the daughter of the person with dementia. Thirty per cent were pensioners. Eighty per cent provided complete care for the person in their own home. Of these, 53 per cent had little time for themselves, 55 per cent reported their own health was deteriorating, 56 per cent were chronically tired, and 51 per cent were not getting enough sleep. Over half were experiencing problems with either the person with Alzheimer's or their own family, and a similar percentage was experiencing problems with their work. Nearly a third reported they felt they were failing to cope with the situation as well as they would wish, and wanted to be taken out of the situation. According to Ferrara et al., the degree of anxiety and depression experienced by the carers was proportional to the severity of the Alzheimer's, the degree of memory loss, and 'feeling sick of the patient'. Other factors associated with distress include time spent caring and the pre-disease quality of relationship between the couple.

Old age doesn't come alone

Social context

According to Jokela et al. (2013), old age brings increases in psychological problems, the prevalence of which rise gradually over the age of 50, and steeply over the age of 75 years. In their study, the prevalence of psychiatric problems rose from 24 to 43 per cent between these ages. In a detailed study of community-dwelling older people, Olivera et al. (2011) found that 46 per cent suffered from some psychiatric symptom or other: 16 per cent had cognitive impairment, 16 per cent anxiety, 14 per cent depression, 6 per cent hallucinations and delusions, 7 per cent excessive worries about illness, and 4 per cent obsessive symptoms. Women were between three and four times more likely to experience depression or anxiety than men.

These findings should not be surprising, as older people typically experience more of the negative events and outcomes that have already been discussed in this chapter, including 'acute life events' such as bereavement and medical illness, negative interactions with family, financial crises, and longer-term stressors such as being a carer, loneliness, and sensory loss (Ormel et al. 2001). Living in a residential home also increases risk for depression, as it is associated with a loss of independence and poor physical health. Gallagher et al. (2013) added to this list by including physical impairment and functional decline as predictors of depression. Levels of depression in women are frequently greater than those among men. This may be a consequence of the loss of their traditional 'homemaker's role' due to disability, the retirement of their partner with his consequent 'intrusion' into the home, grief or loneliness following the death of their husband/partner, and the loss of motherhood and role as domestic head of family.

The power of these factors to influence mood is highlighted by Olivera et al. (2011). They found that women were three times more likely to become depressed than men, and cognitively impaired people were four times more likely to become depressed than those with no cognitive problems. Socially isolated people were 16 times more likely than socially engaged people to develop depression, while seriously chronically ill people were 62 times more at risk than those with no such disorder. In a meta-analysis of risk factors for poor mental health among older adults, Xiu-Ying et al. (2012) found that older people living alone were one and a half times more likely to be depressed than those living with partners or families. People in nursing homes were three times more likely to be depressed than those living at home. Unfortunately, not only does living in this setting increase risk for depression, those that become depressed become increasingly isolated and depressed over time (Drageset et al. 2012). There are also factors that may protect or buffer against depression. These include good medical care, positive coping styles, and social support. Treatment of remediable physical problems that may interfere with social and other activities, such as the use of hearing aids and medical treatment of heart disease, can also reduce depression.

Cognitive functioning

As we age, our cognitive function changes. Based on global measures of cognitive functioning such as IQ scores, our peak abilities occur between the ages of 25 and 30 years, before declining gradually until around 65 years and then decreasing more rapidly. These changes reflect a general slowing of cognitive processes that influence most, if not all, cognitive abilities. More optimistically, perhaps, Schaie (2005) found participants in their longitudinal survey showed evidence of decline in one or more of five cognitive domains by the age of 60, but that virtually no-one declined in all five, even by the age of 80 years. Around 10 per cent of individuals in their seventies and eighties even evidenced an increase in general cognitive abilities. How important these losses of processing power are in terms of day-to-day living is unclear. Indeed, due to changes in demands on their cognitive facilities as a result of retirement, older people may retain or even enhance skills and abilities in domains they choose to focus on.

Despite this optimistic view, a percentage of individuals will go on to develop significant neurological impairment. However, this is a relatively small, and possibly falling, percentage of the population. Matthews et al. (2013), for example, reported that 6.5 per cent of their sample of nearly 8000 people over 64 years were diagnosed as having some form of **dementia**. A less severe form of cognitive decline that may be a precursor to dementia, known as mild cognitive decline, is found in a significant proportion of older adults, with a prevalence of around 20 per cent in its mildest form. Up to one-third of people with dementia become clinically depressed at some time, while just under half of those with mild cognitive impairment experience the same (Enache et al. 2011). The latter figure may be higher, as these people have better awareness of their diminished cognitive ability and may fear for the future.

End of life

Proximity to death is often associated with a need to put life into context, to complete life tasks that remain possible, and to resolve difficulties in order to gain a sense of fulfilment and a feeling of having made a contribution to the lives of others. As Erikson (1980) described it, the final stage of life can be described as a period of 'integrity versus despair', in which people look back on their life and consider whether it was well-ordered and meaningful (resulting in feelings of integrity) or unproductive and meaningless (resulting in despair). For those who have concerns about the events of their lives, it may be a time of reconciliation and attempts at making life more meaningful. Exline et al. (2012), for example, identified some of the processes considered by older patients and their home caregivers as being particularly important. These included forgiveness-related communications, expressions of love, gratitude, and making farewells. A failure to express forgiveness, where appropriate, was associated with more depressive symptoms, as were unresolved differences between individuals. Close proximity to death may also trigger an exploration of personal grounds for faith. Not surprisingly, levels of depression can be high in the weeks and months before death among people who know they are going to die. Up to a third experience clinically relevant levels of depression, while around 20 per cent are clinically anxious at some time (Hotopf et al. 2002).

Chapter summary

1. Almost all mental health problems are more prevalent among the less well off in society. This can be attributable to social drift and social causation. The latter is the most important of these processes, although both may occur.
2. Explanations for this phenomenon include the higher rates of negative life events and hassles, and the lower levels of coping resources, experienced by people in lower socio-economic groups.
3. Women are more at risk for mental health problems than men. Originally thought to be a consequence of women's willingness to report such problems, this is now being seen as an objective finding.
4. Women appear more at risk as a consequence of things that happen to women: work–home spill-over, economic and work factors, violence. It may also be a consequence of their higher dependence on disrupted social networks than men and their need for attachment to children and others within the family.
5. Minority status can increase risk for mental health problems, although risk due to ethnicity may be a consequence of socio-economic factors more than socio-cultural ones. Indeed, many minority ethnic groups experience higher levels of good mental health than majority populations.
6. The apparent increased risk of schizophrenia among African-Americans is now considered to be a consequence of bias in diagnostic processes.
7. Factors associated with risk among ethnic minorities include experiencing discrimination and immigrant status. The prognosis for the latter group is generally worse for immigrants who fail to engage with society or who are economically deprived in their new country of residence. Refugees may experience particularly high levels of distress.
8. Other minorities, including sexual minorities, may also experience additional stress as a consequence of discrimination that can lead to higher levels of mental health problems than the majority population.
9. Repeat episodes of schizophrenia (but not onset) are associated with high levels of negative expressed emotion. Risk is enhanced by spending significant amounts of time living in this context, and if the affected individual has poor cognitive function.
10. Stress, particularly that associated with economic instability and high workload, may contribute risk for mental health problems among single parents.
11. Caring for people with long-term mental or physical health problems markedly increases risk for mental health problems.
12. The social problems and poorer health associated with older age both increase risk for mental health problems.
13. Deteriorating cognitive capacity may also contribute to risk for mental health problems.
14. Proximity to death results in attempts to engage in life review and increases risk for depression and anxiety.

Further reading

Fernando, S. and Keating, F. (eds.) (2009) *Mental Health in a Multi-ethnic Society: A multidisciplinary handbook*. London: Routledge.

Freeman, D. and Freeman, J. (2013) *The Stressed Sex: Uncovering the truth about men, women, and mental health*. Oxford: Oxford University Press.

Fryers, T., Jenkins, R. and Melzer, D. (2013) *Social Inequalities and the Distribution of the Common Mental Health Disorders*. Hove: Psychology Press.

Godfrey, M. and Denby, T. (2004) *Depression and Older People: Towards securing well-being in later life*. Bristol: Policy Press.

Reder, P., McClure, M. and Jolley, A. (eds.) (2005) *Family Matters: Interfaces between child and adult mental health*. London: Routledge.

Chapter 4

Biological processes and interventions

Most mental health or behavioural problems are influenced by the activity of brain systems. Activity within these systems is mediated by the actions of neurotransmitters, chemical messengers that alter the activity of individual neurons and entire brain systems. These form the primary target for pharmacological treatments of mental health problems, increasing or decreasing neurotransmitter activity as appropriate.

Early biological models of mental health problems typically linked disorders to the activity of one neurotransmitter. Depression, for example, was associated with dysregulation of the neurotransmitter serotonin. More recently, it has become evident that multiple brain systems and neurotransmitters may be involved in the development of many disorders. This chapter provides a brief 'primer' of the relevant neuroanatomy, the neurotransmitters, and the drugs that can affect them.

By the end of this chapter, you should have an understanding of:

- The brain areas associated with emotional and behavioural disorders
- The neurotransmitters associated with emotional and behavioural disorders
- The autonomic nervous system and the neurotransmitters and hormones that influence its activity
- The major pharmacological treatments of emotional and behavioural disorders
- The problem of adherence to medication
- The costs and benefits of psychological and pharmacological interventions
- Neurological treatments: electroconvulsive therapy, transcranial magnetic stimulation
- Psychosurgery

The brain

Brain function or dysfunction is central to most mental health problems. These may relate to problems in the regulation of mood or behaviour.

The regulation of mood

Many of the brain areas that influence mood and behaviour are situated in the forebrain. These include the:

- *Thalamus*: a 'relay station' linking basic sensory information to higher cortical areas and regulating motor function. It is important in the regulation of emotion, as it modulates levels of arousal and influences the attention given to differing sensory events.
- *Hypothalamus*: regulates appetite, sexual arousal, and thirst. It also appears to have some control over emotions.
- *Amygdala*: links sensory information to emotionally relevant behaviours, particularly responses to fear and anger. It has been called the 'emotional computer' because of its role in coordinating the process that begins with the evaluation of sensory information for significance (such as threat) and then controls the resulting behavioural and autonomic responses. It is also involved in social processing, and in particular evaluating the meaning of facial expressions and trustworthiness. Finally, it is involved in the laying down and retrieval of episodic memories.
- *Hippocampus*: involved in the consolidation of short-term to long-term memories, in particular spatial memories. This function makes the hippocampus central to learning new information and associative learning.

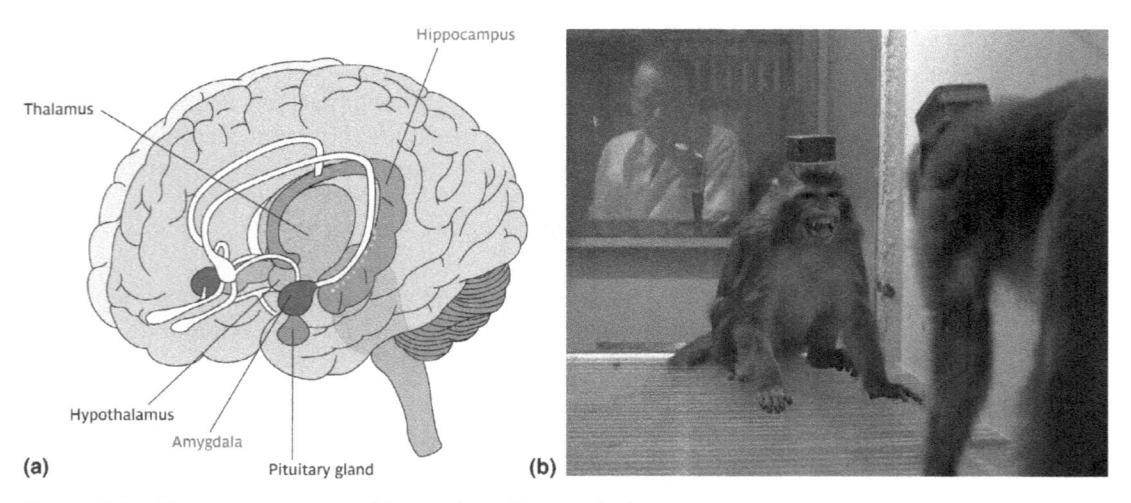

Figure 4.1 The nerve, axon, and its modes of transmission

These brain areas (Figure 4.1) have individual roles in the regulation of emotions or factors that influence our emotions, such as the memories we consolidate and the attention we give to them; both of these are now seen as central to psychopathology (e.g. Wells 2000). Some are also linked together in a network known as the limbic system, which regulates our emotions among other functions. This comprises brain areas known as the Circuit of Papez, with the following neural pathway: hippocampus–fornix–mammillary bodies–thalamus–cingulated cortex–hippocampus, and the hippocampal–fornix–mammillary bodies circuit. But these are not the only brain areas involved in the regulation of emotions. Others include:

- *The ventral tegmental area*: links to nerve cells in the nucleus accumbens and the frontal cortex. This mesolimbic dopamine system forms the brain's primary reward pathway, making it central to intense emotions such as love and (less positively) addiction.
- *Brodmann Area 25*: controls the activity within a number of neural networks, including two related to mood: (1) the hypothalamus and brain stem, which influence appetite and sleep, and (2) the amygdala and insula, which influence mood and anxiety. It also links to, and regulates activity within, the frontal lobes. High levels of activity in Area 25 appear to depress activity in the frontal lobes, preventing them from regulating the distressing thoughts that contribute to depression.
- *Temporal lobes*: although the temporal lobes are not central to the emotional experience, they have an important role in memory and contain systems that preserve the record of conscious experience. They have an intimate connection with the limbic system and link emotions to events and memories. As a consequence, they can influence our mood through linkages with past events and situations.

The regulation of planned behaviour

Many mental health conditions, including schizophrenia, attention deficit hyperactivity disorder (ADHD), and **Alzheimer's disease**, involve a breakdown in planning of behaviour. Central to the planning and control of such behaviours are the frontal lobes, in which control over **executive functions** is largely situated. The frontal cortex has an executive function that coordinates a number of complex processes, including speech, motor coordination, and behavioural planning. Poor executive function, either as a consequence of dysregulation of relevant neurotransmitters or neuronal damage that may occur in conditions such as Alzheimer's disease, can result in a number of outcomes, including: (1) inappropriately low levels of anxiety and concern for the future consequences of any actions, (2) impulsiveness or (3) conversely (particularly following brain damage) a lack of initiative and spontaneity, (iv) impairments in recent memory, poor capacity to think in abstract terms, and (v) an inability to plan and follow through a course of action or to take account of the outcome of actions. Individuals with frontal damage are inflexible and rigid. They have difficulty in shifting from one concept or task to another and changing from one established habit or behaviour to another. The frontal lobes also seem to influence motivation levels. Damage to them can lead to a condition known as adynamia, evidenced through a complete or relative lack of verbal or overt behaviour. The prefrontal lobes are connected to the limbic system via the thalamus and motor system within the cortex. Links between the prefrontal cortex and the limbic system are activated during rewarding behaviours.

Neurons and neurotransmitters

Each of the interconnecting nerves within the brain is known as a neuron. Activation of systems within the brain is the result of small electrical currents progressing along many different neurons. Critical to the flow of this current are the small gaps between neurons, known as synapses. Here, chemicals known as neurotransmitters are responsible for activation of the system.

Each neuron has a number of fine branches known as axons at its terminal. At the end of these is an area known as the presynaptic terminal, which is in close proximity to the postsynaptic terminal within the axon of another neuron. Between them is an enclosed area known as the synaptic space (see Figure 4.2). Neurotransmitter chemicals are stored within the axon in small pockets known as synaptic vesicles. Electrical stimulation of the nerve results in release of the vesicles' contents into the synaptic space. Once the transmitter has been released into the synaptic space, it moves across the gap between the two axons, where it is taken up by specialist cells – the receptor cells – within the postsynaptic membrane. Once in the receiving neuron, chemicals known as second messengers are released and trigger the firing of the neuron, continuing the activity of the activated neurological system. If all the transmitter is not taken up by the postsynaptic receptor, further activation may be inhibited either by re-uptake of the unused molecules back into vesicles in the initiating neuron or by degradation by other chemicals, such as monoamine oxidase released into the synaptic space.

Neuronal activity itself is mediated by small electrical impulses that travel down the nerve axon towards the nerve ending. When a neuron is at rest, the outside of the cell wall is lined with sodium ions, and the inside wall is lined with potassium ions. When the neuron is stimulated by an incoming message at its receptor site, the sodium ions move from the outer

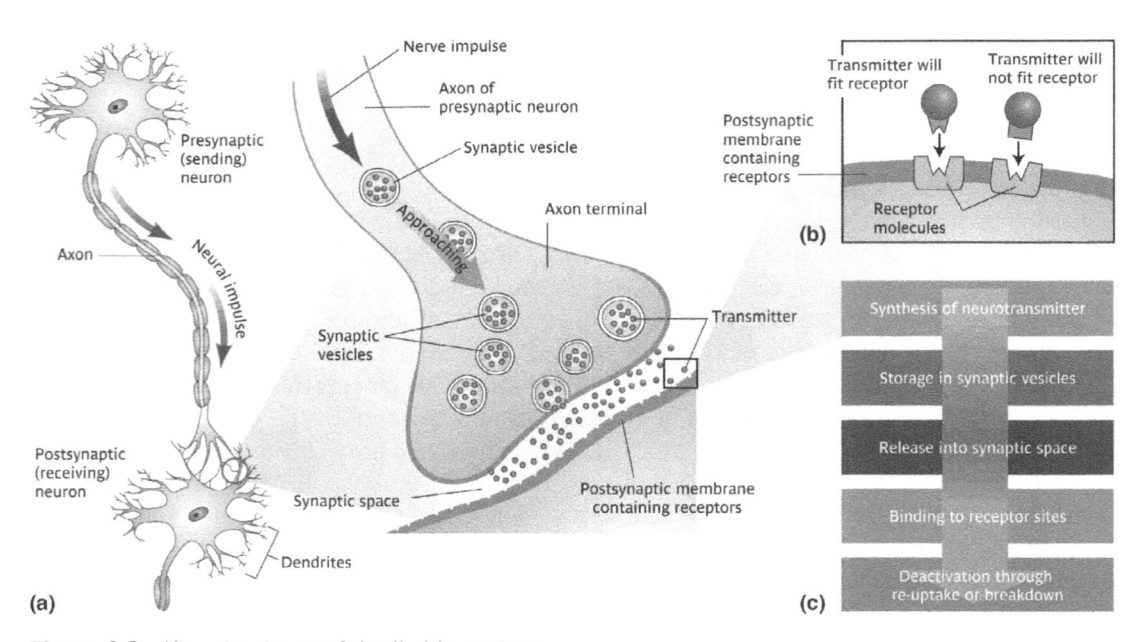

Figure 4.2 Key structures of the limbic system

side of the cell membrane to its inside. This starts a wave of electrochemical activity that continues down the length of the axon and results in it 'firing'. Immediately after this, the potassium ions shift from the inside to the outside of the neuron, returning it to its original resting state.

The neurotransmitters

A relatively small number of neurotransmitters influence activity within the brain systems involved in the regulation of emotions and behaviour, and are implicated in the **aetiology** of the most common mental disorders. They include:

Serotonin

Serotonin is an amino acid, synthesized from its precursor L-tryptophan (which is found in chocolate and may be one reason that eating dark chocolate may influence mood). It is found in the striatum, mesolimbic system, forebrain, cortex, hippocampus, thalamus, and hypothalamus. Low levels or serotonin have been linked to depression, anxiety, obsessive-compulsive disorder, and high levels of impulsivity. The latter may be particularly problematic in people at risk of suicide, with ADHD, and anger control issues.

Norepinephrine

Norepinephrine is the second neurotransmitter involved in depression as well as a number of anxiety disorders. It has also been linked to ADHD, as it is involved in the regulation of attention and concentration, and along with dopamine, has been associated with the development of schizophrenia. Among other areas, it is found in the hypothalamus, cerebellum, and hippocampus. It belongs to a family of chemicals known as catecholamines.

Dopamine

Dopamine is one of the key neurotransmitters involved in schizophrenia. Neurons mediated by dopamine are found in the mesolimbic system, in a brain area known as A10, with links to the thalamus, hippocampus, frontal cortex, and the substantia nigra. Dopaminergic dysregulation has also been associated with conditions as varied as autism and ADHD.

The autonomic nervous system

While most explanations of mental health disorders focus on the role of neurotransmitters within the brain, another system is responsible for the physiological responses associated with anxiety or fear: the autonomic nervous system. This system controls the activity of many of the body's organs, including the heart, smooth muscles, sweat glands, and (in part) the gut. The autonomic system has two sub-systems, both of which innervate the internal organs of the body: the sympathetic and parasympathetic nervous systems. Activity in the sympathetic system increases activity within the target organs, increasing heart rate, smooth muscle tension, gut motility, and so on. Conversely, the role of the parasympathetic system is to reduce arousal. The two systems work antagonistically, and the overall level of physiological activation at any one time is a function of the relative dominance of each system.

The autonomic nervous system is controlled by the hypothalamus. The hypothalamus receives blood-borne and nervous system inputs concerning the state of the body, such as oxygenation and acidity of the blood. It is responsible for automatically increasing muscle tension, heart rate, blood pressure, etc., as the individual shifts from sitting to standing, begins walking, and so on. As such, it allows us to engage in day-to-day activities without conscious thought or preparation. It also regulates our physiological response to emotionally relevant events. It receives inputs from the cortex and limbic system regarding behavioural and emotional factors. Based on these various inputs, the hypothalamus either increases or decreases activity within the different arms of the autonomic nervous system and the various organs it controls. When anxiety or stress is experienced, the sympathetic nervous system becomes dominant, activates the body, and prepares it to respond. At its most dramatic, this response is known as the *fight–flight response*. At such times, sympathetic activity is clearly dominant, the heart beats more quickly and more powerfully, blood is shunted to the muscles and away from the gut (hence the experience of 'butterflies'), skeletal muscles tense in preparation for action, and so on. Extreme activation can result in symptoms that include very high levels of tension, over-breathing (hyperventilation), high heart rate, and sweating: a 'panic attack'.

Norepinephrine and epinephrine

These two chemical messengers are involved in activation of the sympathetic nervous system. The organs innervated by the sympathetic nervous system (including smooth muscles, gut, heart, sweat glands) are initially activated directly through nerve fibres linked to the hypothalamus. However, continued activation of the sympathetic nervous system is maintained by the hormonal counterpart of the neurotransmitter norepinephrine (and to a lesser extent epinephrine), which is released into the blood stream and taken to the affected organs from the adrenal medulla within the adrenal glands, situated above the kidneys.

Acetylcholine

This neurotransmitter, with links between the hypothalamus and target organs, is responsible for activation of the parasympathetic nervous system. It inhibits the action of norepinephrine and epinephrine.

Gamma-aminobutyric acid

Gamma-aminobutyric acid (GABA) is known as an inhibitory neurotransmitter, as it is responsible for the inhibition of neuronal firing. It is widely distributed throughout the brain, including the brain stem, cerebellum, and limbic system. It is also found in the sympathetic nervous system. GABA acts as a form of 'brake' on neuronal activity, and low levels of GABA may contribute to over-activation of the sympathetic nervous system and the experience of anxiety.

Pharmacotherapy

Activation of brain systems is dependent on the activity of neurotransmitters. Problems can occur as a result of too little neurotransmitter being released into the synapses connecting neurons in the relevant brain systems, too much being released, or too much or too little being taken up at the postsynaptic receptor sites. The goal of drug therapies is to ensure appropriate levels of key neurotransmitters. They do this by one of two actions:

- *Increasing the availability* of the neurotransmitter by preventing re-uptake at the synapse, preventing degradation within the synaptic cleft, or replacing low levels of a particular neurotransmitter with its pharmacological equivalent. Drugs that increase the action of a neurotransmitter are known as agonists.
- *Decreasing the availability* of the neurotransmitter by depleting levels of the available transmitter or replacing the active transmitters with an inert chemical. Drugs that inhibit the action of a neurotransmitter are known as antagonists.

Using pharmacotherapy can be a complex process. Prescribing is based on an empirical process. Drugs are prescribed and their effectiveness assessed over a period of time, perhaps a few weeks, to assess their effectiveness. Some drugs may be expected to have an immediate effect; others, including many antidepressants, take some time to be effective. Assessment may involve the person prescribed the drug attending a clinic held by a psychiatrist of other clinician. Or a psychiatric nurse could assess them in their own home. If the drug is proving effective, they may be maintained on the drug. If it is less than optimally effective, the prescriber can take one of two actions. First, the prescriber could increase the dosage. Many drugs are initially prescribed at relatively low doses to minimize side-effects, before the dosage is increased over time to maximize their effectiveness. Second, the person could be taken off one drug and, following a wash-out period while the drug leaves the system, start taking an alternative. Sometimes this may be from the same class of drugs: the effectiveness of the same type of drug may vary across individuals. Sometimes, the person may be prescribed a different type of drug to determine its effectiveness. So, treatment with psychiatric medication is far from simple and requires both skill and significant contact with those prescribed the medication to ensure its optimal effectiveness.

Treating depression

Drugs that increase norepinephrine: MAOIs

The first drug family to be considered here, the monoamine oxidase inhibitors (MAOIs), are included mostly as a consequence of their historical role in the treatment of depression. They were the first antidepressant in regular use in the 1960s and 1970s. Their primary mode of action involves preventing degradation of norepinephrine within the synaptic cleft, thereby sustaining its action. They have a similar, but much more limited action on serotonin. They are now rarely used for two reasons: first, research since this time has shown serotonin to be the primary neurotransmitter associated with depression; and second, MAOIs have to be used with caution. As well as influencing neurotransmitter levels, they also prevent the production of monoamine oxidase in the liver and intestines. This breaks down tyramine, a chemical that can result in potentially fatal and sudden increases in blood pressure if it accumulates within the body. To prevent this, people who take MAOIs have to avoid foods containing tyramine, including cheese, red wines, bananas, and some fish. Some newer MAOIs, known as reversible selective MAOIs, avoid these problems. However, drugs that increase serotonin levels are now the drug of choice for depression.

Drugs that increase serotonin: tricyclics, SSRIs, and SNRIs

Three drug types, listed in order of their introduction, increase serotonin levels by inhibiting its re-uptake once released into the presynaptic terminal: (1) tricyclics (e.g. imipramine, amitriptyline), (2) selective serotonin re-uptake inhibitors (SSRIs: e.g. fluoxetine, sertraline), and (3) serotonin–norepinephrine re-uptake inhibitors (SNRIs: e.g. venlafaxine, duloxetine). Tricyclics and SNRIs also increase levels of norepinephrine.

After proving unsuccessful in the treatment of schizophrenia, tricyclics were found to be effective in the treatment of depression and by the mid-1960s they formed the principal treatment for the disorder. They increase levels of both serotonin and, to a lesser extent, norepinephrine. As such, they influence both key neurotransmitters involved in the development of depression. In retrospect, this may have proven a therapeutic advantage, but at the time of their use this was not recognized. Instead, by the mid-1980s, the pharmaceutical companies had found a family of drugs that more clearly targeted serotonin alone. The advantage of this new class of drugs, selective serotonin re-uptake inhibitors (SSRIs), was that they had many fewer side-effects, such as dry mouth, reduced appetite, and constipation than tricyclics, and were less dangerous in overdose. This was an important benefit, as these side-effects significantly impacted on adherence to treatment regimens. Despite this clear advantage, the use of SSRIs has not been without problems. First, from a therapeutic perspective, care has to be taken on their discontinuation. The 'SSRI discontinuation syndrome' is usually mild, commences within a week of stopping treatment, resolves spontaneously within 3 weeks, and consists of a number of physical and psychological symptoms, of which the most frequent are dizziness, nausea, lethargy, and headache. Restarting use of an SSRI leads to resolution within 48 hours. To minimize this risk, SSRIs, like other antidepressants, need to be withdrawn gradually.

Even more problematic were the political and social issues surrounding the most famous of SSRIs: Prozac. Introduced in 1987, Prozac was marketed by its makers, Eli Lilly, as the leading drug in a new generation of antidepressants free of side-effects. It rapidly gained a reputation as not only being able to help people who were depressed, but also able to improve the quality of life of people who were not. It seemed to increase confidence and sociability, and to reduce shyness and social anxiety. As a result, Prozac was widely prescribed in the USA, for both those who were depressed and those who needed this emotional lift. This widespread use became problematic when a number of serious side-effects emerged, the most important of which involved a condition known as akathisia. This is characterized by high levels of agitation and impulsiveness and was linked to high levels of suicide and a number of high-profile news stories, including that of Joseph Wesbecker, who shot 20 people in his former workplace, eight of them fatally, before killing himself while taking Prozac. Behind this sensationalism, more careful empirical studies provided clearer evidence of the effects of Prozac. Jick et al. (1995), for example, compared suicide rates of over 170,000 people prescribed a range of antidepressants, reporting them as the 'rate of suicide per 10,000 person years'. The lowest rate of suicide, 4.7, was found among people taking Lofepramine (a tricyclic); the mean rate was 10.8 suicides per 10,000 years. The highest rate of suicide was found among those taking Prozac: 19.0 suicides per 10,000 person years. However, many of the people taking Prozac were at particularly high risk of suicide as a result of factors other than their medication. They may, for example, have been prescribed Prozac after failing to benefit from treatment with tricyclics. After accounting for these factors, suicide rates among people prescribed Prozac remained a little higher than the average but did not differ significantly from the norm. Over time, the controversy has eased, and SSRIs are now the primary drug of choice in the treatment of depression. Because tricyclics work on both serotonin and norepinephrine levels, they appear to be more effective in the treatment of depression than SSRIs. However, like tricyclics, they may have more severe side-effects and discontinuation symptoms.

Treating anxiety

Drugs that enhance the action of GABA: benzodiazepines

Benzodiazepines remain perhaps the best-known treatment of anxiety. Indeed, in the mid-1980s, they were the most widely prescribed psychotropic medication. They enhance the effect of GABA throughout the brain and sympathetic nervous system, resulting in sedative, hypnotic, and anxiolytic effects. The first benzodiazepine was chlordiazepoxide (Librium). The best known, Valium, was marketed several years later. Unfortunately, early optimism concerning the benefits of benzodiazepines was tempered by problems of addiction and withdrawal. An estimated 40 per cent of people who take benzodiazepines for longer than 6 weeks, and up to 80 per cent of those who take them over a longer term, are likely to become addicted and experience significant withdrawal symptoms if they stop taking them. These may include feeling tense and agitated, dizziness, a 'metallic taste' in the mouth, blurred vision, and sensitivity to light. More extreme symptoms may include confusion, hallucinations, and epileptic fits. For this reason, prescription of benzodiazepines is now generally restricted to relatively short periods of time to help people over acute crises.

Drugs that increase norepinephrine and serotonin: SSRIs and SNRIs

Fortunately, alternative long-term treatments to benzodiazepines are now available. There is increasing evidence that some anxiety conditions, and in particular panic disorder, are mediated, at least in part, by norepinephrine. Serotonin may also be involved in the aetiology of anxiety disorders such as panic and obsessive-compulsive disorder For these conditions, treatment with antidepressants has now proven more effective than with traditional anxiolytics, and these disorders are increasingly treated with SSRIs or SNRIs.

Treating schizophrenia

Drugs that reduce dopamine levels: phenothiazines

The first drug used to treat schizophrenia was called chlorpromazine. It belongs to a group of drugs variously described as phenothiazines, neuroleptics or major tranquillizers. Its use revolutionized mental health care in the 1950s, leading to the pharmacological treatment of a wide range of disorders. They reduce dopamine activity by blocking postsynaptic dopamine receptor sites. Unfortunately, while successful in the short term, their use eventually results in a proliferation of dopamine receptor sites, adding further to the sensitivity of the postsynaptic receptors and resulting in the need for long-term treatment and increased dosage. These drugs also have a number of significant side-effects, both reversible and potentially permanent. Accordingly, clinicians maintain people with schizophrenia on the lowest effective dose or may gradually reduce or even stop treatment at times when the individual is functioning normally.

The side-effects associated with phenothiazines occur as a result of their impact on the extrapyramidal areas of the brain, including the substantia nigra. These so-called 'extrapyramidal symptoms' mimic those found in Parkinson's disease and include stiffness in the arms and legs, inexpressive face, and tremors, particularly in the hands. These symptoms can usually be relieved by drugs known as anticholinergic agents, which influence nervous control over muscles, or by a reduction in the amount of phenothiazine prescribed. However, about 20 per cent of people who take phenothiazines for an extended time develop a second condition, known as tardive dyskinesia. Its primary symptoms include restlessness, involuntary writhing or tic-like movements of the face or whole body. These symptoms can be irreversible. If detected early, and treatment is stopped immediately, most symptoms will remit. However, many symptoms are similar to those found in schizophrenia and may not be observed; or even result in increased phenothiazine being prescribed.

Increasing NMDA activity

The latest approach to the treatment of schizophrenia involves drugs known as **atypical neuroleptics**. This family of drugs, which includes clozapine and risperidone, achieves their action primarily through their influence on N-methyl-D-aspartate (NMDA) receptors. These, in turn, influence activity within both the dopamine and serotonin systems. They reduce dopamine activity, and thereby reduce **positive symptoms** such as hallucinations, and increase serotonin levels, resulting in a reduction in negative symptoms such as amotivation and thought disorder.

This family of drugs is probably more effective than the phenothiazines and they have fewer extrapyramidal side-effects. Success rates with phenothiazines of about 65 per cent are typical; for the new drugs, the success rate is as high as 85 per cent (Attard and Taylor 2012). Unfortunately, one of the first drugs of this type, olanzapine, was also found to increase the risk for a potentially fatal reduction in white blood cells, known as **agranulocytosis**, resulting in a need for all those prescribed these drugs to have regular blood tests (weekly for the first 6 months, and then fortnightly for a further 6 months) so they could be withdrawn before this disorder became problematic. Although the risk of this effect was reduced in later drugs of this type, it still may occur, as may problems of inflammation of the heart muscle (myocarditis). For this reason, despite their therapeutic advantage over phenothiazines, these drugs are frequently prescribed for people who have not responded to phenothiazines rather than form a first-line treatment.

Adherence to drug treatments

Medication is only effective if it is taken, and taken regularly. This may appear obvious, but full adherence to medication regimes is only modest. Bulloch and Patten (2009), for example, calculated that 35 per cent of people prescribed antipsychotics or sedatives, and 46 per cent of those prescribed antidepressants were either not taking them at all or taking them too intermittently to be effective. More recently, Kaplan et al. (2013) found that up to 44 per cent of people prescribed antipsychotic medication were not taking their medication at all, while around 65 per cent were 'partially non-adherent'. The most frequent reason for non-adherence was forgetting, and for this reason a small number of medications (and in particular some antipsychotics) can be given in long-lasting injection form.

More active decisions to reduce or stop medication use are frequently based on a cost–benefit analysis: weighing up the benefits in terms of symptom reduction and the costs, usually involving side-effects. The more side-effects a drug has, the less likely its use, especially if there are no immediate changes in symptoms when doses of a drug are taken or missed, as is the case for many psychiatric drugs. The chapter has already noted that SSRIs have significantly fewer side-effects than tricyclics, and this is reflected in their respective adherence rates: 64 per cent for tricyclics and 94 per cent for SSRIs (Demyttenaere et al. 1998). The side-effects that influence adherence may also be surprising. In a study of adherence to phenothiazines, those prescribed them reported that feelings of fatigue and sleepiness, weight gain, tension and 'inner unrest', and difficulties in concentration were more important in their decision to not take medication than the experience of extrapyramidal effects, which were the main concern of the prescribing clinicians (Lingjaerde et al. 1987).

Subtler and more global factors may also influence adherence. Day et al. (2005), for example, found that adherence to medication regimes was greatest when the individual prescribed them had a good relationship with the prescribing clinician and had not experienced any real coercion when they were admitted to hospital. A positive attitude towards medication or treatment in general, and a lack of perceived stigma attached to taking medication, have also been found to be associated with adherence, as has viewing the taking of medication as 'necessary'.

Medication: a cost-effective treatment?

Medication is cheap – psychological therapy is expensive. Therefore, if the two approaches have similar outcomes, medication may be the best approach. This is not an unreasonable argument, but it can be countered from a number of perspectives. First, the two approaches may be equally effective at the beginning of therapy: pharmacological therapy may even be more effective than psychotherapy. However, over the longer term, psychotherapy frequently begins to take the lead and to prove equally or more effective. The two approaches generally run pretty close while the person is taking medication, but withdrawal of medication is often associated with marked increases in symptoms. Hollon et al. (2005), for example, compared relapse rates of people successfully treated with either cognitive behaviour therapy (CBT) or pharmacotherapy over a 12-month period. During this time, 31 per cent of those who had received CBT and 76 per cent who had received pharmacological treatment experienced a relapse following the cessation of treatment. This difference in long-term effectiveness is reflected in the costs of treatment. In general, CBT interventions are delivered over 8–12 group or individual sessions by a single therapist. By contrast, because of the problems of relapse, patients may be kept on many pharmacological interventions for a year or more, maybe for much longer. So the costs of pharmacological therapies may extend over significant periods of time and often eventually exceed those of psychotherapy. As a consequence of these extended payments, Antonuccio et al. (1997) found the costs of treatment for depression 2 years following the initiation of treatment were 33 per cent higher among those prescribed an SSRI (Prozac) than those receiving CBT.

Good evidence-based psychotherapy appears in many cases to be more effective than pharmacotherapy, so much so that the UK government has made a significant financial investment in a programme of CBT-type interventions, at varying levels of complexity, in an attempt to reduce the costs of mental health care in the UK. Known as IAPT (Increasing Access to

Psychological Therapies), this programme varies from the provision of self-help to complex individual interventions and is widely available throughout England (but not the devolved nations). Of course, it would be rather too much to claim that medication is redundant in the care of people with mental health disorders. Some conditions, such as acute psychosis, may require medication in both the short and long terms. Many people do not benefit from psychotherapy even in conditions in which this approach is relatively successful, and may need to receive alternative interventions. In addition, access to psychotherapy is often significantly limited due to the lack of skilled therapists. Finally, many people may actively choose to be given pharmacotherapy and reject psychotherapeutic approaches. Both pharmacotherapy and psychotherapy will continue to be used in parallel by health care systems for many years yet, and perhaps more so than the next form of treatment discussed in this chapter.

Current affairs

Increasingly, health care systems are supposed to be responsive to 'patient choice'. So, what would your choice be? If you had a mental health problem that could be treated equally effectively with psychological treatment or pharmacological treatment, which would you prefer? What are the pros and cons of each approach? What sort of person is more likely to chose and benefit from pharmacotherapy and who is likely to benefit most from psychotherapy?

Drugs come with a caveat

The text so far has reflected the conventional view of pharmacological treatment of drug therapies, and has generally been supportive of their use. As such, it is consistent with the majority view. However, this is not the only view, and some shouting from the side-lines suggests we should adopt a degree of caution in considering the use of pharmacological treatments. The first to be considered here is a general critique of 'big pharma' companies developed by Goldacre. In his text, *Bad Pharma*, Goldacre (2012) provided evidence of how many pharmaceutical companies hide or dissimilate the findings of their own research, including that related to antidepressants, when this does not support the use of their drugs. He also noted the frequent inappropriate use of drugs: for example, using adult certified antidepressants for younger people, who may be more prone to their side-effects.

A differing, but more intriguing critique of the development of antidepressants was provided by Kirsch (2009). He identified a hierarchy of evidence that should be used to determine the effectiveness of any drug. The first level is that drugs are more effective than no treatment. This, he argued, is clearly the case for antidepressant medication. The next level of argument is that drugs are more effective than **placebo**. This is the 'gold standard' level of evidence accepted by most researchers and clinicians. He noted that, again, antidepressants achieve this criterion, although the additional benefit from receiving the drug is significantly less than that between the drug and no treatment. In other words, a significant element of the effectiveness of antidepressants is the result of a placebo effect. Kirsch then argued that this traditional view of effectiveness is not as strong as it may appear. He noted that many people in drug trials and the doctors prescribing them are pretty much aware whether they are receiving an active drug or an inert placebo. The presence of side-effects (or lack of them) may indicate which condition the person is a part of. He therefore argued that the optimum way to evaluate any drug is to compare it, not with an inert placebo as is the case in the vast majority of drug trials (the 'gold standard'), but to compare it with a placebo that has some mild side-effects (ideally not dissimilar to those that may be expected if the individual were receiving an active medication similar to that being tested). When antidepressant medication is subjected to this rare manipulation, the difference between active intervention and placebo is minimal. In other words, according to Kirsch the apparent effects of at least one antidepressant treatment can be attributed almost entirely to the placebo effect. Finally, in a challenging editorial in the *British Journal of Psychiatry*, Morrison et al. (2012) highlighted antipsychotics as frequently achieving less than minimal clinical improvements, while carrying more significant and frequent side-effects, including risk of sudden death, than was once thought. It may be worth reconsidering your response to the 'current affairs' question in the light of this type of critique!

Neurological treatments

Electroconvulsive therapy

Electroconvulsive therapy (ECT) involves the brief discharge of electric current through the brain in order to induce a controlled epileptic convulsion. Its origins lie in observations made in the 1930s that stunned pigs appeared particularly sedated and quiet in abattoirs, as well as anecdotal evidence that people who had epilepsy rarely evidenced any form of psychosis and that mood following epileptic seizures often improved. As a result of these observations and emerging evidence of its effectiveness, ECT became a standard form of treatment for both depression and schizophrenia in the 1940s and 1950s, and remained so until the introduction of antipsychotics and antidepressants. It is still in limited use and is recommended by the British National Institute for Health and Care Excellence (NICE: publications.nice.org.uk/guidance-on-the-use-of-electroconvulsive-therapy-ta59) for the treatment of depression that is resistant to pharmacological intervention or where there is a strong likelihood of suicide. Its use in the treatment of schizophrenia is no longer recommended. Treatment usually involves a course of 4–12 treatments over a period of 2–3 weeks, although in 'maintenance ECT' it may be given fortnightly or monthly for 6 months or longer to prevent relapse. It is thought to achieve its actions through an increase in the sensitivity of postsynaptic neurons to serotonin in the hippocampus, increased levels of GABA, and reduced levels of dopamine (Ishihara and Sasa 1999).

Originally given 'straight', ECT frequently resulted in dislocation of the jaw and broken bones, and was highly distressing for those receiving it. Now, it is only given after patients have been given a strong muscle relaxant to prevent the muscular effects of the seizure and anaesthesia to prevent them being aware of both the procedure itself and the complete loss of muscle tone (including not being able to breath voluntarily) resulting from this procedure. Although this has clearly reduced the risks of physical harm during or following the procedure, a second side-effect remains. Immediately after the procedure, people typically take some time to orient themselves in terms of time and place. Perhaps more problematic are the long-term memory problems that many people experience. Feliu et al. (2008), for example, found that nearly one month following ECT, people diagnosed with depression evidenced improvements in mood, but also performed less well on measures of recognition memory, and short-term verbal and visual memory. In an attempt to reduce but not eliminate these problems, the shock given in ECT is now passed through only one electrode on the non-dominant lobe.

Transcranial magnetic stimulation

Given the cognitive problems associated with ECT, a number of research groups are seeking less problematic alternatives, the leading contender of which is transcranial magnetic stimulation (TMS). This involves passing a series of electrical pulses close to the brain. A coil is held close to the scalp. Small, induced currents within the coil can then make brain areas below it more or less active, depending on the settings used. Transcranial magnetic stimulation can influence many brain functions, including movement, visual perception, memory, reaction time, speech, and mood. The obvious effects of TMS last very short times following stimulation. However, the procedure may have longer-term effects on mood. Schulze-Rauschenbach et al. (2005), for example, found 44 per cent of those treated with TMS showed significant clinical improvements and no memory deficits. This compared with a 46 per cent response rate following ECT. Despite this finding, a report published by NICE in 2011 (http://guidance.nice.org.uk/IPG242) maintained its 2007 recommendation that sufficient high-quality research into the efficacy of TMS remains lacking and that it cannot yet be recommended for routine clinical use.

Psychosurgery

The most radical of all biological interventions involves direct surgery on the brain for the treatment of depression and anxiety. Treatment of severe, intractable depression involves destruction of the subcaudate brain area using radioactive rods, which give a brief, destructive burst of radioactivity into the brain area. Treatment of anxiety disorders, in particular debilitating obsessive-compulsive disorder, involves a procedure known as stereotactic cingulotomy, in which electrodes are placed within the cingulate bundle in each hemisphere and heated to 85°C for around 100 seconds. Psychosurgery is now rarely conducted and in some countries such as Germany and some US states it is banned. In the UK, around 20 operations are presently conducted each year. To be a candidate for psychosurgery in the UK, very strict criteria need to be met, including the individual having made two or more serious suicide attempts, having experienced episodic depressive episodes for at least 18 years, and their present episode having lasted at least 7 years. They should also have received large doses of antidepressants and at least 30 ECT treatments. The decision to operate is not made by a single psychiatrist: a panel of three representatives unknown to the individual need to agree the procedure and ensure that the individual concerned is capable of making a reasoned decision to have the operation.

Why such a restricted group of patients, and why so many safeguards? Well, the effects of any intervention – both good and bad – are clearly irreversible. Data from the 1960s, when the procedures were much more frequent, indicated a 4 per cent death rate, 60 per cent of patients developed 'troublesome' personality changes including profound lethargy and loss of motivation, while 15 per cent developed epilepsy. Around 20 per cent of people with schizophrenia and 50 per cent of those with depression gained some degree of benefit (Malizia 2000). Procedures and the accuracy of lesions have clearly improved since this time, and rates of deaths and unwanted effects are significantly reduced. In addition, success rates for some conditions such as obsessive-compulsive disorder have been estimated to be as high as 93 per cent (Jenike 1998). Nevertheless, the operation remains a 'last chance' approach.

Chapter summary

1. The brain is divided into a number of anatomical areas, many of which are in some way related to functions that influence mood or behaviour.
2. Damage to most brain areas will result in deficits that may be evident as emotional or mental health problems.
3. Activity within the brain is mediated by neurotransmitters, which act at the neuronal synapse.
4. Neurotransmitters mediate the activity within brain systems that are responsible for mood and behaviour. The most important to mental health are serotonin, dopamine, GABA, and norepinephrine.
5. Drug therapies affect the activity within brain systems by increasing or decreasing levels of neurotransmitters or their availability within the synaptic cleft.
6. Among other effects, antidepressants typically increase the availability of serotonin (and to a lesser extent norepinephrine); anxiolytics increase levels of GABA; and neuroleptics decrease levels of dopamine.
7. Adherence to medical treatment is far from optimal, and can be influenced by a range of factors, including the frequency and severity of side-effects, and more general factors such as the relationship with the prescribing clinician.
8. While pharmacological treatment is frequently cheaper than psychological therapy in the short term, higher relapse rates and the frequent need for long-term treatment may mean psychological treatments are more cost-effective in the long term.
9. Some critics suggest that evidence in relation to the effectiveness of drugs should be considered with considerable caution.
10. Electroconvulsive therapy involves passing an electrical current through the temporal lobes of the brain to induce a seizure.
11. Treatment with ECT remains controversial. Although it is now much safer than previously, it still evokes strong emotional arguments among both those who support its use and those who oppose it. A number of medical authorities recommend its use in cases of depression that resist treatment using other methods.
12. Electroconvulsive therapy is linked to significant measurable memory problems that last a significant period of time. A new alternative, transcranial magnetic stimulation, may prove effective and have fewer such side-effects.
13. Psychosurgery is now used only in extreme cases of obsessive-compulsive disorder or depression. It achieves a moderate degree of clinical benefit in a population where previous, more conservative treatments have failed, but carries with it a small but significant risk of irreversible cognitive deficits.

Further reading

Bentall, R. (2009) *Doctoring the Mind: Why psychiatric treatments fail.* London: Allen Lane.
Gibb, B. (2007) *A Rough Guide to the Brain.* London: Rough Guides.
Healy, D. (2008) *Psychiatric Drugs Explained.* Edinburgh: Churchill Livingstone.
Kirsch, I. (2009). *The Emperor's New Drugs: Exploding the antidepressant myth.* London: Bodley Head.
Ledoux, J. (1999) *The Emotional Brain: The mysterious underpinnings of emotional life.* London: Orion Books.
National Institute for Clinical Excellence (2003) *Guidance on the Use of Electroconvulsive Therapy.* London: NICE.
Stahl, S. (2008) *Stahl's Essential Psychopharmacology: Neuroscientific basis and practical applications.* Cambridge: Cambridge University Press.

Chapter 5

A psychotherapy primer

This chapter is intended to act as a primer, outlining the underlying principles and key therapeutic approaches of a range of psychological interventions you will encounter later in this book. The space given to each section reflects the importance or frequency of use of each approach, at least in western health care systems. The one exception to this is applied behaviour analysis. It receives relatively little attention, but is, in fact, a widely used approach; just not in the context of most disorders considered in this book.

The dominance of behavioural and cognitive behavioural interventions is not coincidental. Decisions about the use of differing therapeutic approaches within most health care systems are now based on evidence of their effectiveness. This evidence-based approach clearly identifies cognitive behavioural interventions to be most effective, and guidelines such as those provided in the UK by the National Institute for Health and Care Effectiveness (NICE) firmly recommend them as the first line psychological treatment for most disorders. Advocates of psychoanalytic and humanistic therapies may argue that the evidence on which these decisions are made is biased towards easily observable symptoms and does not consider some of the unconscious and unobservable processes underpinning pathologies relevant to these approaches. However, the existing evidence makes their use difficult to justify in economically driven public health care systems. They are still widely available in private health care settings.

By the end of this chapter, you should have an understanding of the basic principles of:

- Psychoanalysis
- Humanistic therapies
- Behaviour therapy
- Cognitive behaviour therapy
- Acceptance and commitment therapy
- Systemic approaches: structural and strategic family therapy
- Applied behaviour analysis

Psychoanalysis

The originator of psychoanalysis was Sigmund Freud. His therapeutic endeavours were based on the premise that adult psychopathology has its origins in trauma and difficulties during children's development. This trauma may be so distressing that it is kept hidden from the individual by their ego defences. As a consequence, the individual may experience emotional difficulties or anxieties without any insight into their origins or means of resolving them. Until these ego defences can be circumvented, and insight achieved, the individual continues in their state of psychological distress. Freud developed three strategies to achieve this insight:

- *Free association* facilitates the recall of traumatic or problematic childhood events previously withheld from consciousness by ego defence mechanisms. It involves the client speaking aloud whatever comes to mind, with the therapist making no conscious effort to monitor or censor their speech. The **client** lies down so they are unable to see the therapist's face and are not influenced by any facial expressions resulting from their flow of thoughts. Insight is not necessarily gained directly, and may continue to be withheld through a process known as resistance. Accordingly, the therapist may be guided more by what the client does *not* say than what they do say. Absences, where the client is unable to think of a word or finish a sentence, or abrupt changes in topic may indicate the proximity of sensitive issues. Errors, in which an individual means to say one thing but actually says something quite different (the so-called 'Freudian slip'), may also be indicative of sensitive issues that the therapist can explore more deeply.
- *Dream interpretation* was considered by Freud to be 'the Royal Road to the unconscious'. An example can be found in Freud's (1900) interpretation of one woman's dream, which included images of flowers as table decorations for a party. When asked to freely associate to the elements in her dream, she associated the word *violet* with *violate*, a word carrying both sexual and aggressive connotations. Freud interpreted the flowers as symbols of fertility and the birthday as a symbol of an impending birth or pregnancy. Accordingly, Freud believed her dreams symbolized her desire to become impregnated by her fiancé.
- *Transference* describes the relationship between client and therapist. Positive transference may involve the client becoming dependent on the therapist or even falling in love with them. Negative transference includes resentment and anger. According to Freud, these feelings reflect those held for significant others earlier in the client's life. If they fall in love with their therapist, for example, this may mean they have failed to resolve an earlier Oedipal conflict. Freud used the transference process in two ways: first, as a diagnostic process, and second, for resolving earlier conflicts by 'working through' the transference process.

Each of these processes can provide insight into the historical origins of present conflicts and distress. Once having achieved this insight, the individual may still need to work through the issues raised by their understanding of the trauma. In a process known as catharsis, the individual is encouraged to express the emotions previously damped down by their defence mechanisms.

Psychoanalysis beyond Freud

Since Freud, a number of alternative schools of psychoanalysis have developed, including those of Otto Rank, Jacques Lacan, and Harry Stack Sullivan, to name but a few. Each approach, clearly, involves a different theoretical and intervention perspective. However, they all have some common tenets that define them as psychoanalytic, and a number of common goals or processes can be identified within them. In an attempt to summarize these therapeutic goals and strategies, Boesky (1990) identified the following processes and outcomes that he considered to occur, to a greater or lesser degree, in all psychoanalytic therapy:

- Gradual and progressive revealing of historic material relevant to the presenting symptoms. A convincing demonstration of the links between childhood sexual and aggressive conflicts, both pre-Oedipal and post-Oedipal, and adult symptoms.
- Cooperative interest in understanding the symptoms, associations, dreams, and behaviour.
- Change in the relationship with the analyst, characterized by less disguised behaviour and ultimately by more realistic patterns of perception, attitude, and behaviour.
- Shifts in images of the self, family members, and the analyst.
- Increased tolerance for the expression of sexual and aggressive derivatives, together with increased coherence and clarity of the associations, behaviour, dreams, and communication.
- Improved capacity to cope with unpleasant mood states.
- Diminished need for self-punishment.
- Increased capacity for realistic gratification.

Classical psychoanalysis was extremely lengthy. Freud saw his clients up to six times a week, and even 'mild' cases were seen for three sessions a week. In addition, because psychoanalysis used free association to allow insight into clients' problems, and there may have been weeks or even months between sessions in which significant insights were attained, analysis took many months or even years. More recent versions of psychoanalysis tend to be shorter, typically lasting no more than 25 sessions (still many more than the typical limits of cognitive behaviour therapy of 6–12 sessions). They have three distinct phases: beginning, an active phase, and termination. Beginning involves assessment, developing a therapeutic alliance, and preparing the client for therapy. In the active phase, the therapist determines the direction of therapy and the issues to be addressed within it. Strategies may involve the use of interpretation of current feelings in terms of past experiences, and the elicitation of emotions experienced at the time of any trauma. Issues of transference are deliberately minimized to discourage client dependence. The end of therapy is a negotiated process, in which issues of loss and separation are considered and dealt with.

Humanistic therapy

There are several schools of humanistic therapy, with the person-centred therapy of Rogers (1961) being pre-eminent. Rogers considered pathology to be a consequence of deviation from the self-actualizing process, usually as a consequence of experiencing inappropriate conditional positive regard. Therapy involves the individual realigning with their actualizing tendency.

The goal of person-centred therapy, as Rogers called his approach, is to provide an environment in which the individual can identify their own life goals and how they wish to determine them: to place them on the pathway to self-actualization. Rogers stated that therapy does not rely on techniques or doing things *to* the client. Rather, the quality of the interpersonal encounter is paramount in determining effectiveness. The goal of the therapist is to provide a setting in which the individual is not judged but is free to explore new ways of being. That is, therapy provides the conditions necessary for growth. To achieve this, the therapist must have three characteristics:

- They are integrated and genuine in their relationship with the client. Being genuine means that the therapist shares feelings or provides feedback about how they feel as a consequence of what the client is telling them. They respond to information or client behaviour in ways that reflect their true response, not a therapeutically formal response. In one glorious (possibly apocryphal) example of this, Rogers himself told the story of how he fell asleep during therapy. When challenged by the client, he told them that yes, he had fallen asleep – because they were boring him!
- They are able to gain an empathic understanding of the client's perspective and communicate this to them. Importantly, empathy is not sympathy. It involves gaining an understanding of the individual's own understanding of their world: their phenomenological field. This understanding has to be conveyed to the individual by showing interest and active engagement with the client's discourse. It can also be shown through empathic statements: reflections involving a re-statement or summary of information given by the client, and perhaps a link to their emotional state: 'I can see you were very upset while telling me about…This must be a very important issue for you.' These increase the level of engagement between client and therapist and encourage further exploration of issues relevant to the client. This non-directive means of exploration is central to Rogers' approach, and is in contrast with the use of more directive questioning.
- They are able to provide unconditional positive regard. In contrast to the conditional positive regard Rogers considered to be the cause of mental health problems, the therapist shows care and involvement with their client, regardless of the issues that may be raised in therapy. This process does not condone inappropriate or problematic attitudes or behaviours that may be uncovered or discussed during therapy. Rather, Rogers believed that the therapist needs to separate the individual from their behaviour: 'I cannot condone your behaviour, but I still respect and value you as an individual.'

Rogers suggested these three therapist characteristics can facilitate a shift from the externally imposed standards of others to the identification of, and progress towards, the pathway to self-actualization. This is thought to be achieved through a series of seven stages (Rogers 1961), in which the client:

1. fails to acknowledge feelings, and considers personal relationships as dangerous;
2. is able to describe their behaviour, but rarely their feelings, which are not 'owned';

3. can begin to describe their emotional reactions to past events, and recognize contradictions in their experience;
4. develops an awareness of their current feelings, but finds it difficult to cope with them;
5. begins to explore their inner life in a more meaningful and emotional way;
6. is able to fully experience feelings while talking of past events; and
7. develops a basic trust in their own inner processes: feelings are experienced with immediacy and intensity.

The therapist's actions facilitate each of these processes. Empathic feedback encourages and validates the exploration and expression of personal feelings and meanings of statements made in therapy. Acceptance and genuineness encourage the growth of trust in the self and increased risk-taking in the expression of previously withheld thoughts or emotions.

Rogers (1957) considered his approach to provide both 'the necessary and sufficient conditions' for 'therapeutic personality change'. Empirical evidence suggests that the approach may be effective for some individuals, including those with good coping resources and who are considering relatively positive issues of change. Such individuals have been described using the acronym YAVIS: young, attractive, verbally able, intelligent, and successful. The approach is less beneficial for people with more severe pathologies, who may benefit more from structured interventions such as cognitive behaviour therapy (Smith et al. 1980).

Accordingly, Rogers' approach may not be 'sufficient' to promote therapeutic change in most contexts. However, elements of the therapeutic approach may be 'necessary' for effective therapeutic change. A key issue in any therapeutic approach is the rapport between therapist and client – the therapeutic alliance. Hovarth and Symonds (1991), for example, calculated that 26 per cent of the variance in therapy outcome was attributable to how well the therapist and client worked together in therapy. The approach and methods used by Rogers can significantly strengthen this alliance. Accordingly, one may consider the core elements of this approach (warmth, empathy, and genuineness) as necessary but not sufficient for effective therapy in most psychiatric settings. They may need to be linked with more structured approaches to behavioural and emotional change – and it is to these approaches the chapter now turns.

Behaviour therapy

Unlike psychoanalysis and humanistic therapies, which essentially attempt to change personality, behaviour therapy – and its subsequent development into cognitive behaviour therapy – targets specific mental health problems. For this reason, a brief introduction to behavioural and cognitive behavioural theory is necessary to understand the rationale for the techniques used. These are also considered in more detail in Chapters 8 and 11.

Behavioural explanations of anxiety

Behavioural explanations of anxiety consider it to result from a conditioning experience in which an inappropriately feared object or context is associated with the experience of fear or anxiety. This conditioned stimulus subsequently triggers a conditioned fear response. Being in a frightening car crash, for example, may condition a fear reaction that is evoked each time the person subsequently travels by car. According to behavioural explanations of fear, this reaction will comprise three factors: the emotion of fear, heightened physiological activity as the individual prepares to either confront the feared stimulus or run away, and (typically) an attempt to move away from the feared stimulus. Unfortunately, while this avoidance is rewarding in the short term as the individual feels relief at the reduction of fear, in the long run it prevents the individual from habituating to the feared stimulus, and maintains the anxiety over the longer term (Mowrer 1947). The goal of behaviour therapy is to prevent this avoidance and place the individual in situations that allow habituation to occur. In contrast to both psychoanalysis and humanistic therapies, the interventions are highly structured and more controlled by the therapist.

Behaviour therapy for anxiety

One of the earliest behavioural interventions involved the treatment of phobias. This involved bringing the client in contact with a feared stimulus in one of two, very different ways: gradually, through a process known as 'systematic desensitization', or more rapidly, through 'flooding'. Systematic desensitization involves first teaching the client a number of relaxation techniques and developing a hierarchy of stimuli that progressively resemble the feared object or situation. In the case of a driving or car phobia, this may include: sitting in a stationary car, sitting in a car with its engine running, sitting in a moving car for short distance down a quiet street, and so on). The client is sequentially exposed to stimuli within the hierarchy, starting with the most distant stimulus from the feared object or situation. On each occasion, they remain in the presence of the stimulus and utilize the relaxation techniques to help them reduce their physiological arousal. This process is repeated several times until the stimulus no longer elicits an anxiety response. They then progress along the hierarchy, repeating the same procedure until they are able to cope in the presence of their feared stimulus or situation. The relaxation response has a number of benefits. From a behavioural perspective, it facilitates a state of relaxation in the presence of the feared stimulus that may speed up the habituation process or even result in a process known as 'counter-conditioning', in which the lack of fear may itself become associated with the object through classical conditioning, and facilitate the relaxation response in future encounters.

The type of relaxation most commonly taught is a derivative of Jacobson's deep muscle relaxation technique. This involves alternately tensing and then relaxing muscle groups throughout the body in an ordered sequence: hands and forearms, upper arms, shoulders and lower neck, and so on. Initially, this is practised in a comfortable and quiet place, such as a bed or supportive chair. However, as the individual becomes more skilled, the emphasis of practice shifts towards relaxation without prior tension, and to begin to use relaxation in the presence of a feared stimulus. It may be augmented by simple breathing exercises: learning to take slow deep breaths using the diaphragm to draw air to the base of the lungs.

It can be difficult to set up a graded exposure programme using real stimuli. They may be difficult to obtain (e.g. snakes) or control (e.g. driving in traffic). In such circumstances, the 'traditional' approach may have involved progressing through an 'imaginal hierarchy'. Now, technology allows us to produce a much more immersive experience, and the use of virtual reality allows the development of closely controlled and constructed hierarchies not previously thought possible.

Systematic desensitization is effective but relatively slow. An alternative approach, known as flooding, significantly speeds up the process. Flooding is based on the premise that even a strong fear response will eventually diminish if the individual remains with the feared object for a sufficiently long period. The process therefore involves the client being directly exposed to a feared stimulus with no attenuation associated with systematic desensitization. The critical issue here is that the client must stay with the feared stimulus until they no longer experience any fear, a process that may take an hour or more. Flooding has the benefit of being quicker than desensitization. However, desensitization may still be used in some cases, as it does not provoke the high levels of client distress associated with flooding. Nor does it run the risk of the recipient leaving before extinction of the fear is achieved; something that may actually add to their problems, as avoidance of the feared stimulus is once more reinforced.

The cognitive shift

Behavioural therapies can be extremely effective. However, they were largely superseded in the 1970s by an approach that placed cognitive factors at the centre of behavioural and emotional change. Cognitive behaviour therapy (CBT), as this new form of intervention became known, has a number of characteristics. Like its predecessor, it focuses on specific emotional problems. It is short-term (typically lasting 6–12 therapy sessions) and directive: the therapist actively helps the client identify and change cognitive errors and problematic behaviours. Two broad approaches are now in common use.

- *Mood disorders*: if the individual is severely depressed, gradually increase pleasurable events; for less depressed individuals, cognitive restructuring through the use of Socratic dialogue and behavioural hypothesis testing.
- *Anxiety disorders*, including generalized anxiety disorder, phobias, and obsessive-compulsive disorder: encounter the feared context through graded exposure or flooding and remain in it until fear has diminished (exposure with response prevention).

Cognitive therapy for mood disorders involved a paradigm change, with the new focus of therapy almost entirely involving cognitive change. This shift was not so marked in the treatment of anxiety disorders, where the principles of exposure to the feared stimulus remain central to treatment, although those may be augmented by the addition of cognitive and other coping strategies.

Cognitive therapy for mood disorders

In the mid-twentieth century, two American therapists, Albert Ellis and Aaron Beck, independently established very similar interventions that changed the therapy world. Ellis's (e.g. 1957) therapeutic ideas pre-dated Beck by some years, and his therapeutic approach known as rational emotive therapy focused on the role of irrational thoughts as precursors to mood disorders and the need to change these irrational thoughts by cognitive or behavioural challenges. Despite this precedence, the work of Beck (1977), which is very similar, is now much more widely known. Beck, like Ellis, argued that depression is the result of incorrect and negatively biased interpretations of day-to-day events. These evoke negative mood states and behavioural responses that may reinforce the original misinterpretation. As a simple example, if you wave to a friend and they do not wave back, this may be seen as having a benign explanation ('They did not see me') or a more emotionally difficult explanation ('They ignored me because I have done something to upset them'). If you are already depressed or low in mood, the latter explanation may be the first that springs to mind. If you subsequently avoid them, because you fear further rejection, this may exacerbate your depressed mood and prevent you from learning the benign explanation is true: they simply did not notice you. Beck referred to these misinterpretations as negative automatic thoughts (NATS). Having an influence on these cognitions, which are conscious and accessible to the individual, are unconscious core beliefs about ourselves and our world, incorporated into cognitive schema (referred to in the plural as schemata). In this example, the schema that 'I am a bad person and not worthy of love' may make interpretation of the friend's behaviour as some form of rejection more likely. These processes are discussed in more depth in Chapter 11.

Changing cognitions

Given the centrality of 'inappropriate' cognitions to mood disorders, it should be no surprise that the most important element of cognitive therapy for mood disorders involves attempts to replace 'faulty' cognitions (NATS) with more realistic and appropriate ones. The ultimate aim is to teach the individual to identify such thoughts at the time they occur, and to replace them with more realistic, positive cognitions, a process known as cognitive challenge:

- 'My friend ignored me. I must have done something bad. Perhaps they don't like me any more.'
- 'There may be a different explanation here. Perhaps they did not notice me. Perhaps they were rushing somewhere. I cannot think of anything I may have done to upset them – so why should I assume this is the case?'

The ability to identify and challenge NATS is not easy, and has to be learned over time. Typically, the therapist initiates this learning process through the use of 'guided discovery' or 'Socratic dialogue'. This involves a detailed exploration of specific instances of inappropriate interpretations, and the types of cognitive errors typically made by the individual. The therapist then gently questions the bases of these assumptions in each situation. As the individual gains insight into their cognitive errors and how they may be challenged, they will be encouraged to identify and challenge them in real time. Many therapists provide a checklist of questions that may trigger this exploration, which include:

Am I confusing a thought with a fact?
Am I jumping to conclusions?
Am I assuming my view of things is the only one possible?
Am I thinking in all or nothing terms?
Am I concentrating on my weaknesses and forgetting my strengths?
Am I blaming myself for something that is not really my fault?
Am I taking things personally?
Am I expecting myself to be perfect?

Am I only paying attention to the black side of things?
Am I exaggerating the importance of events?
Am I predicting the future?

Although challenging NATS may result in immediate improvements in mood, fundamental changes in schemata are necessary to achieve longer-term change. This is much more difficult, as these are unconscious fundamental beliefs about ourselves and the world, established during childhood and maintained over long periods of time. Exploration and challenge of these takes more time, and more therapist skill. Nevertheless, a number of strategies to achieve this have been developed, of which the 'downward arrow' technique is probably the best known. Here, the implications of NATS are followed through to their (il)logical conclusion, and the fundamental schema underpinning them is identified. The case of Stephen provides a simple example. He was held up in traffic and was late for a meeting. His emotional response was one of anger directed at the car drivers slowing him down. The downward arrow technique explored his more fundamental thoughts:

What are the implications of being late?	People will be frustrated and angry with me.
What does it mean if others get angry with you?	It means they are unhappy with me, they think I am not doing my job properly.
What does it mean to you if others think you are not doing your job properly?	They will think I am a failure and incompetent.
What does it mean to you if think you are a failure and incompetent?	I know I am incompetent, and fear that others have discovered my lack of ability.

This exploration identified the fundamental anxiety and low self-esteem underpinning his apparent anger and aggressive responses. Intervention therefore needs to focus on strategies of challenging his low self-esteem through Socratic dialogue or other means. One way this can be achieved is through the use of behavioural experiments designed to show competence and effectiveness in work and other relevant situations.

Changing behaviour

Socratic dialogue and cognitive challenge may change interpretations of events and mood. However, just like the NATs they are designed to change, these new interpretations remain a hypothesis: a more positive hypothesis, perhaps, but still a hypothesis. They are not verified in fact. Although you are able to consider the possibility your friend did not see you, this will not be verified until you have had a positive social interaction with them. With this in mind, a strategy called behavioural hypothesis testing (or experiments) is frequently used to challenge faulty cognitions. The aim of this strategy is to disprove negative beliefs an individual may hold about themselves or their future. Behavioural experiments may occur in the therapy session or as homework. Someone who believes they cannot cope in social situations without drinking excessive amounts of alcohol, for example, may be challenged to go to a party and not drink alcohol, to see whether this truly has the disastrous consequences they originally hypothesized. The hope is, of course, that all will go well and the irrational beliefs are disproved.

A final behavioural intervention that is frequently used for people who are severely depressed involves some form of behavioural activation or scheduling of pleasant events.

Behavioural activation involves establishing a simple plan of 'doing things' (getting up, making a snack, and so on) in order to reduce the somatic slowing down and avolition associated with depression. Pleasant event scheduling, as its name suggests, involves planning pleasures during the day to provide uplifts in mood. Planning these may take some thought, as they should ideally be different to those normally encountered, as negative comparisons with previous levels of pleasure may reinforce low mood rather than lift it.

Cognitive behaviour therapy for anxiety disorders

Cognitive behavioural treatment for anxiety follows a similar paradigm to flooding and systematic desensitization described earlier in the chapter. Known as 'exposure with response prevention', it involves the individual being exposed to a feared stimulus and remaining with it until their fear subsides. This may occur in either a graded or direct manner as outlined earlier. The stimuli involved may be external to the individual (phobic objects such as spiders and cars) or internal ('interoceptive') experiences such as breathing or heart rate, both of which may become triggers for anxiety or panic (see Chapter 8).

Where CBT differs from behavioural therapy is in explanations why this approach is successful and the coping strategies participants may use when exposed to the feared stimulus. The process can now be seen as a series of experiments in which the individual is exposed to the feared stimulus and comes to learn that any fears they may have are unfounded and not true: no harm will occur. That is, their cognitive appraisal of the stimulus or context is challenged just as in cognitive therapy for depression. Treatment gains are no longer interpreted in terms of conditioning or habituation.

While engaging with the feared stimulus, individuals can use a range of coping strategies to help reduce any anxiety they may experience. Just as in behaviour therapy, relaxation may be used to reduce any physiological drive; but its effects are interpreted as gaining control over panic symptoms. More specifically, cognitive challenge or a process known as self-instruction training, in which the individual gives themselves pre-prepared calming messages and reminders to use coping strategies such as relaxation, may be used to counter any anxiety-provoking thoughts they may have either before or during their exposure. Some interventions also include a completely different way of coping with anxiety-provoking cognitions: mindfulness.

Mindfulness

So far, all the cognitive interventions discussed have involved direct engagement with the negative thoughts a person is experiencing. In sharp contrast, mindfulness is a strategy through which the individual learns to recognize the presence of the negative thoughts while remaining emotionally disengaged from them. Mindfulness has a long history, and is central to Buddhist philosophy. It can be achieved through meditation, but can also be evoked, with practice, while engaged in day-to-day activities. Bishop et al. (2004) proposed a two-component model of mindfulness:

- *Self-regulation of attention.* Mindfulness involves being fully aware of our current experience – observing and attending to our changing thoughts, feelings, and sensations as they occur. This allows us to be aware of these phenomena, but not to

elaborate on them. Rather than getting caught up in ruminative thoughts, mindfulness involves a direct non-judgemental experience of events in the mind and body.
- *An orientation towards one's experiences in the present moment characterized by curiosity, openness, and acceptance.* The lack of cognitive effort given to the engagement and elaboration of our experiences allows us to focus on our present experience. Rather than observing experience through the filter of our beliefs and assumptions, mindfulness involves a direct, unfiltered awareness of our experiences.

In essence, mindfulness involves a focus on our whole experience at any one time, not just focusing on panicky, anxious or depressed thoughts. These become just part of our experience, one which we can learn to observe rather than allow to dominate our consciousness. Achieving this level of simultaneous awareness and disengagement is not easy, and most programmes that teach mindfulness do so over sessions spread over many weeks or months. One of the most widely recognized training programmes is the mindfulness-based stress reduction programme of Kabat-Zinn (e.g. 1990). This involves an 8- to 10-week course for groups of participants who meet weekly for practice in mindfulness meditation skills, together with discussion of stress, coping, and homework assignments. An all-day mindfulness training session is also included. Several mindfulness meditation skills are taught. These include the 'body scan', involving a 45-minute exercise in which attention is directed sequentially to numerous areas of the body while lying down with eyes closed. Sensations in each area are carefully observed. In sitting meditation, participants are instructed to sit in a relaxed and wakeful posture with eyes closed and to direct attention to the sensations of breathing. Hatha yoga postures are used to teach mindfulness of bodily sensations during gentle movements and stretching. Participants also practise mindfulness during day-to-day activities such as walking, standing, and eating. For all mindfulness exercises, participants are instructed to focus attention on the target of observation and to be aware of it in each moment. When emotions, sensations or cognitions arise, they are observed non-judgementally. If participants notice their mind has wandered into thoughts, memories or fantasies, their nature or content is briefly noted, and then attention is returned to the present moment. An important consequence of mindfulness practice is the realization that most sensations, thoughts, and emotions fluctuate, or are transient, passing by 'like waves in the sea'.

Mindfulness can act as a 'stand-alone' intervention. It can also be integrated into other therapies and used to help people cope with challenging behavioural experiments or distressing thoughts as part of the treatment of mood and anxiety disorders.

Current affairs

As well as differences in theory and the techniques used, each of the different interventions discussed so far feel very different to the individuals experiencing them. Psychoanalysis may feel opaque and unstructured, with insight or therapeutic change occurring relatively infrequently. Humanistic therapy may feel equally unstructured, but have a shorter and clearer time line. Behaviour therapy and cognitive behaviour therapy are much more structured, focused on skills, and led by the therapist. Which approach would best suit you, and why? Would this differ according to the problems you are experiencing, and if so, why?

Back to basics? The third wave

While CBT remains the dominant therapeutic model in western society, a number of variants have arisen almost from its very inception. Known as third-wave therapies, some of these add or emphasize particular therapeutic strategies that may be of particular benefit for certain types of disorders. The dialectical behaviour therapy of Linehan, considered in Chapter 8, is a good example of this. By contrast, one increasingly popular form of therapy, known as acceptance and commitment therapy (ACT, pronounced 'act'; Strosahl et al. 2004), rejects the need for cognitive change and remains clearly located within its behavioural roots.

Acceptance and commitment therapy

Adopting a radical behavioural perspective, theorists such as Strosahl et al. (2004) have argued that emotional responses occur as a consequence of learned associations between certain contexts and emotional states: their 'relational frame'. According to Hayes et al. (2006), we are able to abstract elements from one set of frames and transfer them to other situations. A child who is trapped inside a wooden box and experiences great fear may later experience the same fear when trapped in other contexts, such as relationships. Although the contexts are very different, the responses are similar because the relational frame is the same.

Because relational frames are verbally accessible (i.e. we are able to understand and describe them), they are also changeable. As a consequence, we may develop distorted concepts of relationships between elements within relational frames, and begin to respond to these distorted relational frames rather than the 'real' relational frames. We take our cognitively distorted view as being an accurate representation of a relational frame: worry about the future becomes worry about an actual future, rather than a potential future. As a result of inappropriate relational framing, we may begin to avoid contexts in which negative emotions and behaviours are triggered. This avoidance results in a state of psychological rigidity, inappropriate coping attempts to minimize any distress we may experience, and we fail to learn that our fears are exaggerated and we can cope effectively with the feared situation. Although the language is different, this process is not dissimilar to a combination of the two-factor theory of anxiety (Mowrer 1947) and the cognitive distortions identified by Beck.

To change emotions, we need to change these learned associations, rather than attempt to change internal processes such as cognitions, emotions, and so on. All ACT interventions aim to increase the individual's flexibility in responding to situations and difficulties they face and, if necessary, to achieve new and valued goals. This flexibility is established through a focus on six, related, core processes:

- *Acceptance* involves becoming aware of thoughts, feelings, and bodily sensations as they occur, but not being driven by them. Attempts at inappropriate cognitive or emotional control are considered costly and stressful and frequently maintain any distress the individual is experiencing: 'control is the problem, not the solution'. Acceptance is taught through a variety of techniques, including mindfulness. Clients learn through graded exercises that it is possible to feel intense feelings or notice intense bodily sensations without harm.

- *Cognitive defusion* involves learning that thoughts are thoughts, feelings are feelings, memories are memories, and physical sensations are physical sensations. None of these experiences are inherently damaging. Thoughts are seen as just one interpretation of events, and many others may be equally appropriate, just as identified by Rogers and Beck. However, rather than attempt to identify and change any 'faulty thinking', the individual learns to accept their presence. This process may be facilitated by a number of exercises that attempt to show the disconnectedness between thoughts and emotions. Participants may be encouraged to sing their thoughts, or to repeat them several times as quickly as they can, for example, in order to show them as observable stimuli that can be treated much the same as any other stimuli. We can choose to focus on them or ignore them.
- *Contact with the present moment* involves effective unrestricted contact with the present moment. First, by observing and noticing what is present in the environment and in private experience (thoughts and emotions). Second, by labelling and describing them without excessive judgement or evaluation. Together these actions establish a sense of 'self as a process of ongoing awareness' of events and experiences. Essentially, the use of mindfulness or similar techniques.
- *Values* relate to the motivation for change. In order for an individual to face feared psychological obstacles, they need a purpose for doing so. Acceptance and commitment therapy aims not just to rid the person of their problems, but also to help them build a more vital, purposeful life. Its central goal is to enable the individual to progress towards valued life goals without being constrained by previous worries, memories, and emotions.
- *Committed action* involves the individual developing strategies for achieving desired goals. Once they have begun to understand how their thoughts and avoidance are preventing them from moving towards such goals, clients are encouraged to define goals in specific areas and to progress towards them. Essentially, a form of exposure and response prevention in which the individual stops avoiding feared situations and learns to cope with the emotions and difficulties associated with engaging with them, and by doing so learning they can be effective in achieving their goals.

In essence, both CBT and ACT acknowledge that much psychopathology is a consequence of inappropriate cognitive interpretations of threat associated with a range of situations, in the case of anxiety, or inappropriate beliefs about one's coping ability and self-worth, in the case of depression. Both attempt to achieve cognitive and behavioural change through enactment of previously avoided behaviours and behavioural experiments. They also encourage users to consider their faulty beliefs that drive their mood or avoidance behaviours as hypotheses not truths. Where they differ is that CBT typically attempts to achieve change by directly confronting cognitions and challenging their veracity, while ACT attempts to teach users to accept the thoughts may exist, but not to focus on them through the use of defusion techniques or mindfulness. That is, CBT generally works by controlling the cognitive antecedents to emotions; ACT does not attempt to change these antecedents, but focuses on teaching effective emotion-regulation skills.

A systems approach

So far, all the intervention approaches have focused on working with individuals. But sometimes whole families or other 'systems' may be experiencing problems, or individuals within families may be experiencing significant problems because of how a family functions. Addressing these issues requires a very different way of working – working at a systemic level.

There are several 'schools' of systemic therapy, each of which has a different model of the causes of family problems, and their remediation. Nevertheless, they all share a common understanding that the family operates as an interrelated and interacting system, in which the behaviour of each person does not occur in isolation. Instead, behaviour follows a principle of circularity in which no one behaviour is seen as starting or being the outcome of events. The behaviour of X affects Y, whose behaviour reciprocally affects X, whose response to this affects C, and so on. Behaviours form a continuous causal loop, with no beginning or endpoint. Change within this continuous set of behaviours can be achieved by intervening at any point in the system.

The experience of family therapy is very different to that of individual therapy. There are frequently two or more therapists, one or more of which may not be obvious to the family. Sometimes a team of therapists sits behind a one-way mirror and tracks the progress of therapy. They provide support to the therapist with the family, who may be too involved in managing the process of therapy to notice all the complex interrelationships that occur. They may discuss issues raised within the session, identify the nature of the interactions among family members, and develop intervention strategies. They may even tell the therapist to take a particular action or ask a specific question. These may be communicated to the therapist in the room by telephone or the therapist stepping out of the room for consultations with them.

Structural family therapy

Structural family therapy (Minuchin et al. 1978) is a widely practised approach to the treatment of family dysfunction. Its core premise is that well-functioning families have a clear structure. Where this is lacking, the family struggles to deal with any challenges it faces from internal or external sources. Central to the family structure are a number of subsystems that combine to determine its organization and style of interaction. Each subsystem shares a common element: generation, gender, interest, and so on. One individual may be a member of several subsystems. They are organized hierarchically, and require clear boundaries between them in order to carry out their specific functions. The parental subsystem is generally considered to be superordinate to others, such as sibling subsystems, and to have an executive function. It makes key family decisions. Problems arise when inappropriate boundaries are established. A child may collude with one parent against the other for a short period of time ('Don't tell mum I broke the vase'), for example, with no harm to the family. But if this inappropriate boundary is maintained, the family will become dysfunctional.

If the boundaries between subsystems are permeable and information flows readily between them, family members become extremely close. Indeed, they may become too close, leading to a state of enmeshment in which individual members do not experience a state of autonomy or independence. Conversely, boundaries that are too rigid prevent information flow between subsystems, resulting in disengagement and emotional detachment between family members. Functional families have clear boundaries, appropriate hierarchies, and sufficiently flexible alignments to adjust, change, and foster individuals within them.

The goal of therapy is to identify where any dysfunctions lie and to change them: to establish a 'normal' family structure in which the parental subsystem has executive powers, the boundaries between and around generations are clear, and long-term alliances do not exist. Each family member should have age-appropriate independence while still feeling part of the family. Therapy is behavioural, directive, and dynamic. The therapist is highly active. They may move about, change the positions of family members to develop or disrupt alliances, interrupt particular allegiance patterns or align with different members of the family. Treatment involves three elements: challenging the family's perception of reality, providing alternative possibilities that make sense to them, and developing new relationships and structures that are self-sustaining. This involves a series of stages:

1. *Joining with the family*: the therapist enters the system, joining or establishing rapport by accommodating to the family's culture, mood, style, and language. The therapist may physically sit within the family and engage with them.
2. *Evaluating the family structure*: the therapist examines boundaries, hierarchies, and alliances. This is a dynamic process. Individuals or subsystems may be observed interacting using role-play. The therapist may even set up conditions for these to be real interactions. Minuchin et al. (1978), for example, frequently observed the families of young people with anorexia eating a meal together. This could demonstrate, for example, the inability of parents to work together to encourage their child to eat, or a shifting pattern of coalitions between parents and child.
3. *Unbalancing the system*: the therapist deliberately unbalances existing, dysfunctional, behavioural patterns, putting the family into a state of disequilibrium. This process is highly directive and may involve the therapist aligning him or herself with different subsystems or alliances. An example of this process can be found in the case of a depressed woman who was pessimistic and hopeless at the start of a therapy session, but whose mood improved as she vented feelings of frustration with her husband and his critical and demanding family. Rather than remain neutral, the therapist sided with her husband, sympathizing with his difficulties in keeping everyone in the family happy, but also suggested they sit down and attempt to establish limits to the intrusiveness of his family on their relationship.
4. *Restructuring operations*: once the system has been unbalanced, a new normative family structure is constructed. This involves a series of strategies, including:
   (a) *Actualizing family transactional patterns*: developing more appropriate transactional patterns through role-play, guided practice, and physical manipulation of individuals into appropriate subsystems (e.g. sitting mother and father together, jointly interacting with members of other systems).
   (b) *Escalating stress*: blocking recurrent inappropriate transactional patterns, and developing conflict in order to encourage new alliances within more appropriate subsystems.

It is assumed that any changes are mutually reinforcing and that the family will continue to develop without the need for further intervention. Nevertheless, therapy may continue at weekly intervals for several months.

Strategic family therapy

In sharp contrast to the highly structured nature of Minuchin's approach, Watzlawick and colleagues' (1974) strategic therapy was less formal and more flexible. Their interventions were based on the understanding that when a family faces a problem, its members typically engage in previously used strategies to deal with the problem. If the problem is not resolved, and the family lacks the flexibility to develop new ways of coping, repeated use of unsuccessful strategies may itself become problematic. An example of this process can be found in the man who becomes upset at his wife's lack of engagement with him. In his frustration, he attempts to persuade her to be more forthcoming in their relationship. Unfortunately, in response to these rather clumsy attempts she becomes more withdrawn and avoidant, which results in him trying to become more persuasive, her becoming increasingly avoidant, and so on. Here, his attempts at persuasion have become part of the problem, as has her withdrawal. It is important to note that *both* repetitive responses exacerbate the problem, not just his frustration or her lack of communication.

The goal of therapy is to identify and change these repetitive and, ultimately, destructive sequences of attempted problem resolution. It follows a number of discrete stages. Therapy focuses on two key, and quite radical, strategies of change: positive reframing and paradoxical interventions.

- *Positive reframing* involves placing a positive interpretation on the behaviours contributing to the problem. A couple who are constantly arguing, for example, may be told this is 'a good thing', as it shows they both have a strong commitment to the relationship as they keep fighting to try and make it work. The goal of reframing is to challenge the family's perception of the presenting problem and to encourage them to redefine and give new meaning to it. Having redefined the problem, the family can no longer apply the same solutions, and new solutions and patterns of interaction become possible.
- *Paradoxical intervention* involves family members being asked to engage in tasks that are paradoxical or contrary to common sense. The arguing couple, for example, may be asked to *continue* arguing, linked to the positive reframe of 'because this shows your continuing care for each other'. By the use of paradox, the therapist creates a therapeutic bind by suggesting that there are good reasons why it is advisable *not* to change – while hoping to have the opposite effect. The paradox is intended to give the problem a new meaning so that those involved will be forced to decide on change or no change – itself a change within the system.

A number of paradoxical strategies have been identified. The above example is known as 'symptom prescription'. A similar technique, known as 'pretending', involves a family member pretending to have a particular problem, with the family enacting their usual pattern around the presenting 'symptom'. Again, this is meant to disrupt the normal family interactions and facilitate behavioural change. The approach has a number of strengths, and the strategic group have reported some impressive therapeutic gains (Watzlawick et al. 1974). However, the ethics of the approach have been strongly questioned, as the power lies with the therapist and the method of treatment is not clear to its recipient.

Applied behaviour analysis

So far, all the therapeutic approaches considered involve working with (more or less) willing participants. But sometimes, it may be necessary to work with individuals who do not choose or do not have the intellectual capacity to engage in this process. To address the needs of these individuals, a very different technology of change is necessary, usually involving some form of environmental manipulation based on the principles of operant conditioning, under the rubric of applied behaviour analysis (ABA).

The goals of ABA are to encourage appropriate behaviours and discourage inappropriate behaviours through the use of the principles of operant conditioning. These may be applied to a range of populations and behaviours, from whole classes of children to encourage being on-task and reduce disruptive behaviour to individuals with significant learning difficulties with the aim of achieving basic functions such as increased eye contact or verbalizations.

Teaching simple behaviours

Applied behaviour analysis is based on operant conditioning principles. At its heart is the basic Skinnerian premise that behaviour that is rewarded is likely to be repeated and/or maintained. If these rewards are not intrinsic to the behaviour, some external reward is necessary. Thus, a child with autism spectrum disorder may gain no intrinsic reward from increasing eye contact with others around them, but may do so in order to gain rewards they do value. Basing an intervention on rewarding appropriate behaviours only works if the person involved is already showing some evidence of these, or similar, behaviours. A more complex process is necessary to initiate and then reinforce behaviours that are yet to emerge. This may incorporate a number of strategies, including prompting, modelling, fading, and reinforcement. Teaching a child to initiate or increase eye contact, for example, may involve the following steps:

- *Prompting*: trainer says 'look at me'. They may then gently move the child's head so that brief eye contact is made, or move into their line of sight.
- *Reward*: once any eye contact is made, however brief, behaviour is immediately reinforced with a known reinforcer. It may not be immediately obvious what will act as a reinforcer, so this needs to be assessed prior to the learning trials. However, this is likely to be a sweet, chocolate or something similar.
- Once a behaviour is regularly elicited by relevant prompts, the reinforcement schedule is changed, so the number of successful trials necessary to gain the reward increases (a process known as *fading*). The behaviour may also be accompanied by social rewards (verbal praise), which do not fade over time. In this way, the verbal praise takes on a rewarding role and serves to maintain behaviour over time. Alternatively, behaviour is shaped towards more sustained eye contact by gradually increasing the duration of eye contact required before it is rewarded. The behaviour may also be practised in other environments or with other trainers to foster its generalization.

A more complex procedure involves a process known as shaping. In the case of teaching basic language skills, for example, this may initially involve the trainer modelling a single word or sound. Any utterance, however distant from this sound, is then rewarded. This procedure is repeated, and utterances again reinforced. However, rewards may only be given if the utterance becomes increasingly accurate and close to the sound made by the trainer. Once the pronunciation of a word is established, a second phase of training may involve rewarding use of the word in the context of a particular stimulus. Training a child to say 'car' in the presence of a toy car, for example, may allow him or her subsequently to draw attention to when they want to play with a car.

Teaching complex behaviours

The principles of ABA can also be used to teach complex behavioural sequences. A process known as 'chaining' (or in reverse, 'backward chaining') allows the training of individual behaviours, which then link together to form a behavioural sequence. To achieve this, a complex skill or sequence of behaviours is first broken down into discrete units. Making a sandwich, for example, involves a clear sequence of behaviours. In forward chaining, each step is taught in a sequential manner. The first step, for example, is verbally prompted ('make sandwich'), modelled (take bread out of packet), and rewarded. Once this behaviour is reliably established, further training trials will prompt the child to 'make sandwich', but having completed this phase they are not rewarded. Instead, a second phase of the sequence (get ham) will be prompted, modelled, and rewarded. Once this is learned, further steps in the making of the sandwich are added, with the reward only being given after all the sequences so far taught are completed. Backward chaining involves the same procedures conducted in reverse and has the advantage, in this case, that the child immediately has the reward of being able to eat the sandwich they have made.

Discouraging inappropriate behaviours

Functional analysis

Over the years, inappropriate or maladaptive behaviour has frequently been discouraged by the use of punishment: some of it, far from subtle. This is unacceptable in modern practice, and more sophisticated approaches are now regularly used. One key approach involves a process known as functional analysis. This assumes that even apparently aimless or aggressive behaviour is goal directed. If the trigger to any such behaviour can be identified or changed, or if the individual can be helped to gain the desired effect by other means, this may prevent its enactment. Functional analysis usually involves a number of stages:

- Observation of the behaviour over a period of time to determine its ABC: regularities in its antecedents, the nature of the behaviour, and its consequences.
- Analysis of these data to determine what causes the behaviour, what its effects are, and by deduction, what its function is. Episodes of screaming in a profoundly learning disabled individual may be triggered by attempts to maintain on-task behaviour beyond a certain time limit, the close proximity of a certain individual, and so on. This may be followed by increased attention by health care staff and removal from

the task/individual involved. The function of the screaming may therefore be: (1) the desire to stop the on-task behaviour, (2) avoid the individual, and/or (3) gain attention from a desired source.
- Implementation of a change plan, based on these hypotheses, that may involve shorter on-task time and attention from staff at times other than when the screaming occurs.
- Further observation of both the implementation of the programme and the behaviour to ensure the desired changes are achieved.

The token economy

For people with less profound difficulties than those so far addressed, the token economy can act as a powerful behavioural control. Its basic premise is that appropriate behaviours are rewarded by the provision of tokens, while inappropriate behaviour is punished by their removal. Tokens may be given immediately following the enactment of an appropriate behaviour or after this behaviour has been maintained for some time. Children with conduct disorder, for example, may be given a token (either physically or more often on a visible chart, such as a star chart) for behaving appropriately during an entire lesson at school. Of course, a token has little or no intrinsic value. The key to this approach is that tokens can be exchanged for more desired rewards after pre-determined periods of time up to, for example, one week. The more tokens obtained over this period, the better the reward. This approach is inappropriate for use with people who have profound cognitive deficits. For it to be useful, those involved need to have relatively high levels of abstract thought and to be able to delay gratification. Nevertheless, is has been used in a wide range of contexts. It can involve one individual or be used to influence the behaviour of entire groups of people. The approach has been used, for example, in the context of psychiatric wards with long-term patients in order to reward pro-social and appropriate self-care behaviours prior to their discharge into the community, school classes, as well as individuals.

Chapter summary

1. Although there are many variants of psychoanalytic therapy, Boesky (1990) identified a number of commonalities between many of them, including: drawing links between childhood sexual and aggressive conflicts and adult symptoms; understanding symptoms, associations, dreams, and behaviour; becoming more open in the relationship between client and analyst; increased tolerance for the expression of sexual and aggressive derivatives; increased coherence and clarity of the associations, behaviour, dreams, and communication; and increased capacity for realistic gratification.
2. Rogerian therapy aims to help the individual regain their path to self-actualization. Rogers considered this could be achieved through three key therapeutic processes: empathy, genuineness, and unconditional positive regard.

3. Rogerian therapy is most effective with psychologically intact and capable individuals. Nevertheless, the core aspects of the approach remain at the heart of high-quality therapy.
4. Behaviour therapy is based on classical and operant conditioning principles. It targets specific behavioural problems, and in particular anxiety-related conditions.
5. The key approach used in behaviour therapy for anxiety conditions involves a process known as exposure and response prevention.
6. Cognitive behaviour therapy aims to change the faulty cognitions that contribute to inappropriate mood states or behaviour. In depression, the key to cognitive change involves the use of Socratic dialogue and behavioural experiments. In anxiety, exposure with response prevention is the key approach.
7. Acceptance and commitment therapy is based on an operant conditioning model (relational frames theory), and attempts to help people engage in new and valued behaviours, some of which may be completely novel; and some of which may have been prevented by fear or other emotional responses.
8. Family therapy is based on a model of systemic circularity. Structural family therapy achieves its aims by changing family structure. Strategic family therapy uses positive reframing and paradoxical intention.
9. Applied behaviour analysis uses a range of behavioural techniques, including prompting, modelling, shaping, rewarding, and chaining to train simple and more complex behaviours.

Further reading

Cooper, J., Heron, T. and Heward, W. (2013) *Applied Behavior Analysis*. Harlow: Pearson.
Crane, R. (2013) *Mindfulness-based Cognitive Therapy: Distinctive features*. Routledge: London.
Dallos, R. (2010) *An Introduction to Family Therapy*. Maidenhead: Open University Press.
Feltham, C. and Horton, I. (eds.) (2012) *The Sage Handbook of Counselling and Psychotherapy*. London: Sage.
Hayes, S. and Strosahl, K. (eds.) (2004) *A Practical Guide to Acceptance and Commitment Therapy*. New York: Springer.
Hennerley, H., Westbrook, D. and Kirk, J. (2012) *An Introduction to Cognitive Behaviour Therapy: Skills and applications*. London: Sage.

Chapter 6

Behavioural disorders in childhood and adolescence

The DSM-5 specifies a number of 'behavioural disorders' in childhood, focusing on those that are considered disruptive and 'externalizing'. However, the issues considered here are wider than those within this limited DSM category and include what are termed 'disruptive disorders' (attention-deficit/hyperactivity disorder and conduct disorder) as well as another two other disorders that can be considered primarily behavioural in nature: school refusal and eating disorders (anorexia and bulimia nervosa). Quite a mixture!

By the end of this chapter, you will have an understanding of factors that contribute to the development and treatment of:

- Attention-deficit/hyperactivity disorder (ADHD)
- Conduct disorder
- School refusal
- Eating disorders: anorexia and bulimia nervosa

A word of warning

Before addressing individual disorders, it is important to note that around 40 per cent of young people identified as having one of the disorders considered in this chapter are likely to have at least one other disorder of either mood or behaviour (Merikangas et al. 2010). Many have similar causes as well as having similar defining characteristics (see Chapter 2), so this **co-morbidity** should not really be surprising. Accordingly, although it may be helpful, if only for the sake of simplicity, to consider each disorder separately, the distress many young people face will be far more multi-dimensional than at first it may appear. This co-morbidity also questions the value of a diagnosis-led approach to defining the problems individuals face. A far more appropriate method may be the formulation-led approach outlined in the introduction to the book, which identifies specific issues an individual is facing and addresses each of them within the therapeutic environment. The diagnosis actually provides little information necessary for a psychological intervention: the formulation provides it all. Unfortunately, a diagnosis is not only of limited use to the psychological treatment of some of the problems identified in this chapter, it may actually be detrimental to the young person involved. Mental health problems are highly stigmatizing in society in general and among young people in particular (Rose et al. 2007). This stigma may result in a number of immediate negative impacts on young people diagnosed with mental health problems, including social isolation and bullying by peers and being devalued by health professionals. It may exacerbate any problems an individual is facing, and can increase the likelihood of them being inappropriately diagnosed with mental health problems in the future. The label 'sticks', and diagnoses should be made with caution.

Attention-deficit/hyperactivity disorder

As its name suggests, attention-deficit/hyperactivity disorder (ADHD) is characterized by significant problems in attention and/or hyperactive and impulsive behaviour. These problems are disruptive in a number of settings and 'inconsistent' with the young person's developmental level.

- *Inattention* is characterized by the child having difficulties keeping attention on tasks or play, being easily distracted by extraneous stimuli, and finding it difficult to organize activities and tasks. They may perform badly at school as a consequence of rushed and careless work, and have difficulties following instructions and completing tasks.
- *Hyperactivity* is characterized by the child always feeling restless and 'on the go'. They may squirm or find it difficult to remain seated for any period to time, talk excessively, and interrupt or intrude on others.

Young people with ADHD find it difficult to determine what is, and what is not, important in their environment. They respond to all stimuli that grab their attention with equal interest and with little thought. They have difficulty establishing friendships and fail to recognize when their behaviour is annoying others. About 25 per cent of children with ADHD have some form of learning difficulty, and many are placed in special education units as a consequence of their disruptive behaviour. They are more likely to drop out of school than those without the disorder.

Although clearly defined in DSM, the diagnosis of ADHD is not without controversy, in particular because of the large number of children given the diagnosis and the medical treatment this is used to justify, particularly in the USA. Clinicians, educators, and parents have all expressed a concern. The concerns of the latter are perhaps exemplified on the website ritalindeath.com, established by the National Alliance against Mandated Mental Health Screening and Psychiatric Drugging of Children. The arguments of such groups can be summarized as follows:

- *Some children with attentional deficits do not receive appropriate help*: a child may have significant problems in one particular area, but not receive help because they do not fulfil the diagnostic requirements for ADHD.

- *Some children may receive inappropriate medical treatment*: a diagnosis of ADHD may be used to justify potentially harmful drug treatments where other approaches may be more beneficial to the child.

This first of these issues reflects a wider concern that attempts to dichotomize behaviours such as ADHD as either 'normal' or 'abnormal' are neither valid nor useful. A number of authors have argued that rather than simply dividing people into those with or without ADHD, it may be more useful to consider them in terms of the difficulties they experience across a range of cognitive abilities and situational contexts. This 'dimensional approach' is both more helpful in targeting interventions and more predictive of long-term outcomes than the broad-brush approach of a general diagnosis (Semiz et al. 2008).

The second concern is that ADHD is over-diagnosed. In the USA, prevalence rates vary between 3 and 6 per cent across states, suggesting differences in diagnostic criteria are being applied. Perhaps of more concern to those who challenge the medical treatment of ADHD are findings of an increase in both the frequency of its diagnosis and medical treatment over time. In the UK, for example, McCarthy et al. (2012) found the percentage of children aged 6–12 years receiving pharmacological treatment for ADHD doubled between 2003 and 2008. In view of the potentially problematic side-effects associated with such treatment, this increase should be viewed with some concern. Of children identified with ADHD, 40 per cent continue to have these problems in late adolescence, and about 10 per cent have some level of symptoms in adulthood (Mannuzza and Klein 2000).

Biological explanations

There is clearly a biological component to ADHD. The main neurotransmitter involved is dopamine, although both norepinephrine and serotonin also contribute to the disorder. Low levels of dopamine impact on three brain systems (Sagvolden et al. 2005):

- *Frontal lobe*: leading to poor attention, behavioural organization, and executive control. The individual responds to stimuli and events with little prior thought or planning.
- *Mesolimbic system*: increasing the salience of short-term rewards and reducing the ability to work towards longer-term rewards.
- *Basal ganglia*: leading to clumsiness, and poor habit learning.

Low levels of norepinephrine and serotonin have an impact through their influence on one brain area:

- *Prefrontal lobe*: leading to an inability to determine what is important in the 'present environment'. The child responds indiscriminately to many stimuli with little or no planning.

These biological processes are influenced to a considerable extent by genetic factors. An estimated 60–80 per cent of the variance in attentional problems experienced by children with ADHD has been attributed to genetic factors (Coghill and Banaschewski 2009). Not surprisingly, the gene alleles identified are associated with the regulation of dopamine (DRD4, DRD5), serotonin (5HTT-LPR), and norepinephrine (NET).

Psychosocial explanations

Two quite separate, distinct, and antagonistic psychological approaches are evident in explanations of ADHD (see, for example, Galves and Walker 2012). One approach appears to concede that ADHD is the outcome of neurochemical dysregulation and that psychological models of the disorder should focus on understanding the psychological processes resulting from the underlying biochemical dysregulation. The alternative approach explores psychological causes for the disruptive behaviour and/or biological disruption.

In the first of these explanations, Sagvolden et al. (2005) suggested that low levels of dopamine lead to poor attention and behavioural organization, a failure to learn appropriate behavioural sequences, a sensitivity to short-term reinforcers, and a lack of response to longer-term outcomes. Similarly, Barkley (2005) considered children with ADHD to be more emotionally responsive to environmental events than average and unable to inhibit inappropriate responses to them. They find it difficult to control their feelings and to tolerate negative emotions. As a consequence, they find it difficult to maintain goal-oriented behaviour when this is associated with some type of negative emotion. Schoolwork and other boring or frustrating tasks fail to hold their attention and they quickly shift to other more immediately rewarding activities.

From the more explanatory perspective, Bettelheim (1967) believed that ADHD develops when children with a biological predisposition to hyperactivity are raised in an environment in which their parents make continued attempts to control this behaviour; and show their frustration and anger when they fail to do so. This becomes a continuous, emotionally demanding, and challenging battle between child and parents which generalizes to other contexts and eventually results in what may be termed ADHD. More recently, attachment theorists have argued the symptoms can be considered an outcome of insecure attachments, and may be considered a 'normal and understandable reaction' of an insecure child to a stressful situation (Galves and Walker 2012). In support of this contention, Storebo et al. (2013) reviewed the outcome of 29 relevant studies and concluded that rates of parental attachment problems were higher among both children and adults with ADHD than in the general population, suggesting a causal association between the two. A related theory (Galves and Walker 2012) suggests that traumatic experiences in early life may adversely impact on the individual's ability to modulate their emotions and make them more likely to see threat and respond impulsively or by withdrawing into themselves; both of these responses can be seen in children and young people diagnosed with ADHD.

The trauma considered to trigger ADHD does not need to have been overwhelming, and in support of both attachment and trauma theories, there is now evidence that adverse family relationships, instability, critical parents, parental hostility, disharmony between mother and child, and a range of factors that can lead to insecure attachment and trauma are associated with ADHD. The trauma–ADHD link is not without its critics, however, and some have argued that it may arise from confusion between the symptoms of post-traumatic stress disorder (see Chapter 11) and ADHD. Both involve cognitive and emotional disruptions, such as difficulty concentrating, dysregulated affect, irritability, and hyperarousal. But, argue the critics, they may occur for different reasons. Children who are traumatized, for example, may exhibit high levels of impulsivity because they have become hypervigilant to potential threats within the environment and over-respond when they think they occur; children with ADHD do so for other reasons. In clinical settings, these different diagnoses become moot.

There is clearly significant overlap between the symptoms of childhood ADHD and PTSD and their causes. The role of the clinician is to ascertain the meaning and cause of symptoms for the individual child and to establish a treatment plan based on them.

Treatment

Given the dominance of biochemical models of ADHD, it should be no surprise that the primary treatment of the condition involves some form of medication, of which the best known is a drug called methylphenidate (Ritalin). It seems odd to prescribe this amphetamine to children who already appear to be too active. However, by increasing levels of dopamine, it paradoxically reduces levels of inattention and hyperactivity, with a 50–60 per cent success rate (Hazell et al. 2011). But prescription is not without problems, with potential side-effects that include high levels of aggression or hostility, loss of appetite, abdominal pain, weight loss, insomnia, increased heart rate, and a slowing of body growth (King et al. 2009). It has also been found to trigger psychotic symptoms and mania in up to 9 per cent of children prescribed the drug (Cherland and Fitzpatrick 1999). Tangentially, easy access to the drug also allows the possibility of its abuse by people without ADHD. For these reasons, alternative drugs are now increasingly used. Atomoxetine, an SNRI, increases levels of norepinephrine, and has fewer side-effects than Ritalin. However, these are still serious and include anorexia, nausea, and vomiting, and are experienced by up to a third of those receiving the drug. Atomoxetine is recommended as an alternative to Ritalin if Ritalin proves ineffective or the child has unacceptably severe side-effects. However, the two drugs are equally effective, and around 50 per cent of young people who do not respond to Ritalin will respond to Atomoxetine (Hazell et al. 2011).

While medication may remain the mainstream treatment for ADHD, psychosocial interventions can enhance its effects. Attentional training programmes work directly with affected children to improve their attention. One such programme included, among other tasks, the use of attention tapes requiring the user to press a buzzer when they heard target words or specific word/number sequences, listening to a paragraph and testing comprehension, and mental arithmetic exercises (Semrud-Clikeman et al. 1999). The young people who received this intervention showed marked improvements on visual and auditory attention tasks. More cautiously, Rutledge et al. (2012) concluded the benefits of attentional training programmes frequently failed to generalize beyond the specific training tasks, and did not impact on wider measures such as teacher-rated classroom behaviours. Other interesting approaches that still need to show effectiveness include intense aerobic exercise, training in mindfulness and social skills.

An alternative, more systemic approach involves working with families to help them manage the difficult behaviours and their highly emotive consequences within the family. This approach typically involves teaching parents behavioural approaches to the management of their child using operant procedures, and family problem-solving and communication training. Families learn to avoid setting up situations likely to trigger inappropriate behaviour, children are rewarded for appropriate behaviour, and families are taught to work together to function and communicate more effectively. From an attachment perspective, this may be considered a means of helping the child achieve a more secure attachment with its parents. This approach may be of some benefit, particularly in reducing parental stress and increasing parental confidence (Zwi et al. 2011).

A second type of systemic intervention involves operant conditioning-based interventions such as a token economy within the school environment. These have been shown to improve measures of academic scores, behaviour, and antisocial behaviour (Miranda et al. 2002). Perhaps of even more benefit are approaches that involve both school and home. In one study using this approach, the *Family–School Success* programme (Power et al. 2012) comprised 12 sessions in which parents were taught parenting skills and met with teachers to develop joint strategies to resolve any problems their child was experiencing. These included teachers setting manageable levels of homework and parents reinforcing its completion, and teachers providing daily report cards recording children's performance on pre-specified target behaviours that were seen by parents on a daily basis. Parents were trained to reinforce appropriate goal attainment on the required behaviours. Even when the children involved were on optimal Ritalin treatment, the intervention still achieved significant gains on measures that included homework performance, parent–school relationships, and parent behaviour; but not sadly, parent–child relationships. Adopting a very different approach, Mikami et al. (2013) worked to reduce the social isolation experienced by many children with ADHD by teaching their peers to be more inclusive. As a consequence, although the children with ADHD did not change their behaviour, boys (but not girls) were more included in social groups by their peers.

Conduct disorder

When does inappropriate behaviour and defiance become sufficient to justify a psychiatric diagnosis? Conduct disorder may be one of a number of 'psychiatric conditions' that ought to be considered at the extreme end of a spectrum of negative behaviours rather than a distinct diagnosis. As a consequence, there is significant debate regarding the validity and utility of diagnosing young children with this condition. This is particularly important because some children have been given this diagnosis when they are engaging in developmentally appropriate disruptive behaviour (Volkmar 2002), with potentially detrimental effects on their future.

Conduct disorder is a repetitive and persistent pattern of behaviour in children and adolescents in which the rights of others or basic social rules are violated. Behaviours may involve bullying and cruelty, destructiveness (which may be as serious as arson or other types of destruction of property), lying and stealing (often involving some degree of confrontation or violence), truancy and running away from home. These behaviours occur in a variety of settings, including home, school, and social contexts.

Although they behave in similar ways, boys may be more disruptive and problematic than girls. Because of their overreaction to situations and outbursts of temper or defiance, children with conduct disorder may have few friends and be socially awkward. The long-term outcome of the condition appears to depend on the age of onset: the earlier the onset, the more likely it is to continue into adulthood. Indeed, late-onset conduct disorder may be considered an exaggeration of the defiance and anger typically expressed during adolescence, which, as the individual develops, remits (Moffitt and Caspi 2001). Early-onset conduct disorder (before the age of 10 years), by contrast, is more likely to be associated with ADHD, neurological deficits, school problems, family dysfunction, aggression, and violence (Powell et al. 2007). Such individuals are also more likely to abuse drugs and have a relatively poor prognosis.

In the UK, the prevalence of conduct disorder in children aged 5–15 years has been estimated to be 1.7 per cent for boys and 0.6 per cent for girls (Maughan et al. 2004). Rates of conduct disorder are higher among lower socio-economic groups and in urban rather than rural settings. In addition, according to the National Collaborating Centre (2013), 30 per cent of a typical family doctor's child consultations and 45 per cent of community child health referrals involve conduct disorders.

Biological explanations

Children diagnosed with conduct disorder frequently exhibit deficits in verbal reasoning and executive function (Moffitt and Lynam 1994). These may reflect deficits in brain regions, including the amygdala, insula, anterior cingulate, and orbitofrontal cortex, all of which have been shown to be associated with antisocial behaviour (e.g. Fairchild et al. 2011). Lower than normal volume in the orbitofrontal regions may explain their poor decision-making, while the same in the amygdala may account for low levels of fear conditioning.

In addition to their neurological structure, people with conduct disorder may also have relatively low levels of **cortisol** and high levels of testosterone. The imbalance between these two hormones (the testosterone–cortisol ratio) may result in a propensity for social aggression (Montoya et al. 2012), and may be exacerbated by low levels of serotonin resulting in high levels of impulsivity. An individual with low cortisol, low serotonin, and high testosterone levels may be at particular risk of impulsive socially aggressive acts. Low levels of dopamine have also been found among people with conduct disorder. This renders them relatively insensitive to social and other rewards that might otherwise control their behaviour, and increases their likelihood of engaging in risk-taking behaviours. These biological processes may be influenced by genetic processes. In the Minnesota Twin Family Study, for example, Bornovalova et al. (2010) found that what they termed 'externalizing disorders', including conduct disorder, alcohol dependence, and drug dependence, were all highly heritable. In addition, separation from a father diagnosed with antisocial personality disorder (see Chapter 9) does not appear to reduce the risk for conduct disorder in children expressing high levels of callous-unemotional traits, suggesting this association may be more strongly linked to genetic factors than social context (Wootton et al. 1997). More specifically, a number of alleles of genes known to regulate dopamine levels have been associated with antisocial behaviour, including those of the COMT, DRD2, and DRD4 genes.

Current affairs

Evidence that antisocial behaviour such as that linked to conduct disorder has some genetic roots raises a number of interesting legal questions. Recently, discussion of the so-called 'warrior gene' – an allele of the monoamine oxidase A gene (MAOA), which has an influence on levels of dopamine, serotonin, and norepinephrine – has raised the question: how responsible are those individuals with a genetic propensity to aggression for their antisocial behaviour? And how should the state, and the legal system, respond to them? Should an individual who commits an aggressive crime (with the appropriate gene allele) be punished for engaging in a behaviour over which they may arguably have little or no control? And is this sort of crime worse and more punishable if they do not have the allele?

Psychosocial explanations

Psychosocial factors interact with biological factors to influence the expression of any genetic risk. The prime candidate here appears to be issues within the family, including parental rejection and coerciveness, physical abuse and inter-parent violence, low levels of discipline and supervision, marital conflict, and parental deviance. Having a parent who themselves engages in criminal or coercive behaviour also increases risk (Rhule et al. 2004), as the child learns inappropriate ways of responding to the world and (equally importantly) fails to learn appropriate ways of responding.

But more subtle processes may also be involved. Patterson and Bank (1989), for example, noted that the parents of children with conduct disorder responded somewhat inconsistently to their misbehaving child. They often reinforced coercive child behaviours by giving them attention or giving in to their demands. At the same time, they ignored more positive behaviours. As a consequence, the child was rewarded for inappropriate antisocial behaviour, and increasingly used such behaviours to obtain parental attention or to manipulate their parents. A similar explanation is drawn from attachment theory. Bowlby (1969) argued that parental responsiveness is critical to the development of self-regulation skills. Poor interactions with parents result in poor attachment, and low attachment security, which in turn leads to high levels of externalizing behaviour as the child acts disruptively to gain their mother's love and has little to lose in terms of love or attention.

Interactions with their peers may also shape and support children's conflictual behaviour. Adolescents with high levels of externalizing behaviours typically associate more with deviant peers and respond to their wider peer group with increasing levels of challenging behaviours (Burt et al. 2009). In addition, the climate at school can mirror that of many children's families. Relationships with teachers may become increasingly conflictual, coercive, and negative in tone, increasing the risk of disruptive behaviour and academic failure. The classroom can itself become a risk factor for conduct disorder. Aggressive children placed in classrooms with high rates of aggression become more aggressive themselves, while living in neighbourhoods that are impoverished, with high levels of residential instability, exposure to community violence or being a victim of a crime, have all been associated with increased risk of conduct disorder (McCabe et al. 2005).

The behavioural impact of these social factors is driven at least in part by the attitudes and beliefs they generate. Aggressive children are hypervigilant to potentially hostile cues within their environment, more likely to interpret ambiguous cues as hostile, and to respond to them with 'action-oriented and aggressive solutions' (Larson and Lochman 2002). These cognitive biases may be exacerbated by poor problem-solving skills that result in an aggressive response to complex or threatening situations. Lopez and Emmer (2002), for example, found that many adolescents who engaged in crime believed aggression to be an effective and appropriate response to threat.

Treatment

Interventions targeted at conduct disorder have worked with the child directly or through their family and school; many have adopted a multi-faceted approach. One such programme, the Incredible Years Training Series, is used widely around the world and targets parents, children, and teachers. The intervention teaches a range of parenting skills through the use of interactive video sessions. These include ways of enhancing positive relationships with children, employing non-violent discipline techniques, and learning to teach children to solve social problems effectively. Where necessary they may be augmented by working with family members to reduce parental mental health problems, and marital discord. The child treatment component also uses interactive videos to teach the young person social emotional skills. Finally, the teacher curriculum includes strategies for strengthening home–school connections, improving teachers' classroom management skills, fostering teachers' use of effective discipline strategies, and increasing teachers' ability to teach and reinforce social-emotional skills in the classroom. Thankfully, given the complexity of the programme, evidence of its effectiveness is strong, achieving clinically significant reductions in oppositional behaviour. In one study, for example, 50 per cent of children with significant externalizing symptoms no longer evidenced them one year after taking part in the programme (Webster-Stratton et al. 2013).

A different approach to the treatment of antisocial behaviour does not involve the identification of particular individuals with particular problems. Preventive programmes may target all 'at-risk' individuals. The best way to run such programmes may be within the normal day to-day running of schools. An example of this approach is the 'good behaviour game', a widely used classroom management approach in the USA that rewards children for engaging in appropriate on-task behaviour during teaching. In this game, the class is divided into two teams and a point is awarded to each team for any inappropriate behaviour involving one of its members. The team with the least points at the end of each day wins a group reward. If both teams keep their points below a pre-set level, they share the reward. The intervention therefore both establishes and reinforces group pressure and norms supporting appropriate behaviour. In one study of this approach, Petras et al. (2008) compared rates of antisocial, violent, and criminal behaviour in young men aged 19–21 years who had attended schools in poor lower-middle-class areas of the USA that had either implemented or not implemented the programme. Men who had shown signs of early problems prior to the intervention were significantly less likely to be still doing so if they attended the schools that implemented the programme.

An alternative approach to treatment has involved the use of atypical antipsychotics. Loy et al. (2012) identified eight randomized controlled trials that had compared their effects against usual care, and found some evidence of their short-term effectiveness in reducing disruptive behaviour.

Working with: conduct disorder

Jon shows many of the signs of conduct disorder. He is unsettled and has poor attention in class. He defies his teachers and parents, and his relationships with his peers are frequently confrontational and difficult. Working with Jon involves identifying specific factors that contribute to each of these problems. Each incident needs to be explored in some detail: what specific factors led to specific problems and what maintained them? Analysis of the incident becomes a learning tool to facilitate future change.

One recent confrontation involved Jon behaving aggressively towards a classmate, Lenny. Before exploring the incident, the therapist may have some initial hypotheses about factors that could have contributed to the incident, and some potential solutions:

(continued)

> *A cognitive cause and cognitive solution*: Lenny somehow triggered self-talk that supported and led to Jon's aggressive behaviour. The solution may be to change Jon's cognitive response to one that does not support aggression.

What this hypothesis does not really consider is what the trigger to these thoughts was, and why did it evoke such self-talk? Accordingly, a second hypothesis (and solution) may therefore be:

> *A situational cause and a situational solution*: Lenny behaved in a way that upset Jon, who lacked the social or problem-solving skills to respond in a way that did not involve an aggressive response. The solution may be to teach Jon these skills.

When questioned about the incident, Jon stated that he hit Lenny because 'he hates him, because he is a fool'. After some discussion, Jon disclosed that Lenny embarrassed him in front of his classmates by joking about a mistake he had made during a football game that allowed the other team to score a goal. He became embarrassed, angry, and hit Lenny.

This sort of teasing is not unusual among young people, and Jon would benefit from learning how to respond to it. This may involve teaching assertion skills, or particular skills at dealing with being teased – the second of the two potential solutions initially considered. One way to begin to address this issue is to consider how Jon could have responded to Lenny's teasing. With some prompting, this discussion could generate a number of solutions:

- Shout or hit him to show anger at his behaviour
- Tell a story of how Lenny had once made a similar mistake
- Try to laugh and 'go with the joke'
- Remind Lenny how he had scored a goal as well
- Walk away to avoid a confrontation

None of these may be the perfect response, but they can be 'tried out' with a therapist or group to allow Jon to practise them and get some feedback on their effect. In addition, by considering his response in similar situations, Jon may be able to build a repertoire of responses he can practise through role-play and become more confident and skilled in his ability to deal with teasing.

School refusal

Children refuse or are reluctant to go to school for a variety of reasons. Some may simply prefer to do other things; some may find it stressful to attend school for a variety of reasons, which could be related to either school or family. Simply expressed, the former may be considered truancy; the latter, school refusal. Previously referred to as a 'school phobia', suggesting an irrational fear of school, the term 'school refusal' is now used to denote a more complex set of causes that vary across individuals and may reflect well-grounded fears of attending school. The simplest way to consider the causes of school refusal can be found in the definition by Kearney and Albano (2004) of school refusal behaviour: a child's refusal to attend or stay in school, motivated by the desire to:

- avoid school-based stimuli that provoke negative emotions
- escape difficult social or evaluative situations
- gain attention from significant others
- obtain tangible reinforcers (e.g. cinema, shops) outside school.

Approximately 1–5 per cent of school-aged young people are 'school refusers', although levels of anxiety-based school refusal and truancy as high as 8.2 per cent have been reported (Egger et al. 2003). The rate is similar across genders and is more prevalent in some urban areas. It does not appear to differ between socio-economic groups. Some children fail to attend school completely. Some may attend school in the morning, but ask to go home early, often complaining of somatic symptoms such as nausea, palpitations, and headaches. As many as 80 per cent of school refusers report such symptoms, which may be associated with the anxiety they experience or are exaggerated to increase the need to leave or avoid school (Honjo et al. 2001). Others may attend school all day but experience high levels of distress while there and try to persuade their parents to allow them to stay at home: arguments, pleading, and tantrums are common. Many children exhibit several of these patterns at any one time. Perhaps not surprisingly, non-attendance at school is associated with poor peer relationships and academic underachievement, although these may be causes as well as outcomes of non-attendance. If persistent, school refusal can lead to decreased opportunities for further education, difficulties in gaining employment, social isolation, and increased risk of psychiatric disorders (Kearney and Albano 2004).

Psychosocial explanations

Unsurprisingly, school refusal can be clearly linked to aversive experiences at school. It can also occur after stressful events, such as moving home or the death of a pet or relative. Several home situations, including high levels of family conflict, physical punishment by parents, and a history of parental physical or mental health problems, may also act as risk factors (Bahali et al. 2011). These may influence the beliefs held by the child. School refusers report higher levels of negative automatic thoughts concerning personal failure and relatively infrequent positive automatic thoughts (Maric et al. 2012). They also tend to have poor social skills, be socially isolated at school, and lack confidence in coping with stressful situations (Place et al. 2002).

Kearney's (2001) model of school refusal is largely functional. The child dodges school either to avoid aversive consequences of gain positive ones. However, a number of clinicians have argued that school refusal may also reflect wider emotional problems. Bowlby (1973), for example, argued that the condition should be called a **pseudophobia**, as he considered school refusers not to be fearing and avoiding school, but rather fearing loss of an attachment figure: their mother. Giving some credence to this interpretation, Egger et al. (2003) found that anxious school refusal among 9- to 16-year-olds was significantly associated with depression and separation anxiety disorder. By contrast, truancy was associated with oppositional defiant disorder, conduct disorder, and depression.

Treatment

Treating school refusal may never require professional intervention. Indeed, the internet has many sites offering support to teachers of children who refuse to go to school. Here are some suggestions taken from the HandsOnScotland website (http://www.handsonscotland.co.uk/topics/anxiety/school_refusal.html):

- Find out if there is anything specific, such as bullying or stress, that is bothering the young person.
- If there are no genuine problems at school, symptoms can be improved with firm and supportive encouragement to attend school every day.
- Help the young person resolve any specific reasonable worries they have about home or attending school.
- Explain to the young person that you understand how upset they feel, but that experience tells us that this upset will settle fairly quickly if they attend school consistently but will get worse if they continue to avoid attending.
- Give the parents information about school refusal and separation anxiety and discuss with them how they are dealing with the young person's reluctance to attend. Encourage them to be firm in their expectation the young person will attend school.
- Draw up a plan of gradual steps to reintegrate them to full-time schooling with support.
- If appropriate, introduce a reward for attending school.

Professional psychologists or teachers may also be involved in a minority of cases. Positive reinforcement for gradually increasing time at school or in the classroom, and social skills training for handling school situations have been shown to be effective in both the short and longer term. More complex interventions have involved a combination of behavioural and cognitive packages. These include graded exposure to feared stimuli or situations related to school, relaxation training, contingent reinforcement for school attendance, cognitive strategies including recognizing and clarifying distorted cognitions and attributions, and devising coping plans. These approaches have been shown to be effective over periods as long as 3–5 years (King and Bernstein 2001).

Eating disorders

Both anorexia and bulimia nervosa typically begin in late adolescence. Although the two conditions appear very different, they both involve disordered eating and people may shift between the two eating patterns, especially from anorexia to bulimia. For these reasons, theorists such as Fairburn (2008) consider them to have the same or similar causes. This theorizing is strengthened by findings of common genetic and neurobiological pathways in the two conditions. For this reason, this section describes anorexia and bulimia separately, before considering their aetiology together.

Anorexia nervosa

Anorexia nervosa involves attempts to achieve an unrealistically low weight in relation to the individual's age, gender, build, and developmental stage. This is usually achieved by starvation (type 1 anorexia), although a minority of individuals may binge on food before vomiting or using laxatives to lose weight (type 2 anorexia). Despite their avoidance of eating, most people with anorexia are preoccupied with thoughts of food. They frequently think or even dream about food, prepare it for themselves or others, and watch others eat. They may experience significant hunger.

They may also harm themselves as a result of their not eating. Low nutrient intake may result in a number of health problems, including cessation of periods, anaemia, tooth decay and gum infections, and skin disorders. If weight loss is extreme, the individual may experience life-threatening metabolic and electrolyte imbalances. It may also result in reductions in brain volume causing cognitive rigidity and impaired decision-making. As a consequence, some clinicians have argued that people who are close to death due to extreme weight loss are incapable of making appropriate decisions about their health, and have justified force-feeding. Thankfully, Wagner et al. (2007) found these neurological changes were no longer evident in people recovered for over one year.

The prevalence of anorexia is variously estimated to be between 1.2 and 4.2 per cent of women and 0.24 per cent of men across a range of countries (Smink et al. 2012). Onset is typically between 14 and 19 years of age. In marked contrast to most mental health disorders, its prevalence is highest among individuals in higher socio-economic groups and high academic achievers. Those at risk are also likely to score highly on measures of perfectionism (Halmi et al. 2000). It is a long-term condition, with a relatively poor prognosis. According to Loewe et al. (2001), only half of those diagnosed with the condition are likely to recover fully, a quarter will achieve a 'partial recovery', while 10 per cent will remain unchanged. Sixteen per cent will die as a consequence of starvation or suicide. Many will switch to the eating habits typical of bulimia nervosa; that is, maintenance of normal weight while still having abnormal eating and vomiting patterns. People with anorexia frequently experience other psychological problems, including depression, obsessive-compulsive disorder, and anxiety.

Bulimia nervosa

Just as in anorexia, bulimic behaviours are largely intended to control weight. However, weight in this context is usually close to average, and the motive for losing or preventing weight gain is associated with being attractive (see Table 6.1). Eating and dieting are less controlled than in anorexia. The individual is typically able to restrain their eating for periods of time, but then disinhibits and engages in binges, often eating up to 5000 calories or more at a time. Bingeing is usually secretive, rapid, and followed by feelings of guilt, self-disgust, and a lack of control. To reduce the calorific impact of food, physical discomfort, and these negative thoughts and emotions, bingeing is typically followed by vomiting, the use of laxatives, and excessive exercise. Ironically, none of these measures prevents calorific absorption from much of the ingested food. Nevertheless, people with bulimia typically remain within their normal weight range. This method of weight control is less harmful than anorexia, but can still result in digestive problems as a consequence of laxative use and damage to the back of teeth due to acid erosion during vomiting.

The prevalence of bulimia is similar to that of anorexia (1–3 per cent of women and 0.1–0.5 per cent of men: Smink et al. 2012). However, its prognosis is much better. Five years after diagnosis, most people will no longer be bulimic, although they may be at some risk of relapse

Table 6.1 Key differences between anorexia nervosa and bulimia nervosa

Restrictive anorexia	Bulimia nervosa
Body weight significantly below age/height norms	Weight varies: underweight, overweight, close to age/height norms
Less likely to experience intense hunger	More likely to experience intense hunger
Less likely to have been overweight in the past	More likely to have been overweight in the past
More likely to be sexually immature and inexperienced	More likely to be sexually active
Considers behaviour as reasonable and 'normal'	Considers behaviour as abnormal
Less likely to abuse drugs or alcohol	More likely to abuse drugs or alcohol
Less likely to engage in deliberate self-harm	More likely to engage in deliberate self-harm
Tendency to deny family conflict	Acknowledges any family conflict
Age of onset between 14 and 18 years	Age of onset between 15 and 21 years
Relatively independent	Seeks the approval of others; wants to be attractive to others
Weight loss is not driven by a wish to look 'feminine'	Accepts social concepts of 'femininity' and wishes to adhere to them
High self-control	Impulsive and emotional instability

(Grilo et al. 2007). A sub-clinical level of bulimic behaviour is more widely prevalent. Schwitzer et al. (2001), for example, reported that up to 15 per cent of female students engaged in periodic binges and/or purging; but few did so at a level that could be considered problematic.

Biological explanations

Biological models of eating disorders have focused on dysregulation of activity within the hypothalamus, as this is the area of the brain involved in the regulation of appetite. Stimulation of the lateral hypothalamus triggers hunger and eating. Stimulation of the ventromedial hypothalamus, known as the satiety centre, triggers feelings of fullness and inhibits eating. Activity within these hypothalamic areas is largely controlled by two neurotransmitters: dopamine and serotonin.

The early stages of eating are associated with both feelings of hunger and pleasure as the expectation of eating and initial intake of food trigger *dopamine release* within the lateral hypothalamus and the mesolimbic system (the so-called 'pleasure centre'). Dysregulation of this response may result in both bulimia and anorexia. The binge-eating phase of bulimia may be a consequence of low dopamine release at this time (or an insensitivity to dopamine), resulting in additional eating in order to achieve previous levels of reward from eating (Jimerson et al. 1992). Somewhat paradoxically, Wagner et al. (2007) suggested the same process might result in people with anorexia feeling less motivated to eat, as they gain no pleasure from doing so.

Eating ceases, at least in part, as a consequence of *serotonin release* in the ventromedial hypothalamus and mesolimbic system. If levels of serotonin release are sub-optimal, the individual may experience a lack of the pleasure associated with eating and eat more in order to experience them (Kaye et al. 1988). Over the longer term, Kaye also proposed that constant dieting reduces levels of a dietary precursor to serotonin, tryptophan, which is found in high-fat foods including chocolate, cakes, and biscuits often craved by bulimics. He argued that bingeing increases levels of tryptophan, which is converted to serotonin, which, in turn, improves mood. Unfortunately, this model has little empirical support, as people typically feel low in mood following bingeing, the biological transition from tryptophan to serotonin in the short period of time following bingeing is biologically implausible, and the foods most people eat while bingeing generally carry insufficient tryptophan to significantly influence serotonin levels.

More recently, Kaye (2008) argued that anorexia might be the result of *excess* levels of serotonin. These may make the individual feel nervous and 'jittery' after eating: feelings that may be reduced by restraining food intake, reducing tryptophan and then serotonin levels. Unfortunately, even Kaye's own work has not always supported this hypothesis, as Kaye et al. (2005) found low levels of serotonergic activity during periods of both starving *and* recovery among people with anorexia. Despite the exact role of these two neurotransmitters being unclear, alleles of the serotonin 5-HTT transporter gene and dopamine receptor genes D2/D3 and DRD4 have each been implicated in risk for eating disorders.

Psychosocial explanations

Perhaps the most important cultural influence on food consumption is an increasing tendency for social norms to favour thinness. For a woman, 'being thin' is considered attractive in most western cultures and is associated with a range of positive personal characteristics, such as intelligence, competence, and even employability (Rhode 2011). Even social or ethnic groups, such as African-Americans, who have traditionally not held this view, are increasingly adopting it; and as they do, their rates of eating disorders increase (Striegal-Moore and Smolak 2000). Websites such as Pro-Ana (http://proana.info) and Bewitching Bones (http://bewitchingbones.webs.com/promiatips.htm) provide normative support for extreme dieting, even when individuals are physically isolated from others with similar attitudes.

Family processes can also influence eating behaviour. Over half the families in which individuals develop an eating disorder have strong attitudes towards weight and shape (Haworth-Hoeppner 2000). In such a context, successful dieting forms a way of gaining acceptance within the family, especially if the individual has been unsuccessful in other domains that are important to the family. Young people with eating disorders are also likely to come from homes with high levels of family discord or have mothers who are perfectionists (Pike et al. 2008); the behaviour and attitudes of fathers appear to have less impact.

Minuchin et al. (1978) suggested an intriguing family model of anorexia. They defined the characteristic of 'anorexic families' as involving conflict between parents that is controlled and hidden. According to Minuchin, adolescence is a stressful time for such families, and an adolescent's push for independence within the family increases the risk of exposing the parental conflict and causing potentially catastrophic schisms within the family. To avoid this, the adolescent develops the symptoms of anorexia as a sign of being weak and needing family support. They become the focus of family attention, deflecting it away from parental conflict, preventing total dissension within the family as the family unites around the 'identified patient'. Minuchin's group based a highly successful and widely used therapeutic approach on this model. Accordingly, while there is little empirical evidence to support it, this theory has proven highly influential.

Perhaps the most widely acknowledged theoretical model of both anorexia and bulimia was developed by a British clinician. Fairburn (2008) argued that societal and family norms can lead to cognitive distortions central to both anorexia and bulimia. In both conditions, thinness and weight control become highly salient. The young person develops distorted beliefs and attitudes towards their body shape. These generally do not involve physical misjudgements about their size and shape, but do involve significant dissatisfaction (or even disgust) with both. In addition, their self-worth becomes dependent on being thin. All activities are assessed in terms of their impact on weight control, and even small changes in weight have a profound effect on thoughts and feelings. Weight gain decreases perceptions of control and self-esteem; weight loss increases them.

Anorexia and bulimia reflect different responses to these beliefs. Both involve attempts to lose weight, governed by self-generated rules about when and how the individual can eat. These goals are typically perfectionist and difficult to achieve. Nevertheless, people with anorexia achieve success and are able to sustain long-term dietary control and weight loss – partly, perhaps, because of their perfectionist tendencies. By contrast, bulimics are more chaotic and less able to restrain their eating. Worse, once they have begun eating, they typically engage in catastrophic and dichotomous thinking ('I've eaten, so that's the end of my diet. I may as well just eat now... and start again tomorrow'), and a binge occurs. This typically improves mood for a short time, perhaps due to drowsiness associated with eating large amounts of food or feelings of relief following purging, but is then followed by feelings of disgust and shame at overeating. This results in a determined effort to follow the dietary rules set, which places the individual at risk of bingeing, and so the cycle continues.

Hofmann et al. (2007) developed a similar model of dysregulation specific to bulimia. According to these authors, two contradictory processes govern the behaviour of people with bulimia. They are motivated to restrict their food intake while also holding automatic pro-eating attitudes. Maintaining the motivation to diet takes effort, and may at times become difficult to maintain, either because of the sheer duration of this effort or because of other demands made on the individual: a state described as ego depletion. At this point, the automatic attitudes become dominant, the individual loses the motivation to continue restraining their eating, and they binge.

Treatment

Anorexia

Interventions used in the treatment of anorexia frequently involve two stages: (1) in hospital, focusing on weight gain, and (2) as an out-patient, focusing on long-term cognitive and behavioural change. Hospital care is generally considered necessary if an individual weighs less than 75 per cent of normal for their age and height. At this time, the individual has little or no intrinsic motivation to gain weight. Accordingly, interventions focus on providing extrinsic rewards for weight gain. These typically include social and exercise privileges. The ultimate reward is discharge from hospital once the person has achieved a pre-determined weight. Around 75 per cent of individuals achieve their target weight. However, nearly 20 per cent discharge themselves from hospital, while around 30 per cent become so low in weight they require feeding through a **naso-gastric tube.** That nearly one-third of people are essentially 'force fed' is a continuing controversy within the treatment of severe anorexia. Some have argued that the individual has the right to choose whether or not they eat; and whether or not they die. Others have argued that cognitive impairment resulting from severe malnutrition prevents the individual arriving at an informed decision about their eating. In the UK, this cognitive impairment is generally considered sufficient to warrant treatment against the wishes of the patient. This is probably the dominant thinking among clinicians, and has been tested within the UK courts.

The second phase initially involves the therapist getting to know the individual, and exploring (but not challenging) their core beliefs and the costs and benefits of extreme dieting. Once a strong working relationship has been formed, their core pro-anorexia schemata may be challenged using Socratic dialogue. This involves challenging perceptual and attitudinal distortions, the belief that body weight is the prime determinant of self-worth, and exploration of the high emotional costs of anorexic behaviour. Behavioural hypothesis testing ('eat an extra 250 calories a day to explore whether this will put on weight') may be used to test and explore core beliefs. The intervention also involves teaching problem-solving techniques to help with any crises that might occur. It may last a long time, often up to a year, and even then have a relatively modest impact. Carter et al. (2009), for example, found a year-long outpatient CBT intervention to be more effective than usual care in preventing weight loss after participants had achieved a criterion weight. By the end of the year, the relapse rate in the usual care condition was 64 per cent; in the CBT condition, the relapse rate was 35 per cent. By contrast, McIntosh et al. (2005) found non-specific support to be more effective than either CBT or **interpersonal psychotherapy**, which had improvement rates of 56, 32, and 10 per cent, respectively. The researchers speculated that CBT might have been less than optimal, as the cognitive rigidity of the people with anorexia may make it difficult for them to achieve cognitive, and hence behavioural, change.

Finally, the primary pharmacological approach to treating anorexia involves drugs aimed at influencing serotonin and dopamine activity. One drug (Olanzapine), in particular, has proven effective. One of the significant side-effects of this atypical antipsychotic when used in the treatment of other disorders is significant weight gain. It also seems to have this effect, as well as reducing levels of rumination about weight and diet, in the treatment of anorexia (Brewerton 2012).

Bulimia

Interventions to treat bulimia are typically more structured than those treating anorexia. The best-known intervention is probably the cognitive behavioural approach of Fairburn (2008). This involves a series of sequential steps:

- Replace binge eating with three meals a day (and even snacks), without vomiting or purging. Coping strategies may be developed (call a friend, play a computer game) to help distract from the urge to vomit.
- Eat previously avoided types of food: if necessary, starting with those that are the easiest to cope with and working up to more difficult foods.
- Stop hiding body shape: expose body shape through wearing tight clothing, undressing at swimming baths, and so on.
- Learning relapse prevention strategies: plan how to cope with future urges to avoid food or vomit, or to prevent continued bingeing should it occur.

Through this programme, the participants learn that eating regularly will not result in weight gain, and may even result in weight loss, as well as breaking the habit of overeating and purging. Despite its popularity, few outcome studies have been conducted using this programme, although they have shown some success. Fairburn et al. (1995), for example, found that 63 per cent of people diagnosed with a range of eating disorders who received the intervention showed no evidence of bingeing or purging nearly 6 years after the intervention. However, this finding may exaggerate the likely effectiveness of the intervention in people with bulimia. Agüera et al. (2013) reported that only around 30 per cent of women diagnosed with bulimia showed 'full remission' (that is, no binging or purging with laxatives or vomiting) following a 22-week CBT programme. Those with a more moderate form of bingeing achieved a much higher success rate of 70 per cent.

Case formulation: eating disorders

Although there is little empirical evidence to support the family models of Minuchin and Watzlawick considered in Chapter 4, they have proven very popular among certain psychotherapists. One area to which they both may be applicable is the treatment of anorexia. But they will adopt a very different approach. Here are the two contrasting formulations and treatment approaches that they may develop from them, completely different to the interventions more frequently used now.

Jane is an adolescent girl diagnosed with anorexia: the 'identified patient' indicative of structural problems within a family. The therapist has heard how the mother and father try to encourage her to eat, but have so far failed to do so. The therapist diagnosed the issue as one in which the family has failed to accommodate her transitional stage from adolescence. The parents are observed as powerless to persuade her to eat, and seem to put their differences aside and unite in their concern to get her to eat.

A structural approach
A structural view of this situation would be that the family is enmeshed: they are overly concerned about their daughter's behaviour and so close to her that they deprive her of her independence and decision-making autonomy. The power invested in the girl to control the family has inverted the power hierarchy within the family, and the parental system is weak: they cannot get her to eat.

The goal of therapy is to remedy these deficiencies, in particular to strengthen the parental sub-system and restore the appropriate power hierarchy. One way in which this may be achieved is for the therapist to actively change the structure and to support the parents in their attempts to control the behaviour of their daughter.

A strategic approach
A different formulation of the problem may be gained by a strategic approach. One possible formulation is that as Jane entered adolescence, she tried to gain more autonomy and independence. However, her parents were overprotective and controlling and did

not accommodate to these changes. She therefore started to diet as an expression of control and autonomy. However, her dieting and loss of weight simply increased her parents' concern over her health and increased their desire to control her and ensure she ate 'properly'. Accordingly, they increased their attempts at controlling her eating. As a direct consequence, she rebelled and escalated her diet, which, in turn, increased her parents' concern and protective behaviour, which…The cycle continues. The pattern of interaction that is established is the main concern of the strategic therapist – not the initiating problem.

The goal of therapy is to disrupt this cycle of events. A typical paradoxical intervention would involve providing a positive reframe over the dieting ('It's good you both are committed to this issue, and the focus you give it') and the paradox (somewhat easier to determine (!); the parents should support and encourage Jane in her dieting).

Chapter summary

1. Many disorders of childhood are co-morbid. That is, if a child has one disorder there is a significant likelihood they will have at least one other.
2. Attention-deficit/hyperactivity disorder is characterized by poor attention and planning, and high levels of physical restlessness.
3. It is associated with dopaminergic dysregulation in the frontal lobe (affecting executive control), mesolimbic system (the ability to work towards long-term goals), and basal ganglia (poor habit learning).
4. Family dynamics and the experience of trauma influence risk for ADHD.
5. Serotonin and norepinephrine are also involved and influence frontal lobe activity and attention.
6. The most common treatment of ADHD involves the use of Ritalin. This can cause significant side-effects in some children and its over-use has been controversial.
7. Psychosocial interventions include attentional training, teaching parenting skills, and parent–school collaboration. These have had mixed results, although may combine effectively with treatment using Ritalin.
8. Conduct disorder appears to be associated with neural structural deficits as well as high levels of testosterone combined with low levels of cortisol and serotonin.
9. It is also associated with a range of psychosocial factors, including poor family environment and poor supervision and discipline within the family.
10. Treatment may involve teaching children to deal with stress effectively and not to resort to aggression, how to cope with negative emotions as well as engaging parents and teachers.
11. Social classroom strategies, including the 'good behaviour game', have also proved effective.

12. School refusal affects a significant proportion of children and has a number of causes, including fear of attending school and attachment problems.
13. Simple strategies employed by teachers and parents can encourage school attendance in most children, although more complex cognitive behavioural approaches may be necessary for a minority.
14. A number of common biological processes affecting hypothalamic activity may underlie both anorexia and bulimia.
15. According to Fairburn, both eating disorders have a common goal of controlled eating, but people with anorexia are more successful and controlled in doing so. People with bulimia tend to intersperse periods of high control with uncontrolled binges and purging.
16. Treatment of the two conditions differs markedly. Anorexia may be treated by a period of weight gain followed by long-term CBT or family therapy. Bulimia is typically treated using a gradual increase or maintenance of healthy eating patterns and the elimination of purging.

Further reading

Fairburn, C.G. (2008) *Cognitive Behavior Therapy and Eating Disorders.* New York: Guilford Press.

Green, C. and Chee, K. (2011) *Understanding Attention Deficit Disorder.* London: Vermilion.

Kearney, C.A. (2001) *School Refusal Behavior in Youth: A functional approach to assessment and treatment.* Washington, DC: American Psychological Association.

National Collaborating Centre (2013) *Antisocial Behaviour and Conduct Disorders in Children and Young People: The NICE guideline on recognition, intervention and management.* London: Royal College of Psychiatry.

Treasure, J. (2013) *Anorexia Nervosa: A survival guide for families, friends and sufferers.* London: Routledge.

Chapter 7

Life-long problems?

This chapter looks at disorders labelled by DSM-5 as either developmental or personality disorders. Both are characterized as being life-long disorders. We have already considered one such disorder: attention-deficit/hyperactivity disorder. This chapter considers a further developmental disorder, autism, before addressing two important personality disorders.

By the end of this chapter, you should have an understanding of:

- The causes and treatment of autistic spectrum disorder
- The nature and development of personality disorders
- Borderline personality disorder
- Antisocial personality disorder and psychopathy

Autistic spectrum disorder

Leo Kanner first identified autism in 1943. Since then, a wider cluster of conditions, including Asperger syndrome, childhood disintegrative disorder, and Rett syndrome have been linked to autism and form a group of conditions known as autistic spectrum disorder (ASD). Conditions under this heading are characterized by delays or abnormal functioning in three domains: (1) social interaction, (2) communication, and (3) stereotyped patterns of behaviour, interests, and activities.

The behaviours associated with ASD emerge over time, and typically become evident around the age of one year. Children with ASD rarely initiate play with other children, and are usually unresponsive to their attempts to engage with them. By contrast, they frequently develop strong bonds with inanimate objects, and carry them around if possible. Attempts to achieve eye contact appear aversive and are met with avoidance. About half of children with ASD never learn to speak. Those that do evidence a number of odd characteristics, including:

- *Echolalia*: repetition of words or phrases spoken to the child immediately, hours or even days earlier.
- *Pronoun reversal*: the child refers to him or herself in the third person, as he or she has heard others speak about them: e.g. 'How are you, Simon?', 'He's here…'.

Finally, children with ASD rarely engage in symbolic play. More often, they engage in repetitive, stereotypic, and seemingly meaningless behaviours. These include ritualistic hand movements, such as flicking fingers across their face, or repetitive body movements, including rocking or walking on tip-toe. They may become upset if prevented from engaging in these behaviours or when minor elements of their daily routine are changed. Their play often has an obsessive flavour to it, such as lining up toys in a row or constructing complex patterns with household objects.

The abilities and difficulties of children with ASD vary considerably. Around 80 per cent of children with ASD score less than 70 on intelligence tests, placing them in the learning disabilities range. The deficits they experience are quite specific, and relate to abstract thought, symbolism, and sequential logic. Some may have isolated mathematical or memory skills, in a condition known as *idiot savant*. The name reflects that while these skills can be truly prodigious (such as being able to recall all the UK football scores after reading them once), they rarely enhance the individual's ability to cope with day-to-day life. Despite the high prevalence of intellectual disabilities associated with ASD, many consider them to coincide with, rather than form, a characteristic of the disorder. Others have suggested that they are the result of severe communication and social difficulties preventing the childhood experiences necessary to facilitate appropriate neurodevelopment (Vivanti et al. 2013). That is, they are a consequence of ASD, not a feature.

The long-term outcome of children with ASD is mixed. Those with learning difficulties often make a poor adjustment to adulthood, and most need some level of supervised care for life. By contrast, many without learning difficulties can achieve an independent life, gain employment, and live independently. They are able to take an active part in society, with few deficits apparent to the casual observer, although they may have significant problems in establishing and maintaining relationships and little understanding of social and emotional aspects of life. Coping with the unpredictability of the social world is especially demanding, even overwhelming, for adults with ASD, and may lead to high levels of anxiety and feelings of panic. Perhaps the most well-known 'high functioning autistic' (her words) is Temple Grandin, a professor of animal science at Colorado State University, about whom a BBC documentary ('The woman who thinks like a cow') is available on YouTube (http://www.youtube.com/watch?v=PtdTuZp1k5g0).

Psychosocial explanations

Early theories of ASD considered its behaviours to be evidence of the child withdrawing from an intolerably stressful environment. Bettelheim (1967) contended that the parents of children who develop ASD desire to reject the child they never wanted. The child becomes aware of these feelings, their inability to change them, and as a consequence they retreat to the 'empty fortress' of ASD to protect themselves against this pain and disappointment. Evidence of this process in conditions of what may be termed 'typical' deprivation has been difficult to find. However, 10 of 165 children who grew up before the age of 4 years in conditions of extreme deprivation frequently described as 'inhuman' in Romanian orphanages (including being left crying and miserable, unwashed, restrained in beds, and forced to urinate and defecate there) were subsequently diagnosed with autism (Rutter et al. 1999).

Most psychological theories now focus on the nature of the cognitive deficits that are central to the condition. The first of these has been identified as 'weak coherence', reflecting an inability to process visual information in a holistic manner; instead, focusing on, and being unable to defocus from, the constituent parts of any element within the visual field (Frith and Happe 1994). A second explanation involves deficits of executive control, involving problems with planning, working memory, maintenance and shifting of attention, and inhibition of inappropriate responses. Deficits in executive function may explain the repetitive and rigid behaviours associated with ASD, and the impaired ability for social interactions, which typically require flexible and immediate evaluation, then selection of appropriate responses to complex verbal and non-verbal information (Bennetto et al. 1996).

A third, and perhaps the most influential, theory involves deficits in the theory of mind (Baron-Cohen et al. 1985). According to Baron-Cohen, the inability to understand how other people 'work' underpins many of the deficits in ASD, and in particular those involving social reciprocity and communication. In one study of this phenomenon, Tager-Flusberg (2007) noted that when children with ASD are given theory of mind tasks involving intuitive understanding of social situations or jokes, they appear to set about them using logical reasoning: relying on language and non-social cognitive processes instead of the insight typically developing children would use. Not all children with ASD evidence deficits in theory of mind and they do not do it all the time. Nevertheless, this theory remains at the heart of most understandings of the experiences of children with ASD.

Biological explanations

The causes of any neurological deficits underpinning these cognitive deficiencies remain poorly understood. One explanation for ASD is the opioid theory. This theory is based on findings that a number of behaviours similar to those in ASD, including lack of separation distress, low levels of social engagement, and stereotypical behaviour, can be evoked by injection of opioid **agonists** in animals and humans. In the case of ASD, it is hypothesized that incompletely digested dietary **casein** and/or **gluten** found in barley, rye, and oats leaks natural **opioids** into the gut (Reichelt et al. 1991). These pass through the intestinal membrane, which may be excessively permeable in some individuals, and are taken by the blood stream to the brain, where they act as neurotransmitters acting on brain systems normally affected by dopamine and **endorphins**, including the reward and pain systems. Their impact on the latter may explain why people with ASD frequently show a reduced sensitivity to pain, while being hypersensitive to other sensations, such as hugging or cuddling, usually considered benign or pleasurable. It may also explain why people with ASD engage in self-destructive behaviours such as biting or head-banging, as these may stimulate the release of endorphins. Despite these logical connections, evidence to support the theory is weak. There has been no evidence of opioid peptides in the urine of children with ASD, and dietary interventions to reduce these opioids have proved ineffective. One explanation of the latter finding is that the brain may be irreversibly damaged by early exposure to the opioids, which is in line with the child's early exposure to casein or gluten.

Despite any strong evidence in its favour, the opioid theory nevertheless spawned one of the most controversial recent issues in child health: whether to give children a combined measles, mumps, and rubella (MMR) vaccine. This issue arose in the late 1990s, after Wakefield et al. (1998) reported a study in which they claimed to have evidence that the MMR injection caused an inflammation of the bowel wall, leading to a failure to digest casein or gluten, opiate saturation of the brain, resulting in autism. Fortunately, since then, several large studies have shown no increase in population levels of ASD following the introduction of the MMR vaccine. It is now generally acknowledged that the MMR does not cause ASD.

An emerging, and possibly stronger, candidate for some of the problems associated with ASD involves the dysregulation of serotonin both before and after birth. Reviewing the evidence, Whitaker-Azmitia (2005) suggested that in the early stages of development, when the **blood–brain barrier** is not yet fully formed, high levels of serotonin in the blood can enter the brain of genetically vulnerable foetuses and damage serotonin terminals during development. The loss of serotonergic nerve fibres persists throughout subsequent development and contributes to the symptoms of ASD. Exactly where in the brain any damage may occur is still not fully understood, but three areas of the brain appear particularly vulnerable: (1) the amygdala, involved in the response to fear; (2) the hypothalamus, involved in social memory and bonding; and (3) the anterior cingulated area, which is involved in face recognition, motivation for social behaviour, and mood regulation. Dysregulation of serotonin may continue into adulthood among people with ASD (Chugani 2004).

Autistic spectrum disorder has a genetic component, probably associated with the action of many genes. The ones so far implicated include those involved in fundamental issues of brain cell activity (CDH9, Shank3), GABA activity (GABRB3), and neuronal communication (neurexin 1). That said, it appears these genes are not specific to ASD, and are also relevant to a range of other disorders, including attention-deficit/hyperactivity disorder, bipolar disorder, major depressive disorder, and schizophrenia (Cross-Disorder Group of the Psychiatric Genomics Consortium 2013).

Treatment

Perhaps the most widely propagated treatment of ASD involves the dietary restriction of casein and gluten to reduce absorption of opioids from the gut. Unfortunately, evidence of the effectiveness of this approach is lacking (Mari-Bauset et al. 2014), although high-quality, well-controlled studies are still to be conducted. Pharmacological studies of reducing the impact of opioids, involving the use of naltrexone (see Chapter 10), have found it to reduce activity levels, but to have no consistent impact on other behavioural symptoms including stereotypic behaviour and self-injurious behaviour (Dove et al. 2012). Drugs that increase serotonin levels have also proven modestly effective, leading to some improvement on measures of irritability and obsessive behaviour, but also resulting in significant side-effects (Hurwitz et al. 2012). Perhaps the most effective pharmacological intervention involves the use of atypical antipsychotics, which may impact on problem behaviours including aggression, but also carry a high risk of sedation and weight gain (Dove et al. 2012).

The lack of a 'magic bullet' pharmacological intervention means that psychological interventions, and in particular those involving some form of behavioural intervention, remain at the heart of the treatment of ASD. Lovaas developed a somewhat controversial approach in the

1980s. His highly intensive therapy involved working with children for most of their waking day, both at home and at school, initially for a period of 2 years. Children in the programme were rewarded for being less aggressive and more socially appropriate and, against more recent ethical considerations, punished for engaging in **challenging behaviours**. In his original assessment of the intervention, Lovaas (1987) compared this highly intensive intervention with one involving only 10 hours of therapist contact per week. At two-year follow-up, the differences between the two groups were startling. The average IQ of the intervention group was 83 points; that of the comparison group 55. Twelve of 19 children in the intensive intervention group had IQs at or above the norm; two of 40 in the less intensive intervention met this criterion. In addition, nine children in the intensive therapy group were accepted in the same year class as their peers: only one child in the less intensive therapy group achieved this. Four years later, the relative gains made by the children in the intensive therapy group had been maintained. Unfortunately, because these findings were so startling, the study was subject to close scrutiny, and a number of significant methodological shortcomings were identified. In addition, most attempts to replicate these findings have failed (e.g. Smith et al. 2000). Nevertheless, the intervention approach, albeit without the punishment of negative behaviours, is still widely used.

The operant approach of Lovaas has been refined in a number of ways by Koegel and colleagues, who have developed 'pivotal response teaching' (Koegel and Koegel 2012). The first refinement involves targeting what they term primary factors: skills or behaviours that influence other, secondary factors. Poor communication skills, for example, can lead to challenging behaviours such as tantrums or aggression. Interventions improving communication skills, including improving eye contact or reducing stereotypical movements, should therefore also reduce the frequency of such behaviours. A second innovation involves not only using strategies designed to achieve behaviour change, but also those designed to increase motivation to change. This is achieved by not just rewarding the enactment of target behaviours, but also rewarding behaviours similar to the target behaviour. A final innovation involves allowing the child control over the reward they are given for engaging in the targeted behaviours. Perhaps the most extreme, and ultimately most rewarding, examples of this allows the child to engage in stereotypical or ritualistic behaviours, which are intrinsically highly rewarding. These combined strategies have been shown to improve on-task behaviour, and reduce the incidence of aggressive tantrums and other 'off-task' behaviours (Schreibman et al. 2008).

Personality disorders

Personality disorders are considered stable long-term conditions that become evident during childhood and endure throughout adulthood. DSM-5 identified three clusters of disorders, some of which may be considered attenuated and long-term versions of more severe disorders considered elsewhere in the book. Others are profoundly distressing either to the individual or those around them.

- Cluster A: *Odd or eccentric* – paranoid, schizoid, schizotypal
- Cluster B: *Flamboyant or dramatic* – antisocial, histrionic, narcissistic, borderline
- Cluster C: *Fearful or anxious* – avoidant, dependent, obsessive-compulsive.

Despite their differing nature, Beck et al. (1990) argued that common neurocognitive processes link all the personality disorders. In his evolutionary model, Beck suggested we are all genetically pre-programmed to respond to our environment in certain ways. These responses may be adaptive in some evolutionary times, but less adaptive in others. A tendency to be wary of strangers or behave in an aggressive or competitive manner, for example, may be of benefit at times of threat or scarcity but not at times of high social cohesion and mutual cooperation. Beck considered personality disorders to be the inappropriate expression of these pre-programmed responses. The individual responds in ways that reflect their genetic programming, and is unable to adapt to changing contextual demands. This lack of flexibility is a consequence of both genetic and childhood experiences. According to Beck, most of us learn to overcome any 'maladaptive' programming, and to respond appropriately to the situations we experience. However, the childhood experiences of some individuals may prevent them developing this flexibility. A particularly shy child, who is protected by his or her parents from situations that challenge their shyness, may never learn to be socially confident. An aggressive child, who learns to dominate and gain from their aggression, may never learn more cooperative behaviours. Their lack of flexibility leads to problems in adulthood where these behaviours are not supported or tolerated.

Beck's cognitive approach is, of course, strongly reflected in the model. He considered that any behaviours are driven by a set of core schemata, which influence an individual's response to environmental events. Individuals with a dependent personality, for example, may consider themselves to be weak and incompetent, and they need a strong 'caretaker' to help them function and survive. These beliefs are maintained over time through a number of processes identified by Young and Lindemann (1992):

- *Schema maintenance*: paying attention to information that supports the beliefs
- *Avoidance*: avoiding situations that may challenge them
- *Schema compensation*: overcompensating for negative schema by over-reacting in an opposite direction to them

A shy individual, for example, may reject evidence of positive interactions with others that shows they are liked ('they were only being nice'), avoid social situations in which they could experience positive social interactions, or over-react by being overly extrovert, resulting in rejection and reinforcement of their negative schema.

Borderline personality disorder

Borderline personality disorder (BPD) is characterised by frantic attempts to avoid real or imagined abandonment, high levels of impulsivity, unstable relationships that begin by over-valuing and idealizing new friends and end by devaluing them, chronic feelings of emptiness, and recurrent suicidal or self-mutilating behaviour. People diagnosed with the disorder typically seek out relationships, and then become excessively involved and demanding within them, to the point that this becomes intolerable to the other person involved. Attempts to reduce the intensity or withdraw from the relationship are met by threats of self-destructive behaviour, and when the relationship inevitably collapses, the resultant distress is so devastating the person with BPD is almost unable to cope. They may engage in self-destructive behaviour in an ineffectual attempt to diffuse their negative feelings and distress.

Given this repeated cycle of events, depression and suicidal thoughts are very common among people diagnosed with BPD, and up to 10 per cent eventually commit suicide (Zanarini et al. 2005). They may also engage in self-harming behaviours including drug abuse and alcohol misuse, and dangerous behaviours such as driving too fast. Another self-harming behaviour, known as 'cutting', is also widely associated with BPD. The cutting of arms, legs or torso is common. The cuts are not so deep as to cause serious physical damage. Indeed, their main negative effect is that the individual has multiple small scars, which can be difficult to hide.

About 6 per cent of the population is thought to have this disorder, with a slightly higher prevalence among women than men (Grant et al. 2008). It typically begins in adolescence and continues through adulthood. However, it is not as immutable as was once thought. Zanarini et al. (2005), for example, found that only three-quarters of a cohort of people initially given this diagnosis warranted the diagnosis some 6 years later. In addition, only 6 per cent of those people who improved experienced a 'relapse'.

Psychosocial explanations

People diagnosed with BPD report high levels of childhood difficulties and trauma, including sexual abuse, violence, separation from parents, and childhood illness (Bandelow et al. 2005). Not surprisingly, nearly 90 per cent of people diagnosed with BPD have also been found to have insecure adult attachments (Fonagy 2000). Fonagy speculated that this trauma may result in the young person choosing not to try and understand the minds of others, including the person who instigated the abuse. As a consequence, they fail to develop a theory of mind and find it difficult to manage relationships with others. They are unable to recognize the impact of their behaviour (whether positive or negative) and to make appropriate adjustments in response to social and verbal cues. Their behaviour is driven by their fear of being alone, but they fail to see the warning signs of impending relationship problems and are devastated when they occur. This failure may not just reflect a problem in theory of mind. Experimental tasks have shown that while people with BPD are able to discriminate between neutral and negative facial expressions when given time to consider them, they find it difficult to do so immediately on seeing the faces (Dyck et al. 2008): a process that reflects real-life social interactions.

Another theory rooted in childhood experiences, object relations theory, suggests that as a result of negative childhood experiences, the individual develops a weak ego and needs constant reassurance. They frequently engage in a defence mechanism known as *splitting*, dichotomizing objects into 'all good' or 'all bad', and fail to integrate the positive and negative aspects of self or other people into a whole (Klein 1927). This inability to make sense of contradictory elements of self or others causes extreme difficulty in regulating emotions, as the world is constantly viewed as either 'perfect' or 'disastrous'.

From a more cognitive perspective, Young and Lindemann (1992) identified how negative childhood experiences translate into maladaptive schemata about self-identity and relationships with others. They identified three key schemata underpinning BPD:

- 'I am bad', leading to self-punishment;
- 'No one will ever love me', leading to avoidance of closeness;
- 'I cannot cope on my own', leading to over-dependence.

Self-harm, a fundamental aspect of BPD, can be maintained by operant processes: successful control of other people's behaviour by threats of self-harm reinforces its use. However, it may have a more benign and important use – as a means of coping with strong negative emotions. This, indeed, may be its primary function. People diagnosed with BPD experience strong and distressing emotions, and have few resources with which to cope with them. Self-harm appears to be one effective coping mechanism. Engaging in self-harm may distract from emotions or prove a form of self-validation and self-identity. For many, the process of self-harming, and cutting in particular, can trigger a feeling of dissociation from emotions and physical sensations. Such individuals may feel neither pain nor emotions while cutting. Once established, this form of behaviour not only proves highly reinforcing, it also prevents the individual learning less damaging forms of coping.

Biological explanations

Many researchers that have focused on the neurological underpinnings of BPD consider them to be outcomes of childhood neglect and abuse rather than an independent cause (e.g. Pally 2002). Low serotonin levels, particularly in the prefrontal cortex and ventral medial cortex, may contribute to impulsive aggressive behaviour, including self-harming (New et al. 2004). A second, and increasingly interesting area of research, involves the role of oxytocin. This hormone is perhaps best known for triggering breast-feeding following childbirth. However, it is now increasingly seen as impacting on social relationships: oxytocin levels within the amygdala and hypothalamus appear to be involved in empathic responses and social bonding. Appropriate levels of oxytocin may enhance encoding and conceptual recognition of positive social stimuli over social-threat stimuli (Guastella et al. 2008): processes that appear to be disrupted in BDP. Finally, a more familiar neurotransmitter, dopamine, may also be involved in emotional dysregulation, impulsivity, and the cognitive biases associated with BPD (Friedel 2004).

Although family studies of BPD suggest some genetic contribution to risk for the diagnosis (Distel et al. 2008), finding the genes involved is proving difficult and a full understanding of the genetic processes involved in BPD remains elusive.

Case formulation: borderline personality disorder

Mandy was a 26-year-old single woman with a history of self-harming, including cutting her wrists and arms, and overdosing on prescription medication. On occasion, these had formed genuine attempts to end her life. She had previously been seen by a clinical psychologist, but had dropped out of therapy after only a few sessions. She had few acquaintances, and no close friends, living on her own in a bedsit in London. She was unemployed at the time she was seen by a clinical psychologist.

Long-term antecedents
Mandy told her mother she was being sexually abused by her father as a young girl. Initially, her mother did not believe her claims. However, once this was acknowledged, she left the relationship, raising Mandy in the company of a succession of uncaring and

occasionally verbally and physically abusive 'boyfriends' from the age of 11 years. During this time, and until she left the family home aged 18 years, Mandy felt unloved and uncared for. She was often ignored, and at best tolerated. However, she learned to keep a 'good face' on her experiences and hide any distress she felt.

The only way Mandy felt she could gain attention at this time was through engaging in extremes of behaviour. She learned that self-harming, such as cutting, provoked some attention from her mother, even if largely negative, including significant rows between them. Once away from the family home, Mandy lived in a bedsit and had a series of poorly paid jobs. She had no contact with her mother, and often felt lonely. Her low mood would trigger memories of abuse and provoke episodes of self-harm. These led to feelings of dissociation, which provided a 'time out' from her distress. She had a series of short-term relationships with men, all of which were tempestuous, demanding, and ended in significant arguments. After arguments, she would self-harm. After one drug overdose she was taken to the local hospital emergency medical unit, where she was seen by a psychiatric nurse, and then referred to a clinical psychologist. She did not attend.

Formulation

As a consequence of her early history, Mandy had low self-esteem and a strong sense of shame. She had not learned to tolerate or express negative emotions in a meaningful and appropriate way. Indeed, she had learned to express any negative emotion in a histrionic and overly expressive manner. When things were stressful in her life (for example, relationships failing), she felt extremely vulnerable and anxious and experienced high levels of negative affect. She had not learned to manage these emotions appropriately, and frequently tried to do so by becoming overly reliant on support from anyone willing to provide it (usually her boyfriends), or, when this support was not available, she resorted to self-harm as a means of expressing distress, trying to manage this distress, and manipulating others ('Stay with me or I will really hurt myself'). She found therapy challenging and distressing because it addressed issues she was unable to cope with effectively. She therefore dropped out or refused to engage in it.

Treatment

Helping people with BPD can be complex and difficult. The early stages of treatment may increase levels of negative emotions, the very issue people with BPD are struggling to manage, and result in episodes of self-harm. Interventions with people who have significant emotional problems and high levels of impulsivity may therefore involve working with them in a hospital setting until they are safe to continue as an out-patient. The complexities of treating BPD have in the past resulted in a certain amount of nihilism: the belief that people with the disorder cannot be treated. More recent work has begun to challenge this somewhat negative assumption, although some caution is warranted (Stoffers et al. 2012). Two of the most widely used treatment approaches are dialectical behaviour therapy (DBT) and a variant of cognitive behaviour therapy known as schema-focused therapy (SFT: Young 1999).

Dialectical behaviour therapy was specifically developed for working with people diagnosed with BPD by Linehan (1993). It typically involves working with groups, whose key goals are improving social relationships and reducing self-injurious and suicidal behaviours. It is based around the principles of acceptance and commitment therapy and involves teaching four sets of skills: interpersonal effectiveness, core mindfulness, emotion regulation, and distress tolerance. Interpersonal effectiveness involves learning the skills necessary to develop and negotiate interpersonal relationships. The other skills allow the individual to cope with the emotional consequences of these relationships, whether good or bad. Emotional regulation includes learning to identify and label emotions, increasing positive emotional events, and being mindful of emotions and their associated thoughts without necessarily having to respond to them. Distraction involves learning to temporarily distract oneself from negative emotions. This may involve the use strategies that mimic the effects of self-damaging behaviours such as cutting, but in a more benign manner. This often involves physical sensations such as a cold shower or squeezing a squeeze ball until it hurts.

The central element of SFT is that the individual's behaviour and emotions are governed by maladaptive schema. Young and colleagues identified a number of archetypal maladaptive schemata that operate in BPD and drive its associated behaviours: (1) the abandoned and abused child, (2) the angry and impulsive child, (3) the detached protector, (4) the punitive parent, and (5) the healthy adult (Kellogg and Young 2006). Individuals may switch between schemata. For example, the individual may engage with the abandoned child schema when faced with interpersonal rejection, and then shift to angry impulsive child in responding to it in a self-defeating and harmful way. Schema-focused therapy aims to identify and change these modes of thinking, using standard cognitive techniques including cognitive restructuring. However, these are augmented by a range of other strategies, including 'limited reparenting' in which the therapist provides an atmosphere of acceptance and safety within the therapeutic relationship. This quasi-parental relationship, in which the individual can feel safe and wanted, is seen as central to the therapy. Other intervention strategies include direct attempts at changing maladaptive behaviour and re-experiencing the emotions associated with early dysfunctional relationships. This complex intervention can last as long as 3 years, with two sessions per week.

Despite the sophistication and duration of these therapeutic approaches, their effectiveness appears to be modest, albeit consistent. In a meta-analysis of the then available data, Stoffers et al. (2012) concluded that DBT was more effective than usual care on measures of self-harm, anger, parasuicidality, and 'general functioning' in both the short and long terms. There was insufficient data to study the effects of SFT across studies. However, it does appear to be an effective intervention. Arntz et al. (2005), for example, found that one year after treatment with SFT, 52 per cent of participants no longer met the criteria for a diagnosis of BPD, and evidenced significant improvements in social relationships and incidences of self-harm. This compared with a 29 per cent recovery rate in the comparison intervention (transference-focused psychotherapy). These figures are comparable with the outcomes of DBT.

Pharmacological interventions to treat BPD have had mixed results. Linehan et al. (2008) found treatment with an atypical antipsychotic (olanzapine) to have similar effects to a placebo intervention. Unfortunately, while irritability and aggression scores reduced more quickly in the olanzapine group, levels of self-inflicted injury rose more than in the placebo intervention. Schulz et al. (2008) found no benefit of olanzapine over placebo. Rinne et al. (2002) found that treatment with the SSRI, fluvoxamine, proved successful in reducing rapid mood shifts, but not impulsivity and aggression. Overall, it appears that pharmacological interventions may help reduce some aspects of BPD, but make little impact on its core symptoms.

Working with: borderline personality disorder

Dialectical behaviour therapy is a complex and long-term process. Here is a brief snapshot of just one element of the approach: the dialectical process after which it was named. In the context of DBT, dialectism is said to be a method of persuasion and set of assumptions about reality that contains within it a position contradictory to the stated position. The suicidal individual who states, 'I want to commit suicide' is both stating what may be a truth, but by the very fact they are making this statement may allow the observer to take action to prevent it, so it also holds the dialectic: 'I do not want to die'. Neither is true or false: the desires co-exist. Resolution of this statement is achieved by synthesizing these two contradictory beliefs, perhaps by resolving to build a life that is worth living. Identifying and resolving these dialectics is central to the practice of DBT. An example of this dialectic can be found in this conversation between Susan and her therapist following an episode of cutting:

Susan: I felt better after cutting. I felt calm, and detached. And to be honest, the cutting was not as bad as I often do
Therapist: So, it seems that you are saying that the cutting was a good thing... And if you saw someone else feeling similar emotional pain that you would cut them to make them feel better... If your sister was experiencing distress, would you cut her, or suggest she cut herself to make her feel better?
Susan: No, you know I wouldn't.
Therapist: Why not? It works for you.
Susan: It would be bad. I would try and comfort her or talk to her, not cut her!

Here, the dialectic is that cutting herself is an acceptable way of coping with distress, but cutting of or by others is not. The goal of the discussion is to highlight and try to resolve these discrepancies. This process may be started by the therapist simply noting the discrepancy and inviting Susan, in this case, to consider the paradox, its implications, and how it can be resolved.

Antisocial personality and psychopathy

According to DSM-5, antisocial personality and psychopathy are one and the same (and considered under the rubric of antisocial personality disorder). Others, perhaps the majority of researchers, consider them to be different. According to Hare et al. (2000), the DSM understanding of antisocial personality is an individual who is criminally antisocial. They frequently engage in irresponsible and antisocial behaviours and have 'reckless disregard' for the safety of themselves or others. By contrast, his definition of a psychopath (and one that is widely accepted across the scientific community) is an individual who may engage in these behaviours, but is also unable to process emotional information and has no regard for the emotions of others. This additional requirement clearly distinguishes between two groups of individuals. Using his own measure of psychopathy, the Psychopathy Checklist (PCL), Hare found that around 80 per cent of criminals could be categorized as having antisocial personality disorder: only 20 per cent met the criteria for psychopathy (Hare et al. 2000).

In his original description of the psychopath, Cleckley (1941) identified the following characteristics:

- superficial charm and average intelligence
- absence of nervousness or neurotic manifestations
- unreliability
- untruthfulness and insincerity
- lack of remorse or shame
- antisocial behaviour without apparent compunction
- poor judgement and failure to learn from experience
- pathological **egocentricity** and an incapacity to love
- general poverty in major affective reactions
- unresponsiveness in general interpersonal relations.

Psychopaths may lead highly antisocial lives, and many come to the attention of the judicial system. They are often portrayed as cold killers and sadistic criminals. But many relatively pro-social psychopaths lead apparently successful lives. Indeed, many people with strong psychopathic tendencies can be found among leading business and entrepreneurial groups. Their remorseless ambition, ability to manipulate others, and lack of concern for others may be highly rewarded within the corporate world (Babiak and Hare 2007).

Biological explanations

According to Hare, psychopaths lack the ability to experience emotional consequences of their behaviour, because their brains are hardwired in ways that do not permit the experience of (strong) emotions. Studies using functional MRI have illustrated the neural systems responsible for these deficits. In one such study, Kiehl et al. (2001) measured activity within the limbic system of three groups of people during a range of psychological tasks: non-criminals, non-psychopathic criminals, and criminals identified as psychopaths by the Psychopathy Checklist. They asked participants to rehearse and remember lists of neutral words and words describing negative emotions, and to identify them in a subsequent recognition task. Engaging in these processes resulted in activation of the limbic systems of both non-psychopath groups. In psychopaths, it resulted in activation of the frontal lobes, suggesting that they did not experience the negative emotions associated with these words and that their processing primarily involved one of logic rather than emotion.

A subsequent conditioning study by Birbaumer et al. (2005) illustrates how unresponsive to aversive stimuli psychopaths are. Over a series of trials they trained ordinary individuals and psychopaths to anticipate a neutral outcome or painful response following a number of discriminative stimuli. As the ordinary participants learned to anticipate pain, they experienced an anxiety response involving increased sweat gland activity and activation in the limbic–prefrontal circuit. Psychopaths displayed none of these responses. The origins of these neurological deficits are unclear: they may be present at birth; they may be a consequence of negative emotional events during childhood teaching them to 'switch off' their emotions.

Biological involvement in antisocial behaviour is limited to the activity of neurotransmitters. Low levels of serotonin increase risk for impulsivity and aggression (Oades et al. 2008). Low levels of norepinephrine increase risk for risk-taking behaviours. This may appear counter-intuitive, as one may expect high levels of norepinephrine to drive high activity, thrill-seeking, antisocial behaviours. However, Raine et al. (1998) argued that individuals with low levels of norepinephrine have to engage in more extreme behaviours in order to obtain the 'buzz' those with higher natural levels of norepinephrine achieve by less dramatic means.

Psychosocial explanations

While psychopathic behaviour is largely driven by neurological factors, antisocial behaviour is more influenced by environmental context. Childhood factors that increase risk for antisocial behaviour (and possibly contribute to psychopathy) are a lack of emotional closeness with the childhood family, poor parenting, having a convicted parent, large family size, poor school attainment, and disrupted family (Farrington 2000). These may be added to by wider social factors that include high involvement with deviant peers and a criminal sub-culture, and living in an impoverished neighbourhood (Eamon and Mulder 2005). As well as blunting emotional responses, these experiences may contribute to a set of cognitive beliefs that underpin antisocial or psychopathic behaviour. These may include beliefs such as 'people are there to be taken', 'we live in a jungle and only the strong survive', and 'others will get me, if I don't get them first' (Beck et al. 1990). Interestingly, very specific beliefs may support different behaviours. Liau et al. (1998), for example, found that different beliefs supported covert and overt antisocial behaviour ('People need to be roughed up once in a while' versus 'If someone is careless enough to lose a wallet, they deserve to have it stolen'). A combination of these beliefs combined with poor coping skills may result in aggressive or antisocial responses to a range of social or other stressors.

Treatment

Emphasizing the differences between antisocial personality disorder and psychopathy, most interventions aimed at antisocial behaviours have been conducted in young people, whereas those attempting to treat psychopathy have targeted adults.

Individually targeted interventions to treat antisocial behaviour have met with little consistent success, possibly because those involved lack the motivation to engage with them (Gibbon et al. 2010). More useful may be interventions targeted at environments in which these behaviours may occur. An example is the 'good behaviour game', a widely used classroom management approach in the USA that rewards children for engaging in appropriate on-task behaviour during teaching. In the game, the class is divided into two teams with points awarded for any inappropriate behaviour involving one of the members of either team. The team with the fewest points at the end of each day wins a group reward. If both teams keep their points below a pre-set level, they share the reward. The intervention has two benefits. It prevents teachers being seen as a target for dissension and hostile behaviour, and encourages significant peer pressure to behave appropriately: something much harder to challenge. There is a large body of evidence supporting this approach. Petras et al. (2008), for example, found evidence of lower rates of antisocial, violent, and criminal behaviour among young adult men who attended schools using this approach than in similar schools where the intervention was not implemented.

A systemic approach has also been used with individuals already identified as engaging in antisocial behaviour. Borduin et al. (1995), for example, described a complex intervention targeted at individuals, families, and the peers of such individuals. The family component taught parents appropriate parenting skills and to reduce levels of parental stress at home. They were encouraged to monitor and reward progress at school and establish homework routines. The young people involved were encouraged to engage with appropriate peer groups through attending youth groups and other after-school activities, but sanctioned for engaging with antisocial peers. Finally, they were taught social and problem-solving skills to enable them to reduce impulsivity and negative behaviours. The intervention was very intensive, lasting up to 5 months, with initial sessions as frequent as once a day, before tailing off to weekly meetings as therapy progressed. Borduin reported a halving of known re-offending rates compared with a control group (21 vs. 47 per cent) 4 years after the intervention.

Antisocial personality disorder is difficult to treat; psychopathy may be impossible to treat. The lack of emotional response to punishment or threat of punishment is a significant obstacle to change. Psychopaths are unlikely to voluntarily seek treatment (although they may be asked to do so if incarcerated) and are likely to see little value in changing behaviours that may have been effective means-to-an-end in the past. Indeed, therapy can lead to increases rather than decreases in psychopathic behaviour.

One treatment approach has followed the same philosophy as the classroom management approach described above: using peer pressure to influence behaviour. Therapeutic communities form a 24/7 approach to treating psychopaths. All participants live together, and are made responsible for the physical and emotional care of others. Members are required to conform to group norms on the acceptability of behaviour. Communities developed in the UK, under the leadership of Maxwell Jones in the late 1940s, were loosely based on Rogerian principles, and tried to inculcate high levels of honesty, sincerity, and empathy. Their aim was to teach psychopaths to engage with others and to adhere to social 'rules'.

Early evidence suggested this approach to be beneficial, with apparent reductions in recidivism following periods of stay in such communities. However, in a study of the effectiveness of Grendon Prison, now advertised as the only therapeutic community operating in Europe, Gunn et al. (1978) found 70 per cent of its psychopaths were known to re-offend, compared with 62 per cent of a matched group of men incarcerated in a normal prison. A widely cited US study (Rice et al. 1992) also found mixed effects of a therapeutic community: discharged non-psychopaths were less likely to re-offend than those experiencing the standard prison population, while the crime rate among psychopaths increased. It should be noted that this 'community' significantly differed from the UK understanding of a therapeutic community: participation was non-voluntary and members were expected to take part in up to 80 hours of intensive group therapy each week. They had little contact with professional staff and had little opportunity for diversion; access to television and informal social encounters were severely limited. The compulsory nature of the intervention would now be deemed unethical.

More individually targeted interventions have also struggled to achieve consistent benefits. Hare (2002), for example, examined the outcome of a number of short-term, prison-based, CBT programmes and found that they had little effect on re-offence rates of most psychopathic individuals. Among offenders with particularly high levels of psychopathy, re-offence rates actually rose following treatment. Assuming a lack of motivation to change following a typical individual intervention, both Beck et al. (1990) and Wong and Hare (2002) have developed CBT interventions that attempt to alter psychopaths' behaviour to become more pro-social, while allowing them to still achieve their desired ends. The outcome of these approaches has yet to be reported.

Current affairs

If psychopaths are biologically hardwired to experience no remorse or concern for those they manipulate, should they be held responsible for their actions? Some psychopaths achieve high-level jobs within their chosen careers: they are focused, do not deviate from their chosen course, and see no problem in stepping on others who they consider to be weaker or less effective. They achieve a socially acceptable level of dominance and success. So, psychopaths do not necessarily become criminal or antisocial. How responsible are those that do not conform? And how should we treat them? Prison for acts that may not be their 'fault'? Therapy that will not work? What do you think?

Chapter summary

1. Autistic spectrum disorder is characterized by delays or abnormal functioning evident in three domains: (1) social interaction; (2) communication; and (3) stereotyped patterns of behaviour, interests, and activities.
2. People with ASD vary from 'high functioning' individuals with above-average intelligence and minor degrees of social disabilities to profoundly disabled individuals.
3. The potential causes of ASD include excess neurological opiates or serotonin, possibly at a critical phase as a child.
4. The best interventions in ASD appear to be behavioural in nature. Dietary and pharmacological interventions appear of relatively little benefit.
5. Personality disorders may be a result of neurocognitive responses that render the individual unable to respond appropriately to changing contexts.
6. They are characterized by schemata that support inappropriate behaviours and maintained by processes that include schema maintenance, avoidance, and schema compensation.

7. Borderline personality disorder is typified by intense and troubled relationships, which eventually collapse as a consequence of high levels of dependence.
8. People with the disorder have difficulty in managing their emotions and understanding social cues.
9. Dialectical behaviour therapy and schema-focused therapy are two extended CBT approaches used to treat borderline personality disorder, with consistent but modest results.
10. Although considered under the same rubric in DSM-5, antisocial personality disorder and psychopathy may be considered different disorders.
11. The roots of antisocial personality disorder are thought to be broadly social; those of psychopathy neurological.
12. Treatment or prevention of antisocial personality disorder may be achieved through systemic interventions with schools or families.
13. Treatment of psychopathy has proven of limited effectiveness. There is no consistent evidence from well-controlled trials that show any form of intervention is effective.

Further reading

Bateman, A.W. and Krawitz, R. (2013) *Borderline Personality Disorder: An evidence-based guide for generalist mental health professionals.* Oxford: Oxford University Press.

Frith, U. (2008) *Autism: A very short introduction.* Oxford: Oxford University Press.

Heard, H.L. and Swales, M. (2008) *Dialectical Behaviour Therapy: Distinctive features.* London: Routledge.

National Collaborating Centre for Mental Health (2009) *Antisocial Personality Disorder: The NICE guideline on treatment, management and prevention.* London: NICE.

Ronson, J. (2012) *The Psychopath Test.* London: Picador.

Chapter 8

Anxiety disorders

This chapter considers a range of disorders associated with anxiety. Risk of developing them is associated with fundamental neurological processes, and they have many psychological processes in common. For this reason, the chapter begins by considering factors common to most of the disorders considered later in the chapter.

By the end of this chapter, you should have an understanding of the following in both young people and adults:

- Overarching models: neurological and psychosocial factors
- Separation anxiety disorder
- Specific phobias
- Generalized anxiety disorder
- Panic disorder
- Obsessive-compulsive disorder

Neurological factors

Underpinning many anxiety disorders are neurological structures supporting a process known as behavioural inhibition. Excessive behavioural inhibition can be seen in infants, older children, and adults. It is evident through vigilant and withdrawn behaviour in response to novel situations, extreme social avoidance or withdrawal, and over-susceptibility to punishment. These responses are driven by activity in two neural networks that together form the behavioural inhibition system (BIS: Gray 1991). The first comprises the septohippocampal system (linking the septum, amygdala, hippocampus, and fornix); the second is known as the Papez circuit (or the 'circuit of emotion') and links the mammillary bodies, thamalus, cingulate gyrus and hippocampus, prefrontal cortex, amygdala, and septum. Activation of these systems results in the individual inhibiting their ongoing behaviour in order to attend and respond to threat. In some individuals, the criteria for 'threat' may be set too low, resulting in them constantly over-responding to situations as if they carried a high degree of threat. The amygdala is central to this process because this is where emotional memories are stored and the present context is evaluated in terms of its threat value. The prefrontal cortex is responsible for determining how to respond to the threat, and initiates the inhibitory process. The 'low setting' is associated with low levels of GABA and dopamine, and high levels of serotonin.

While enhanced behavioural inhibition is not the same as a diagnosis of anxiety, an active BIS places the individual at risk for anxiety disorders both as a child and adult (Hirshfeld-Becker et al. 2006). However, and apparently paradoxically, clinical levels of anxiety disorders appear to be associated with *low* levels of serotonin, as well as low levels of dopamine and GABA. They are also associated with high levels of norepinephrine, which is responsible for activation of the sympathetic nervous system. This is particularly evident in phobic and panic disorders, which are characterized by high levels of physiological activation and the fight–flight response.

Risk for anxiety disorders appears to be linked to genetic factors. Scaini et al. (2012), for example, reported that 43 per cent of the variance in generalized anxiety symptoms in young people was attributable to genetic factors; only 17 per cent was attributable to environmental factors. Unsurprisingly, the genes involved include alleles of the COMT gene, associated with dopamine regulation, those that control GABA regulation, and alleles of the serotonin transporter gene, 5-HTTLPR.

A trans-diagnostic model of anxiety

The trans-diagnostic approach, first highlighted by Harvey et al. (2004), states that many conditions assigned different diagnoses have a number of psychological factors in common. In the case of anxiety, these include intrusive thoughts, appraisals, safety behaviours, and our beliefs about how to cope with the cause of the anxiety (known as metacognitive beliefs). Wells (2000) provided a theoretical model encompassing these processes to explain a range of anxiety disorders. In this he noted that our levels of anxiety are primarily driven by:

- the thoughts we have about events that happen to us
- the attention we pay to them
- our metacognitive beliefs.

According to Wells, clinical levels of anxiety arise from an appraisal that a stimulus or situation may cause threat or harm to either the self or others. These appraisals may be in relation to external stimuli ('the lift cable will break and I will be killed'), internal stimuli ('my heart is racing I am having a heart attack') or even our own thoughts ('If I think bad things, bad things will happen'). In order to deal with these threats, the individual establishes plans to reduce them. These coping plans are guided by a series of beliefs, or 'metacognitive knowledge', as Wells refers to them. These are often unconscious and automatic, although individuals may be able to verbalize them. An individual with high levels of anxiety may unconsciously scan their environment for threat, and be able to verbalize this as: 'I must be vigilant so I won't be taken by surprise'. Another, quite destructive plan may be to actively attend to anxiety-engendering beliefs. A spider phobic, for example, may hold a number of beliefs, both neutral ('they are small, delicate and fragile') and negative ('spiders can harm me'), about spiders. However, once they are close to a spider, they may only attend to their negative beliefs and ignore more positive ones. They may also evoke memories of fear in the presence of a feared object.

These plans place the individual in a state of high alert, ready to respond to the threat in a way that will reduce its impact on the individual – to engage in so-called safety behaviours. The most obvious means through which this can be done involves avoidance of the feared thoughts, stimulus or situation. The spider phobic may avoid going into a room in which they think there is a spider, or may run away having seen one. Other coping responses may be necessary if the stimulus cannot be avoided. An individual may, for example, engage in some form of compulsive behaviour that they believe will neutralize the threat: washing their hands three times after touching an object believed to contaminated with a virus, and so on. These safety behaviours are of clear and immediate benefit to the individual, as they achieve an immediate reduction in their level of anxiety. However, in the longer term they maintain the fear. The relief from anxiety associated with such behaviours is rewarding and makes the individual more likely to avoid the feared stimulus in the future (see Mowrer 1947; see Chapter 5). In addition, by avoiding confronting the feared situation, they fail to learn that any threat is less than they estimated, and that it will, in reality, do them no harm.

Childhood origins of anxiety

Anxiety may be the consequence of a failure to develop adequate bonds to an attachment figure during childhood (e.g. Ainsworth and Bowlby 1991; see Chapter 2). A number of alternative routes involve more fine-grained, carer–child interactions. In the first few years of life, caregivers can engage and disengage infants' attention from distressing objects in order to moderate their arousal levels. Those who help the child disengage their attention to reduce distress can reduce the child's arousal before it becomes overwhelming. Carers not attuned to infants' needs may exacerbate their distress by preventing them from doing so. This may prevent the child learning to regulate their emotions, resulting in long-term anxiety problems. As the child gets older, authoritarian, intrusive, over-protective or controlling parenting increases risk for anxiety disorders (Varela et al. 2009). This may involve multiple pathways, including parental modelling of anxious responses and reinforcement of the child's own anxieties. By contrast, appropriate parenting reduces the risk of developing anxiety even among children with high levels of behavioural inhibition (Lewis-Morrarty et al. 2012).

Wider influences beyond the family may also impact on childhood anxiety. Anxious children may benefit from being in well-structured childcare environments with other children, whereas anxiety may be increased if a child experiences multiple caregivers (Morrissey 2009). As children get older, interactions with peers become more influential. Being part of a social group is associated with low levels of anxiety, and social anxiety in particular. Being bullied has the opposite effect (Fisher et al. 2012).

These experiences may translate into cognitive distortions that influence the child's anxiety levels and, unless countered by more positive experiences, establish longer-term patterns of thinking. Carthy et al. (2010), for example, found that clinically anxious children shown threatening scenes experienced greater negative emotional responses, were less successful at applying reappraisals (reframing them in a less threatening perspective), and reported less frequent use of reappraisal in everyday life than typical children. Similarly, Muris et al. (2000) found that when listening to ambiguous stories about social situations, socially anxious children needed to hear fewer sentences of a story before deciding it was scary than controls.

Interestingly, Waters et al. (2008) found no evidence of any impact of parental style on children's levels of anxiety. Any differences appeared to lie within the children themselves. Theses authors compared interpretations of a number of ambiguous situations made by three groups of children: (1) children of anxious parents, (2) children of non-anxious parents, and (3) children with some form of anxiety disorder. The children of anxious and non-anxious parents did not differ in their perceptions of threat, control or emotional reaction to these situations. By contrast, children with an anxiety disorder experienced more threat, less control, and more negative emotional responses than either of the other two groups. Accordingly, while family and other childhood experiences may impact on anxiety as a child, the temperaments of children themselves may subsequently contribute to the degree of anxiety they experience. That is, the degree of anxiety they experience may be a function of both the functioning of the behavioural inhibition system and the environment in which the individual is raised and subsequently experiences as an adult.

Treatment consequences

Reflecting these common pathways to anxiety, the treatment of young people with anxiety disorders is frequently non-specific and, in contrast to treatment in adults, addresses the factors underlying a range of problems. This generic approach has been encouraged by findings of equivalent treatment effectiveness across a range of interventions (Manassis et al. 2002). Some interventions are designed to fit within the normal school curriculum. The FRIENDS programme (Essau et al. 2012), for example, teaches children across a range of ages how best to manage day-to-day stress. Content varies across the age groups, but includes learning about anxiety, how to resist peer pressure or bullying, managing intense emotions using relaxation and mindfulness, developing positive and constructive friendships and study skills. Optional sessions allow for parental involvement. The programme has proven highly effective on outcome, including anxiety, depressive symptoms, and perfectionism.

More therapy-focused interventions have also involved parents. Hirshfeld-Becker et al. (2010), for example, compared the effectiveness of three interventions in children aged as young as 4 years: individual CBT, family CBT, and family-based educational support. Family-based CBT involved teaching children the use of self-instruction, relaxation, and gradual exposure to feared situations with response prevention (see Chapter 5). Parents were taught similar techniques and supported their children in developing and using these skills. They were also taught parenting skills and encouraged to reward their child for any successes they achieved. The individual CBT programme taught children the same skills, but without direct involvement of parents. Parents, however, were still involved in supporting their child on CBT homework tasks. Both CBT interventions achieved a 69 per cent success rate, compared with 32 per cent in the education support group.

Overall, CBT appears an effective treatment for childhood anxiety, and gains made in treatment appear to continue over the long term (Saavedra et al. 2010). It may also be possible to provide such interventions using new technologies. Khanna and Kendall (2010), for example, compared the effectiveness of a computer-assisted CBT programme designed for 7- to 13-year-olds with a standard CBT intervention. The computer-assisted CBT programme comprised 12 animation sequences teaching stress management strategies and setting therapist-supported homework tasks involving engaging in a feared activity. The standard CBT intervention comprised sessions with a therapist covering the same issues 'live'. The percentage of children that benefited from the two interventions was 81 and 70 per cent, respectively. It is also possible to combine CBT with pharmacotherapy to increase its effectiveness. Ginsburg et al. (2011), for example, found remission rates after 12 weeks of treatment to be 68 per cent for those who received a combination of CBT and SSRI, 46 per cent for CBT alone, and 27 per cent for a drug placebo condition. Longer-term studies are needed to identify what happens when the drug is discontinued, although it is currently associated with significant relapse.

Separation anxiety disorder

According to Bowlby (1969), separation anxiety is a normal stage in the development of very young children. Once a child is able to recognize and remember its mother's face, it will respond to different faces with various levels of alarm. This usually occurs between the ages of 6 and 18 months. However, some children continue to experience high levels of anxiety when separated or threatened with separation from their mother or other primary attachment figures. This inappropriate anxiety has been labelled separation anxiety disorder (SAD). It is estimated that between 2 and 4 per cent of children will develop SAD, with 30–40 per cent of cases persisting into adulthood: around two-thirds have other disorders, including social phobia, depression, and ADHD (Shear et al. 2006). Although it is more common in primary school children, teenagers may also experience SAD while adjusting to transitions or stressful situations such as parental divorce or the death of a parent.

When separated from their major attachment figures, young people with SAD experience a variety of negative consequences, including sadness, apathy, and social withdrawal. They may express exaggerated fears involving harm to themselves or their family as a result of muggers, burglars, kidnappers, accidents, and so on. Concerns that they or others may die are common. The threat of separation is highly threatening, and something to avoid, through pleading, crying, clinging, and temper tantrums. Young children, in particular, may show anger or even hit someone who is enforcing a separation. Conversely, when they are with adult attachment figures, they may be compliant, involved, and eager to please. The need for the constant attention and proximity of attachment figures can cause frustration, resentment, and family conflict. Children with SAD may be reluctant to sleep away from an attachment figure, and when they do fall asleep they may experience nightmares with a separation theme or involving the death of an attachment figure. They may also experience unusual perceptual experiences such as feeling eyes looking at them or seeing scary creatures before falling asleep. Young people with SAD may experience a range of stress-related physical symptoms, including stomach aches, palpitations, and shortness of breath. They may **hyperventilate** and experience **panic attacks**. As a result of avoidance of school and other interactions with peers, they may become socially isolated and have difficulty developing and maintaining friendships. School refusal may impact negatively on school and examination performance.

Psychosocial explanations

Parental or family factors can be important in the development of SAD. The condition clearly fits within an attachment theory perspective, and the young people involved may be described as having an anxious-ambivalent attachment style. This is associated with authoritarian, over-protective or controlling parenting. An additional factor, known as parental intrusiveness, appears to be a further risk factor for SAD. This involves disproportionate parental regulation of the young person's emotions and behaviour. It is intended to reduce or prevent distress, but instead fosters a dependence on the parents, and minimizes or reduces the young person's perceptions of mastery over their environment (Wood et al. 2003).

The outcome of these various processes is a set of beliefs and attentional processes supporting fear of separation. In-Albon et al. (2010), for example, followed the eye movements of children with or without SAD when presented with two images of children either separating or reuniting with a woman on a computer screen. They found that children with SAD initially paid more attention to the picture of separation, being vigilant to threat, but subsequently avoided looking at the picture as they found it distressing. This attentional bias was reduced following a course of CBT (In-Albon and Schneider 2012).

Treatment

The optimal treatment for SAD involves working with parents to help them manage their child's anxiety. Eisen et al. (2008), for example, taught parents CBT skills that included relaxation and cognitive challenge and how to teach these skills to their children. The parents then helped their children use the skills in a programme of gradually increasing separation from the relevant parent(s). The programme proved highly effective. At the other extreme, Santucci and Ehrenreich-May (2012) found that a one-week CBT intervention provided in a 'camp-like setting' also proved effective on measures of self-report severity, functional impairment, and parental reports.

Specific phobias

A specific phobia is an irrational fear of an object or situation. The individual is aware their fear is disproportionate, but is unable to control it. The most prevalent fear is that of snakes, affecting about 25 per cent of the population. Such phobias have three components:

- *Behavioural*: avoidance or retreat from the feared stimulus.
- *Physiological*: high sympathetic nervous system activity, evident through high levels of muscular tension, increased heart rate, sweating, and reduced gut motility (the 'butterflies').
- *Emotional*: fear and anxiety.

Phobias emerge in an ordered sequence over childhood. Animal-, blood-, storm-, and water-specific phobias typically develop in early childhood. Height phobia develops in teenagers. Situational-specific phobias (e.g. claustrophobia) typically develop during the late teenage years. Around 8 per cent of children will report having one or more phobias (Soo-Jin et al. 2010), while 5 per cent of adults and 2 per cent of older adults will report similar

Table 8.1 Some of the more unusual phobias

Phobia	a fear of...
Turophobia	a fear of cheese
Taphephobia	a fear of being buried alive
Triskaidekaphobia	a fear of the number 13
Ailurophobia	a fear of cats
Ancraphobia	a fear of wind

problems (Grenier et al. 2011). Many phobias, including a fear of spiders and snakes, appear to be universal. Some are highly culturally specific. *Kayak angst*, for example, experienced by Inuit people, is a fear of being alone on the Greenland ice fields (see Table 8.1).

Biological explanations

Risk for phobias is mediated by the behavioural inhibition system. However, the phobic response has a strong physiological component, involving activation of the sympathetic nervous system, driven by the neurotransmitter and hormone norepinephrine and, to a lesser extent, epinephrine (see Chapter 4). This 'fight-flight' response involves a number of symptoms, including sweating, muscular tension, a rapid heart beat, and rapid breathing that may develop into hyperventilation. The one exception to this involves a fear of needles or blood. Exposure to these stimuli in phobic individuals results in high levels of parasympathetic nervous system activity, leading to low blood pressure, dizziness, and even fainting. Symptoms are relieved if the person retreats from the feared stimulus.

There may also be a neurological explanation for the fact that phobias such as fear of relatively benign spiders and snakes (at least in countries such as the UK) are much more common than a fear of guns, knives or other objects that could more realistically harm us. In explaining this apparently paradoxical finding, Seligman (1971) adopted an evolutionary approach. His preparedness theory proposed we acquire phobias more easily to stimuli that have been to our evolutionary benefit. At some time in our distant history, it was beneficial to be frightened of small and potentially dangerous animals such as snakes or spiders, which Seligman referred to as 'phylogenetically relevant' stimuli. People with these fears may have had a survival advantage, and been more likely to pass on their genetic traits. Importantly, he did not suggest we are born with a phobia of such creatures. Rather, we acquire fear to these stimuli more easily than to phylogenetically irrelevant cues, such as cars, guns, and so on. More recently, Mineka and Ohman (2002) have proposed a stronger version of the theory, suggesting that such fears may be acquired involving *no* contact with the feared object, are unconscious and under marginal conscious control, and may be processed by a 'fear module' centred in the amygdala.

Psychosocial explanations

Psychoanalytic models consider phobias reflect a conflict between the id and ego. Based on conflict arising in childhood, the original cause of the phobic response is either repressed or displaced onto the feared object. Thus, the phobic object is not considered to be the original case of anxiety. The case example of 'Little Hans' is described in Chapter 1.

Behavioural explanations of phobias consider them to result from a conditioning experience in which an inappropriately feared object or context becomes associated with the experience of fear or anxiety. This conditioned stimulus subsequently triggers a conditioned fear response. The typical response when this stimulus is encountered in the future is to avoid or escape from it. Unfortunately, while this is rewarding in the short term, as the individual feels relief at the reduction of fear, in the long run it prevents the individual from habituating to the feared stimulus, and maintains the anxiety over the longer term. Put more technically, the two-process model of Mowrer (1947) suggested fear of specific stimuli is acquired through classical conditioning and maintained by operant conditioning: the negative reinforcement associated with avoidance.

Watson and Rayner (1920) reported the most famous early example of this process. Their conditioning of 'Little Albert', an 11-month-old hospitalized child, induced a phobic response to furry animals through the association of loud noises while playing with a furry toy rabbit. His fear generalized to similar-looking stimuli including balls of cotton, white fur, and a Santa Claus mask. Sadly, although Albert was subsequently allowed to play with the toys in the absence of loud noise, he was discharged from hospital with his phobia intact.

This simple model of phobias has been extended in a number of ways. First, people may acquire phobias as a consequence of seeing others expressing phobic fears. Children learn to be frightened of spiders because they see other family members showing fear in the presence of spiders – a process known as vicarious learning (Bandura 1977). Conversely, people may be protected against the development of phobias following a traumatic incident if they experience fear in the presence of a stimulus they have previously encountered without any fear. The greater this contact, the less likely the person is to develop a phobia; multiple previously safe car journeys, for example, may reduce the risk of a phobia developing following a car crash. By contrast, people are more likely to maintain a phobia once established if they are exposed to information justifying the fear (e.g. view a film about the risks of car crashes) or rehearse this information (e.g. think about the risk of crashing before or during any car journey).

Cognitive models have added a further component: a cognitive response involving perceptions of harm. Importantly, Wells (2000) noted that these thoughts are frequently evoked only in the presence of the feared stimulus. People with phobias may be able to rationally understand the feared stimulus will do them no harm when not in its presence, but become overwhelmed by fearful cognitions when close to it.

Treatment

The treatment of phobias in children largely takes place within the general treatment programmes considered earlier in the chapter, with high levels of success (Saavedra et al. 2010). Treatment in adults has largely involved exposure with response prevention, either in the form of systematic desensitization or flooding (see Chapter 5). The latter approach is now generally favoured, as it is relatively quick and has proven highly successful. Hellstrom et al. (1996), for example, found clinically significant improvements in 82 per cent of their participants. However, it is no more successful than more gradual approaches (Zlomke and Davis 2008).

A more novel approach involves the use of virtual reality. This can be particularly beneficial when controlled exposure to a feared stimulus, such as flying or driving, may be difficult.

However, one obvious drawback is that while the images may look real, participants know they are not. So the degree of fear evoked may be less than that evoked by live stimuli, as may the degree of any habituation or cognitive change ('Well, I know I can cope with images of... but still not sure I can cope with the real thing'). For these reasons, perhaps, Michaliszyn et al. (2010) found that a virtual reality programme was less effective than 'live' exposure in the treatment of spider phobics.

Generalized anxiety disorder

As its name suggests, generalized anxiety disorder (GAD) involves anxiety experienced in a wide range of contexts. Worries usually concern everyday issues, but are exaggerated, difficult to control, and cause significant distress. People with GAD may experience:

- Uncontrollable worry about a range of issues and situations.
- Long-term 'hypothetical' fears: 'What if...'
- Multiple physical symptoms associated with high levels of sympathetic arousal: muscle tension, irritability, restlessness, and insomnia.
- Avoidance of difficult or feared circumstances.
- 'Over-responsibility': the belief that negative outcomes are their fault and can be prevented by worrying.
- Difficulty concentrating: as their focus is always on potential future problems.
- 'Contagion by association': the belief that any negative experience that occurs to others will happen to them.
- Constant reviewing of events to ensure they didn't hurt anyone's feelings or do anything untoward.

Between 3 and 4 per cent of young people experience GAD. It has an insidious onset but can be precipitated by a sudden crisis. Their concerns may be quite 'adult', including worry about their family financial situation, the safety of playing on climbing frames, their parents' health, and so on. Exaggerated beliefs about their personal responsibility for potentially catastrophic events and the belief that worry can prevent such outcomes is both typical of the condition and central to recent cognitive models of the disorder (Wells 1995). Once established, the disorder may continue for extended periods. Around 80 per cent of adults with the disorder, for example, experienced similar problems during childhood (Butler et al. 1991) and most adults with GAD are unable to remember a time when they were free of worry or anxiety, even in childhood.

At any one time, 1–5 per cent of the adult population could be diagnosed with GAD. Its prevalence is highest among social groups under pressure, such as the poor, people living alone or experiencing chronic work stress, and ethnic minorities (Melchior et al. 2007). As the demands of daily living seem to increase, so does the prevalence of GAD. Prevalence of GAD in the USA rose from 2.5 per cent in 1975 to 4 per cent by the early 1990s (Regier et al. 1998).

Biological explanations

Biological models of GAD have focused on the role of the behavioural inhibition system (BIS). This receives information about the environment from the sensory cortex. It compares this with expectations based on previous experiences. If a mismatch occurs, the individual interprets these as threatening and inhibits ongoing behaviours in order to respond to the threat. People with GAD tend to be highly attentive to these mismatches, and as a result the BIS is constantly activated. Interestingly, although people with GAD tend to have a chronically overactive sympathetic nervous system, they may respond to acute stress with *less* sympathetic activation than the norm, probably because chronic over-responding renders the receptivity to norepinephrine at postsynaptic sites less sensitive over time (Spiegel and Barlow 2000). Alleles of the RGS2 gene, which influences norepinephrine and serotonin activity, appear to be implicated in risk for the condition.

Psychosocial explanations

Freud considered the origins of adult anxiety to lie in childhood events. He believed that excessive punishment results in a child coming to believe their id impulses are dangerous and need to be controlled. As a consequence, when they become an adult, and their parent is not there to control these impulses, they worry they will not be able to control them. By contrast, a child that is over-protected fails to develop adequate defence mechanisms to deal with the demands of adult life and experiences anxiety in response to relatively innocuous situations.

Humanists such as Rogers (1961) also identified excessive discipline as a precursor to GAD. Rogers believed that if a child is subject to criticism and harsh standards, they adopt the standards of those around them in order to receive conditional positive regard. They deny their own desires and try to meet these externally imposed standards. However, these desires may break through this denial and cause significant anxiety, as they reveal the discrepancy between what the person needs to be to achieve self-actualization and what they want to be to gain the love of their parents and others. Childhood discipline may certainly influence risk. Varela et al. (2009), for example, found over-protectiveness, excessive punishment, and critical comments in childhood were associated with high levels of anxiety in adulthood. More serious trauma may also be predictive (McLaughlin et al. 2010).

The behavioural model of phobias, even in its extended form, struggled to explain this wide-ranging anxiety. More cognitive models were required. In one of the first, Beck (1997) argued that children who experience high levels of generalized anxiety initially interpret a relatively small number of situations as dangerous and threatening. Over time, they apply these assumptions to more and more situations and develop an increasingly generalized anxiety. Beck identified a number of cognitive schemata that underpin this anxiety, including: 'a situation or a person is unsafe until proven safe' and 'it is always best to assume the worst'. As a consequence of such thoughts, the individual becomes alert to the possibilities of danger and threat throughout their everyday life, and respond with the emotion of anxiety. In addition, they may also experience what Beck called 'emotional reasoning', through which the experience of emotions such as anxiety in certain situations can trigger anxiety-based cognitions: 'If I am feeling anxious, there must be something to be anxious about here'. Thus, the individual may enter a cycle of negative emotions driving negative cognitions, which in turn drive negative emotions, and so on.

Adding complexity to Beck's model of GAD, Wells (1995) identified two types of worry experienced by people with the disorder:

- *Type 1 worries*: worries of a kind that most of us experience, related to work, social, and other issues.
- *Type 2 worries*, or 'meta-worries': positive or negative beliefs about type 1 worries ('Worrying will help me cope with this problem'; 'Worrying will drive me mad…').

Most people experience type 1 worries, although perhaps to a lesser degree than people with GAD. However, meta-worries contribute almost uniquely to GAD. Wells noted that this type of worry can be unpleasant but also forms a coping response at times of stress. People with GAD typically believe worrying is an active and beneficial thing to do. As a result, they may actively choose to worry in the expectation that, while unpleasant, it will eventually be of benefit. At other times, they may feel out of control and unable to stop worrying, and that worrying is impacting on their life in many negative ways. Accordingly, they frequently vacillate between trying to use worrying as a means of coping with stress and trying to avoid and stop worrying. Unfortunately, they usually achieve neither goal.

Treatment

Despite the complexity of the disorder, treating children within larger CBT programmes appears as effective as for other disorders (Manassis et al. 2002). In adults, cognitive behavioural treatment of GAD involves exposure and response prevention. A particular form of intervention, known as 'worry exposure', involves inducing anxiety-provoking or catastrophic worries and maintaining a focus on them until they no longer evoke an anxiety response. Participants learn their thoughts can be tolerated, will do them no harm, and become less threatening over time. This may be combined with relaxation or cognitive challenge. Around half those who receive this intervention show clinically significant improvements, compared with 15 per cent who receive no treatment (Hunot et al. 2007). More recent methods that combine this approach with the use of strategies such as mindfulness may achieve slightly higher levels of success, with an average 57 per cent of participants being classified as having 'recovered' at one-year follow-up (Hanrahan et al. 2013).

From a pharmacological perspective, benzodiazepines, SSRIs, and tricyclics have proven moderately effective in treating GAD, with around 30–40 per cent of those treated showing clinically significant gains. The relatively high number of side-effects associated with benzodiazepines and tricyclics suggest SSRIs should be the drug therapy of choice, and therapy should last at least 12 months (Reinhold et al. 2011). These medications may also combine effectively with CBT. Barlow et al. (2000), for example, found that 6 months after cessation of imipramine (a tricylic), only 20 per cent of their sample showed significant improvement. At the same time, 41 per cent of those given the drug plus CBT did so, while 32 per cent of those given CBT alone met the same criterion.

Panic disorder

A panic attack is an episode of intense fear or discomfort that reaches a peak within 10 minutes, and is associated with symptoms including sweating, palpitations, and racing heart. Importantly, these panic attacks appear to 'come out of the blue' with no easily identifiable trigger. One of the most obvious signs of a panic attack is hyperventilation, which contributes to additional symptoms, including dizziness, feeling unable to breathe, and tingling sensations in the arms and fingers. Prevalence rates of 0.5–5 per cent have been found in adults, while in children rates of 0.2–10 per cent have been reported (Diller 2003). Once a panic episode has been experienced (and certainly if it occurs again in the same context), there is a high probability that the individual will avoid going back to the place in which it occurred. This avoidance can itself be highly problematic, and in children may stop them attending school and engaging in a social life.

Biological explanations

As with simple phobias, physiological models implicate sympathetic nervous activation as fundamental to the disorder. The individual is in an intense state of fight or flight, driven by norepinephrine and epinephrine. However, a number of other neurotransmitters are also involved in the condition. These include serotonergic pathways in the raphe nuclei, orbitofrontal cortex, temporal cortex, and amygdala (Nash et al. 2008), and GABA-mediated activity in the amygdala: low levels of GABA lead to high levels of fear (Goddard et al. 2001). The GABA receptors also control activity within the hypothalamus, and its activation of the sympathetic nervous system. Activity of these neurotransmitters is influenced by genetic factors, including alleles of the tryptophan hydroxylase 2 (TPH2) gene, which controls serotonin metabolism.

Psychosocial explanations

Children who develop panic attacks are likely to have parents who themselves have some sort of anxiety disorder (Biederman et al. 2005) and are exposed to the parental and family influences outlined earlier in the chapter. Among adults, the highest rates of panic disorder are among those who are widowed, divorced or separated, who live in cities, and who experience health problems (Klauke et al. 2010).

More theoretical models of panic disorder have focused on short-term predictors. These models explain how feelings of panic and high anxiety occur in the absence of clearly delineated fear stimuli. The most influential theory to date is that of Clark (1986), which suggests an initial episode of panic can be triggered by high levels of physiological arousal associated with emotional states such as anxiety or anger, or physical causes such as high caffeine levels or exercise. Panic begins if the individual misinterprets these arousal states as being indicative of serious health threat: 'I feel faint and my heart is racing...I must be having some sort of heart problem!' These misinterpretations trigger further sympathetic activity and its related sensations, which seems to support the initial catastrophic interpretation ('Yes, my heart really is pounding: I really am heading for a heart attack!'), which leads to higher arousal, hyperventilation associated with a panic attack, increased catastrophizing, and so on.

Following this first episode, many people become hypervigilant, checking for physical sensations they interpret as symptoms of an underlying physical health problem. Unfortunately, this vigilance and its associated anxiety increase levels of arousal and its associated sensations when in the same or similar contexts. Awareness of these 'symptoms', in turn, confirms any negative beliefs the person may have ('I'm having the same symptoms again...there must be a problem!') and can trigger further panic episodes. As a result, they may begin to avoid contexts in which they fear the symptoms will re-occur.

Evidence to support Clark's theory can be found in a number of experimental studies, although the most illustrative was perhaps that reported by Clark et al. (1988). In this study, they asked people with and without panic disorder to read aloud a series of word pairs, some of which included pairings of body sensations and catastrophic thoughts (e.g. 'breathless–suffocate') typically made by people with panic disorder. The manipulation proved unexpectedly strong. Ten of the twelve participants with panic disorder, but no controls, had a panic attack while reading the cards.

Treatment

Therapy typically involves exposure with response prevention. Here, participants are taught relaxation and breathing control to reduce hyper-arousal and hyperventilation, and cognitive restructuring and self-instruction to change catastrophizing thoughts. These skills are then used to help them through a structured behavioural programme involving engaging with previously avoided situations. They may also be encouraged to hyperventilate and induce feelings of panic within the treatment session and to learn to control them.

This approach has proven extremely successful. Clark et al. (1994), for example, compared this approach with the prescription of imipramine (a tricyclic) and a waiting list control. At one-year follow-up, 85 per cent of those in the CBT group were symptom-free, in contrast to 60 per cent in the pharmacological intervention. In addition, 40 per cent of people prescribed imipramine sought an alternative treatment during the follow-up period, compared with only 5 per cent of those who received CBT. Much subsequent research has focused on finding the optimum means of providing this type of intervention. Lessard et al. (2012), for example, compared the effectiveness of a single- and a seven-session intervention with people who presented at a hospital emergency unit complaining of chest pain diagnosed as panic disorder. Both interventions were equally effective. A second approach has shown internet-based interventions, particularly when accompanied by a small number of personal meetings with therapists or email exchanges, also to be of benefit (Pier et al. 2008).

Obsessive-compulsive disorder

Obsessive-compulsive disorder (OCD) is a long-term, potentially disabling condition. Obsessions comprise intrusive thoughts involving fear of harm to the self or others unless action is taken. Compulsions involve the enactment of these protective actions.

In contrast to phobias, which involve a fear of stimuli that can be avoided or escaped from, OCD is a fear of *unavoidable* stimuli, which require other strategies to reduce the anxiety they induce. As a consequence, people with OCD engage in behaviours they come to believe will reduce or obviate the threat. Doors and windows may have to be checked a set number of time before leaving the house, furniture has to be cleaned a number of times, hands may become sore due to repeated washing with scalding hot water, and so on. These compulsions are frequently referred to as safety behaviours: thoughts, images or behaviours the person comes to believe will prevent harm. They are illogical, disproportionate, and intrusive; and cause significant anxiety if they are not completed. They can take significant amounts of time, and severely restrict the individual's quality of life.

Young people's experience of OCD is generally considered to be similar to that of adults. Obsessions involving fear of harm and separation, compulsions without obsessions, and rituals involving family members are more common in younger than older children. Frequent concerns involve fear of contamination, the potential of harm to family members, fears about sexual orientation, and fears of loss of identity (changing into 'someone else'). The Children's Center for OCD and Anxiety (http://www.worrywisekids.org/index.html) identified what they termed 'red flags' to indicate the likelihood of a child having OCD:

- Obsessions and/or compulsions take up more than an hour a day and can significantly interfere with a child's functioning: unable to get dressed on time because of constantly repeating actions, unable to complete homework due to erasing, re-writing, re-reading, etc.
- Intrusive thoughts, images, impulses that make no sense and are diametrically opposed to the child's being: fears or imagines stabbing parent; religious child fears that he or she hates God; innocent child believes he or she was sexually involved, etc.
- Repetitive behaviours: excessive washing, checking, redoing, counting, tapping to relieve anxiety, etc.
- The child fears that he or she is going crazy because of the strangeness of the thoughts.

A number of common obsessions and compulsions in adults are outlined in Table 8.2.

Up to 4 per cent of young people will develop OCD (Geller 2007). Among young children, more boys than girls (ratio of 3:2) develop the condition. By adolescence, slightly more girls than boys develop it. Prevalence peaks among pre-adolescent children. It is often associated with behavioural disorders, including ADHD (see Chapter 6). It may last a long time: 40 per cent of children who develop the disorder will have comparable symptoms 9 years later (Micali et al. 2010).

Similar prevalences are found among adults. Fineberg et al. (2012), for example, found that around 3.5 per cent of their Swiss population sample met the criteria for the disorder,

Table 8.2 Frequent concerns and safety behaviours reported by people with obsessive-compulsive disorder

Fears	Safety behaviours
Concern with cleanliness (dirt, germs, contamination)	Excessive and ritualized bathing, washing, cleaning
Concern about body secretions (saliva, urine, stool)	Rituals to remove contact with body secretions, avoid touching, etc.
Sexual obsessions (forbidden urges or aggressive sexual actions)	Ritualized and rigid sexual relationships
Obsessive fears (harming self or others)	Repeated checking of doors, heaters, locks; when driving, retracing route for fear of having run someone over
Concern with exactness (symmetry, order)	Ritualized arranging and rearranging
Obsessions with health (something terrible will happen and lead to death)	Repeating rituals (checking and rechecking vital signs, rigid dietary intake, constantly checking for new information about health)

while 11 per cent reported sub-clinical levels of the behaviour. The majority of problems first occur among people in their early twenties.

Biological explanations

Biological theorists (e.g. Christian et al. 2008) have implicated two interconnected brain systems in OCD. The first is a loop connecting the orbito-frontal area, where sexual, violent, and other primitive impulses normally arise, to the thalamic region, where the individual initiates more cognitive and perhaps behavioural responses as a result of this activation. A second loop connects the orbito-frontal region to the thalamic region, but via the corpus striatus. The striatal region is thought to control the degree of activity within the systems. It tends to filter out high levels of activity within the orbito-frontal area so that the thalamus does not over-respond to these initial impulses. In OCD, it may fail to correct over-activity in the orbito-frontal–thalamic loop, so the individual over-responds to environmental stimuli, and is unable to prevent their cognitive and behavioural responses to them. The first system is mediated by the excitatory neurotransmitter, glutamic acid. The second system is mediated by a number of neurotransmitters, including serotonin, dopamine, and GABA. Despite the primacy of serotonin mechanisms in the disorder, evidence of a genetically transmitted role of serotonin activity has proven elusive.

Psychosocial explanations

Freud (1922) considered OCD to result from the individual's fear of their id impulses and their use of ego defence mechanisms to reduce this anxiety. This 'battle' between the two opposing forces is not played out in the unconscious. Instead, it involves explicit thoughts and actions. Id impulses are evident through obsessive thoughts, while the compulsions are the result of ego defences. Two ego defence mechanisms are particularly common: undoing and reaction formation. Undoing involves overt behaviours designed to counter the feared outcome, such as washing to avoid contamination. Reaction formation involves adopting behaviours diametrically opposed to the unacceptable impulses. An individual who experiences strong 'inappropriate' sexual compulsions may counter them through cleanliness and orderliness. The origins of OCD lie in the anal phase of development. Freud suggested that children in this stage gain gratification through their bowel movements. If their parents prohibit or curb this pleasure through overzealous potty training, this will result in a state of anger and aggressive id impulses expressed through soiling or other destructive behaviours. If the parents respond to this with further pressure, or if they embarrass the child in attempts to encourage toilet training, the child may feel shame and guilt. So, the pleasure of the id begins to compete with the control of the ego. If this continues, the child may become fixated in this stage and develop an obsessive personality.

The behavioural model of obsessive-compulsive disorder is based on the two-process model of Mowrer (1947). What differentiates OCD from phobic or panic disorders is that anxiety arises in situations from which the individual cannot easily escape. As a result, reductions of distress are achieved by engaging in covert or overt ritual or obsessive behaviours designed to reduce the anxiety associated with the particular stimulus. These avoidant behaviours reduce anxiety in the short term, but maintain it in the longer term, as the affected individual fails to learn that no harm will occur in their absence.

More recent, cognitive behavioural explanations have extended this behavioural model. According to Salkovskis and Kirk (1997), obsessions are intrusive beliefs that the individual will be responsible for harm to themself or others unless they engage in some form of preventive action. In response to this threat, the individual may try to ignore or suppress these thoughts. Unfortunately, this often results in an increase in their frequency. So they shift to the use of safety behaviours, with their consequent maintenance of the problem.

The related, meta-cognitive model of Wells (2000) emphasizes how worrisome 'beliefs' can become 'truths' and drive inappropriate behaviour. According to Wells, people with OCD make a number of cognitive errors, known as fusion beliefs – the belief that a 'bad thought' is the equivalent of a 'bad action':

- *Thought–event fusion*: having a thought means an event has happened or will happen in the future.
- *Thought–action fusion*: thoughts will lead to the uncontrollable enactment of unwanted actions.
- *Thought–object fusion*: thoughts, feelings, and memories can be transferred onto objects and/or 'caught' from objects.

Obsessive-compulsive disorder results from a combination of these beliefs and the additional belief that cognitive rituals prevent the harm associated with them. A developmental pattern in the types of thoughts experienced can be identified. Children with OCD report fewer intrusive thoughts than adolescents or adults. In addition, these thoughts are less distressing and more controllable. They also report fewer beliefs about responsibility, lower probability estimates of harm, and greater use of thought suppression strategies than adolescents and adults (Farrell and Barrett 2006). However, beliefs in relation to thought–action fusion, perceived severity of harm, self-doubt, and cognitive control do not differ with age. Thus, it appears that the cognitive experience of OCD is very similar in adolescence and adulthood, but younger children experience a milder, more controllable form of the disorder.

Case formulation

Jake is 13 years old, lives with his parents in York, and has just moved to secondary school. Jake's older brother, Sam, died from leukaemia when Jake was 12. During Sam's illness, Jake developed significant worries about infection and illness, which led to repetitive checking behaviours regarding contamination and cleanliness. Following Sam's death, Jake and his family have struggled to manage his worries and behaviours, which include frequent washing (to the point of having sore hands) and seeking reassurance from his mother. Jake is often distressed and his mother finds it difficult to resist his demands. Things escalated since his move to secondary school, and his parents report being at 'breaking point'. His mother has had to take significant time off work due to stress.

Long-term antecedents
Jake had a relatively stable early childhood. His mother experienced post-natal depression following his birth and found managing two small boys challenging, but was helped by a supportive family. Sam's diagnosis was traumatic and meant there was a sudden change in family life for Jake. The trauma of his diagnosis made all the family hyper-vigilant to health threats and they often expected the worst. As Sam's health needs became paramount, Jake's needs were often overlooked. His parents spent significant amounts of time at the hospital and Jake was often left with family and friends, unsure of what was happening to his brother. Sam's treatment meant that germs and contamination were real threats to his brother's health.

Short-term antecedents
Jake has recently had his thirteenth birthday and moved to secondary school. His mother returned to work 6 months ago for the first time since Sam's death. The family have begun to talk about the future and think about taking a holiday, although this has not happened due to the severity of Jake's worries and behaviours. Jake's mum remains overwhelmed with grief and finds managing Jake's reassurance-seeking and worries difficult. She finds it hard to say 'no' to him, but also gets very angry with him, which escalates the situation further.

Formulation
Although Jake may be the person referred to the mental health system, his whole family are actually affected by these events and are part of the formulation.

Jake's early attachments are likely to have been insecure as a consequence of his mother's post-natal depression. His brother's illness in middle childhood was devastating for the family and his parents became hyper-vigilant to threat and focused on his brother's physical and emotional needs, often overlooking Jake's needs. This was confusing for Jake and increased the anxiety he already felt about his brother's illness. At times he did not know what was happening to his brother and he often blamed himself or wished he was ill rather than Sam. Jake's obsessive worries and compulsive behaviours have a legitimate origin, in that contamination was a very real threat to his brother's health during his treatment.

Seeking reassurance from his mother not only reduced his anxiety in the short term but acted as a vehicle for securing parental attention and bringing her close. Jake's difficulties become more pronounced following his move to secondary school, which is a big step for many young people, but was also significant for Jake's family in that Sam never attended secondary school, nor celebrated his thirteenth birthday: all markers that life is moving on without Sam. Jake's mum finds it difficult to think about a future without Sam and remains overwhelmed with grief, feeling guilty thinking about the future and unable to move forward. This is likely to be reflected in the wider family system, reinforcing how stuck the family feel and keeping the family locked in the obsessive-compulsive cycle of behaviour and grief, unable to move on.

Treatment

As with other anxiety disorders, the first-line treatment for OCD in both children and adults involves 'exposure with response prevention'. That is, exposure to situations that would normally trigger compulsive behaviours, but not engaging in them. This often involves a gradual exposure to increasingly difficult situations, combined with the use of coping strategies such as relaxation or self-instruction.

In children and young people, this approach will typically result in a 37 per cent reduction in risk for continued problems (O'Kearney 2007) – a better outcome than in many interventions in adults (Olatunji et al. 2012). More effective than CBT alone, however, may be CBT in combination with an SSRI. The Pediatric OCD Treatment Study Team (2004) compared the effectiveness of CBT, sertraline (an SSRI), and the two in combination. Sertraline and CBT alone were equally effective, while the combined intervention was more effective than either of them alone. The rate of clinical remission for the combined treatment was 53.6 per cent; for CBT alone, 39.3 per cent; for sertraline alone, 21.4 per cent; and for placebo, 3.6 per cent. What are unclear are the longer-term outcomes of these interventions, following the cessation of the SSRI. Partly because of this question, and partly due to a reluctance to prescribe children unnecessary medication, the optimal treatment may involve an escalating approach in which CBT forms the first-line treatment, with the addition of an SSRI if the young person fails to respond.

In adults, interventions usually comprise three key elements: mind experiments, challenging inappropriate thoughts, and behavioural exposure and response prevention. Mind experiments allow the individual to test and challenge the validity of their beliefs. Someone who is frightened their thoughts may kill someone, for example, may be encouraged to test the reality of this assumption through a mind experiment in which the therapist and then client think the feared thoughts – hopefully with no negative effects! The other elements involve Socratic challenge of worrisome thoughts, while exposure and response prevention involves exposure to feared stimuli without engaging in safety behaviours, often in a graded exposure programme.

A meta-analysis by Olatunji et al. (2013) found this approach to be better than control conditions both immediately after treatment and at follow-up. However, the authors also found that cognitive behavioural interventions were generally no more effective than pure behavioural interventions, and pure cognitive interventions that involved attempts at cognitive change, addressing inflated responsibility, overestimation of threat, and intolerance of uncertainty in the absence of behavioural exposure and response prevention were least effective. Acceptance and commitment therapy has also proven effective, and better than relaxation training alone (Twohig et al. 2010). However, relaxation is far from the optimal intervention for OCD, and no comparison of this approach with an exposure and response prevention intervention has been conducted.

Pharmacological treatment of OCD now largely involves the use of SSRIs, although success rates are generally lower than those of other anxiety disorders and relapse rates are relatively high following drug cessation. These benefits may, however, be augmented by the use of CBT. Simpson et al. (2008), for example, achieved a 25 per cent reduction in symptom severity following 8 weeks of exposure and response prevention in patients already receiving treatment with SSRIs. In addition, Tolin et al. (2004) found that an exposure and response prevention programme proved beneficial in a group of patients who had not benefited from previous treatment by SSRIs.

Working with: obsessive-compulsive disorder

J had experienced some degree of obsessional behaviour for much of his life. As a child he had been a perfectionist, engaging in frequent checking behaviour. As a young adult, his life gradually became increasingly controlled by his need to check he had completed tasks, not left lights or heaters on, and so on. His behaviour became so problematic that he sought help from both his family doctor, who prescribed SSRIs, and a local hypnotherapist. He benefited from seeing the hypnotherapist until one session in which he believed he experienced 'an existential void', a 'nothingness' he found extremely disturbing. As a consequence, his symptoms increased and were added to by a range of obsessions linked to occult, folk beliefs, and a range of religious contexts. These included:

- The numbers 3, 6, and 9. As examples of this fear, he would not use supermarket checkout aisles with these numbers. If his bill included any of these numbers, he would be unable to use the purchased product, or if it was a relatively trivial purchase (not, for example, food he would consume or something he would keep in the house) he could do so only by repeating the safe number 7, four times. If he saw a car number plate that included these numbers while driving to the supermarket, he would have to drive round the supermarket four times. If he said the numbers, he had to repeat the number 7 four times to counter this action. As a college lecturer in mathematics, this presented him a significant problem!
- Images or situations that represented 'nothingness'. These included a blank wall he drove past to get to work each morning and a Buddhist retreat close to his home. He dealt with these by not looking at either object (and not using some of the rooms in his house). If he did see them, he would find it difficult to manage his anxiety because even the use of safe images or numbers was relatively ineffective.

J provides an unusual example of OCD, as most of his safety behaviours were relatively brief and unobtrusive. However, their use was very frequent (there were many other triggers than those noted here) and they had a significant impact on his life. The issue of shopping was clearly a major problem and meant that on occasion he had not eaten because a food bill added up to the wrong number. He had not been able to make major purchases for a number of years.

Because of the all-pervading nature of his OCD, rather than engage in a highly focused behavioural programme, J's intervention comprised two elements. At each session, he chose between two and three triggers to address over the following week. Depending on his confidence in achieving change, he would either reduce the duration/repetition of safety behaviours or cut them out completely. Because of his fear of existential nothingness, he was unwilling to learn any coping strategies involving mindfulness, but he learned relaxation and used it if he became particularly tense or anxious.

(continued)

Treatment of his shopping anxieties involved a more formal intervention. He identified a hierarchy of situations from least to most anxiety-provoking, and progressed along this hierarchy in an exposure plus response prevention programme. This included shopping in the feared number aisles in supermarkets and shopping for items and taking them home/using them even if their individual prices or the total bill included a forbidden number. This began with things he might need for a short while but were ultimately disposable, such as cleaning items for the kitchen, before moving to more problematic items such as food he would eat, or long-term purchases including a settee. At each level of the hierarchy, he learned not to engage in any safety behaviours and to cope with the anxiety he experienced, which may have lasted from minutes to hours.

Chapter summary

1. Most anxiety disorders have a common neurological basis, involving excess activation of the behavioural inhibition system.
2. They also have a number of common psychological characteristics, including threat-appraisals, high physiological reactivity, fear, and safety behaviours.
3. The origin of many anxiety disorders lies in childhood, involving interactions between parental interactions and child cognitions.
4. Treatment of children with anxiety often follows a generic treatment approach regardless of the specific diagnosis.
5. Separation anxiety disorder is generally found in young people, but may extend into adulthood.
6. It reflects insecure attachments and is best treated by working with parents to reduce the anxiety.
7. Phobias can be acquired through conditioning or vicarious learning. The severity and duration of phobias may be affected by a range of cognitive factors, as well as prior experiences.
8. Treatment involves some exposure with response prevention.
9. Generalized anxiety disorder involves anxious responses to a range of (non-threatening) stimuli.
10. Explanations include psychoanalytic, humanistic, and cognitive factors.
11. Treatment may include worry exposure with response prevention.
12. Panic disorder is characterized as the experience of unexpected panic attacks.
13. According to Clark, it is initiated and maintained by interpretation of the symptoms of arousal as evidence of significant health threat.
14. Treatment involves exposure with response prevention.
15. Obsessive-compulsive disorder involves the experience of anxiety in the absence of means of avoiding feared stimuli. Safety behaviours replace avoidance, but maintain the disorder.
16. Treatment involves exposure with response prevention.

Further reading

Abramowitz, J.S. (2009) *Getting Over OCD: A 10 step workbook for taking back your life.* New York: Guilford Press.

Davey, G.C. and Wells, A. (2006) *Worry and its Psychological Disorders: Theory, assessment and treatment.* Chichester: Wiley.

Eddy, K.T., Dutra, L., Bradley R. et al. (2004) A multidimensional meta-analysis of psychotherapy and pharmacotherapy for obsessive-compulsive disorder, *Clinical Psychology Review*, 24: 1011–30.

Stallard, P. (2008) *Anxiety: Cognitive behaviour therapy with children and young people.* Hove: Routledge.

Wells, A. (2013) *Cognitive Therapy of Anxiety Disorders: A practice manual and conceptual guide.* Chichester: Wiley.

Chapter 9

Disorders of mood

This chapter introduces a range of disorders, all of which are characterized, at least in part, by inappropriate mood.

By the end of this chapter, you should have an understanding of the causes and treatments of the following disorders both in children and adults:

- Depression
- Suicide
- Bipolar disorder
- Seasonal affective disorder

Depression

Most of us experience periods of low mood. However, for people with depression, this low mood becomes chronic and all-pervasive. Severely depressed people can lack motivation or the biological drive to take voluntary action. Getting out of bed and engaging in daily activities can be difficult. They may experience suicidal thoughts, but lack the motivation or drive to follow through on these thoughts. Indeed, people with severe depression may be at increased risk of suicide following the initiation of treatment as they continue to have suicidal thoughts while becoming increasingly motivated to act on them. People with depression often report slow or confused thoughts and difficulties in concentrating or problem-solving. Their thought content is negative, with high levels of pessimism about the future.

Around 5–6 per cent of the adult population in western countries are likely to be depressed at any one time, and of these around a third will be classified as severely depressed. By contrast, very few young children are diagnosed with major depression: prevalence rates range between 0.05 and 3.0 per cent (Birmaher et al. 1996). However, in adolescence, prevalence rates are as high as 8 per cent, and twice as high in girls than boys, possibly as a result of differences in coping styles or hormonal factors related to puberty (Angold et al. 1999). Around 70 per cent of adolescents who have one episode of depression are likely to have a second within 5 years, although the relationship between onset during childhood and adult episodes is much weaker (Hazell 2004).

The average age of a first episode is around 32 years. Prevalence rates among women are about twice those in men. About a quarter of depressive episodes last less than one month, up to a third last for a year, while a further 25 per cent may last 2 years or more (e.g. Kessler et al. 2005). Following an episode of depression, many people will go on to experience further bouts.

One reason for the much lower reported rate of depression in children versus adults may be a consequence of difficulties in its diagnosis. The criteria for a diagnosis of depression in young people are clearly specified and are essentially the same as those for depression in adulthood. Despite this apparent clarity, an estimated 70 per cent of children and adolescents may not receive appropriate diagnosis and treatment (National Institute of Mental Health 2001), for a number of interrelated reasons. First, many children do not spontaneously tell their parents they have a problem, and depression generally has a slow onset and fluctuating course, making it difficult for parents to identify (Hazell 2004). Second, the presentation of depression may differ according to the child's developmental stage. Young children, under the age of 7, have difficulty communicating negative emotions and thoughts, and are likely to report their distress in terms of somatic problems: general aches, pains, headaches, stomach aches, and so on. At a later age, some symptoms may present as behavioural rather than emotional problems. Irritable mood may cause angry, hostile behaviour, while impaired attention may not appear unusual, or even be considered a sign of ADHD. Other frequent signs of depression in young people include: withdrawal from friends and previously enjoyed activities, increased irritability or agitation, missed school or poor school performance, indecision, lack of concentration or forgetfulness, as well perhaps more classic signs of persistent sadness and hopelessness, lack of enthusiasm or motivation, and feelings of worthlessness or excessive guilt.

Biological explanations

Depression is associated with the activity of three neurotransmitters that modulate activity of the limbic system, its connections to 'paralimbic' cortical areas including the ventromedial prefrontal cortex, and the central nervous system: serotonin, norepinephrine, and dopamine. Central to the activity of all these may be serotonin. According to the permissive hypothesis of depression, low levels of serotonin have a direct negative effect on mood, but also permit dysregulation of dopamine and norepinephrine activity. Together, these result in different symptoms associated with depression:

- *Norepinephrine dysregulation*: low levels of alertness or energy, anxiety, and poor attention.
- *Serotonin dysregulation*: anxiety, obsessions, and compulsions.
- *Dopamine dysregulation*: poor attention, low motivation and 'interest in life'.

While drug treatment with SSRIs increases serotonin levels almost immediately, their impact on mood may take weeks to become evident. This may be a consequence of receptor neurons taking time to adapt to the increased levels of serotonin within the synapse.

However, it may be the result of more complex processes. According to Malberg et al. (2000), some symptoms of depression result from damage to neurons in the hippocampus caused by the neurotoxic effects of high levels of the stress hormone cortisol found in depression. The delay in treatment effect may reflect a process of repair and re-growth of neurons damaged in this way, as SSRIs increase levels of neural growth hormone. Once the hippocampus is repaired and normal serotonin activity is resumed, mood improves. Not surprisingly, gene alleles associated with increased risk for depression are linked to serotonin (5-HTT), dopamine (COMT), and norepinephrine (NET) activity.

Psychological explanations

Freud considered depression to be analogous to grieving. According to Freud (1917), depression results from an imagined or symbolic loss. Events that trigger depression involve losing the love or esteem of important individuals. The depressed person introjects their negative feelings towards the individual they consider to be rejecting them. Those most prone to depression are likely to have failed to effectively progress though the oral stage of development. As a consequence, they remain dependent on others for love and approval throughout their lives, and are susceptible to events that trigger anxieties or experiences of loss.

Early behavioural models of depression considered depression to result from a low rate of positive social reinforcement (Lewinsohn et al. 1979) or a lack of control over negative events (Seligman 1975). More recent explanations have focused on cognitive factors. Abramson et al. (1978), for example, argued that individuals are at risk of depression if they make internal, stable, and global attributions for negative events: 'It's my fault, it will always go wrong, and this is just typical of my life.' By contrast, positive outcomes are attributed to external, unstable, specific causes: 'Things went well, but no thanks to me. It was luck and won't happen again.' These attributions combined with the belief that things are unlikely to change places the individual at significant risk for depression.

Perhaps the most well-known cognitive model of depression is that of Beck (1997). According to Beck, depression is associated with what he termed 'cognitive errors' or 'faulty thinking': inaccurate and negative interpretations of events that affect us. Beck identified a wide-ranging series of errors from his clinical work, including absolutist thinking, arbitrary inference, and selective abstraction (see Table 9.1). These cognitions are our automatic and immediate responses to events: negative automatic thoughts (or NATs). They reflect the *cognitive triad*: beliefs about our self, events or other people that affect us now and in the future. In depression, these typically reflect:

- *The self*: 'I am worthless.'
- *The world/environment*: 'The world is unfair and is against me.'
- *The future*: 'My future is hopeless.'

It is important to note that Beck did not claim these distorted beliefs cause depression; rather, they *maintain* depression once it has begun. The causes of depression lie in deeper, unconscious processes. According to Beck, as a result of childhood experiences, we develop fundamental beliefs about ourselves and the world. These unconscious cognitive schemata influence our conscious thoughts and our mood (see Chapter 1). Negative events in childhood,

Table 9.1 Some examples of Beck's depressogenic thinking errors

Absolutistic thinking	Thinking in 'all-or-nothing' terms: 'If I don't succeed in this task, I am an absolute failure. I am either the best teacher, or I am nothing…'
Over-generalization	Drawing a general (negative) conclusion on the basis of a single incident: 'That's it – I always fail at this sort of thing…I can't do it!'
Personalization	Interpreting events as personal affronts or obstacles: 'Why do they always pick on ME!…even when I'm not to blame?'
Arbitrary inference	Drawing a conclusion without sufficient evidence to support it: 'They don't like me…I could tell from the moment we met…'
Selective abstraction	Focusing on an insignificant detail taken out of context: 'I thought my lecture went well. But that student who left early may have been unhappy with it. Perhaps the others were as well but didn't show it…'

such as those resulting from parental rejection, can establish negative cognitive schemata about the self and the world.

Among children, these negative beliefs may have a more direct impact on mood. Bishop et al. (2004), for example, found that depressed children paid more attention to, and remembered more, negative aspects of stories than children who were not depressed. The cognitive model of depression appears appropriate to both children and adults. As the individual grows older, however, these negative schemata may become less salient over time, or else the individual would be chronically depressed. However, when they encounter stressful circumstances later in childhood or adulthood, and particularly those that echo previous childhood experiences, these may trigger low mood. This increases the salience of relevant negative schemata, activation of which triggers their related NATs. Together, these maintain low mood and the development of depression.

Reflecting Beck's initial training as a psychoanalyst, his theory suggested a critical childhood period during which schemata are established that will have a lifelong impact. Others, such as Meichenbaum (1985), have suggested that schemata can change and evolve over time. They are certainly amenable to change, for this is the core precept of cognitive behaviour therapy (CBT). But how flexible they are over the lifespan is difficult to determine, at least in part because our behaviour and experiences tend to reinforce rather than challenge existing schema.

Psychosocial explanations

A range of psychosocial factors can trigger depression in children, including bullying in school, medical illness, life stress, or the loss of an important person. Depression rates are higher among children from high stress households, and among those in which one or more parents is experiencing depression. Interestingly, children may be more vulnerable to marital dissatisfaction experienced by their father than their mother. Wang and Crane (2001) speculated this may be because mothers continue to provide care for their children even when distressed, while fathers may disengage from the family and abandon their child caring role. Men are also more likely to overtly express signs of distress through anger, aggression, and lack of affection. By contrast, when mothers experience marital instability, they frequently become more involved with their children than previously. Depressed mothers may, however, contribute to risk for childhood depression as a result of poor bonding and attachment with their children. Women with post-natal depression may achieve less strong bonds with their children, and engage in less appropriate and caring parental behaviours (Muzik et al. 2012).

Ironically, excessive care or control by parents may also be problematic. Parental attempts to exercise excessive control over their child, which they would interpret as 'monitoring' or 'support', may implicitly communicate to the child they consider them to be incompetent and incapable: beliefs that may be internalized and result in low mood or depression (Pomerantz 2001).

Among adults, prevalence rates for depression are highest among populations under social pressures, including the economically deprived and unemployed, ethnic minorities, and people with poor social or marital support. People with a low income, for example, are almost ten times more likely to become depressed than the economically better off (Andersen et al. 2009). Explanations for the higher rates of depression among women than men include higher levels of 'work–home spill-over' (working at both home and place of work), the adverse effects of social disruption, and the greater ability of men to distract from negative thoughts at times of pressure (Holen-Hoeksema 1990). Elder abuse is a significant risk factor for depression among older people (Dong et al. 2009), as is the experience of chronic health problems (Tsai et al. 2005).

Treatment

The most widely used psychological intervention for depression for both children and adults is called cognitive therapy (Beck 1977), although it actually maintains a significant behavioural component (see Chapter 5). Following an educational phase in which the individual is taught the basic model of depression, this approach typically involves a number of strategies, including:

- *behavioural activation* and *pleasant event scheduling* to increase physiological arousal and engagement in functional, social, and other rewarding activities. This is of particular benefit to individuals who are significantly depressed.
- *cognitive challenge*, in which the individual identifies errors of thinking and challenges them either in the therapy session or in their lives. Within therapy, this process is likely to be led by the therapist using Socratic dialogue.
- *behavioural hypothesis testing*, in which the individual deliberately tests the validity of their negative assumptions, in the hope of disproving them.

In what is still the most recent meta-analysis of the relevant data, Harrington et al. (1998) concluded that this type of intervention achieved remission rates of 62 per cent among young people aged 8–19 years, compared with 36 per cent for those who received standard care. Among young people with relatively low levels of depression, alternative approaches to one-to-one counselling have been considered. In one interesting New Zealand study, Merry et al. (2012) compared the effectiveness of a computerized self-help programme based on CBT principles with usual care, usually some form of counselling with a counsellor or psychologist.

They hoped to show that their intervention was equally effective as 'live' therapy, thereby justifying its future use as a cost-effective treatment. Indeed, remission rates were better in the computer-based approach: 44 versus 32 per cent – a significant difference.

Among children with moderate to high levels of depression, research has taken another approach: examining the effectiveness of CBT combined with medication. In one such study, March et al. (2004) compared the effectiveness of CBT alone or in combination with fluoxetine (an SSRI) in a group of young people aged 12–17 years with moderate to severe depression. By the end of therapy, 73 per cent of those receiving the combined therapy were no longer diagnosable with depression. Success rates in the other conditions were 62 per cent for fluoxetine and 48 per cent for CBT. The relatively poor short-term outcome of CBT is a fairly common finding, as it can take some time for people to become skilled and gain benefit. Thankfully, the 6-month success rates were more reassuring: 86 per cent for the combined intervention, and 81 per cent for both fluoxetine and CBT. A key issue is whether the gains made in the pharmacologically treated group continued after the drug was no longer prescribed. We await these data.

This study involved the use of fluoxetine for a good reason. The development of most antidepressants is based on their impact on adults, and they may prove less effective and more toxic in children. Indeed, concerns about their safety and potential side-effects, including dizziness, headache, hostility, and agitation, have led both the UK and USA to ban the use of all SSRIs except fluoxetine in the treatment of children aged 8–17 years. With this cautionary note, these data suggest that the primary intervention for mild depression in young people should be CBT. In more severe cases, a combined intervention may be optimal, particularly if CBT does not prove effective on its own.

Parents have also increasingly become involved in CBT-based programmes designed to help them support their depressed children. The interventions typically provide knowledge and skills to help the whole family cope better with the issue. Although this approach has received relatively little research attention, it is frequently used, and appears to be successful both in helping depressed young people and in reducing their risk of becoming depressed as a result of parental depression (Compas et al. 2011).

Among adults, evidence of the effectiveness of cognitive therapy has been built up over several decades. A recent meta-analysis by Cuijpers et al. (2014), for example, identified nine studies comparing the effects of cognitive therapy with pharmacological interventions including tricylics and SSRIs. The two types of intervention proved equally effective in the short term. However, participants receiving pharmacotherapy were over two and half times more likely to relapse following the cessation of therapy than those receiving cognitive therapy. They were also twice as likely to relapse over long-term follow-up periods even if they continued on pharmacotherapy. Given the clear benefits of cognitive therapy, recent studies have attempted to determine the most cost-effective way of providing it – using, for example, computerized and internet interventions. For example, the Increasing Access to Psychological Therapies (IAPT) programme in England, which provides computerized cognitive therapy for people with mild depression, is achieving significant short-term benefits, although the longer-term outcomes may be more modest (Gyani et al. 2013).

An increasingly used alternative approach involves the use of mindfulness or a broader acceptance and commitment approach. In one evaluation of this approach, Forman et al. (2012) compared the effectiveness of acceptance and commitment therapy and cognitive therapy in the treatment of people experiencing anxiety or depression. In the short term, the two interventions proved equally effective; in the longer term, cognitive therapy appeared to be superior. However, mindfulness may be more effective for people who have relapsed following cognitive therapy, particularly those that have experienced three or more previous depressive episodes (Coelho et al. 2007).

Case formulation: depression

A was a recently divorced secretary. She had always been anxious within her 4-year marriage, but had been devastated when her ex-husband had asked for a divorce. In the months following the divorce, she had become increasingly depressed, stopped seeing her friends, and was taking significant time off work.

Long-term antecedents
A was a lone child. She had been sexually abused by a close friend of the family for 2–3 years from around the age of 6. She felt disgust at the abuser's behaviour, but also blamed herself for much of what happened. She believed she deserved to be abused because: (1) she was a bad person, because of all the people that he could have abused, he chose her, which must indicate he saw something bad in her; (2) her parents did not love her, because they did nothing to prevent the abuse; and (3) God did not love her. These beliefs were strengthened by the occasions, for example, when her parents left her alone with the abuser while they went away on weekend trips.

Short-term antecedents
A had several early relationships with boys, none of which became sexual by her choice, and few girl friends. On leaving school following her GCSEs, she took a secretary's job at a local small business. There, she met a junior manager who asked her out. Their relationship was 'steady' rather than 'whirlwind', and even at the beginning of the relationship sex was not a priority for either partner. They married after a relationship lasting just over 18 months. Over the months before the end of their relationship, her husband spent more and more time away from home, and the quality of the relationship deteriorated. She became low in spirits, felt unloved, and found any sexual relationship increasingly difficult to deal with: eventually they stopped having intercourse.

Formulation
A had chronic low self-esteem because of events that had occurred in her childhood – and her failure to challenge the basis of those beliefs. She felt unloved and did not love herself. She was frightened of sexual relationships, but nevertheless desired 'safe' relationships with men. The one safe relationship with an adult she had achieved was not strong, but had protected her against her negative self-beliefs and self-disgust. The absence of this relationship, the lack of any supportive relationships, combined with a re-activation of her negative beliefs about herself, resulted in significant distress and depression.

Working with: depression

Ms V was a lone child, brought up in a small village some miles from Gloucester. She had been sexually abused by a close family member for 2–3 years from around the age of 6 years. Over time, she came to believe that she deserved to be abused because, like A: (1) she thought she was a bad person – of all the people that he could have abused, he chose her; (2) her parents did not love her – they did nothing to prevent the abuse; and (3) God did not love her – he allowed it to happen.

As a consequence of her low self-esteem and self-disgust, Ms V had a poor social life and her relationship with her parents was poor. She did not have any boyfriends and became significantly overweight, partly because she gained pleasure from eating, partly because it made her unattractive to men. The one safe relationship with a male adult she had achieved was not strong, but had protected her against her negative self-beliefs and self-disgust. The unfortunate death of this individual, the lack of any supportive relationships, combined with re-activation of her negative beliefs about herself, resulted in significant distress and depression.

Her key beliefs were challenged through Socratic dialogue:

- One key dialogue reflected on the fact that Ms V spent occasional nights with the abuser while her parents were away for the weekend. She took this as a clear sign that her parents both knew what was happening and condoned it. However, close questioning on this issue reminded Ms V that she did not want her parents to worry about her, or the abuser to tell her parents what was occurring, so when she went to stay with him she had pretended to be looking forward to it and smiled and laughed while her parents were there. As a consequence, they could not have been aware of her concerns and distress.
- Through similar questioning, she began to believe that she was chosen not because of who she was, but because of her availability and, as a consequence, began to challenge her beliefs that she was a bad person and that God did not love her.

Of note is that while Ms V was able to reappraise her beliefs about herself and the abuse, these changes did not immediately transform her into a happy and carefree person. Nevertheless, she was able to establish a warmer and more loving relationship with her mother, and began to develop stronger acquaintanceships and then friendships with people she knew, including one man with whom she developed a strong, if asexual, relationship. This reciprocity and evidence of being loved gradually resulted in improvements in mood, maintained over a period of months. She remained a vulnerable individual, but was coping with life.

Suicide

Suicide is the third leading cause of death among Americans aged 15–24 years (Anderson and Smith 2003). Among 10-year-olds, suicide is rare but gradually increases over time to rates of 19 per 100,000 boys and three per 100,000 girls during adolescence. While suicide rates are higher among boys than girls, girls have higher rates of suicidal ideation and attempted suicide. Among adults, suicide is not limited to individuals who are depressed. In fact, its highest prevalence may be among people with acute psychosis. In addition, many people with no evidence of mental health problems report having had suicidal ideas, and 2 per cent have made a suicide attempt. Exact figures for the prevalence of suicide are difficult to ascertain. However, an estimated 0.4 per cent of the US adult population attempt suicide in any one year. Around 3.5 per cent experience suicidal thoughts, and 1 per cent make suicidal plans (Crosby et al. 2011).

Not surprisingly, suicide rates are highest among populations under severe stress. Among young people, triggers to suicide include:

- a recent or serious loss
- struggling with sexual orientation
- a lack of social support
- bullying.

Risk may also be moderated by a range of factors, including access to lethal means (e.g. pills or weapons), fear of stigma while seeking help, difficulties in accessing help, and cultural and religious beliefs that suicide is a noble way to resolve personal difficulties. Among adults, other types of stressors may emerge. Rates as high as 19 per cent, for example, have been found among sex workers in Goa (Shahmanesh et al. 2009). Less dramatically, suicide rates are lower among married and co-habiting people than those who are divorced. They are also relatively high among men, with rates four times higher than among women and young people who experience abuse, bullying or examination stress (Anderson and Smith 2003), and those of all ages in sexual minorities (King et al. 2008). Among older people, suicide may occur as a consequence of increasing disability: 44 per cent of one sample of elderly people apparently committed suicide to prevent being placed in a nursing home (Loebel et al. 1991). Suicide rates among the recently bereaved are also high. Finally, suicide may be influenced by social factors that are significantly removed from the individual. Won et al. (2013), for example, found celebrity suicides predicted the incidence of suicides within the general population, and appeared to be more important than classical indices of economic hardship.

A recent phenomenon has been the development of suicide pacts made through the internet, often between people who did not previously know each other. However, this is not new. Although suicide pacts account for less than 1 per cent of the total number of suicides in the UK (Brown and Barraclough 1997), one pact occurs, on average, every month (Rajagopal 2004). In contrast to internet pacts, the relationship between individuals in these pacts is typically exclusive, isolated from others, and the immediate trigger is frequently a threat to the continuation of the relationship, such as the impending death of one member. Both people involved typically employ the same method.

Psychosocial explanations

According to Freud (1920), suicide is an aggressive act targeted not at the person involved, but a lost 'love object': an important individual who has rejected the person taking their own life. It is an act of revenge. Hendin (1992) identified other psychoanalytic processes that may lead to suicide, including ideas of effecting a rebirth or reunion with a lost object as well as self-punishment and atonement. More recently, Rudd (2000) suggested that people who attempt suicide are likely to be experiencing a number of emotions, including hopelessness, worthlessness, despair, and agitation. They may also have high levels of impulsivity, irritability, poor problem-solving skills, aggression, and a history of drug or alcohol abuse. When these various elements collide, the person feels worthless, helpless, and is unable to problem-solve their way out of these feelings. Their impulsivity may lead them to take an aggressive response to the feelings, perhaps aided by the use of drugs or alcohol. They make a suicide attempt.

Of course, not all people who attempt suicide succeed, and many do not wish to. So-called 'parasuicide' involves an apparent attempt at suicide that is not designed to result in death. It is most prevalent among young people and females (National Center for Health Statistics 2013). It is often seen as a call for help, to alert others to the distress the individual is experiencing.

Treatment

Key elements of interventions to reduce risk of further suicide attempts involve identifying realistic goals whose achievement would make the individual less unhappy and strategies by which they could be achieved. Other approaches focus more on the immediate determinants of risk and may involve techniques including **thought-stopping** and cognitive challenge. Few formal evaluations of these types of approach have been reported, but do report some degree of benefit. Brown et al. (2005), for example, found the number of further suicide attempts over an 18-month follow-up period was almost halved in people who took part in a ten-session cognitive therapy intervention versus those in a usual care group: 24 versus 43 per cent. Other studies have focused on helping the bereaved relatives of people who have committed suicide. Bereavement groups in which people share their bereavement experience and provide support for others have shown some, limited benefit.

Thinking about...

Assisted suicide is a highly contentious issue, with strong advocates both for and against. An argument can be made in support of this process. It affords respect for the autonomy of the individual to make decisions consistent with their values and beliefs, and acknowledges that it is reasonable to make personal choices that reduce the experience of suffering. Arguments against include the notion that it is inappropriate to support an autonomous action that prevents the possibility of future autonomous desires (e.g. the finality of suicide prevents one changing one's mind) and it could provide a mechanism for 'state-approved' deaths. More pragmatic questions include, who would assist in the suicides, and would certain individuals be pressured to accept suicide? So, should the state support some individuals in ending their lives, and if so what types of individuals? Or should no one be allowed to commit suicide?

Bipolar disorder

Bipolar disorder was formally known as manic-depression, and this name reflects the nature of the problem. People with the disorder experience periods of profound depression alternating with periods of mania or elation. Two broad natural histories of the disorder have been identified:

- alternating episodes of depression and mania, often with long periods of stabilized mood in between;
- episodes of depression, with less frequent periods of 'hypomania'.

During periods of mania, the person moves rapidly, talks rapidly and loudly, and their conversation is filled with jokes and attempts at cleverness. Flamboyance is common. Judgement is poor, and they may engage in risky behaviours they later regret: spending significant amounts of money, inappropriate sexual behaviour, and so on. They may also become extremely frustrated by the actions of others, who they see as preventing them succeeding in their grand plan. During severe manic or depressed episodes, some people may have symptoms that overwhelm their ability to deal with everyday life, and even reality. They may experience significant sleep disturbance, psychotic symptoms such as hearing voices, paranoia, visual hallucinations, and believe they have special powers. Periods of high positive emotion can be of benefit to the individual and can help them perform at work and deal with other people (Seal et al. 2008). However, they can also lead to family conflict or financial problems, especially when the person appears to behave erratically and irresponsibly without reason.

Problems associated with bipolar disorder often begin in late adolescence or early adulthood, and around 2 per cent of the adult population are likely to be diagnosed with bipolar disorder at any one time (Boyd et al. 2011). Rates are higher among high stress groups including the economically deprived, those living alone, and some minority ethnic groups (Grant et al. 2005). Men seem to have more manic episodes than women, while women may experience more depressive episodes (APA 2000). It is a debilitating condition, and around half of those with the disorder will make a full recovery within 2 years of its development.

Biological explanations

Low levels of serotonin are linked to both manic and depressed phases of bipolar disorder (Mahmood and Silverstone 2001). To account for this apparent paradox, the permissive theory of bipolar disorder (Findling et al. 2003) states that low serotonin levels permit the activity of norepinephrine to determine mood. Low serotonin combined with low norepinephrine results in depression; combined with high norepinephrine, it results in mania. Another neuronal mechanism that appears to be involved in bipolar disorder is associated with the electrical conduction of whole neurons. Disturbances in the activity of a second messenger known as protein kinase c (PKC), which controls the firing of neurons and levels of serotonin and norepinephrine released into the synaptic space, may be implicated in both depression and mania. Excessive PKC activation can disrupt prefrontal cortical regulation of thinking and behaviour (Szabo et al. 2009), resulting in the grandiose, illogical thinking associated with mania. Although family history studies indicate a clear contribution of genetic factors to risk for bipolar disorder (Cosgrove and Suppes 2013), the genes that contribute to this risk are far from clearly delineated.

Psychosocial explanations

Vulnerability to bipolar disorder may be established in childhood, with difficulties or trauma in childhood predicting more frequent fluctuations of mood as an adult (Dienes et al. 2006). It may also be triggered by a range of stressors in adulthood. These may be long-term in nature, such as high levels of critical communication within a family (Miklowitz et al., 2003), or short-term stressors we all encounter from time to time, the impact of which may be exaggerated in people diagnosed with bipolar disorder, as they may find coping with day-to-day problems more stressful than other people (Myin-Germeys et al., 2003). This impact may be moderated by the presence of good social support (Johnson et al. 2003).

Psychological explanations of the disorder suggest it may be related to individual 'thinking styles'. Jones (2005) identified that people diagnosed with bipolar disorder evidenced a 'fragile' cognitive style that made them vulnerable to the impact of stress. During periods of depression, they tend to have cognitions similar to those in depression to ruminate on. When in a high emotional state, they experience the opposite thinking style: they believe they are capable of great things, of achieving more, and attribute any positive aspects of their life to their own abilities. This drives them to engage in more activities, have less sleep, and so on – a process that may lead to exhaustion and low mood as they fail to achieve the (unrealistic) goals they have established. Some individuals appear to have either or both of these thinking styles between acute episodes. They may, for example, believe any elevation of mood is an excellent opportunity to achieve their goals while also fearing that their mood might escalate to the point they will be admitted to hospital. Both thinking styles can leave them vulnerable to changes in mood when faced with external stressors or difficulties.

A second cognitive model was proposed by Winters and Neale (1985), who hypothesized that the disorder results from a combination of low self-esteem and unrealistically high standards of success. Their model suggests that when at-risk individuals experience either depression or cognitions associated with low self-esteem, their response is to adopt the *manic disguise*: a manic coping style involving attempts to maintain social rewards from people around them, which are needed to bolster their self-esteem. This prevents the onset of a true depressive episode. However, if the social reinforcement they gain is inadequate or they are unable to maintain the behaviours for a protracted period, depression 'breaks through' and an episode of depression begins.

In an experimental test of this hypothesis, Lyon et al. (1999) found evidence of the unconscious processing that could underpin the process. They found that when asked to endorse a series of self-descriptors, people with bipolar disorder in the depressive phase were more likely to endorse negative items than a comparison group of non-depressed individuals. Those who were in the manic phase were more likely to endorse positive self-descriptors. However, and critically, when asked to recall the words they had seen, *both* groups recalled more negative descriptors than the control group. Lyon and colleagues took this pattern of results to indicate that while people with mania explicitly made positive attributions about themselves, underlying this was a set of negative beliefs about self.

Treatment

The treatment for bipolar disorder is primarily pharmacological in nature. Unfortunately, treatment with SSRIs or SNRIs frequently results in rapid mood swings rather than stable changes of mood, and is rarely used. A more frequently used approach involves lithium bicarbonate. This stabilizes mood swings, and significantly increases the time between manic or depressive episodes (Suppes et al. 1991). How it achieves these effects is not fully understood. It has only a modest impact on serotonin activity (Chenu and Bourin 2006), but may influence neuronal sodium and potassium activity or reduce inflammation in the brain, although how and where is not yet clear.

Lithium has to be taken consistently to minimize risk of relapse, even when the person taking it feels 'well'. Unfortunately, this may have a significant impact on their emotional life: users feel emotionally 'flat', with little variation in mood. Many prefer to risk a further episode rather than continue with this experience. Other side-effects include weight gain, compromised coordination, tremor, excessive thirst, and memory disturbances. A further disincentive is that the window between ineffective and toxic doses of lithium is narrow. Too high a dose results in lithium intoxication, the consequences of which include nausea, vomiting, tremors, kidney dysfunction and, potentially, death. This, and the regular blood check-ups necessary to ensure a safe but effective dose also deter adherence.

The biological model of bipolar disorder has been dominant for some years, and attempts to change the course of the disorder using CBT are only relatively recent. Nevertheless, Prasko et al. (2013) concluded that various psychological strategies can provide significant additional benefit to those already prescribed medication. These are usually initiated during a period of stable mood, and are intended to prevent relapse. They include:

- cognitive behavioural methods of symptom management, including establishing regular activity patterns and time management, and challenging dysfunctional thoughts;
- anti-relapse techniques involving strategies for managing medication, coping with stress, and seeking help at the onset of relapse.

In one evaluation of this approach, Lam et al. (2005) reported relapse rates over one year of 44 per cent in a psycho-education plus medication group and 75 per cent in a medication-only group. At 3-year follow-up, smaller but significant gains had been maintained in the combined therapy group. Mindfulness may also be of benefit, but only if participants regularly practise meditation (Perich et al. 2013).

An alternative approach involves working with families. The goals of these interventions are to reduce family stress and criticality, and establish a family context supportive of the individual and their adherence to medication. These, too, have proven reasonably successful. Miklowitz et al. (2003), for example, found an approach designed to improve communication, problem-solving, and coping strategies within the family resulted in a significant improvement in relapse rates compared with standard treatment. Relapse rates over one year were 71 per cent in the standard intervention, and 47 per cent in the family therapy intervention.

Seasonal affective disorder

The final mood disorder here is very different to those described above, and was only recognized as a distinct disorder in the mid-1980s (Rosenthal et al. 1984). Seasonal affective disorder (SAD) is evident as a regular temporal relationship between the onset of an episode of depression when the days shorten and there is less sunlight, and remission as the days get longer. It appears to be quite different from major depression, with symptoms including increased appetite, weight, and duration of sleep, as well as other depressive symptoms such as sadness, decreased activity, anxiety, work problems, decreased libido, and day-time tiredness (Magnusson and Partonen 2005). Its severity is seldom so severe that it results in absence from work.

Age of onset is typically between 20 and 30 years. It may prove a chronically recurring problem: up to 42 per cent of patients have recurring episodes for up to 11 years following initial onset, some of which may occur in winter and some of which may become non-seasonal (Thompson et al. 1995). Its prevalence varies across the world, with higher prevalence rates in countries farther away from the equator (Magnusson and Partonen 2005). Interestingly, symptoms become worse if people move from south to north and improve if they move in the opposite direction (Rosenthal et al. 1984). The opposite pattern occurs in the southern hemisphere.

Those whose symptoms are so severe that they receive a diagnosis of SAD may be a subset of a larger group of people who experience a range of negative symptoms over the winter. Terman (1988), for example, reported that 50 per cent of the general population reported lowered energy levels, 47 per cent reported increased weight, while 31 per cent reported decreased social activity in the winter months. Twenty-five per cent reported that these changes were sufficiently marked to signify a personal problem.

Biological explanations

Explanations of SAD are almost uniquely biological, and focus on chemicals affected by exposure to sunlight. The 'circadian hypothesis' (e.g. Lewy et al. 1998) sees the hormone melatonin as central to the condition. Release of melatonin from the pineal gland in the base of the brain controls activity in the midbrain and hypothalamus, especially sleeping and eating. Its release is triggered by darkness, and in free-living mammals increased melatonin levels as the days get shorter reduces their activity, slows them down, and prepares them for winter rest or hibernation. Early melatonin models thought that SAD resulted from a similar process in less free-living humans who cannot slow down or hibernate, causing sleepiness, increased appetite, and the range of symptoms described earlier. More recently, Lewy et al. (1998) suggested that rather than the level of melatonin determining mood, it is the times at which it is secreted that are important. They suggest that changes in the times of dawn and dusk in the transition from summer to winter affect the time that melatonin is released, shifting the circadian rhythm of sleep, and taking it out of alignment with other biological rhythms.

The dominant form of treatment for SAD involves exposing individuals to bright light in order to reduce melatonin release. Lewy and colleagues' hypothesis suggests that for this approach to be effective, exposure to light should be early in the morning, which helps maintain the summer wake–sleep cycle and delays the secretion of melatonin until later in the day. Their own work has supported this hypothesis, although contradictory data have been reported. Terman (1988), for example, found bright light treatment in the morning and evening to be equally effective, allowing the possibility that there may be two sub-groups of SAD: one with a general melatonin disorder, and one with a distorted circadian rhythm.

A second hypothesis suggests that at least some of the mechanisms underlying SAD may be those that underpin other forms of depression. Serotonin dysregulation is implicated in the aetiology of classic depression, and its level appears to vary across the seasons, with it falling over the winter. Increasing serotonin levels may improve mood, although less so than that achieved by therapies such as light therapy (Partonen and Lonnqvist 1998). The approach may also work best with people who have not responded to light therapy (Pjerk et al. 2004), suggesting that while serotonin levels may be implicated in SAD, they do not provide the entire picture. Risk for SAD appears to be influenced by genes, including those that both influence serotonergic transmission (Sher 2001) and circadian rhythms (Kripke et al. 2009).

Treatment

The recognized treatment of SAD is known as 'bright light' treatment, which lowers levels of melatonin. The individual is typically exposed to high levels of artificial light, varying from 2500 lux for a period of 2 hours to 10,000 lux for half an hour each day over a period of 1–3 weeks. For comparison, light indoors typically measures 100 lux or less. Outside lux levels may vary between 2000 lux or less on a rainy winter day and 10,000 lux in direct sunshine. Exposure is increasingly done in the morning to help shift individuals into an appropriate melatonin day–night rhythm.

These interventions can be effective. Sumaya et al. (2001) reported a trial in which participants were subject to three conditions in random order: (1) a therapeutic dose of 10,000 lux for 30 minutes daily for one week; (2) a non-therapeutic dose of 300 lux over the same time period (placebo); and (3) and a no-treatment period. After light treatment, 50 per cent of those receiving the active treatment no longer met the criteria for depression. Levels of depression did not change following either the placebo or no-treatment phases. Building on this success, more recent studies have tried to find the optimal wavelength of the light to improve mood. In one such study, Strong et al. (2009) compared the effects of short wavelength light (blue light) against dim red LED lights. The blue light proved the more effective of the two. Despite these successes, not all studies have shown light therapy to be effective. Wileman et al. (2001) randomly allocated people with SAD to either an active (4 weeks of 10,000 lux exposure) or what they considered to be a placebo (4 weeks of 300 lux) condition. Immediately after treatment, 30 per cent of those in the active treatment and 33 per cent of those in the placebo treatment were no longer depressed; 63 per cent of those in the active group and 57 per cent of the placebo group showed 'significant' improvements. The authors took this to indicate either a high level of placebo response among people with SAD, or that the threshold for light therapy was lower than initially thought.

Although light therapy remains the pre-eminent treatment for SAD, some people prefer to take medication. The use of SSRIs results in greater improvements than those achieved by placebo and achieves significant gains among people who have benefited little from light therapy (Pjerk et al. 2005). A further candidate treatment involves the use of noradrenaline reuptake inhibitors (NARI), which have been shown to have a similar benefit to SSRIs (Pjerk et al. 2009).

Chapter summary

1. Depression is a consequence of dysregulation of serotonin, norepinephrine, and dopamine.
2. According to Beck, psychological explanations indicate the role of long-term cognitive schemata and NATS.
3. Treatment with CBT appears to be more beneficial than with SSRIs.
4. Suicide is typically the result of a congruence of high impulsivity, poor problem-solving skills, and low mood.
5. Treatment involves remedying each of these elements.
6. Bipolar disorder appears to be a consequence of serotonin and norepinephrine dysregulation.
7. Psychological explanations suggest the disorder may be associated with particular styles of thinking, childhood difficulties, and adult stressors.
8. The 'manic defence may be thought of as an attempt to maintain mood at times of depression through apparently manic behaviour.
9. Treatment with lithium appears to be the best medical option, but the high incidence of side-effects reduces adherence. These may be improved through individual or family therapy.
10. Psychological therapy may also have a direct impact on risk for episodes of bipolar disorder as a consequence of reduced stress or changes in thinking.
11. Seasonal affective disorder is a distinctive disorder that is associated with lack of sunlight in winter months.
12. It may be associated with disruption of melatonin or serotonin mechanisms.
13. Treatment typically involves exposure to 'bright light' during the morning, although drugs that increase serotonin levels may also be of benefit.

Further reading

Fry, S. (2008) *Stephen Fry's the Secret Life of the Manic Depressive* (DVD). London: BBC.
Gilbert, P. (2014) *Depression: The evolution of powerlessness*. London: Routledge.
NICE (2009) *Depression in Adults: The treatment and management of depression in adults*. London: NICE.
Verduyn, C., Rogers, J. and Wood, A. (2009) *Depression: Cognitive behaviour therapy with children and young people*. Hove: Routledge.
Williams, M. (2014) *Cry of Pain: Understanding suicide and the suicidal mind*. London: Piatkus.

Chapter 10

Trauma

> Several chapters in this book identify trauma as a precursor to a range of mental health problems. This chapter focuses on two additional conditions in which trauma is seen as a central and perhaps the only antecedent. The first, post-traumatic stress disorder is widely recognized as a direct consequence of traumatic events. The second, dissociative identity disorder (perhaps better known as multiple personality disorder), is more controversial. Indeed, some have questioned its very existence.
>
> By the end of the chapter, you should have an understanding of:
>
> - The nature and treatment of post-traumatic stress disorder
> - The controversy surrounding dissociative identity disorder

Post-traumatic stress disorder

Post-traumatic stress disorder (PTSD) occurs as a consequence of being exposed to a range of potentially traumatizing events that result in fear and threat to personal safety or integrity. These may be external (e.g. being involved in or witnessing a fatal car crash) or internal (e.g. fear of being close to death as a consequence of a heart attack). They may even involve indirect exposure to trauma: many people, for example, were diagnosed with PTSD after watching television images of people jumping off the Twin Towers in the 9/11 terrorist attack. The traumas most commonly experienced by children involve physical or sexual abuse and domestic violence, which are more often responsible than non-interpersonal stressors such as accidents, disasters or illnesses (Van der Kolk 2005).

Immediately following such trauma, those affected may react with agitation and confusion, or they may withdraw, become unresponsive and depressed. They may express a range of emotions, including intense fear, helplessness, anger or horror. In the longer term, three characteristics dominate:

- *Intrusive memories*: Two distinct types of trauma memories have been identified. The first involves memories the individual may choose to access and can change as a result of thinking about the event. A second type of memory is known colloquially as flashbacks. These can be triggered by reminders of the event or occur at times when the mind is not actively engaged. They frequently occur at night, and take the form of nightmares. They cannot be stopped or interrupted and involve re-living the experience of the trauma. The person experiences the emotions and the physical sensations they experienced at the time. It feels like 'being there'.
- *Avoidance*: Because these memories can be so distressing, people with the disorder generally try to avoid events that may trigger any reminder of them.
- *Chronic arousal*: The individual is in a constant state of alertness or readiness to respond to danger. This may result in difficulty concentrating, impulsiveness, irritability or anger, and related physical symptoms. They may have extremely disturbed sleep.

These core symptoms may be accompanied in children by worrying about dying, physical symptoms such as stomach pains or headache, episodes of anger, and behavioural regression to that of a younger age.

Biological explanations

Like the anxiety disorders, risk for PTSD is heightened for those with high levels of behavioural inhibition (see Chapter 8). However, the brain areas involved in PTSD are thought to be those involved in processing emotions and memory, the amygdala and hippocampus in particular. The amygdala is associated with the formation of conditioned fear responses, the hippocampus for storing and retrieving relevant memories.

Two stress hormones are also implicated in establishing traumatic memories: norepinephrine and cortisol. Increases in these hormones generally enhance memory, although the levels that may occur at times of traumatic stress may actually be toxic to brain tissue and result in neuronal death, damaging the memory systems. The hippocampus, for example, may experience irreversible damage following severe trauma, leading to problems in working memory and an exaggerated conditioned fear response (Bonne et al. 2008). Norepinephrine release can also produce high states of arousal and fear, and intense visual flashbacks in some individuals. Brewin (2001) speculated that flashbacks may occur when information is transferred from the amygdala to the hippocampus.

The sympathetic nervous system (see Chapter 3), controlled by the hypothalamus and levels of norepinephrine, is also responsible for the high levels of physiological arousal associated with the condition. Genetic factors may influence dopamine and norepinephrine reactivity in response to trauma, and hence risk of PTSD (Voisey et al. 2009).

Psychosocial explanations

The conditioning model of PTSD (Foa and Kozak 1986) is an extension of Mowrer's two-factor theory of phobias (see Chapter 8). That is, PTSD is a classically conditioned emotional response. According to Foa and Kozak (1986), at the time of the traumatic event, the individual establishes a **neural network** of memories of the event, linking images, thoughts, and the fear experienced at the time of the event. Re-exposure to similar contexts or stimuli triggers the network and its conditioned fear response. As with anxiety, avoidance of reminders of the trauma prevents distress, but also prevents habituation of the fear response.

The first schema model of PTSD, developed by Horowitz (1986), had its roots in psychoanalytic theory. He suggested that PTSD occurs when the individual is involved in events that are so horrific they cannot be reconciled with an existing view (schema) of the world as inherently safe. The belief that one may die in an incident may shatter previous beliefs of invincibility, leaving the individual feeling unsafe and vulnerable. To avoid this ego-damaging discrepancy, defence mechanisms of numbing, avoidance or denial are evoked. However, these compete with a second innate drive, known as the 'completion tendency'. This requires the individual to integrate memories of trauma into existing world models or schemata: either to make sense of the memories according to currently held beliefs about the world or to change those beliefs. The completion tendency maintains trauma-related information in active memory in an attempt to process it. Defence mechanisms try to stop these memories entering consciousness. The symptoms the individual experiences are the result of fluctuating strengths of these competing processes. When the completion tendency breaks through the defence mechanisms, memories intrude into consciousness in the form of flashbacks, nightmares, and unwanted thoughts or emotional memories. When defence mechanisms are effective, the individual experiences periods of numbness or denial. Once trauma-related information is integrated into general belief systems, the symptoms cease.

Brewin (2001) considered these processes to occur in two distinct memory systems:

- *Verbally accessible memories (VAMs)*: these are memories of the incident that can be deliberately accessed. Memories tend to be fragmented, based on normal recall processes, and can be changed as the person processes information about the traumatic incident. They may, for example, become less traumatic as the individual thinks about and reframes the incident as being less threatening than they initially thought; they may become more traumatic if they later consider the event to have been more personally threatening.
- *Situationally accessible memories (SAMs)*: these memories, known as flashbacks, cannot be deliberately accessed, but come to consciousness in response to cues that remind the individual of the incident or when the VAM system is activated – which is why people with PTSD try to avoid thinking about the traumatic incident. They may also occur when the brain is not actively processing information, as the completion tendency leads to them being triggered in an attempt to process the memories into the general memory system. They are frightening, the person experiences them as if they are 'in the event', and they cannot be deliberately changed.

According to Brewin, resolution of PTSD requires both sets of memories to enter the normal memory system. Resolution of VAMs involves deliberate recall and reframing of information. This leads to an integration of the VAMs with pre-existing beliefs and models of the world, and restores a sense of safety and control over both self and the world. The SAMs gradually change over time and become less emotion-laden and frightening as a consequence of integration of new, non-threatening information or, more frequently, through the creation of new SAMs. Brewin identified the hippocampus as the neural centre involved in processing VAMs and the amygdala as being involved in processing the more emotionally laden SAMs.

Repeated trauma in children

Children may experience trauma as a consequence of involvement in a range of single traumatic situations. However, they may also experience longer-term and repeated trauma such as sexual or physical abuse. This may result in trauma-related symptoms of a different nature. According to van der Kolk (2005), young children lack the capacity to effectively regulate their own emotions, particularly at times of high stress, and rely on their parents to facilitate this outcome. If a parent is unable to do this, or is the cause of distress, the child is unable to regulate their internal emotional state and experiences strong negative emotions, even terror. If this experience is repeated, the child learns to dissociate, experiences a complex but dislocated series of cognitions and emotions, and is unable to fully comprehend what is happening or develop plans to cope with it. Repeated trauma by a parent leads to a child's chronic inability to regulate their emotions, and excessive anxiety, anger, and helplessness beyond the time of trauma. These feelings may become so severe they trigger a dissociative state even at times the trauma is not occurring. This combination of outcomes may be responsible for a range of debilitating problems (Cook et al. 2003), including:

- *Problems of attachment*: distrust and suspiciousness, interpersonal difficulties, uncertainty about the reliability and predictability of others.
- *Physiological symptoms*: hypersensitivity to physical touch, somatization, increased medical problems including pelvic pain and **pseudoseizures**.
- *Difficulties in affect regulation*: difficulty in controlling emotions, describing feelings, communicating wishes and desires.
- *Dissociation*: amnesia, **depersonalization**, and **derealization**.
- *Impaired behavioural control*: poor control of impulses, self-destructive behaviour, aggression against others, sleep disturbance, eating disorders, oppositional behaviour or excessive compliance.
- *Cognitive difficulties*: difficulties regulating attention, problems processing novel information or completing tasks, learning difficulties, problems with language development.
- *Disturbance in self-concept*: lack of continuous and predictable sense of self, disturbances of body image.

Treatment

The most frequently used approach to treating post-traumatic stress involves a process known as trauma-focused exposure CBT. Its underpinning theoretical rationale is that the individual will ultimately benefit from exposure to memories of the event and their associated emotions. Such exposure leads to reconciliation between memories and the meaning of the traumatic event and pre-existing world schemata, and their integration into general memory systems.

Reactivation of memories by this procedure involves describing the experience in detail, focusing on what happened, the thoughts and emotions experienced at the time, and any memories that the incident triggered. This may be augmented by participants listening to their own recorded stories of the trauma or even (especially children) drawing trauma-related pictures. These may be augmented by a variety of cognitive behavioural techniques, including relaxation training and cognitive restructuring. Relaxation may help the individual control their arousal at the time of recalling the event or at other times in the day when they are feeling tense or on edge. Cognitive restructuring may help them address any distorted cognitions they had in response to the event and make those thoughts less threatening ('I'm going to die!... It felt like I was going to die, but actually that was more my panic than reality').

Even with the use of these coping strategies, this process can lead to exacerbation of distress particularly at the beginning of therapy, as upsetting images, previously avoided where possible, are deliberately recalled. To minimize this distress and to prevent drop-out from therapy, Leskin et al. (1998) recommended a graded exposure process in which the individual initially talks about particular elements of the traumatic event at a level of detail they choose over several occasions until they no longer respond with a stress response. Any new, and potentially more distressing, memories are avoided at this time, and become the focus of the next levels of intervention.

This approach has proven effective in the treatment of children with both one-off and repeated traumas. Nixon et al. (2012), for example, achieved a 65 per cent remission rate following trauma-focused CBT after a one-off trauma experienced by a group of 7- to 17-year-olds. Deblinger et al. (2006) found trauma-focused CBT was more effective than child-centred therapy following sexual abuse in children aged 8–14 years. Those in the trauma-focused CBT group reported fewer symptoms of PTSD and less shame at both 6 and 12 months following the end of treatment. In a similarly aged group of young people who had experienced familial violence, Cohen et al. (2011) found trauma-focused CBT to be more effective than usual care on a range of PTSD symptoms. Finally, and of particular note, Scheeringa et al. (2011) achieved similar benefits in a group of children aged 3–6 years.

Working with: post-traumatic stress syndrome

Twelve-year-old Andrew was referred to the child mental health services as a result of his disclosure to school officers that a male relative had sexually abused him. As a consequence, he had stopped attending school, and experienced a range of symptoms, including flashbacks to the events, disturbed sleep and nightmares, poor concentration, quickly aroused anger and irritability, and strong mood swings including anger, depression, and anxiety. He has also experienced panic attacks when experiencing flashbacks to events. He was angry with the perpetrator, himself for allowing the events to happen, and his family for (unknowingly) encouraging the relationship. He felt a strong sense of shame about events, and spent much time ruminating about the abuse and blaming himself for allowing it to occur.

Although the 'standard' approach to treating Andrew would involve trauma-focused CBT, other adjunctive approaches might be of benefit to address the wide range of problems he was experiencing. Accordingly, a package of interventions was developed, including:

- *Education about abuse and grooming*: to put his role in the events into context, to minimize any self-blame or shame, and normalize his reaction to events.
- *Trauma-focused exposure*: involving a gradual exposure to talking and thinking about increasingly difficult memories of events.
- *Cognitive challenge*: identification, for example, of self- or family-blame thoughts, and challenging them through education and Socratic dialogue: 'I must have led him on in some way for him to try and abuse me...He was a clever and manipulative individual who chose me because I was easy to access through the family.'
- *Relaxation skills*: to help reduce hyper-arousal both during the day and at night.
- *Sleep hygiene strategies*: aimed at reducing arousal prior to going to bed, including relaxation, not using Xbox in the hour before going to bed, avoiding energy drinks, and so on.
- *Imagining a more positive life*: beginning to consider a life after the feelings of shame and trauma; planning getting back to a positive life.
- *Re-establishing family relationships and trust*: through engagement with his parents in one session to obtain their perspective on events and to allow him to express his feelings about the family's response to them.
- *Planned activities during the day*: to minimize time spent ruminating on distressing issues.

The basic approach of trauma-focused therapy was key to the intervention. However, additional elements based on a formulation of the problems, and addressing a range of problems, made a much stronger intervention.

In adults, trauma-focused therapy has also been found to be superior to no treatment or alternative active interventions, including supportive counselling and relaxation therapy without exposure (Bisson et al. 2007). Marks et al. (1996), for example, reported a comparison of relaxation, exposure alone, cognitive restructuring alone, and exposure plus cognitive restructuring. By the end of the intervention phase, all the other treatments proved superior to relaxation, with no differences in effectiveness between them. At 3- and 6-month follow-up, the exposure programme proved superior. It would appear that self-instruction and other cognitive techniques may help participants cope with the anxiety and other emotions evoked in the early stages of exposure programmes, while exposure to traumatic memories is critical to long-term benefit. The optimal treatment seems to involve a combination of self-instruction training or other cognitive strategies in the early stages of therapy combined with gradual exposure to traumatic memories.

The most recent treatment of PTSD, known as eye movement desensitization and reprocessing (EMDR), was discovered by chance by Shapiro (1995). She noticed that while walking in the woods her disturbing thoughts began to disappear, and when recalled were less upsetting than previously. She associated this change with her eyes spontaneously moving rapidly backwards and forwards in an upward diagonal. Since then, the procedure has been developed into a standardized intervention and subject to a number of clinical trials in the treatment of PTSD.

Treatment typically involves recall of target memories by the client as visual images along with a negative cognition that goes with the image, framed in the present tense ('I am terrified'). The client next rates the strength of emotion evoked by this process. They are then asked to track the therapist's finger as it is moved increasingly quickly back and forth across their line of vision. After 24 such movements, the client is instructed to 'Blank it out' or 'Let it go', and asked to rate their level of emotion. This procedure is repeated until the client experiences minimal distress to the presence of the image and negative cognition. If no changes occur, the direction of eye movements is changed.

Eye movement desensitization and reprocessing incorporates exposure to elements of the trauma stimulus. An important question is therefore whether the addition of the eye movements enhances the effect of exposure. This does not seem to be the case. Bisson and Andrew (2009) used meta-analysis to examine the effectiveness of EMDR in the treatment of PTSD compared with no treatment, non-specific treatment, and the exposure methods described above. While their analyses indicated a benefit for EMDR compared with no treatment or non-specific treatments, its benefits were similar to those resulting from exposure approaches, although in its favour these results were achieved more quickly than with the other therapies.

Finally, a variety of drug types have been used in the treatment of PTSD to some effect, including antidepressant MAOIs, SSRIs, and tricyclics (see Chapter 3). Ipser et al. (2006), for example, conducted a meta-analysis on studies of antidepressants in the treatment of PTSD, finding that SSRIs achieved significantly greater improvements than placebo on measures of functioning and the core PTSD symptoms of intrusion and avoidance.

Case formulation

Mr F was a police officer in a small town in the west of England. At six feet four inches, he was a big strong man, fond of playing rugby for a local team, and drinking with his mates. He was happily married with three young children.

Long-term antecedents
As is often the case with PTSD, there were very few long-term antecedents for Mr F's development of PTSD. He had no history of mental health problems, and had no work- or home-related problems.

Short-term antecedents
The trigger to Mr F's PTSD was a simple event. He was attempting to deal with a group of aggressive youths in an area he routinely patrolled when he slipped and fell. At the time he was on his own, and the youths took this opportunity to beat and kick him around the body and head. The force of the beating was such that he was briefly knocked unconscious. The last thought he had before losing consciousness was that he was going to die. He was found by his patrol colleague and fellow officers and was taken to hospital before being sent home to recover from his injuries.

Over the next few months he experienced a significant number of flashbacks, feeling the force of the blows to him and experiencing the fear of dying. Many occurred at night, while in bed. Every flashback was terrifying, and in the hour following them he had to get out of bed and try to watch television or read a book to help him calm down. He regularly had two or more flashbacks per night. As a consequence, he became increasingly exhausted. In addition, he spent much of the day mulling over the causes and consequence of the attack: why the youths were so aggressive, what he could have done differently, what might have happened if his colleagues had not arrived when they did, and so on. He would spend many hours ('A day may disappear') looking out of a house window dwelling on the attack.

As a result of these various processes, his mood became increasingly depressed. He was able to engage with his wife and children for brief periods in the day – helping prepare breakfast, for example – but found these periods increasingly difficult to manage and he became more and more isolated even within the family home. He also isolated himself from the home, spending hours away in peaceful places dwelling on the events and their consequences. He was unable to go into the area where the attack occurred or where he was likely to encounter similar youths because he was unsure whether he would be able to cope at the sight of them, expecting to be extremely frightened but also maybe expressing his anger. In a relatively small town, this severely limited where he was able to go.

Formulation
Mr F had a significant post-traumatic response. The critical factor in its development was his belief that he was going to die as a result of his beating. He continued to hold this belief, believing that it was only the intervention of his colleagues that prevented him from dying. This continued catastrophic belief helped maintain his anxieties. He experienced the three key symptoms of PTSD: flashbacks, when his mind was unoccupied, pre-occupation and rumination on the originating incident, and heightened arousal. His depression stemmed from the belief that some of the youths wanted him dead and that the actions of his beat colleague, who had left him alone to deal with another incident, had left him vulnerable. His rumination constantly focused on his negative beliefs about the incident and how close to death he had been, and his anger towards those involved. Accordingly, although he chronically ruminated about the incident, he failed to normalize or reappraise it as something less threatening, both of which may have reduced the frequency and severity of his flashbacks. The time spent dwelling on these negative thoughts combined with exhaustion due to lack of sleep and his dislocation from his family and friends led to depression, and a vicious cycle of rumination, flashbacks, avoidance of positive aspects of life, low mood, rumination… and so on.

Dissociative identity disorder

Traumatic events often evoke a process known as dissociation: a state of psychological detachment or disengagement from the emotional consequences of the experience. This can be experienced in a number of ways, including feeling detached from events, that time is standing still, or as a total or partial loss of memory of the event or events. This response may form a one-off, immediate, and unconscious response to a highly traumatic situation. It can also be learned and deliberately used to help cope with repeated traumas, including those associated with child sexual abuse. Some theorists consider that this process can result in a condition known as dissociative identify disorder (DID).

The nature, causes, and even existence of DID are controversial. Previously known as multiple personality disorder, its defining feature is that the individual behaves as if they possess two or more distinct and separate personalities, known as 'alters'. The number of alters reported can be ten or more. Each has their own enduring pattern of perceiving, relating to, and thinking about the environment and self. They are relatively independent of each other, and often unaware of ongoing information or events relevant to other alters. Most protect the host personality from memories of the trauma. They do not 'see' themselves in the physical body they are in: children see themselves as four feet tall, girls see themselves as girls, and so on. Some may speak different languages.

There are many types of alters, which have been named by people familiar with the disorder:

- *Host*: the main personality presented to the outside world.
- *Original birth child*: sometimes referred to as the core personality, this alter may be awake and functioning, or 'asleep'.
- *Child alters*: these alters experienced much of the abuse, and have many trauma-related memories and associated distress; their behaviour is childlike.
- *Gatekeepers*: some systems have a gatekeeper, who directs and has control of the body and other alters; they may control the length of time a particular alter is in the body, but are rarely evident to others.
- *Protectors*: these protect the system from outside threats. They usually talk hard, or fight, or do whatever is necessary to keep the system safe. They often use anger as a defence. They are especially protective of the child alters.

People with DID are said to have an 'ecosystem' of alters who compete with each other to gain control over the output channels. Switches between alters controlling the body may occur following stress or upset caused by factors as trivial as an unexpected touch or as overpowering as seeing an abuser. The alter that most successfully maintains an emotional equilibrium is likely to be most evident.

Psychosocial explanations

The nature – and, indeed, existence – of DID has been hotly debated. Two dominant, and completely antagonistic, theories are that the condition is either the result of childhood trauma (e.g. Gleaves 1996) or a socially constructed system created and shaped by the affected individual and therapist in the course of therapy (e.g. Spanos 1994).

According to Gleaves (1996), repeated trauma leads the child to use dissociation, a self-induced hypnotic state, to defend against the trauma, and to locate the memories of abuse within their subconscious. During episodes of abuse they deliberately dissociate, separating themselves from the emotional consequences of these acts. Memories of the event are therefore prevented from entering consciousness, but form isolated unconscious memoires, linked to these dissociative states. Over time, the dissociated parts of the individual, with their atomized memories, 'split' into alter personalities. These emerge in adulthood to help the individual cope with stressful situations or express negative emotions and resentments that are unacceptable to the primary personality.

The opposing view is that DID comprises a set of beliefs and behaviours constructed by the individual in response to personal stress, therapist pressure, and societal acceptance of the concept of 'multiple personality'. According to this argument, some therapists both encourage clients to construe themselves in this way and provide legitimation of the different identities such individuals enact. These people learn to portray themselves as possessing multiple selves and to organize and elaborate their personal history to make it consistent with their understanding of what it means to be a 'multiple'. Such individuals are not necessarily 'faking' their multiplicity. Rather, they come to adopt a view of themselves that is congruent with the view conveyed to them by their therapist.

Arguments supporting the reality of DID have received robust counter-arguments by its critics. Evidence that DID is associated with the experience of childhood trauma, for example, has been countered by findings that when traumatized children have been followed prospectively, none have been found to develop DID (Kihlstrom 2005). In addition, the timing of memories of abuse is often inconsistent with the neurological development required to maintain such memories. Ross et al. (1991), for example, reported that over a quarter of their sample of people diagnosed with DID reported having memories of abuse before the age of three, and 10 per cent reported such memories before the age of one. These ages are both much younger than is typical in cases of sexual abuse and before the development of neural substrates that would permit such long-term recall.

Many people with DID do not remember being abused until this is discovered in the course of therapy, often involving hypnosis. Such 'recovered memories' should be treated with caution. Confidentiality issues mean that evidence of therapist persuasion is hard to acquire. However, DID-like symptoms have been generated through suggestion in experimental settings. Spanos et al. (1985), for example, was able to 'induce' a range of DID-like symptoms, which were maintained over two sessions and on a range of psychological tests, through hypnotic suggestion in naïve participants. Supporters of DID have argued that while such studies are interesting, their participants did not experience or report key features of DID, including episodes of time loss, depersonalization or derealization. In addition, Reinders et al. (2012) found significant differences in neural activation patterns between people diagnosed with DID and both high and low fantasy-prone individuals instructed to enact two DID identity states. They concluded that although high fantasy individuals may be able to mimic the overt behaviours associated with DID, this is not reflected in their neurological or physiological responses.

Other experimental evidence has examined memory systems in DID. A central phenomenon of DID is that memories are 'locked' within each alter to prevent them becoming conscious and distressing other alters or the host. This allows experimental exploration of this phenomenon. In a study by Elzinga et al. (2003), for example, people with a diagnosis of DID were presented with a series of words, half of which had a threatening or sexual connotation. Following a series of explicit and implicit memory tests given to both the alter initially shown the words and one other alter, they found that the alter shown the words achieved a higher recall than the second alter. However, the second alter still recalled a significant number of words. Levels of threat-related words recalled, for example, were 36 per cent in the same state and 21 per cent in the second state. In addition, both alters performed equally well on measures of implicit memory. Similar findings in other studies suggest memory issues reported by people with DID may not reflect actual memory retrieval inability, but rather a 'meta-memory disorder': inaccurate beliefs about memory functioning.

Unfortunately, research investigating DID may be considered at something of an impasse. Boysen and VanBergen (2013) summed up the situation in their paper in which they noted that an average of only nine papers per year had explored the aetiology of DID between 2000 and 2010, and that many of the central criticisms of the disorder remain unaddressed. Most cases of DID are reported by a relatively small number of clinicians (suggesting a bias in diagnosis by 'believers' in the condition), and most people simulating DID in the laboratory are indistinguishable from those diagnosed with DID. Boysen and VanBergen concluded that DID research lacks the productivity and focus needed to resolve ongoing controversies surrounding the disorder – a somewhat disappointing outcome for a rather dramatic condition.

Treatment

Not surprisingly, protagonists for and against the concept of DID have differing ideas about its treatment. For those therapists who believe in the concept, a key goal is to integrate the alters into a coherent whole, known as fusion. Incidentally, this goal may not actually be shared by many people or alters, who reject integration, which they see as a form of death (Spiegel 1999). Most studies to date have involved single-case or multiple-case reports: a relatively limited form of evidence. These have shown a range of interventions to be of some benefit, including analytical therapy, cognitive analytic therapy, guided imagery, and group therapy (e.g. Kellett 2005). However, the lack of therapeutic detail in most reports, as well as the lack of control condition and potential bias in reporting successes (most clinicians do not like to advertise their therapeutic failures), means it is unclear what the best treatment for DID is.

Current affairs

To some people, the concept of DID may appear fantastical and unbelievable. To others, it appears a reasonable concept that, however bizarre, has some grounding in reality. Mainstream neurocognitive models of trauma memories have identified how dissociation can result in isolated memories separate from the main memory stores. We also know from work with children that children can chose to dissociate during repeated trauma in order to reduce the distress they experience at such times. Thus, some of the concepts of DID do have a plausible basis. But does it exist? Or, perhaps more pertinently, is it a 'real' or 'constructed' phenomenon?

Chapter summary

1. PTSD has three central symptoms: (1) intrusive memories; (2) attempts at avoidance of these memories; and (3) high levels of arousal.
2. The neurological substrates of PTSD are the amygdala and hippocampus that together mediate fear and memory, and link the two together. High arousal is mediated by the sympathetic nervous system.
3. The conditioning model of PTSD provides a partial explanation of the phenomenon, but cognitive models such as that of Brewin provide a more in-depth understanding.
4. Exposure methods may prove the best intervention for PTSD, particularly when combined with strategies to help clients cope with any emotional distress triggered by the therapeutic process.
5. Eye movement desensitization and reprocessing appears to be of benefit, but no more so than exposure methods.
6. Dissociative identity disorder may be a response to repeated childhood sexual trauma involving severe dissociation at the time of the trauma, resulting in the development of 'alters' or alternative personalities.
7. The socio-cognitive model suggests this is a response to therapist and social pressure to behave in a way that suggests multiple personalities.
8. Debate about which of these models is best has focused on differing explanations of the prevalence of the disorder, whether therapists can 'teach multiplicity', social and therapist pressures to present with DID, and the relationship between childhood abuse and DID.
9. While some cases of DID may be created by the process of therapy, others may represent a 'real' clinical condition. Each case should be considered on its own merits.

Further reading

Brewin, C.R. and Holmes, E.A. (2003) Psychological theories of posttraumatic stress disorder, *Clinical Psychology Review*, 23: 339–76.
Feather, J.S. and Ronnan, K. (2010) *Cognitive Behavioural Therapy for Child Trauma and Abuse*. London: Jessica Kingsley.
Gillig, P.M. (2009) Dissociative identity disorder: a controversial diagnosis, *Psychiatry*, 6: 24–9.
Joseph, S., Williams, R. and Yule, W. (1995) Psychosocial perspectives on posttraumatic stress, *Clinical Psychology Review*, 15: 515–44.
Kihlstrom, J.F. (2005) Dissociative disorders, *Annual Review of Clinical Psychology*, 1: 227–53.

Chapter 11

Psychosis

> The focus of this chapter is on a condition frequently referred to as schizophrenia, although as you will see, this name is not without its problems – hence the title of the chapter being psychosis (the experience of hallucinations and/or delusions). The chapter considers the issue on its own, with no links to other conditions. This is partly a function of the organization of the book: it has to go somewhere, and all the other chapters are full! However, it also reflects the important impact of the condition on the lives of those experiencing it.
>
> By the end of this chapter, you should have an understanding of:
>
> - The causes and treatment of schizophrenia or psychosis
> - Challenges to the diagnosis of schizophrenia
> - The treatment of schizophrenia
> - The treatment of delusions and hallucinations

Introduction

Originally identified by Kraepelin in 1883, and termed dementia praecox, the condition was considered to be a progressive and deteriorating condition, with no chance of recovery. Redefined some 25 years later by Blueler as 'schizophrenia' (literally, split mind), it was then considered to involve ambivalence, disturbance of association and mood, and a preference for fantasy over reality. Today, schizophrenia is characterized by disorders of perception and thinking, the most obvious of which are:

- *Delusions*: strong and unshakeable beliefs including: (1) *control* over other people or being controlled by others; (2) *grandeur*, being somehow special or famous; and (3) *reference*, believing the behaviour of others relates directly to oneself.

Table 11.1 Some of the most frequent symptoms of acute schizophrenia

Symptom	Percentage of cases
Lack of insight	97
Auditory hallucinations	74
Ideas of reference	70
Flattened affect	66
Suspiciousness	66
Delusions of persecution	64
Thought alienation	52

- *Hallucinations*: anomalous perceptual experiences, which may affect all senses, but are most often auditory. They may appear in the voice of the individual or others, and can be malicious, commanding or benevolent.

Conversations with people diagnosed with schizophrenia, at the height of their disturbance, may seem bizarre and incoherent. They may invent new words (neologisms), or make bizarre associations between words, known as 'word salads'. Their emotion is often flattened, although they may experience apparently inappropriate mood states such as elation or depression as a consequence of their thoughts or hallucinations. Table 11.1 lists some of the more frequent symptoms reported by people diagnosed with the disorder.

About 1 per cent of the adult population are likely to have a diagnosis of schizophrenia at any one time (APA 2000). The disorder is episodic, with periods of recovery between periods of acute symptoms. The age of first episode is typically between 20 and 35 years, and although most episodes will remit, the condition has a poor prognosis and risk of relapse is high. Around half those who have one episode of schizophrenia will experience significant levels of recovery for 5 years or more. However, only 12 per cent are likely to remain completely symptom-free (Robinson et al. 2004), and most will experience further psychotic episodes and a gradual decline in cognitive function, partly as a consequence of the disorder, partly because of the medical treatment they may receive. Early treatment and good social support maximize the chance for sustained recovery.

Challenging the diagnosis

For a diagnosis of schizophrenia to be made, DSM-5 requires a range of symptoms of which at least one symptom is the experience of delusions, hallucinations or disorganized speech. These may be added to by grossly disorganized or **catatonic behaviour**, and negative symptoms involving an absence of activation, evident through apathy, lack of motivation or poverty of speech.

A key problem with the DSM diagnostic criteria for schizophrenia is that the same diagnosis can be given to individuals who present with very different experiences and problems. This contradicts the notion of a disorder that has one underlying mechanism: if this were the case, all people should present with the same cluster of symptoms. A related point is that different people with schizophrenia respond to different medications, including neuroleptics, lithium, and benzodiazepines (see Chapter 5). Others fail to respond to any of these medications. As Bentall (1993: 227) noted: 'We are inevitably drawn to an important conclusion: "schizophrenia" appears to be a disease which has no particular symptoms, no particular course, and responds to no particular treatment.' On these grounds, he suggested that the diagnosis has no validity and that the concept of schizophrenia should be abandoned. Rather than attempting to explain multiple syndromes, future efforts should focus on explanations of particular behaviours or experiences: each of the various symptoms of 'schizophrenia' should be considered as a disorder in its own right, with differing underlying causes and treatments.

A further issue of relevance here is that the experiences of people diagnosed with schizophrenia are not exclusive to them. Many people who do not come to the attention of the psychiatric services also hear voices. What distinguishes between them and people who seek help for their 'problem' appears to be differences in their responses to the voices and their ability to cope with them. Positive coping strategies include setting limits to the time spent listening to voices, talking back to them, and listening selectively to more positive voices (Romme and Escher 2000).

This diversity of opinion presents a challenge when writing about the disorder. Biological explanations tend to focus on the broad diagnosis of schizophrenia, while psychological explanations focus on more discrete explanations of hallucinations and delusions. Similarly, while most intervention studies have been conducted under the rubric of schizophrenia, a number have now specifically targeted the influence and emotional impact of delusional thinking. Reflecting these historical processes, some parts of this chapter will use the term schizophrenia. Elsewhere, the terms psychosis, hallucinations or delusions are preferred and used to describe the relevant phenomena.

Psychosocial explanations

The biological substrates and developmental processes, including childhood trauma, associated with schizophrenia are outlined in Chapter 1, and will not be reiterated here. This section focuses on psychosocial factors that influence risk for the disorder in adulthood. As with many mental health problems, risk is associated with psychosocial stress. It is most prevalent among those of low socio-economic status About 25 per cent of episodes are precipitated by acute life stress (L. Phillips et al. 2007), although lesser stresses known as 'daily hassles' may also trigger psychotic relapse in vulnerable individuals (Norman and Malla 1994).

Perhaps the strongest risk factor for *recurrent* psychotic episodes involves critical family dynamics. Negative expressed emotion (NEE) is characterized by high levels of criticism and negativity within the family towards an affected individual. First identified by Vaughn and Leff (1976), this dynamic has now been found to significantly increase risk of relapse across many countries and cultures (Miklowitz 2004). Importantly, this effect is only found in those who spend a significant time in the home environment: being out of the house and engaged in other contexts is protective against high NEE. The theory seems to place the 'blame' for recurrence on the family, but this may be unfair, as high levels of NEE tend to be a response to odd behaviours rather than a cause. High NEE is likely to occur if the family considers these behaviours to be wilful or difficult (Yang et al. 2004). It has also been associated with a range of other problems including borderline personality and bipolar disorders.

Explaining hallucinations and delusions

More symptom-specific psychological models of psychosis have focused on attentional processes and the theory of mind. The central premise of attentional models is that psychosis reflects an inability to identify and filter out irrelevant environmental stimuli. As a result, affected individuals are overwhelmed by sensory experiences. Hemsley (1996), for example, suggested that people who experience hallucinations and delusions have two significant information-processing deficits:

- an impairment in the rapid and automatic assessment of sensory input;
- a breakdown in the relationship between stored memories and current sensory input.

Hemsley hypothesized that we select stimuli to which we pay attention as a result of previous experiences. We store what he referred to as 'regularities': memories of consistent relations between particular contexts and the events that may occur in them. These allow us to respond to familiar (or partially familiar) contexts appropriately, and to determine what is, and is not, important to attend to. According to Hemsley, these automatic processes are compromised in psychosis, and the individual is unable to focus their attention appropriately. They attend to everything within their environment, and become overwhelmed by sensory information. Two key problems arise from this sensory barrage:

- *Hallucinations* result from a failure to filter out redundant information and giving all stimuli equal weight. Critically, the individual's thoughts cannot be distinguished from external stimuli, and are perceived as an external voice.
- *Delusions* occur when trying to impose meaning on this barrage of confusing internal and external stimuli.

Hughdahl et al. (2013) suggested a further processing problem may occur. Once an individual begins to experience 'voices', they frequently have difficulty disengaging from them. They become a key focus of attention. As a consequence, the individual may try to reduce their perceptual and cognitive overload through social withdrawal or impoverished speech.

Experimental studies support these models. People who experience hallucinations or delusions have more difficulty locating the spatial location of sounds and are less able to identify the meaning of words when spoken against a background of white noise: despite being confident they can do so. They are particularly poor at distinguishing words with an affective meaning, leaving them susceptible to misinterpret emotionally laden words in ordinary life (Rossell and Boundy 2005). In addition, they may pay more attention to what they consider malevolent voices, and less to more benign ones (Kråkvik et al. 2013). This makes sense, as these would apparently carry high levels of threat – but in this context, the threat is not real, and the focus of attention inappropriate.

Theory of mind explanations of psychosis (e.g. Frith and Corcoran 1996) are based on the premise that in order to engage successfully in social situations, we need to understand the thoughts and feelings of the people with whom we are interacting. To achieve this, we need to understand our own thinking and feeling. We need a theory of mind. According to Frith, the central deficit of psychosis is a failure to develop this understanding. As a consequence, individuals with this disorder have fundamental difficulties in social interactions and understanding their our own cognitive processes. They may have difficulties in understanding their intentions, and feel not in control of their own decisions and actions. They may also believe that thoughts are being inserted into their mind or they are inserting their thoughts into the minds of others. Finally, their lack of understanding of others' motives and actions may lead to feelings of paranoia. As a consequence of this confusion, they may retreat into social isolation.

A number of experimental studies have explored this issue. One approach has involved the use of jokes that involve deception and require an intact theory of mind to understand them. Marjoram et al. (2005), for example, presented people diagnosed with schizophrenia and controls with a series of single-image cartoons, half of which required an understanding of the theory of mind to 'get' the joke as it involved attributing a mental state (e.g. ignorance, deception) to one of its characters. The other jokes were of a more slapstick nature, and did not require an intact theory of mind. People diagnosed with schizophrenia 'got' less of both kinds of jokes, but were particularly poor at understanding the theory of mind jokes.

A more recent study explored the neurological processes underpinning this finding. Brüne et al. (2011) recorded fMRI scans of people with a diagnosis of schizophrenia, people considered at risk for schizophrenia, and 'healthy controls' while they were engaging in a task similar to that of Marjoram et al. They examined activation of the so-called 'theory of mind network', which comprises the medial prefrontal cortex, the anterior part of the cingulate cortex, the posterior cingulate/precuneus region, the middle temporal lobes, superior temporal sulcus, and the temporo-parietal junction. Within this neural network the prefrontal cortex and the cingulate cortex are involved in distinguishing self from other, in error monitoring and prediction, and in 'decoupling' hypothetical states from reality (Frith and Frith 2003). Brüne et al. reported levels of activation of this network were lower in people diagnosed with schizophrenia than in 'healthy controls'. By contrast, the at-risk group evidenced greater activation of the network, perhaps as a form of compensatory action as they attempted to understand the motives of the cartoon characters.

While the theory of mind approach to understanding cognitive deficits in psychosis is generally supported by relevant research (Bora and Pantellis 2013), not all data are supportive. In an interview study by McCabe et al. (2004), for example, one participant diagnosed with schizophrenia stated that he did not tell people he had intrusive thoughts, as he believed others would think him odd, and he felt ashamed – understandings that required an intact theory of mind. Furthermore, it remains unclear how any impairment fluctuates between acute and stable periods within the disorder or how it affects individuals' use of language or social behaviour.

Explaining persecutory delusions

Delusions are at the extreme end of a continuum of thought that runs from 'ordinary thoughts' to those that are bizarre and impossible. They may be rational attempts to make sense of anomalous circumstances or experiences (Bentall and Fernyhough 2008). Accordingly, while the content of such thoughts may be out of the ordinary, the psychological processes underpinning them are not.

In a model elaborating these process, Freeman et al. (2002) argued that persecutory delusions are the outcome of several processes: (1) environmental events, (2) 'psychotic processes', (3) pre-existing beliefs, and (4) personality and emotion. According to their model, the inception of delusions begins with a 'precipitator' (stress, drug misuse, etc.). This results in increased arousal and poor sleep. These combine in vulnerable individuals to trigger anomalous experiences such as hearing voices, subtle perceptual anomalies, and experiencing actions as unintended. In response, the individual searches for meaning: why did they happen, why are they taking the form they do? If the individual has pre-existing negative views about themselves, others, and the world, they are likely to develop strong persecutory delusions. These may be augmented if the individual is typically anxious and already primed to anticipate threat. The risk for such inappropriate conclusions is also high as a result of a general tendency to 'jump to conclusions' typical of these individuals. Alternative explanations for their experiences are neither searched for nor considered. These biases are maintained by a number of processes, not unlike those involved in the maintenance of other emotional states, including the avoidance of disconfirmatory evidence through social withdrawal and/or continued drug use (Woodard et al. 2007).

An alternative approach to understanding persecutory beliefs, based on a more humanistic model, was developed by Bentall (e.g. Bentall et al. 2001). He suggested that many people with schizophrenia have a poor self-image and experience significant discrepancies between how they would like to be and how they consider themselves to actually be. This may be maintained by attributional biases (good things that happen to me are accidental and undeserved; bad things are my own fault) and may result in low mood or depression. Persecutory delusional beliefs may act as a psychological defence against this process. By attributing their own negative beliefs to others ('They may not think well of me, but I think I am OK'), the individual may be able to reduce their feelings of inadequacy. According to Bentall, such negative attributional styles may be learned from other family members, and parental criticism may precipitate relapse by triggering actual–ideal self-discrepancies. They may be the result of long-term victimization and poor attachment in childhood.

Case formulation

John was a 23-year-old man who lived with three other people in a rented flat in a suburb of Birmingham. He had experienced problems in childhood as a consequence of both his parents' violence to each other and their neglect of their children. He had been moved from the family home, and away from his siblings, to a foster home as a consequence of these problems. He was quite happy in the foster home and school, and gained a number of A-levels. However, after leaving home to go to college, he began a history of significant drug and alcohol use, and had dropped out of college in his first year. Since then, he had had a number of short-term casual jobs, but nothing long term. He continued to be a heavy user of drugs, including marijuana, amphetamines, and cocaine over a period of years. To sustain his drug use, he had engaged in petty crime and occasionally dealt drugs. He

(continued)

was known to the local police force, which had detained him on a number of occasions, although he had not been to prison. He was well known to local probation officers.

John was admitted into a local hospital following the onset of an acute psychotic episode, which appeared to follow a break-up with a girlfriend several weeks previously. His flatmates had noticed that his behaviour had become increasingly strange and withdrawn over that period. He was telling them that he was hearing voices indicating that the police were after him and that they had put out a contract for him to be killed because of his history of crime and the way he had treated his girlfriend. He could hear the voices because they were being transmitted through the police radio system, which he was able to detect through radio receivers in his brain. He had locked himself in his room, closed the curtains, and was not eating. He felt frightened and believed that if he left the house, the police would find him and that he would be taken to prison or killed. In order to calm himself down he was using significant amounts of marijuana and alcohol. His flatmates' concern was such that they had contacted their family doctor, who had visited John in his flat. Under the guise of doing some tests to check out the reality of the changes to his brain and to try and sort them out, the doctor had persuaded John to be admitted to a local psychiatric hospital on a voluntary basis.

Once in hospital he was assessed by a psychiatrist, and placed on antipsychotic medication. After a few weeks, although he felt calm and safe in hospital, he still appeared depressed and believed that the police were still 'after him'. He was therefore referred to a clinical psychologist in the hope that they could change his paranoid beliefs.

Formulation

John was a vulnerable individual as a consequence of his damaged upbringing, difficulties in engaging with others, and the stresses associated with relationships and use of non-prescription drugs. The incident appears to have been triggered by his breaking up of a relationship with a woman he had been seeing for several months. He had not treated her well during the relationship and the break-up had been quite uncaring and disrespectful to her. According to Bentall, this may have evoked memories of his childhood and the pain he experienced at this time, making him feel guilty for his behaviour, which was like that of his parents, for whom he little respect or love. He differed significantly from an ideal self of being caring and cared for. This guilt led to ruminations and worry about how he had behaved, its implications for him, and the belief that he was a bad person. Exacerbated by the use of drugs, he had externalized these feelings of guilt and self-deprecation onto the police.

Treatment

Antipsychotic medication

Most people diagnosed with schizophrenia receive some form of medication, although dosages may be reduced or even discontinued during periods of remission. The types of drugs used, their mode of action, and some important side-effects are considered in Chapter 4.

Adherence to the required treatment regimen is crucial to gain benefit. Morken et al. (2008), for example, found that people in remission who stopped taking their medication were ten times more likely to experience a relapse and four times more likely to be re-hospitalized than those who continued taking it. Unfortunately, adherence rates as low as 20 per cent have been reported (Ascher-Svanum et al. 2006). This may be a consequence of a range of factors, including symptom severity, negative attitudes towards medication, substance misuse, low expectations of drug effectiveness, poor therapeutic alliance, and acute side-effects. Based on these findings, a number of studies have evaluated a range of strategies for maximizing adherence. Simple approaches involve the use of memory aids or prescription of drugs in pre-prepared plastic packaging, each containing separate pop-out sections containing all the medication to be taken at each time of the day across one week (Valenstein et al. 2011). Other approaches involve good planning at the time of discharge and maintaining good contact between the individual and their care team when they are not in hospital. Educational programmes, while increasing knowledge, have had little impact on adherence. By contrast, cognitive interventions designed to improve attitudes towards medication have proved of benefit, as have family interventions that have addressed increasing adherence. In general, the more types of intervention, the better the effect (Barkhofa et al. 2012).

Early signs

It is generally accepted that the earlier any intervention the better. With this in mind, there is now an increasing emphasis on not waiting for a first psychotic episode to become problematic, but trying to prevent this from occurring at all. Such interventions target individuals who are showing 'odd behaviours' or experiencing anomalous experiences but who do not fulfil the diagnostic criteria for schizophrenia. These 'early signs' may include:

- changes in sleep or eating patterns
- mood swings and increased anxiety or low mood
- ideas of reference: the belief that 'everything is about' the individual
- loss of energy and feeling withdrawn
- thoughts being faster or slower
- thoughts 'being put into [the individual's] head' or disappearing
- thoughts being spoken aloud
- hearing, smelling, and seeing things that other people do not.

Such interventions work. A meta-analysis by Stafford et al. (2013) concluded that CBT reduced risk of progression from these often rather vague symptoms to frank psychosis by around 50 per cent. The same approach may also help minimize pharmacological treatment following successful treatment of a psychotic episode. This involves a gradual reduction or cessation of medication at the same time as the individual or their family monitor for early signs that indicate potential onset of a further episode. If this occurs, they seek help and medication is initiated or increased. In a typical study of the effectiveness of this approach, Gaebel et al. (2002) found people adopting the early signs approach used less medication over a 2-year period than those in a continuous medication condition. There were no between-group differences on measures of psychopathology, social adjustment or subjective well-being. Despite this success, some have questioned the effectiveness of this approach. Gaebel and Riesbeck (2007), for example, found that the early signs identified by many individuals were not predictive of relapse.

Family interventions

The recognition that high negative expressed emotion was contributing to relapse in schizophrenia resulted in a number of studies of family interventions targeted at its reduction. In one of the earliest of these, Leff and Vaughn (1985) randomly assigned people with schizophrenia who had at least 35 hours per week face-to-face contact with family members in a high NEE household to a family intervention or usual care condition. The intervention included a psycho-educational programme that focused on methods of reducing NEE within the household, family support, and the opportunity for family therapy. The programme was highly successful. Nine months after the end of therapy, 8 per cent of the people in the treatment group had relapsed, in contrast to 50 per cent of those in the comparison group. At 2-year follow-up, 40 per cent of the treatment group and 78 per cent of the control group had relapsed.

Falloon et al. (1982) adopted a similar therapeutic approach. Their intervention included education about the role of family stress in triggering episodes of schizophrenia and working with the family to develop family problem-solving skills. Their results were equally impressive. At 9-month follow-up, 5 per cent of the people in families receiving treatment had relapsed, compared with 44 per cent of those receiving standard medical treatment. At 2-year follow-up, relapse rates were 16 per cent and 83 per cent respectively. On the basis of this and other related evidence, Pharoah et al. (2010) concluded that family interventions reduce risk of relapse by about half compared with standard medical care. They also noted that family interventions decreased the frequency of admissions to hospital, time spent in hospital, and improved compliance with medication regimens.

Cognitive behaviour therapy

Two forms of CBT are increasingly being used with people with a diagnosis of schizophrenia. The first, stress management, involves working with individuals to help them cope with the stress leading to or associated with psychotic experiences. The second, known as belief modification, involves attempts to change the nature of delusional beliefs the individual may hold.

Stress management approaches involve a detailed evaluation of the problems and experiences an individual is having, their triggers and consequences, and developing strategies to help cope with them. These include cognitive techniques such as distraction from intrusive thoughts or cognitive challenge, increasing or decreasing social activity as a means of distraction from intrusive thoughts or low mood, and using relaxation techniques (see Chapter 2).

This approach has proved successful in preventing or delaying individuals at high risk of developing schizophrenia moving into a first episode (Salokangas and McGlashan 2008). McGorry et al. (2002), for example, randomized such individuals into what they termed an intervention involving supportive psychotherapy focusing on social, work or family issues, or low-dose risperidone therapy combined with CBT. Each intervention lasted for 6 months. By the end of treatment, 36 per cent of the people who received supportive psychotherapy progressed to first-episode psychosis compared with 10 per cent in the combined CBT/risperidone group. Morrison et al. (2007) also found short-term gains following a purely cognitive intervention, but at 3-year follow-up the intervention proved no more successful than usual care.

Other studies have evaluated interventions intended to promote recovery following an acute episode of schizophrenia. In one such study, Tarrier et al. (2000) randomly assigned individuals to either drug therapy alone or in combination with stress management or supportive counselling. The stress management intervention involved 20 sessions in 10 weeks, followed by four booster sessions over the following year. By the end of the first phase of treatment, those who received this intervention evidenced a greater improvement than those in the supportive counselling group, while people who received only drug therapy showed a slight deterioration. One-third of the people who received stress management achieved a 50 per cent reduction in psychotic experiences; only 15 per cent of the supportive counselling group achieved this level of benefit: 15 per cent of the stress management group and 7 per cent of the supportive counselling condition were free of all positive symptoms. None of those in the drug therapy group achieved this criterion. One year later, there remained significant differences between the three groups, favouring those in the stress management condition. At 2-year follow-up, those who received only drug therapy had significantly more problems than those in the psychological treatment groups. However, the two psychological interventions proved equally effective.

Belief modification involves the use of verbal challenge and behavioural hypothesis testing to counter delusional beliefs and/or hallucinations. Verbal challenge encourages the individual to view a delusional belief as just one of several possibilities. The person is not told that the belief is wrong, but is asked to consider an alternative view provided by the therapist. New possibilities may then be tested in the 'real world' as appropriate. A similar process is used to challenge hallucinations, focusing on the patient's beliefs about their power, identity, and purpose. Behavioural hypothesis testing involves challenging any thoughts in a more direct, behavioural way (see also discussion of these issues in Chapter 2).

Reflecting the novelty of this approach, relatively few studies have evaluated this type of intervention. Nevertheless, from their meta-analysis of four randomized controlled trials, Jones et al. (2000) concluded that these interventions reduced both the frequency and the impact of hallucinations. In addition, while they had a limited impact on measures of conviction in delusional beliefs, they reduced the amount of distress associated with them. Overall, people who were taught ways of challenging their delusional beliefs or hallucinations were half as likely to relapse as those who were not.

Trower et al. (2004) followed a group of 38 individuals with **command hallucinations** who were randomly allocated to usual care or a cognitive intervention. The results were impressive. At both 6- and 12-month follow-up, those in the cognitive intervention group reported significantly less compliance with the commands, as well as less belief in their power or superiority. Drury et al. (2000) reported a more multifaceted intervention that involved both individual and group cognitive therapy in which participants learned to cope with delusions and hallucinations. In addition, they took part in a 6-month family psycho-education programme and an activity programme including life-skills groups. The effects of this intervention were compared with those of an activity programme involving participants in sports, leisure, and social groups. The short- and mid-term impacts of the intervention were impressive. Those in the active therapeutic programme recovered more quickly following the relapse that brought them into therapy. At 9-month follow-up, 56 per cent of the control group still had moderate or severe problems, compared with 5 per cent of the intervention group. At 5-year follow-up, however, there was no evidence of any differences between the two groups on measures of relapse rates or levels of positive symptoms. To achieve longer-term benefits, it may be necessary to introduce a second, perhaps less extensive, 'booster' intervention.

Working with: psychosis

David, aged 28 years, was experiencing significant delusional beliefs. He believed other people could 'listen to and understand his thoughts', and that by doing so they had the potential to control his behaviour. He also believed he held a number of military secrets that were central to the safety of the country. To avoid these becoming known to others, he had withdrawn from contact with other people for the past 2 weeks, and was living in one room in his parents' house. His sleep was poor. He was eating little and had clearly lost weight. He was not taking his prescribed medication, but was using significant amounts of cannabis and cigarettes to help keep calm during periods of acute agitation. He was admitted into hospital under Section 3 of the Mental Health Act, which allowed him to be treated in hospital for a period of 6 months without his consent. As soon as he was admitted, he was prescribed antipsychotic medication and observed taking it.

After 2 weeks on the ward, he was less anxious and agitated. He was seen by a therapist, with a view to helping him achieve a more rational understanding of his experiences and to reduce the risk of future admissions. These two requirements allowed the possibility of at least three approaches to his treatment:

- An 'early signs' approach to help David and his family to identify early signs of his shift into delusional thinking and to seek psychiatric support.
- Using CBT to identify and modify any delusional thinking David may still have.
- Working with his family to reduce any stress and criticism within the household.

Of these approaches, the first two were considered the most likely to be of benefit, as discussions with both David and his family found them to be highly supportive with little stress in the household.

Early signs
The early signs approach is based around a formulation of the triggers and maintaining factors of the present psychotic episode (and others if relevant). Long-term factors included David's time in the army when he was in the Royal Corp of Signals, from which he was discharged following his use of drugs and odd behaviour. His present episode seems to have been triggered initially by his breaking up with a girlfriend, after which he began to smoke more cannabis, and to sleep poorly – both of which may have contributed to his odd experiences and thinking. He stopped leaving the house, and

eventually remained in his room, leaving him deprived of social and other inputs, allowing him time to become immersed in his own thinking and worries. His use of cannabis and cigarettes may have contributed to his experience of paranoid beliefs. Any shift towards this sort of behaviour should result in immediate contact with his **community mental health team**, who would send a community nurse to make an immediate assessment and coordinate psychiatric treatment at home, and hopefully prevent him from being admitted to hospital.

CBT for delusional thinking
This typically involves a more gentle and less challenging approach to cognitive change than may occur, for example, in the treatment of depression. The goal is often not to directly challenge and change the individual's way of thinking, but rather to reduce the strength with which they believe their delusional thoughts. So, initial discussions with David involved an exploration of his thoughts, with no attempt to challenge them. Only once a good therapeutic alliance was established could his beliefs be challenged. Specific examples of triggers to his thinking were identified: for example, his belief that someone was watching him and reading his thoughts in a cafe. He was asked: 'What made him think this?'; 'Was there any other explanation for what he saw the man do?'; 'Why may he have behaved like he did if he was not listening in to your thoughts?', and so on. This gentle approach may not completely change David's way of thinking, but it allows the possibility of other explanations and weakens the strength with which he believes his delusional thoughts.

Chapter summary

1. Schizophrenia is characterized by a number of experiences, although the most central are lack of insight, delusions and hallucinations.
2. The DSM diagnosis has been challenged from a variety of perspectives, and to avoid some of the confusion surrounding the concept, it is now frequently considered under the more precise rubric of psychosis.
3. Psychosocial factors in adulthood that combine with genetic factors to contribute to risk of psychosis now largely focus on family stress and negative expressed emotion (NEE).
4. Psychological explanations of various manifestations of psychosis include information overload, lack of congruence between actual and desired states, and a complex combination of (a) environmental events, (b) 'psychotic processes', (c) pre-existing beliefs, and (d) personality and emotion.
5. Treatment usually involves medication, although this may be minimized through the use of early signs interventions.
6. Cognitive behaviour therapy may be used in the treatment of delusions, while family interventions aimed at NEE or family stress are also efficacious.

Further reading

Bentall, R.P. (2003) *Madness Explained: Psychosis and human nature*. London: Penguin.

Cooke, A. (2014) *Understanding Psychosis and Schizophrenia*. Report by the Division of Clinical Psychology. Leicester: British Psychological Society.

Morrison, A.P., Renton, J., French P. et al. (2008) *Think You're Crazy? Think again: a resource book for cognitive therapy for psychosis*. Oxford: Routledge.

Steel, C. (2012) *CBT for Schizophrenia: Evidence-based interventions and future directions*. Chichester: Wiley.

Chapter 12

The problem with pleasure

This chapter focuses on addictions and sex. An odd combination, perhaps, but they are both are driven by desire and the seeking of pleasure. So they share, at least in part, some commonality. The chapter addresses several issues linked to the use of, and dependence on, a number of drugs; and a non-drug-related addiction, gambling, that shares many of the same characteristics. It then addresses three sexual issues, two of which involve men dressing in women's clothing, but for very different reasons: transvestism and gender dysphoria. Finally, the chapter considers the causes and potential treatments of paedophilia.

By the end of this chapter, you should have an understanding of:

- Factors associated with drug use and addiction
- Common pathways to addiction
- The use and abuse of alcohol, cannabis, and heroin
- The causes and treatment of gambling addiction
- The causes and questionable diagnoses of gender dysphoria and transvestic disorder
- The causes and treatment of paedophilic disorder

Drug use and addiction

Most cultures engage in some form of escape from reality through the use of naturally occurring drugs such as peyote, cannabis or 'magic mushrooms'. Even animals have been known to eat fermenting fruit in order to enjoy its alcoholic effects. It should therefore come as no surprise that despite potential legal sanctions, many people use drugs, and often use many drugs. In Europe alone, an estimated 12 million adults used cannabis in 2011 (European Monitoring Centre for Drugs and Drug Addiction 2012). Drug use tends to be highest among young people, the socially marginalized and homeless, and those involved in particular drug cultures such as 'raves'. Among the latter, polydrug use can involve up to ten drugs, including alcohol, cannabis, ecstasy, amphetamines, and cocaine. Only 3 per cent of the drug-using population injects. The APA (2000) distinguished between two 'levels' of problems associated with drug use:

- *Drug abuse*: a maladaptive pattern of substance use leading to significant impairment or distress and outcomes including failure to fulfil major role obligations at work or home, use in situations in which it is physically hazardous, legal problems, and social or interpersonal problems.
- *Drug dependence*: the individual is psychologically or physically dependent on a drug. They develop a tolerance to the drug, need more of it to achieve the desired experience, and experience withdrawal symptoms if they stop using it. Other outcomes include social impairment, devoting substantial time and effort to obtaining the drug, and a history of repeated, unsuccessful attempts to stop using.

Common pathways to addiction

Addiction to drugs involves a number of neural pathways. The most important, with the possible exception of cannabis, involves the so-called 'reward system'. This includes the mesolimbic and mesocortical pathways, with the mesolimbic pathway – from the ventral tegmental area via the medial forebrain bundle to the nucleus accumbens – being the most important. Activity within this system is mediated by the neurotransmitter dopamine, the activity of which can be increased by use of a drug, or in strongly addicted individuals by the sight of drug paraphernalia or expectation of drug use (Boileau et al. 2007). Over time, regular drug use appears to reduce the sensitivity of the reward system, and the individual needs more of the drug, and more frequently, to maintain the same level of reward. If they cannot access the drug, they may experience withdrawal effects.

Some differences in individual risk of addiction appear to be mediated by genetic factors. One variant of the D2 dopamine receptor gene, the DRD A1 allele, for example, is highly prevalent in individuals with a dependence on alcohol, while alleles of the DRD2 dopamine gene are involved in determining risk for opiate dependence.

These biological processes are mirrored by psychological processes. From a behavioural perspective, drug use initially results in feelings of pleasure. However, as the individual becomes biologically dependent on the drug, other outcomes may become evident. If an individual chooses not to take a drug, or cannot access it, they may experience withdrawal effects. These can be extremely unpleasant, and in behavioural terms, highly punishing. Relief from them, by further use of the drug (negative reinforcement), is highly reinforcing. As a consequence, long-term use of some drugs may be driven as much by attempts to avoid withdrawal effects as the expectation or experience of pleasure.

Alcohol

Access to alcohol varies across the world. In Muslim countries, the Qur'an prohibits its consumption. But even where consumption is legal, many countries try to limit its accessibility through pricing or by restricting the number of outlets in which alcohol can be purchased. These restrictions are in place because of the harm that may result from alcohol consumption. 'Safe' limits to alcohol consumption are not clear, and depend on an individual's genetic make-up. 'Safe' may also be defined in terms of both the short- and long-term consequences of excessive consumption. Short-term consequences include increased risk of drink-drive accidents, unsafe sex, violent crime, accidents, admission to mental and general hospitals, burns and suicide (Allan et al. 2001). Long-term excessive consumption can result in significant health problems, including liver cirrhosis, hepatitis, hypertension, various cancers, and neurological problems.

The path to alcohol dependence is gradual, beginning with social drinking, progressing to drinking at times of stress or difficulty, and then an increasing 'need' to drink in order to cope with daily stresses or prevent withdrawal symptoms. In the early stages of dependence, the individual may need a lunchtime drink to prevent feelings of discomfort. This may progress to needing an early morning drink and continued drinking through the day. Periods of abstinence as short as 3–4 hours may become difficult, and result in symptoms including tremor, nausea, sweating, and mood disturbance. Longer periods of abstinence result in *delirium tremens* ('the DTs'). These are highly distressing symptoms, usually beginning 3–4 days after cessation and lasting up to 3 days. They include fluctuations in consciousness, impairment of memory, insomnia, and frightening auditory or visual hallucinations.

Biological explanations

Many young people drink alcohol, often to excess, but then moderate their consumption as they take on more responsibilities: jobs, family, and so on. Thus, the key question may not be why do people start drinking alcohol, but rather, why do some people continue to drink alcohol to excess? The answer in part may be genetic. Some individuals with variants of the DRD A1 and CNR1 genes, which influence dopamine activity within the pleasure centre, appear to be particularly sensitive to the effects of alcohol (Bowirrat and Oscar-Berman 2005). These individuals may be encouraged to initiate alcohol use because they find it easy to gain a 'high'. Unfortunately, continued use of alcohol reduces the response of the reward system to other potential reinforcers, leading to a dependence on alcohol to maintain a desired mood state. At the same time as its influence on dopamine, alcohol enhances the action of GABA within the hypothalamus and sympathetic nervous system, helping calm mood and behaviour. Over time, this causes a reduction in the natural production of GABA, leading to a dependence on alcohol to maintain desired emotional states. Abstinence results in sub-optimal levels of GABA, increases in anxiety and agitation, and the onset of physical withdrawal symptoms. These are relieved by continued drinking or, in time, the body's resumption of normal levels of GABA.

Psychosocial explanations

From a psychological perspective, consumption is rewarded by feelings of pleasure and disinhibition. Later, once an individual has begun to develop a dependence on alcohol, drinking may prevent or stop withdrawal effects: it becomes a negative reinforcer. Cognitions known as addictive beliefs ('I need a drink to get through the day'; Beck et al. 1993) may also support consumption. It is believed that alcohol is often used as a means to reduce stress, although empirical evidence of this role is surprisingly mixed. It has been shown to reduce stress, increase stress, or have no impact on stress at all (Sayette 1999). These differences may be explained by Sayette's appraisal-disruption model, which states that alcohol reduces situational stress by inhibiting the activation of negative appraisals and stressful memories of similar situations. If an individual drinks alcohol *before* encountering a situation, they will experience a lower level of stress than if they had not had a drink. If they start drinking *during* it, their negative appraisals/memories will already have been activated and they will experience no reduction in stress.

A number of social factors may also contribute to risk for alcohol dependence. Consumption may be encouraged by positive portrayals of alcohol use on television or in films (Engels et al. 2009). More immediate social factors may also encourage consumption. Round-buying, cheap drinks, standing drinking, even loud music in bars (Guéguen et al. 2008), all can increase consumption. Finally, adverse life-events may increase consumption, while groups under social pressure, including blue-collar workers and originating populations in the USA and Australia, also drink more alcohol than others (Guiao and Thompson 2004).

Treatment

Treatment of people who are alcohol dependent usually begins with a period of withdrawal: 'drying out'. This is an unpleasant time during which those involved may experience significant withdrawal effects. These may be partially relieved by the use of benzodiazepines. Withdrawal usually takes place over a period of 3–4 days and can be conducted in hospital or at home with the support of nurses.

Once withdrawn, a range of treatments is possible. Two types of drug treatment are particularly common. The first involves a type of drug known as an antidipstrotrophic, of which the most well known is Antabuse. This works by preventing alcohol being broken down by the liver beyond its immediate metabolite, acetaldehyde. This accumulates in the body and causes a number of unpleasant symptoms, including flushing, headache, vertigo, and 'copious vomiting', around 15–20 minutes after consumption. The knowledge these effects will occur if alcohol is consumed is intended to prevent drinking. Of course, treatment using this drug is voluntary, and not taking the drug allows consumption without these effects. Nevertheless, around 50 per cent of individuals achieve long-term abstinence using this approach (Krampe et al. 2006).

A second type of drug treatment involves the use of opioid agonists, such as naltrexone, which reduce cravings for alcohol. This approach, of course, encounters the same problems as those involving Antabuse: if people want to drink, they simply stop taking the medication. However, a slow-release version of naltrexone, which is therapeutically effective for one month, appears to reduce this risk. One evaluation of this version of the drug (O'Malley et al. 2007) found alcohol-dependent individuals were likely to remain abstinent for longer than those treated with placebo (41 vs. 12 days). In addition, 70 per cent of the treated group were considered 'responders' (that is, they had less than 2 days' heavy drinking in any 28-day period) compared with 30 per cent in the placebo-treated group.

Psychosocial approaches to the treatment of alcohol dependence differ markedly in their philosophy. One approach, typified by the 12-step treatment programme of Alcoholics Anonymous (AA), is often referred to as the Minnesota model. This approach is based on the belief that alcohol dependence is a physical, psychological, and spiritual illness that cannot be cured, but can be controlled by total abstinence from alcohol. Alcoholics Anonymous provides a strong social support network and encourages regular attendance at its meetings. Attenders are encouraged to accept that they are powerless to control their drinking, to cease their struggle, and to allow a 'higher power' to take control. Millions of people throughout the world follow the programme, with some success. Timko et al. (2000), for example, found 64 per cent of those who had gone through an AA programme reported maintaining a 'benign' drinking pattern: an interesting finding not only because of the high success rate (albeit self-reported) but because it appears that many people who went through this abstinence-based programme were actually drinking at relatively safe levels.

More time-limited programmes have adopted a number of approaches. A popular method, known as motivational interviewing (Miller and Rollnick 2002), can involve a single interview designed, as its name suggests, to increase motivation to reduce consumption. Motivational interviewing uses a non-judgemental interview to encourage participants to consider the costs and benefits of their drinking and to reduce their consumption. It has proved effective in people early in their drinking career, achieving reductions in consumption among young people identified as drinking excessively (Daeppen et al. 2011), drink-driving and other traffic violations, alcohol-related injuries and alcohol-related problems when given to young drivers admitted to casualty departments following an alcohol-related accident (Monti et al. 1999).

Among people with longer-term problems, motivational interviewing may be the first step of a more extensive process of behavioural change. This often involves a programme, based on cognitive behavioural principles, designed to teach interpersonal and assertive skills to help participants cope more effectively with stressful situations and with refusing drinks, and relapse prevention skills including challenging addictive beliefs and coping with cravings to drink. The goal here is to help people remain abstinent or, more frequently, to help them drink at a moderate and non-damaging level. In an attempt to find the most effective treatment, Project MATCH compared the effectiveness of CBT, 12-step, and an intervention based on a long-term motivational support called motivational enhancement therapy (MET). Costing around US$27 million, and involving 1726 problem drinkers followed up for 8 years (Waldron et al. 2001), it was found that the three interventions were equally effective! However, people who entered treatment with high levels of anger fared best with MET; those whose social support systems favoured continued drinking, who had higher levels of dependence, and higher levels of mental health problems benefited most from the 12-step approach; those with lower levels of dependence fared best with CBT.

Cannabis

It is estimated that 147 million people use cannabis worldwide (World Health Organization: http://www.who.int/substance_abuse/facts/cannabis/en/), making it the most widely used illegal drug in the world. An estimated 10 per cent of users at any one time are dependent to some extent on the drug, evidenced by its use to prevent withdrawal symptoms, unsuccessful attempts to control its use, and using more cannabis and for a longer time than intended (Swift et al. 2001).

Biological explanations

The main active ingredient of cannabis is delta-9-tetrahydrocannabilol (THC). When smoked, this chemical reaches the brain almost instantly: if eaten, the effects take longer to achieve and are less potent, but may last for up to 4 hours. The amount of THC in herbal cannabis varies between 1 and 15 per cent. However, newer strains, including 'skunk', can have up to 20 per cent THC, making it much more potent than 'traditional' cannabis.

THC acts on cannabinoid receptors within the endocannabinoid system, which impacts on a range of behaviours and emotions. The system includes the:

- Hypothalamus: appetite and sexual behaviour
- Basal ganglia: motor control and planning
- Ventral striatum: prediction and 'experience' of reward
- Amygdala: anxiety, emotion, and fear
- Hippocampus: memory and learning.

Because of the wide range of psychological processes influenced by the endocannabinoid system, the effects of cannabis are wide-ranging and not all relate to mood or pleasure. It evokes a mild 'high', feelings of relaxation, creative thinking, as well as medical benefits of reduced pain and nausea. It is also associated with increased appetite and impairment of cognition (primarily memory for information given while under the influence of the drug) and psychomotor performance. For some, the acute effects may be more negative, and include anxiety, agitation, and paranoia. In the longer term, smoking cannabis can lead to lung and trachea damage and may contribute to long-term impairment of cognitive functioning involving organization and integration of complex information (Solowij et al. 2002).

Cannabis use can also lead to psychosis, particularly in vulnerable individuals. Henquet et al. (2005), for example, followed a large group of young people aged 14–24 years for over a 4-year period. Within this group, they identified a number of people who showed evidence at entry into the study of risk for psychosis, with their scores on a symptom checklist showing high levels of 'paranoid ideation' and 'psychoticism'. Overall, cannabis users were significantly more at risk of developing psychosis than non-smokers. However, most of the risk was among those people already at risk for psychosis. In this group, cannabis users were 24 per cent more likely to develop psychosis than non-users. The risk for low-risk individuals was 6 per cent greater if they smoked cannabis. Risk is mediated by genetic factors, with the latest candidate being alleles of the AKT1 gene involved in dopamine regulation.

Treatment

Most people who seek help for dependence on cannabis have other significant problems, including risky sexual behaviours, delinquency, legal problems, and pregnancy. This clearly complicates any intervention that may be used, although a number of trials have been conducted. Summarizing their findings, Budney et al. (2007) concluded that both CBT and motivational enhancement therapy have proved effective, although a combination of approaches is best. Even so, across studies, abstinence rates at one year have been shown to be relatively modest: only 19–29 per cent for studies combining CBT and MET. These relatively modest findings reflect the multiple problems faced by participants in the studies, and how difficult cannabis dependence can be to treat. They may also suggest a goal of total abstention may be inappropriate, and may be better replaced by one of controlled cannabis use.

Heroin

Heroin can be injected, smoked, snorted or taken as a suppository. Ingestion results in profound feelings of relaxation, euphoria, and warmth: worries are forgotten and self-confidence increases for periods of 4–6 hours. Smoking heroin ('chasing the dragon') may now be the most frequent means of using the drug, and provides the most instant high. Once an individual is chemically dependent on the drug, withdrawal symptoms are extremely unpleasant, typically begin 8 hours after cessation, and include muscle pain, sweating, cramps, chills, vomiting, and diarrhoea. They may last for up to 10 days, although the first 72 hours are the worst. For obvious reasons, the prevalence of heroin use is difficult to ascertain with absolute certainty, but is around 0.25–0.5 per cent of populations across Europe and the USA (Bargagli et al. 2006). Users frequently use multiple drugs, and may switch between them depending on their relative availability and price (Degenhardt et al. 2005).

Biological explanations

Heroin has an impact via a number of neurological pathways. It influences dopaminergic activity within the 'pleasure centre' of the brain. It also influences the perception of pain and our emotions through binding to receptor sites that normally bind to so-called naturally occurring opiates. These receptor sites are found throughout the brain, although they are particularly prevalent in the thalamus, midbrain, hypothalamus, and spinal cord. Regular heroin users may also develop a generalized dysfunctional lack of connectivity throughout the brain, including the prefrontal cortex, amygdala, and hippocampus, resulting in impaired self-control and inhibitory function as well as deficits in stress regulation.

Psychosocial explanations

The behavioural model of pleasure followed by avoidance of withdrawal effects outlined earlier in the chapter is clearly relevant to heroin use, as is the sensitization to drug cues. Meyer (1995), for example, reported that the sight of a needle may decrease the severity of withdrawal symptoms when coming off heroin. In contrast, cues conditioned to withdrawal may trigger withdrawal symptoms, even years after stopping using heroin. Cognitive factors are also involved in expectancies of both pleasure and, ultimately, fear of withdrawal.

Key social factors that lead to heroin use include seeking pleasure, relief from stress, social pressure, and seeking mystical experiences (Nutt and Law 2000). The benefits of heroin, and the specificity of its role as a stress reducer, can be found in the estimated 40 per cent of US soldiers who used the drug during action in the Vietnam War and the 1 per cent who continued using when back home in the USA (Grinspoon and Bakalar 1986). Use can escalate to abuse, and then to dependence, involving increased tolerance of the drug, compulsive drug taking, and withdrawal symptoms if the drug is not taken regularly. Sharing needles is relatively common and may contain a social or ritual element. Use is often maintained by stealing: more than 95 per cent of American opiate-dependent individuals reported committing crimes to maintain their drug use (NIH Consensus Development Panel 1998).

Treatment

Interventions used to address heroin addiction are aimed at reducing its use or limiting the harm associated with it. Needle exchange schemes, for example, aim to reduce risk of infection from viruses and other pathogens associated with shared needle use. They involve exchanging old needles for new at venues accessible to users, such as pharmacies or clinics. This approach is now used across the world, and has achieved significant reductions in the transmission of viruses such as HIV and hepatitis. Despite these successes, use of such schemes is not universal. Some US states, for example, have argued that needle exchanges maintain heroin use, and have rejected their use on moral grounds.

Another harm prevention approach involves the use of drugs considered less harmful (and prone to overdose) than heroin. Drugs such as the synthetic opioid methadone do not give the same 'high' as heroin, but do prevent the onset of withdrawal symptoms if used to replace heroin. They are usually dispensed once a day from treatment clinics or pharmacies. This approach is widely used: around half the UK family doctors are prescribing methadone at any one time. However, it is not universally popular among users, many of whom complain of its toxicity and the feeling they are not being given a sufficient dose. Low adherence may also be a consequence of the lack of a 'high' as is having a partner or friends still using heroin. A more recent approach has involved the use of diacetylmorphine, essentially pure heroin, again prescribed by doctors and accessed via pharmacies in an injectable form twice a day. This has less toxicity than methadone, and higher levels of adherence. In one study comparing the two approaches, Oviedo-Joekes et al. (2009) found that 88 per cent of people receiving diacetylmorphine and 54 per cent receiving methadone remained in treatment over a one-year period.

The second treatment approach involves cessation of heroin or drug-substitutes. Just as in the treatment of alcohol problems, treatment usually begins with a period of detoxification and can involve pharmacological or psychological approaches. Pharmacological treatment involves the use of opiate antagonists such as naltrexone. These inert chemicals bind to opioid receptors in the brain, preventing the 'high' following the use of heroin. Unfortunately, as few as 3 per cent of people engage in this form of treatment, and many of them use it irregularly. Accordingly, despite the relatively high levels of success achieved when people use the drug (31–64 per cent abstinence rates: Tucker and Ritter 2000), the approach can be considered to have limited success only.

People who use heroin often lead chaotic lives, and find it difficult to follow formal therapeutic programmes. Accordingly, interventions such as CBT are also difficult to institute and drop-out rates are very high. For this reason, perhaps, Scherbaum et al. (2005) found a one-session group cognitive behavioural intervention to be as effective as a long-term equivalent. An alternative approach to attempts at individual change has involved a form of contingency management. Gruber et al. (2000), for example, provided 'rewards' including free weekend recreational activities or rent payment if weekly blood tests found ex-heroin or -methadone users to be following their required regimen. After one month, 61 per cent of participants in the programme continued to be enrolled in treatment, while 50 per cent on an abstinence regimen remained abstinent. The equivalent figures in a group not receiving the intervention were 17 and 21 per cent respectively.

Gambling disorder

Not all addictions have physical causes. For example, around 1–2 per cent of gamblers have some degree of gambling addiction (Delfabbro and Thrupp 2003). That is, they experience biologically mediated highs associated with gambling and withdrawal symptoms when unable to gamble. The prevalence of gambling disorders does not appear to differ according to the availability of gambling outlets. Nevada residents are about eight times more exposed to gambling than New Jersey residents and nine times more so than Iowa residents, yet their levels of gambling disorders are lower than either of the other two populations (Shaffer 2005). Nevertheless, more subtle factors may influence levels of gambling problems. Both on-line access and gaming machines that produce instant wins increase gambling levels among gamblers exposed to them (Yau et al. 2014).

Biological explanations

As with people addicted to drugs, the process of developing an addiction occurs over time, is mediated by dopaminergic activity within the brain's pleasure centre, and is influenced by genes that affect the degree of this activity (Comings et al. 2001). Perhaps because of common genetic pathways, around 30 per cent of pathological gamblers also experience alcohol-related problems.

Psychosocial explanations

Psychosocial factors also influence gambling levels. Sharpe (2002), for example, identified a combination of personality and learning history that influences risk for developing a gambling disorder:

- *Impulsivity*: high impulsivity measured between the ages of 11 and 15 years is associated with a doubling of risk for problem gambling at age 19 (Liu et al. 2012).
- *An early 'big win'*: a 'big win' early in a gambling career can build resistance to loss, and increase risk for continued gambling in the face of subsequent losses. Unfortunately, while this process has some intuitive appeal, at least one experimental study has failed to find this effect (Weatherly et al. 2004).
- *Pro-gambling beliefs and attitudes*: once started, problem gamblers typically maintain their gambling through the use of irrational, positive beliefs. They may, for example, discount losses, believing they have some degree of control over outcomes: 'If I lose four times, I must win on the fifth...'. Pro-gambling beliefs among family and peers are also strongly predictive of uptake and continued gambling among young people (Delfabbro and Thrupp 2003).
- *Negative emotions*: among pathological gamblers, low mood is frequently a trigger to gambling, in the expectation of the 'buzz' associated with gambling.

Treatment

In their meta-analysis of the relatively few relevant studies, Cowlishaw et al. (2012) reported that most had relatively short follow-up periods making long-term outcomes difficult to determine. However, those studies that have been conducted have shown significant benefits following CBT on measures of financial losses and gambling frequency. A typical CBT intervention, reported by Ladouceur et al. (2003), involved challenging irrational pro-gambling beliefs using Socratic dialogue, rehearsal of challenges to be made while gambling, and developing strategies to disengage from high-risk situations. The intervention proved successful in both the short and long terms: 54 per cent of participants reduced their gambling by at least 50 per cent, compared with only 7 per cent of a control group. These gains were maintained for up to 2 years. Interventions based on motivational interview alone have also shown benefit, although these have generally involved people with less severe problems. Self-help programmes such as the Gamblers Anonymous 12-step programme may achieve significant gains, although well-designed studies of its effect are lacking (Hodgins et al. 2011).

Working with: addiction

A common element of all interventions for addiction is the experience of craving, whether for a drug or to gamble. The strategies to help people cope with these feelings remain fairly basic, but can be effective. These may involve:

Distraction
- Focus on surroundings such as cars, people, and so on. What can they see? How many open windows have they passed, and so on?
- Talking: start a conversation, concentrate on what is being said.
- Avoid 'cue-laden environments': go for a walk, visit a library, visit a 'clean' friend.

Activity scheduling
A rather more long-term approach to distraction is planning activities for whole days to avoid tempting situations or having time to begin to think about drug use.

Flashcards
To avoid having to think how best to cope with severe temptation or cravings at the time they occur, flashcards can be pre-prepared. These can include coping strategies or motivational statements, carried in a bag or pocket, and taken out at times of pressure. They may say, for example:

- Keeping clean feels much better than strung out.
- Things are going good with X: keep it up.
- Get out now before you give in!

Imagery
A number of imagery techniques can be of value, including:

- *Image refocusing*: essentially a thought-stopping technique involving shouting (internally) 'Stop!', combined with the mental image of a stop sign, police officer or other relevant negative image.
- *Negative image replacement*: if someone begins to image the positive pleasures of using, shift to more negative images of withdrawing, being caught with drugs, and so on.
- *Positive image replacement*: if, conversely, the individual gets caught up in worries and negativity, replace such thoughts with images reflecting positive outcomes of keeping clean.
- *Imagery rehearsal*: using imagery to image and rehearse positive coping when experiencing cravings.

Cognitive challenge
This may be difficult at times of craving, and may benefit from preparing and planning in the comfort of the therapy session before using challenges in 'real life'. The individual can record in a 'thought diary' the thoughts they experience at times of craving. These thoughts are then discussed in therapy, and more rational, less 'risky' responses determined. These can them be implemented the next time such thoughts are experienced: 'I'm bored, and lonely...I really need a hit to keep me going' versus 'OK, if feel bored...but there are things I can do to feel better...call my buddy, play a video game...', 'I can make friends that don't take drugs. I can go to an NA meeting, meet some people...'.

None of these strategies is 'high-tech', but they are doable, which is much more important and can make the difference between remaining abstinent or engaging in addicted behaviour.

Transvestic disorder

Although differing markedly from the norm, prominent celebrities such as the artist Perry Grayson and comedian Eddy Izzard have begun to increase the public acceptance of transvestism. Nevertheless, DSM still continues to classify transvestism as a disorder if it is associated with significant distress.

In some cultures, cross-dressing has a cultural or ceremonial role. In India, for example, devotees of the Hindu god Krishna dress as females in order to pose as his consort, the goddess Radha. More widely, around 3 per cent of men in western cultures cross-dress with some regularity and most begin to do so around puberty (Långström and Zucker 2005). Initially, cross-dressing typically instigates sexual excitement, although this frequently recedes over time and is replaced by a feeling of comfort and well-being (Docter and Prince 1997). The desire to cross-dress often increases over time and many transvestites covertly wear female clothes under their male clothes.

Men who cross-dress behave according to masculine stereotypes. As children, they have typically male hobbies, enjoy rough and tumble games, and so on, and these masculine characteristics continue in adulthood. The majority are exclusively heterosexual (although sex may be enhanced by the use of feminine 'props') and are, or have been, married at some time. A significant minority of Docter and Prince's (1997) large US sample had cross-dressed in public: 10 per cent had travelled on public transport, 26 per cent had used a women's toilet, and 22 per cent had tried on women's clothing in shops. Despite this public bravado, many people reported having been distressed as a consequence of their cross-dressing, and felt some degree of guilt or shame: 70 per cent reported having purged their wardrobe on at least one occasion, while 45 per cent had sought counselling. Many also hide their behaviour or stop cross-dressing at the beginning of new relationships. The reactions of partners vary. According to Docter and Prince (1997), 28 per cent were 'completely accepting' of the behaviour, while 19 per cent were 'completely antagonistic'. The majority experienced an uneasy relationship with this behaviour.

Current affairs

As a diagnostic system, DSM has a history of classifying a number of sexual behaviours as 'disorders'. Most controversially, DSM-III (APA 1987) stated that homosexuality warranted a psychiatric diagnosis. Now, the APA is more constrained in its judgements about what or is not a disorder. Nevertheless, it is still possible to question whether some sexual disorders, including transvestism, are indeed disorders. Perhaps it may better be considered as one of a range of sexual behaviours that are neither 'normal' nor 'abnormal'. They simply 'are'. The one defence of this diagnostic assignment is that transvestism is only considered a disorder if it causes distress to those involved. However, it is questionable whether there is anything inherently distressing in engaging in transvestic behaviours, or whether any distress is a result of social attitudes towards the behaviour. So, is transvestism a psychiatric disorder? And does this argument hold for more 'problematic' behaviours such as sadism, exhibitionism, and paedophilia?

Psychosocial explanations

Men who cross-dress do so because of its associated sexual thrill or feelings of comfort. However, the long-term origins of these needs are unclear. Newcomb (1985) suggested that parents of cross-dressers provide weak or ambivalent role models, so the child does not learn gender stereotypical behaviours. However, most cross-dressers behave in 'boyish' ways as children, so this theory is not strong. A second approach suggested that cross-dressers may come from families with a strong negative attitude towards men, so dressing as a woman involves some form of defence mechanism (Zucker and Bradley 1995). Again, the predominantly masculine lives led by cross-dressers mitigates against this theory. A third theory, referred to as 'petticoat punishment' suggests cross-dressers may have been forced to dress as girls by their parents as a form of punishment. Subsequent cross-dressing is considered to be a way of mastering and overcoming this punishment or the punishers (Stoller 1968). Once more, there is little evidence to support this theory.

Ovesey and Person (1973) offered a more complex psychoanalytic model. They suggested that in cases in which a boy's father shows no emotional warmth towards the boy's mother, she may seek this (and unconscious sexual gratification) from her male child. In order to hide her sexual interest in the boy and protect him from his father's anger, she dresses him in girl's clothing. As a consequence, the boy fails to bond with his father and is unable to achieve a successful resolution of the Oedipal complex. In addition, he develops a long-term dependence on his mother and, in adulthood, seeks out other women who will accept or even encourage his cross-dressing. According to Ovesey and Person, dressing in women's clothes empowers the adult male. The female clothes hide his masculinity, disarm his sexual rivals, and allow him to gain sexual gratification without threat from potential rivals.

Less dramatically, but probably more accurately, a final model of the development of cross-dressing involves a conditioning approach, in which early experiences with female clothing (which may have been accidental) while experiencing sexual excitement result in a classically conditioned association between women's clothing and sexual excitement (Crawford et al. 1993).

Treatment

Although cross-dressing may not be considered a disorder that requires treatment, some people who cross-dress do experience emotional distress, perhaps because of partner or societal responses to their behaviour. The numbers of people seeking formal therapy are relatively small, and studies of the impact of therapy have largely involved individual case studies. Masturbatory retraining (see below) and CBT appear to be of some benefit (Laws and Marshall 2003).

Gender dysphoria

Just like transvestites, men diagnosed with gender dysphoria frequently desire to dress as women. But their need to do so is driven by different motives. Such men, and their female equivalents, hold the strong belief that they truly are of the opposite gender, and experience a strong need to change their sex. They feel 'trapped' in a wrong body. This need typically becomes evident as early as 3 years of age and the childhood behaviour of such individuals is stereotypical of the gender they wish to be. Girls adopt stereotypical male behaviours and attitudes, preferring, for example, 'rough and tumble' play and even rejecting urinating in the sitting position. By contrast, boys reject 'rough and tumble' and wish their genitalia to change to those of a female. By adolescence, about 40 per cent of such children no longer want to change their gender, and their behaviour becomes more gender-appropriate over time (Wallien and Cohen-Kettenis 2008). However, the remaining 60 per cent frequently become preoccupied with their inappropriate gender and experience clinical levels of distress.

Many men adopt cross-dressing as a means of reducing this distress. Others may take the more radical step of physically changing their gender through the use of surgical and hormonal treatments. Such treatments, known as sex reassignment, are clearly not simple. Transformation from male to female involves two stages. In the UK, the person is required to live as a female for a period of a year prior to irreversible surgery. During this year, they start taking the female hormone oestrogen, which softens the skin and leads to the development of breasts and 'feminine' hips. At the same time, they may receive electrolysis to remove facial hair or have cosmetic surgery to feminize their facial appearance. They are trained to increase the pitch of their voice. If this period is successful, and the person wishes to proceed, it is followed by surgical removal of the penis and construction of an artificial vagina. This new vagina allows natural and enjoyable sexual intercourse. For women becoming men, the outlook is less positive. They too take hormone therapy, to redistribute fat away from the hips and breasts and deepen the voice. Unfortunately, surgery to build a penis from the clitoris is generally less successful and the penis is usually small and incapable of a normal erection. Surgery may also involve removal of breasts and the uterus.

Biological explanations

Explanations of gender dysphoria are almost uniquely biological, although a definitive cause has yet to be identified. It may have some genetic basis. Heylens et al. (2012), for example, reported that of 23 identified MZ twins with gender dysphoria, nine had a twin also with the disorder. In DZ twins, no such relationship was found. Although twin studies in intact families cannot exclude the role of parental influence, these data certainly suggest the possibility of a genetic basis to the disorder. A neural pathway has also been tentatively identified. Male-to-female transsexuals have been found to have a smaller area of the hypothalamus known as the bed nucleus of the stria terminalis (BST) than typical males and for it to contain less somatostatin-expressing neurons (Kruijver et al. 2000). In female-to-male transsexuals, the BST appears to have more somatostatin-expressing neurons than average. Although the BST has been found to regulate sexual activity in rats, its influence on gender choice remains unclear.

Psychosocial explanations

Psychological explanations have struggled to explain gender dysphoria. While conditioning models involving parents who model and reward non-gender-related behaviour may explain the development of non-gender-consistent behaviours (Zucker et al. 1994), they have greater difficulty explaining the extremely strongly held beliefs about their gender that such people hold, and their resistance to any form of psychological therapy.

Treatment

Physical treatments are very effective in the case of gender dysphoria. Around 80 per cent of both men and women taking hormones prior to surgery report improvements in mood and quality of life (Murad et al. 2009). Following surgery, most male-to-female transsexuals express high levels of satisfaction with their self-image as a woman, although sexual intercourse is rated as less pleasurable than the norm (Weyers et al. 2009). Most people who have undergone surgery report improvements in cosmetic appearance, sexual functioning, self-esteem, body image, family life, social relationships, psychological status, and life satisfaction. However, a minority also experience difficulties in previous relationships or working environments, and may have to move home or work. A very small number request reversal of the operation, which is not possible, and may experience significant low mood or even commit suicide.

An especially controversial issue has been whether to allow young people with gender dysphoria to receive hormonal and surgical treatment. Those in support argue that such individuals will benefit from an early change in gender and be able to integrate into adult life with less disruption than at a later age. Those against suggest that young people do not have the maturity to make such life-changing decisions and may change their desired gender as they mature. The evidence suggests that when available, surgical treatment is beneficial. In a 4-year follow-up of a cohort of young people with gender dysphoria who were either allowed or denied surgery, Smith et al. (2001) found that none of those who had surgery regretted their choice, and reported higher levels of body satisfaction and lower levels of body dysphoria than those not undergoing surgery.

Given the lack of evidence of a psychological cause, and the resistance of individuals with the disorder to seek or receive psychological therapy, it is not surprising that there are few reports of psychological interventions in this population. However, based on findings that many young people who express gender dysphoria eventually become reconciled to their gender of birth, Meyer-Bahlburg (2002) attempted to facilitate this process. Working with 11 boys and their parents, they provided a home environment that encouraged gender-appropriate behaviours and attitudes. The boys were encouraged to play with their father more, and their mother less. They were rewarded with increased attention for engaging in gender-typical behaviour and distracted from non-gender-typical behaviour. They were also encouraged to play with boys, join male sports groups, and so on. The majority of children showed some change as a consequence of the intervention.

Paedophilic disorder

Paedophilia involves engaging in some sort of sexual activity with children under the age of sexual consent, or wanting to do so. Importantly, while two young people engaging in sexual intercourse may be illegal, it would be inappropriate to consider this as 'paedophilia'. For a diagnosis of paedophilic disorder to be given, DSM requires a 5-year age difference between the perpetrator and young person and that the perpetrator is age 16 years or older.

The age of sexual consent is socio-culturally determined, and has been subject to change over time and across countries. It is not based on biological norms of attraction. A majority of men find post-pubescent girls of any age to be physically attractive, although they generally inhibit expression of this attraction (O'Donnell et al. 2014). Evidence of this can certainly be found in history. Early Greek, Roman, and Samurai warrior writings frequently referred to what would now be considered paedophilic relations between men and young boys. At the beginning of the twentieth century, the age of consent was 12 years in most countries. Since then, the age of consent has generally increased, although some countries have resisted or delayed this change. In 2014, the age of sexual consent in Bulgaria, for example, was 14 years, while it rose from 14 to 16 years in Canada only in 2008.

Paedophilic behaviours vary from looking but not touching to oral sex and touching of genitals. Penetrative sex is more common in older children, and is frequently instigated following a period of grooming or preparing the child. The prevalence of paedophile behaviour is, for obvious reasons, somewhat difficult to ascertain with any accuracy. However, Seto (2004) estimated that less than 5 per cent of adult males engaged in paedophile behaviour and a much smaller proportion did so exclusively. A much smaller proportion (between 0.4 and 4 per cent of known sexual offenders) are female. Ward et al. (1995) considered there to be broadly two types of paedophiles: those they referred to as 'situational offenders' who engage in paedophile behaviour at times of stress and frequently offend with family members, and 'paedophilic offenders' who have a larger number of victims beyond the family, are more motivated to offend, and hold strongly pro-paedophile attitudes.

Case formulation

Mr J was a 30-year-old man, admitted to hospital following a period of severe depression. Before this time he had been a teacher in the north of England. Some months before he came to the notice of the mental health services, his name was found on a distribution list for child pornography, his house was raided, and paedophile materials were found on his computer. He was charged and found guilty of using child pornography. He was dismissed from his job. He was married at the time, but was immediately asked to leave the marital home and his wife began divorce proceedings. He moved to London, where he could be 'lost among the crowd'. There, he became profoundly depressed, and was admitted to hospital for treatment of his depression.

Long-term antecedents
Mr J was homosexual. During his adolescence he had no sexual relationships with either boys or girls. However, while masturbating his imagery focused on young adolescent boys. As he aged and left home to go to university, he found his homosexuality and sexual interest in young boys both shaming and inappropriate. He therefore did not seek sex with young men, but did have a number of age-appropriate homosexual relationships. Unfortunately, these relationships ended disastrously and as a consequence, and in an attempt to conform to both his and his parents' perceived norms, he began to date women. He was able to establish a long-term relationship with a woman with a low sex drive whom he later married. His marriage had been functional and pleasant, but not sexually satisfying. During it, he had regularly used child pornography, with a particular interest in young adolescent boys. He taught physical education at school, so clearly had the opportunity of seeing young boys with little or no clothing. However, he denied ever having abused his positiony, and no complaints had been made against him.

Formulation
Mr J did not fit the 'classic' profile of a paedophile. He was able to develop age-appropriate social (and to a more limited extent sexual) relationships both with men and women. He was not 'driven' to paedophilia as a consequence of an inability to engage with age-appropriate individuals. In addition, he considered his sexual interest to be inappropriate and felt ashamed by it. He considered that child pornography was exploitative and morally unacceptable. Nevertheless, his interest in young boys was maintained by masturbation to their images. His depression was a consequence of the loss of his job and his marriage, the probability that he would never find work again, and the shame he felt as his behaviour had been made public.

Psychosocial explanations

The childhood experiences of paedophiles are difficult to explore, as many embellish negative or abusive experiences to justify their behaviour. In addition, they may offer a series of other justifications for their behaviour, including: denial ('Is it wrong to give a child a hug?'), minimization ('It only happened once'), justification ('I am a boy lover, not a child molester'), and fabrication (activities were 'research for a scholarly project'). Nevertheless, careful and detailed work by Dhawan and Marshall (1996) indicated that around half of men who abuse children were themselves subject to abuse as a child. Why this should translate into later abusive behaviour with others is not clear, although explanations include trying to gain a new identity by becoming an abuser or engaging in an imprinted sexual arousal pattern (Cohen et al. 2002).

Behavioural theories suggest that paedophilia is the outcome of continued pairing of sexual pleasure through masturbation to images of children during childhood and beyond. Unfortunately, this simple explanation fails to explain why as a child or adolescent grows older, the images used in masturbation do not. It also cannot explain the findings of Barbaree and Marshall (1989), who reported that around half their sample of paedophiles evidenced greater sexual responses to images of mature women than those of young children. Of note also was that 15 per cent of non-paedophiles were more aroused by pictures of female children than more mature women. Clearly, there is more to these sexual choices than simply sexual attraction. Finkelhor (1984) suggested four conditions that lead an individual to engage in paedophile behaviour:

- the belief that sex with children is emotionally satisfying;
- the belief that sex with children is sexually satisfying;
- an inability to meet sexual needs in a more socially appropriate manner;
- disinhibited behaviour at times of stress.

This can be considered a 'push–pull' theory, in that the individual is pulled towards young people as a result of their beliefs that they enjoy sex and are easy to befriend and manipulate, and is pushed towards them by their inability to engage with more age-appropriate sexual partners. In a more complex model, Ward and Siegert (2002) identified a number of types of paedophile, each with different motives and 'pathways' to their behaviour:

- *Intimacy deficits*: the individual can engage in age-appropriate sexual behaviour. However, they may be driven to paedophile behaviour when an appropriate partner is not available or during periods of sustained loneliness.
- *Deviant sexual scripts*: the individual prefers age-appropriate sex and equates sexual relationships with emotional intimate relationships. However, they fear rejection by adults. When they feel lonely or want emotional intimacy, they seek sex with children to avoid these threats.
- *Antisocial cognitions*: the individual holds strong antisocial beliefs and engaging in inappropriate sexual activity forms an exciting way of expressing their antisocial attitudes.
- *Multiple pathway dysfunction*: the 'classic' paedophile. The individual prefers sex with children. In addition, they lack the intimacy and social skills necessary to engage in age-appropriate sexual behaviour. They engage in age-inappropriate

sexual behaviour to reduce dysphoria, and consider children to be sexual beings that enjoy sex and have the ability to actively choose to be involved in sexual acts.

Pithers (1990) focused on the short-term process leading to high-risk behaviours that are relevant to some of these groups. He noted the desire to engage in paedophile behaviour is frequently triggered by low mood, and forms an attempt to reduce this dysphoria. As a consequence, an individual may enter a high-risk situation, often as a consequence of a series of seemingly irrelevant decisions that place them in increasing proximity to potential victims. Once in this situation, they are overwhelmed by the potentially rewarding excitement associated with paedophile acts. They focus on these rather than the long-term negative outcomes to the situation, and as a result engage in some form of paedophile behaviour. Once the immediate 'rush' has receded, they may once more experience remorse, but feel out of control of their behaviour, a negative mood state that may trigger the cycle again.

Treatment

Paedophilic behaviour is against the law and subject to legal sanctions. In addition to imprisonment, sex offenders in many countries are placed on a 'register' that records a number of details about them, including their address: failure to register can result in imprisonment or fine. The aim of the register is to ensure that the whereabouts of all potential sex offenders is known. This ensures they do not live too close to risky areas such as schools and that the police can monitor them as appropriate. In the UK, parents, guardians, and third parties can now enquire whether a person who has access to a child is a registered sex offender or poses a risk to the child, although access to information remains at the discretion of the police. 'Megan's law' in some US states goes one step further, requiring individuals to tell their neighbours they are a paedophile and to place a notice in their window with this information. Perhaps because of the potential problems that can result from this disclosure, the known whereabouts of paedophiles is much lower in the USA than in the UK.

Knowing the location of paedophiles may have been less pertinent if paedophilia had proven amenable to change. However, many paedophiles do not volunteer for treatment, up to 86 per cent drop out from treatment (Larochelle et al. 2011), and the effectiveness of treatment programmes is far from guaranteed. Perhaps the most radical form of treatment involves castration or neurosurgery, both of which have been used in the past but are now deemed unethical. Drugs may provide a less permanent means of reducing sexual desire, but do not change the object of that desire. Androgen blocking drugs have proven moderately successful, although quality data are lacking. In one of few studies, Rösler and Witztum (1998) examined the impact of monthly drug injections of a gonadotropin-releasing hormone combined with supportive psychotherapy for up to $3\frac{1}{2}$ years in a series of 30 patients. All participants reported a reduction in inappropriate sexual fantasies and a reduction to zero 'incidents' per month while taking the medication. An alternative medication involves the use of luteinizing hormone-releasing hormone (LHRH) agonists, which also prevent the production of testosterone, and have similar levels of effect. Of course, treatment does not come without its problems, which as well as sexual dysfunction include loss of body hair, increased size of testes, hot flushes, mood swings, breast growth, and weight gain. For these reasons, as well as the desire to reoffend, many individuals choose not to receive this treatment or stop taking it once initiated.

Psychological interventions have also proven of mixed effectiveness. Behavioural interventions have involved aversion therapy, which has proven relatively ineffective, and masturbatory retraining. In this, the individual initiates a sexual response using their favoured imagery (which may include inappropriate images). However, once initiated the individual masturbates until orgasm while thinking more appropriate images. The aim is to condition sexual excitement to the experience of appropriate adult sexual imagery. While this may not present the ethical challenges of aversion therapy, it has proven no more effective, and it is used relatively sparingly (Fagan et al. 2002).

The dominant psychological approach now involves the use of relapse prevention. This involves teaching participants to:

- identify situations in which they are at high risk of offending;
- get out of the risky situation;
- consider lapses as something to be learned from;
- identify factors that led to relapse and plan how these could be avoided in the future.

Unfortunately, while this approach (combined with attempts at changing **core beliefs** associated with offending) may be the best we have, data to support its use are limited. Nevertheless, what evidence there is suggests this is the most effective treatment presently available, halving re-offence rates up to a year following treatment (Lösel and Schmucker 2005). Overall, around 11 per cent of treated offenders (by whatever treatment) are known to have re-offended; the equivalent figure for those not treated is 17 per cent.

Chapter summary

1. Drug abuse results in impairments in some aspects of life. Drug dependence implies a biological dependence resulting in withdrawal symptoms following cessation.
2. The key neural system involved in all forms of addiction involves the mesolimbic and mesocortical pathways. The key neurotransmitter is dopamine.
3. Alcohol dependence is also associated with its effects on GABA within the hypothalamus and sympathetic nervous system.
4. Consumption of alcohol is influenced by a variety of psychosocial factors, including purchasing rounds, stress, and addictive beliefs. Risk is also associated with genetic factors.
5. Pharmacological treatment of alcohol dependence involves drugs such as antidipstrotrophics, which induce significant aversive symptoms following alcohol consumption, and opioid agonists that reduce cravings.
6. Psychological treatment involves either complete abstinence or controlled drinking. Approaches include the Minnesota model, CBT, and motivational interviewing.

7. Cannabis is a widely used drug. While most users will experience no harm, some individuals may become dependent on the drug, and some may develop psychosis. Genetic factors significantly influence risk for psychosis.
8. The impact of psychological interventions for cannabis-dependent users is modest.
9. Heroin impacts on both dopamine and endorphin activity within the brain.
10. Interventions targeted at heroin users have frequently adopted a harm reduction approach, involving, for example, needle exchange schemes and prescription of safer alternatives.
11. The effectiveness of both pharmacological and psychological interventions is modest.
12. Gambling can become addictive and is influenced by the same neural systems as drugs.
13. Risk for gambling disorder is associated with a range of psychosocial factors, including high levels of impulsivity, social norms that support gambling, and (more proximally) low mood.
14. CBT approaches have proven effective in helping people control their gambling.
15. Transvestic disorder involves men dressing as women and a degree of associated distress.
16. Psychoanalytic explanations implicate a failure to resolve the Oedipal complex. The behavioural model appears to be the best single cause model.
17. Few treatment studies have been reported, although some people experiencing distress as a result of their behaviour may show some benefit from CBT.
18. Gender dysphoria involves feeling trapped in a body of the wrong gender.
19. It becomes evident early in life, and although some individuals become more comfortable with their gender, can be a strong and consistent experience.
20. Treatment usually involves gender reassignment, the outcomes of which are generally positive.
21. Paedophilic behaviour involves individuals over the age of 15 years. It may involve fantasy, touching or penetrative sex.
22. A number of complex models of its development have been proposed, including Finkelhor's four conditions model and Ward and Siegert's identification pathways to paedophilia.
23. Responses to paedophilia include legal, social, and psychological measures. Response prevention appears to be the most effective psychological approach, although its impact remains modest.

Further reading

Aard, T., Polashek, D. and Beech, A. (2006) *Theories of Sexual Offending*. Chichester: Wiley.

Jones, W. (2012) *Grayson Perry: Portrait of the artist as a young girl*. London: Random House.

Långström, N., Enebrink, P., Laurén, E.M. et al. (2013) Preventing sexual abusers of children from reoffending: systematic review of medical and psychological interventions, *British Medical Journal*, 347: f4630.

Marlatt, G.A. and Donovan, D.M. (2008) *Relapse Prevention: Maintenance strategies in the treatment of addictive behaviors*. New York: Guilford Press.

Nutt, D. (2012) *Drugs – Without the Hot Air: Minimising the harms of legal and illegal drugs*. Cambridge: UIT.

Peterson, T. and McBride, A. (eds.) (2005) *Working with Substance Misusers: A guide to theory and practice*. London: Routledge.

Chapter 13

Mind and body

This chapter considers a number of disorders involving both mind and body. It starts by addressing conditions in which individuals experience undue anxiety in relation to their perceived physical health or appearance. It then examines a mysterious and relatively little understood disorder, conversion disorder, characterized by neurological symptoms such as paralysis or pain in the absence of any known medical pathology. Finally, it considers the cognitive, behavioural, and emotional consequences of a condition with a clear neurological cause: Alzheimer's disease.

By the end of this chapter, you should have an understanding of the causes and interventions relevant to the following disorders:

- Somatic symptom disorder
- Illness anxiety disorder
- Body dysmorphic disorder
- Conversion disorder
- Alzheimer's disease

Somatic symptom disorder

Somatic symptom disorder is characterized by the experience of physical symptoms that cause distress in the absence of any known physical pathology. An individual with the disorder typically makes repeated and frequent visits to their doctor complaining of a range of physical symptoms. They are often referred to hospital consultants to ensure there really is no organic cause for the symptoms, but also, in many cases, to ease the pressure on family doctors to 'do something' about the symptoms the individual is experiencing. These may be diffuse, can cause considerable disability and distress, and include:

- *Gastrointestinal*: nausea, vomiting, abdominal pain.
- *Sexual*: painful sensations, pain during sex.
- *Pseudoneurological*: amnesia, difficulty swallowing, dizziness, difficulty walking,
- *Pain*: diffuse pain throughout the body or limbs, headaches, 'pins and needles'.
- *Heart and lungs*: difficulties breathing, palpitations, chest pain.

Somatic symptom disorder was previously known as somatization disorder, with abridged somatization disorder a milder form of the disorder. Prevalence rates among children and young people admitted to paediatric hospital services can be high as 7 per cent (Janiak-Baluch and Lehmkuhl 2013). Among people admitted to medical wards, the prevalence of the disorder can be as high as 5 per cent (4 per cent of men; 8 per cent of women; Fink et al. 2004). Around 0.1–0.7 per cent of the general population will have the disorder (Creed and Barsky 2004), while nearly 20 per cent of patients attending their general practitioner in Australia were considered to have somatic complaints 'mostly explained by psychological disturbance' (Clarke et al. 2008). It often co-occurs with other anxiety disorders and can last a considerable time.

Case formulation: somatic symptom disorder

Theresa was a woman in her late fifties. She lived with her son in a working-class area of Bristol. At the time she was seen by a psychologist, she had been complaining of complex and distressing 'physical symptoms' for over 10 years. They included tingling down both sides of her body, dizziness, feeling weak, headaches, and collapsing. Sometimes the symptoms became worse, sometimes better, but never disappeared. At times, they were sufficient to stop her leaving the house.

Repeated tests failed to find a physical cause for her problems. Every family doctor in her local area had struck her off their list of patients because of her very frequent visits. They felt unable to treat her and had become increasingly frustrated and then frankly annoyed by her. She was the classic 'heart sink patient', who they could not help, but who took up significant amounts of their time. She had also sought treatment from a variety of alternative practitioners, including herbalists, chiropractors, reflexologists, and shiatsu practitioners. None had been of help.

She lived with her 40-year-old son, who spent much of his time out of the house or in his own room. She occasionally socialized with one or two long-term psychiatric patients she had met through her contact with the psychiatric services. She was aware that she had worn out her other friends, recounting her worries and symptoms, who now refused to see her. She rarely left the house, and then only to go shopping at her local shops.

When first seen by a psychologist, she was able to provide a diary of her symptoms, recorded on an hourly basis over many months. Investigation of relevant psychological issues proved difficult, as the sessions were, at least initially, somewhat overwhelmed by her repeated descriptions of her physical symptoms. However, a time line of key issues did emerge.

(continued)

Long-term antecedents
Theresa came from a working-class family. She had three siblings, and a history of illness within the family. Her father worked long hours, and competition for parental attention was strong. She was unhappy at times, feeling neglected and estranged from her parents and she had few friends. She was often sick as a child, and gained some attention within the family at these times. She left school with no qualifications, but met a man who she married and with whom she had a baby. Unfortunately, the marriage was unhappy and she described him as 'a little odd'. She divorced him after a few years and brought up the child on her own. She described some physical health problems at the time of her marriage, which gradually became worse in the following years.

Short-term antecedents
Theresa's son had lived with her all his life. He was relatively happy, had a job and good social relationships, and had made it clear that he wanted to move out of the house to develop on his own. However, he was also concerned about his mother's health and continued to live at home in case she became acutely ill. He coped with living at home by spending much of his time in his own room to avoid her constant complaints of physical problems.

Formulation
Theresa was brought up in a family of little emotional warmth, in which the emotional needs of the children were not recognized or responded to. She did, however, gain some parental attention when she was ill. She learned to signal emotional distress, and to gain emotional support, by reporting physical symptoms. Her experience and reporting of symptoms varied across her life, with the distress associated with a poor marriage and subsequent divorce being obvious triggers. The most recent contributor to her symptoms was her social isolation and worry that her son would leave home, leaving her with little social contact. Her symptoms could therefore be seen as both her typical response to stress and a means of keeping her son close to home and a source of companionship. The style of her attachment to him could be described as anxious attachment, as she feared that if he left home he would also leave her. Her total focus on her symptoms, to the extent of maintaining a diary in which she recorded them, increased her awareness of her symptoms and their impact. The symptoms were therefore a response to stress, formed a core attentional focus from which she found it difficult to withdraw, and had the function of keeping her son close.

Psychosocial explanations

Psychoanalytical theories of somatic symptom disorder focus on childhood experiences. Guthrie (1996), for example, suggested that poor mother–child relationships make the individual deficient in their use of imagination and the language they use to describe and control stress. This is conceptualized in terms of physical sensations: feeling tense, having stomach-ache, being light-headed, and so on. They also find it difficult to develop appropriate adult relationships, seeking out partners who are willing to act as their carer, and adopting the role of the invalid. The reporting of physical symptoms therefore serves both as an expression of emotional distress and as a means of eliciting the care of one's partner. There is evidence of maltreatment during the childhood of many people with somatic symptom disorder (e.g. Spitzer et al. 2008). In addition, van Dijke (2012) found several modes of dysfunctional emotional regulation linked to childhood adversity in people diagnosed with the disorder.

From a more psychobiological perspective, Rief and Barsky (2005) argued that all bodily organs continuously produce sensory information that is transmitted to higher cortical structures. For most people, most of the time, these sensations are filtered out as background 'sensory noise'. Attention is only paid to exceptions to those expected. The level at which this filter is set differs across individuals. People who are anxious about their health, for example, may notice and pay attention to more sensations than those without such concerns. The individual may then fall into a repeated cycle of checking and paying continued attention to these sensations, as they are thought to be 'symptoms' that imply the presence of some sort of health threat. This process inevitably results in significant and prolonged anxiety.

Risk for somatic symptom disorder is influenced by the experience of parental illness and childhood illness, particularly if this is associated with a lack of parental care. But other, more subtle carer–child interactions may also influence risk. Craig et al. (2004), for example, observed that mothers with somatic symptom disorder were emotionally flatter and gave their children less attention than other mothers during a free play period. However, they were more responsive than other mothers when their child played with a medical box. Interestingly, these psychosocial factors appear to be the prime determinant of risk. There is little evidence that neurological or genetic factors have a significant role in the disorder, although inflammatory processes within the spinal cord and hypothalamus may be implicated in the heightened perception of pain (Dimsdale and Dantzer 2007).

Treatment

Somatic symptom disorder has proven hard to treat, and there are relatively few intervention trials indicating the best treatment approach. One approach, reported by Lidbeck (2003), involved relaxation training and education designed to change attribution of symptoms from being signs of health problems to being signs of stress. Compared with no treatment, the programme achieved significant reductions in worry and medication use immediately following treatment and at 6-month follow-up. Escobar et al. (2007) examined the effectiveness of a CBT programme targeted at a people with medically explained symptoms (insufficient to warrant a diagnosis of somatic symptom disorder), comparing it with usual care. By the end of therapy, 60 per cent of the intervention group reported their physical symptoms to be significantly improved. This compared with 25 per cent in the control condition. Unfortunately, this benefit had faded at 6-month follow-up. In another group of people with relatively low levels of symptoms, Moreno et al. (2013) compared the effectiveness of group or individual CBT, and found the individual intervention to be more effective on both measures of somatic symptoms and mood.

Working with: somatic symptom disorder

Working with Theresa (see the Case formulation box above) proved a complex challenge, as she did not accept the formulation described. If she had, then the ideal approach may have been:

- Help Theresa and her son gain insight into the psychological factors contributing to her problems.
- Teach cognitive strategies to challenge her worries.
- Teach strategies such as mindfulness to help Theresa tolerate her distress. Identify other ways of distracting from distress and worries.
- Negotiate with her son a mutually agreeable plan in which he would leave home, but maintain regular contact with his mother

The actual intervention was more complex and involved more people:

- Establishing regular and pre-arranged appointments with one family doctor during which Theresa could discuss her symptoms. Both Theresa and the doctor acknowledged that these appointments would not result in a 'cure', but would limit the number of repeated and increasingly fractious appointments.
- Leaving the house more often to engage in things to distract from her worries. This included going out with one of her friends and attending a day hospital one day a week, joining in the activities there.
- Using conversations with friends and her son to discuss non-health-related issues: discussion of her symptoms at these times was not 'allowed'.
- Her son agreed to consider negotiating leaving home but only after he could see some improvement in his mother's health.
- Regular meetings with a community mental health nurse to discuss issues of a psychological nature and help Theresa keep to the plan.

The intervention proved reasonably successful, but was not without its problems. While Theresa did reduce her visits to GP surgeries, she increased her attendance at the local hospital emergency medical units: at one time attending three in one week. This was addressed through Socratic dialogue. Her symptoms had lasted many years without becoming so serious they had required medical treatment, and her visits to doctors had not resulted in any effective treatment. Accordingly, delaying seeing a doctor by, say, a week would be unlikely to lead to a sudden deterioration in her health or stop her accessing an effective cure. She agreed to reduce her visits to the hospitals. To help her cope with the consequent anxiety, she talked with friends made in the day hospital on the phone about non-health-related issues or kept herself busy to distract from her worries. This proved an effective approach. Over the following 6 months, she showed some improvements. Her mood lifted, she was more social, and went on day trips with friends.

> She focused less on her symptoms and did not let them dominate her life as much as they had done. She still experienced unusual physical sensations, but was better able to cope with them. Her son continued to live at home, but life was better as Theresa talked less about her symptoms and they spent more time together.

Illness anxiety disorder

The difference between somatic symptom disorder and illness anxiety disorder (previously known as hypochondriasis) is subtle. People with somatic symptom disorder experience various unexplained symptoms, whereas those with illness anxiety disorder both experience 'symptoms' and/or consider they have an illness. They may also believe they may develop an illness in the future, even if they have no ongoing symptoms. They are highly sensitive to medical or health-related information, suggesting they may have a disease, and highly resistant to counter-information. Importantly, they do not experience such anxiety in relation to other parts of their life. The disorder has a slightly lower prevalence than somatic symptom disorder, averaging around 1.5 per cent of the general population and 1.5 per cent of men and 6 per cent of women admitted to general medical wards (Fink et al. 2004).

Psychosocial explanations

Unsurprisingly, perhaps, risk factors for illness anxiety disorder are similar to those for somatic symptom disorder. They include high levels of physical and sexual abuse, inattentive parenting, high levels of childhood sickness, parental overprotection, and encouragement of sick-role behaviour (Portegijs et al. 1996).

Freud (1914) considered the disorder to result from challenges to the 'ego libido': the love of one's own body. He contended that if this becomes excessive, the individual's focus on external sources of love diminishes, and they develop anxiety about their physical state. They focus on the love of their body and physicality, while at the same time becoming anxious that they may lose the object of their love. Accordingly, they focus not only on the good things about their body, but also on potential health threats that may destroy it.

A second model, proposed by Stuart and Noyes (1999), is similar to the psychoanalytic model of somatic symptom disorder described above. That is, the model considers illness anxiety disorder to involve seeking emotional care from family and friends through reporting physical complaints or symptoms. According to Stuart and Noyes, lack of consistent parental care causes a child to view others as unreliable caregivers and to develop anxious and insecure attachments. Parents who are unresponsive to psychological needs may respond more to physical ones. As a consequence, these become the child's primary means of gaining adult attention and feelings of attachment. Unfortunately, the corollary of this strategy is that they also fail to learn other ways of eliciting care and attention from their environment. As an adult, the still insecurely attached person therefore continues to communicate his or her need for care through complaints of illness. Unfortunately, these complaints are frequently ignored, and even viewed with suspicion, potentially reinforcing the original fear of lack of attachment and supportive relationships.

In a cognitive model of the outcome of these childhood experiences, Warwick and Salkovskis (1990) suggested the experience of stress or noticing bodily signs can activate faulty, alarming or pessimistic cognitive schemata about health and disease. This leads to a number of sequelae:

- *Selective attention to schema-consistent information*: the individual pays particular attention to physical experiences, including raised heart rate, gastric motility and lumps and bumps such as moles, that are interpreted as signs of disease.
- *Cognitive errors*: disconfirmatory information, such as medical reassurance, is ignored. Instead, the individual focuses on, and ruminates about, the potential adverse health consequences of any experiences they have or 'symptoms' they detect.
- *Physiological changes*: sympathetic nervous system activity may increase due to anxiety the person experiences, resulting in changes in bowel habits, sleeping, and so on. Each 'symptom' confirms the presence of a health problem.
- *Safety behaviours*: these include avoiding activities that trigger health rumination, repeated checking, taking unnecessary preventive medication, and reassurance-seeking. Unfortunately, these safety behaviours serve to maintain the problem, as the person never comes to learn that they are unnecessary.

A variant of this model includes the symptom sensitivity central to somatic symptom disorder. According to Marcus et al. (2006), people with illness anxiety disorder are both more sensitive to physical sensations than the norm, and more likely to label them as symptoms of a medical 'illness'. Focusing on benign bodily sensations increases awareness of them, increases the amount of attention paid to them, and confirms the presence of a disease. This seems a plausible process, but whether such individuals can both experience and accurately detect physical symptoms has been questioned. Steptoe and Noll (1997), for example, found people diagnosed with illness anxiety disorder were actually *less* able to accurately measure their heart rate and sweat gland activity then those with less health concerns. So, such individuals may feel they are sensitive to their body, but this sensitivity may be illusory.

Treatment

Both CBT and acceptance and commitment therapy (ACT) have been used to treat illness anxiety disorder, with some success. Cognitive behaviour therapy adopts the exposure plus response prevention approach, which involves reducing checking behaviour and the frequency of medical consultations. This may be augmented by strategies designed to change fundamental illness beliefs, including behavioural hypothesis testing and cognitive challenge. In a study of this approach, Clark et al. (1998) compared their illness anxiety disorder treatment programme with a non-specific CBT intervention that targeted stress-related cognitions and emotions unrelated to health concerns. Both treatments were more effective than no therapy. In addition, both interventions appeared to have very specific benefits: CBT for illness anxiety disorder resulted in less checking and health anxiety, while stress management reduced levels of reported stress. However, one year after treatment, both interventions appeared equally effective on all measures.

People with illness anxiety disorder may have very fixed illness beliefs that are difficult to address using cognitive challenge. For these people, mindfulness approaches may be of particular benefit. McManus et al. (2012), for example, found a mindfulness-based cognitive therapy intervention to be more effective than usual care. Immediately following the intervention, 47 per cent of the intervention group and 78 per cent of the usual care group met the criteria for a diagnosis of illness anxiety disorder. The gains in the intervention group were even greater at one-year follow-up, with 28 per cent of the intervention group and 75 per cent of the usual care group meeting the same criterion.

Until relatively recently, there was a general consensus among psychiatrists that pharmacotherapy was likely to be of little value to people with illness anxiety disorder. However, some recent attempts have been made to treat the condition using SSRIs, with some short-term success (Fallon et al. 2008). More importantly, perhaps, a study comparing psychological and pharmacological treatments (Greeven et al. 2009) found a better response following CBT than medication. After 16 weeks of treatment, 45 per cent of people in the CBT group achieved significant reductions in symptoms, compared with 30 per cent of those treated with an SSRI and 14 per cent given placebo. At 18-month follow-up, the gains made following therapy were largely maintained, although neither intervention proved better than the other at this time.

Body dysmorphic disorder

Many of us experience some degree of dissatisfaction with our body. Fortunately, few of us are so unhappy that this dissatisfaction reaches pathological proportions. Bohne et al. (2002), for example, found that while 74 per cent of American university students had body image concerns, only 29 per cent were preoccupied by them, and only 4 per cent met the diagnostic criteria for body dysmorphic disorder. This disorder involves a preoccupation with an imagined defect in appearance that is associated with significant distress or handicap in social and other situations. This preoccupation and strength of belief can be so strong and resistant to change in some individuals, it can be considered a delusional belief on a par with those found in psychotic disorders.

The targets of concern differ according to gender, and reflect societal norms of desired physical characteristics. Accordingly, men typically worry about their body build, genitals, and hair; women are preoccupied with their legs, hips, and breasts (Phillips et al. 2006). As a result of their concerns, people with body dysmorphic disorder frequently camouflage the perceived defect (through clothing, make-up) or change it through excessive exercise, dieting or surgery. They will avoid social situations in which the apparent defect will be exposed and often feel anxious or self-conscious – so much so that Didie et al. (2008) found that 80 per cent of people with the disorder reported some degree of impairment in work, while 39 per cent reported not having worked in the previous month as a consequence of appearance concerns. Around a quarter of the people with the disorder will attempt suicide (K. Phillips et al. 2007). Young people may also engage in ritualistic behaviours typically associated with extreme anxiety, including body rocking, skin picking, as well as experiencing poor sleep, appetite and concentration, lack of empathy, lethargy, social withdrawal, aggressive outbursts, and suicidal ideation (Phillips 1996). These symptoms are similar to those in a range of other disorders, indicating both the trans-theoretical nature of the problem and difficulties in diagnosis. Rates of spontaneous remission are low (Phillips et al. 2008).

Psychosocial explanations

The APA (2013) considers body dysmorphic disorder to be an obsessive-compulsive disorder. It does so because the preoccupations held by people with the disorder resemble obsessions. They are anxiety-producing, recurrent, and difficult to control. In addition, such individuals engage in time-consuming, repetitive, compulsive behaviours, including mirror checking and measuring the perceived defect, and avoid situations likely to trigger body dysmorphic cognitions, such as social situations, mirrors, and posing for photographs. According to Rosen (1996), this focus on physical appearance stems from critical events related to an individual's appearance during childhood or early adolescence, the most common being teased about weight or size. Other, more general, vulnerability factors include being neglected as a child, with consequent feelings of being unloved and rejected (Phillips 1991). According to Rosen, these critical events activate dysfunctional assumptions about physical appearance and their implications for self-worth and acceptance. Once established, the disorder may be maintained by selective attention to perceived physical problems or information that supports this belief. Rehearsal of negative and distorted self-statements results in them becoming automatic and believable. Finally, the positive emotional responses associated with avoidance, checking, and reassurance-seeking behaviours reinforce and maintain the condition.

A psychoanalytic perspective suggests that body dysmorphic disorder arises from an individual's unconscious displacement of sexual or emotional conflict or feelings of guilt and poor self-image to specific parts of the body (Sobanski and Schmidt 2000). The displacement is thought to occur because the underlying problem is so threatening to the ego that it is unconsciously displaced into the more ego-acceptable issue of appearance. However, the body part of concern, such as the nose, will represent another, more emotionally threatening body part, such as the penis.

Biological explanations

Both body dysmorphic disorder and obsessive-compulsive disorder are thought to be underpinned by the same neurological processes: dysregulation of serotonergic and dopaminergic activity associated with the mediation of threat and anxiety (see Chapter 11). The role of these neurotransmitters in body dysmorphic disorder is largely justified by the effectiveness of treatments using SSRIs, discussed below. Evidence from twin studies indicates a significant genetic risk, with the genes thought to overlap those that moderate risk for obsessive-compulsive disorder (Monzani et al. 2012).

Treatment

Many people with body dysmorphic disorder approach plastic surgeons to try to rid themselves of the supposed flaws in their appearance. However, this approach is out of the reach of most people, and even among those that do receive surgery, the outcome of the treatment is likely to be disappointing.

The most common psychological treatment involves CBT, following the exposure plus response prevention approach. Exposure to avoided situations includes exposure of the individual's body or their perceived defect in social and other relevant situation, often in a graded exposure programme. Prevention of checking or self-reassuring behaviours is used to counteract checking rituals. Finally, cognitive restructuring, in which dysfunctional thoughts are identified and then challenged, is a key component of any intervention. Research into the effectiveness of CBT is still rather sparse, although optimistic (Prazeres et al. 2013). Rosen et al. (1995), for example, achieved an 82 per cent success rate immediately following treatment, and 77 per cent at follow-up. This compared with a 7 per cent improvement rate during a no-treatment phase of their study. Evidence from pharmacological trials is also sparse. In their review of the relevant pharmacological trials, Somashekar et al. (2013) concluded that SSRIs were an effective treatment of body dysmorphic (and illness anxiety) disorder, but also noted that conclusive evidence was still lacking.

Conversion disorder

In one of the most intriguing of all mental health conditions, people with conversion disorder present with striking neurological symptoms such as weakness, lack of coordination, paralysis, sensory disorders or memory loss, in the absence of any medical pathology. In addition, despite their significant symptoms, many appear totally unconcerned about their symptoms: a process labelled *la belle indifférence*. Up to 4 per cent of those attending neurology outpatient clinics in the UK are thought to have conversion disorders (Perkin 1989). Prevalence rates in the general population are more difficult to determine, but are estimated to be around 0.3 per cent. Women are more likely to be diagnosed with the condition than men. Bizarrely, Ahmad et al. (2008) found the rate of admissions to hospital with a diagnosis of conversion disorder was highest during a full moon. Another odd finding was reported by Burneo et al. (2003), who identified a key diagnostic feature of the disorder to be what they termed 'the teddy bear' sign: 87 per cent of the 903 cases they diagnosed with conversion disorder brought a teddy bear to the diagnostic testing process.

The disorder has an equally strange history. Originally termed 'hysteria', the condition was thought to result from the uterus travelling around the body, resulting (depending where it was in the body) in symptoms including feelings of suffocation, paralysis, fits, fainting, and an inability to eat. Treatment involved repositioning the uterus through physical manipulation. The condition was also evident in the First World War, when it was known as 'shell shock'. This condition, exemplified by blindness, paralysis, and profound amnesias, was originally thought to be a consequence of micro-haemorrhaging in the brain as a result of the shock of shell bursts close to those affected. However, autopsies revealed no such pathology, and the condition was later ascribed to conversion disorder.

Incidents of so-called 'mass hysteria', when groups of individuals develop strange and unexplained symptoms, are also fairly common. One of the most famous involved the so-called 'toxic lady' in California. Admitted for cervical cancer, it was claimed that her body and breath exuded an odd garlicky smell. Unfortunately, the woman became acutely ill while in hospital, and during her unsuccessful treatment one of her physicians felt faint and left the room. A second member of staff who checked on the health of this physician also fainted. Another clinician also fainted. Over the next few days, several other staff members developed symptoms including loss of consciousness, shortness of breath, and muscle spasms. Findings that subsequent blood tests were normal and that more women than men were affected by these symptoms led to the conclusion that these symptoms were essentially 'hysterical' in nature.

Psychological explanations

Psychoanalytic explanations consider the condition to be the result of an unconscious ego conflict being converted to physical symptoms (Freud and Breuer 2004). Perhaps the most famous case of conversion disorder is that of Anna O. She became ill while nursing her terminally ill father. Her illness began with a severe cough, and subsequently included paralysis of the extremities of her right side, disturbances of vision, lapses of consciousness, and hallucinations. Her original therapist, Joseph Breuer, believed these symptoms were the physical expression of her resentment at having to look after her father. Unfortunately, Anna also began to believe she was pregnant with Breuer's baby – an example of transference, indicating she was in love with Breuer. As a consequence, care passed to Freud, who believed some of her hysterical symptoms were the result of these secret sexual desires and the need to maintain contact with Breuer.

Although eschewing the idea of unconscious processes, behavioural explanations of Anna O's disorder are quite similar to this formulation. These suggest that conversion symptoms are functional and under the control of the individual expressing them. They are shaped and maintained by operant conditioning. In the case of soldiers in the trenches, this involved avoidance of situations in which they could be killed. For Anna, it involved maintaining contact with someone she loved. Central to this assumption is that individuals actively choose to engage in these behaviours. Attempts to determine whether this is the case have tried to find 'loopholes' in the behaviours of people presenting with conversion disorders. In one such analysis, Zimmerman and Grosz (1966) asked a patient with hysterical blindness to identify which of three visual stimuli was being presented to them. Initially, the patient performed at below chance levels: itself somewhat suspicious. However, after the patient was 'allowed' to overhear a conversation made by a confederate suggesting that 'the doctors reckon that the patient can see because he makes fewer correct responses by chance than a blind man would make', his performance improved significantly. This was taken to indicate the individual was dissimilating.

Biological explanations

A third, neurological, explanation of conversion disorder involves disordered cortical or subcortical functioning. A small number of studies have shown that attempts at movement of paralysed limbs by people with hysterical paralysis appear to be countered by alternate and opposing neurological processes (Vuilleumier et al. 2001). In one example of this process, Marshall et al. (1997) identified the neural processes of a lady with conversion disorder when asked to move her paralysed left leg.

- *Preparing* to move her leg resulted in activation of her left premotor cortex and both cerebellar hemispheres – the same processes that occurred when she was preparing to move her non-paralysed right leg. The authors interpreted this as an indication of her 'genuine' preparation to move her left leg.
- *Trying* to move her leg resulted in activation of the appropriate movement-related brain areas, including the left dorsolateral prefrontal cortex and both cerebellar hemispheres. There was no activation of the right premotor areas or the right primary sensorimotor cortex necessary for movement. However, areas of the brain not

usually involved in movement (the right cingulated cortex and right orbitofrontal cortex) *did* show activation. The authors proposed that this activation somehow inhibited movement of her left leg.

These neurological processes are similar to those found in people placed under hypnosis and who are given hypnotic commands that mimic the paralysis of conversion disorder (Halligan et al. 2000), findings that led Oakley (1999) to speculate that conversion disorder may be similar to some forms of hypnotic process. He marshalled a number of arguments in favour of this hypothesis:

- Many 'symptoms' evident in hypnotized individuals are similar to those reported in conversion disorder. These include paralysis, increased or decreased pain sensation, and blindness.
- Both hypnotized individuals and many people with conversion disorder do not appear to be concerned about their odd symptoms.
- The physical states associated with both conversion disorder and hypnosis involve a lack of volition. People would like to move but cannot. 'They say "I cannot"; it looks like "I will not"; but it is "I cannot will".'

Based on these findings, Oakley provided a plausible neural explanation for what the behaviourists considered to be 'faking' symptoms. His contention was based on cognitive models that indicate much of our behaviour is controlled by unconscious processes (e.g. Baddeley 2007). Whether or not this information becomes conscious is governed by an executive system that controls conscious attentional and other processes. In the case of hypnotic suggestion, the executive system may withhold sensory information from the individual's consciousness so the person is genuinely unaware of visual or painful stimuli, despite having an intact sensory system. Similarly, it may unconsciously inhibit muscular activation to produce paralysis. Oakley suggests that the lack of conscious control over movement or sensory awareness in conversion disorder may result from the same process – but in this case, not as a result of an external 'command' (as in hypnosis), but as a result of unconscious internal processes. In this case, the executive 'chooses' in some way to allow or disallow various information into awareness. This may be the result of a variety of unconscious 'internal dynamics and motivations in the interests of providing a solution to what may be an otherwise insoluble psychological problem' (Oakley 1999). In this model, the condition is indeed functional, in that it involves a means of escape from unmanageable stresses, but it is not a conscious or deliberate 'faking'. What is not yet clear is *why* this extreme stress response may be evoked in some individuals.

Treatment

Its rarity and the wide range of problems associated with conversion disorder makes formal randomized controlled treatment trials difficult to conduct. Nevertheless, Moene et al. (2003) was able to assign people with motor conversion disorders (including paralysis, gait disturbance, **aphonia**, and pseudo-epileptic seizures) into either ten sessions of hypnosis focusing on suggestions of symptom reduction and age regression to enable emotional insight, or a waiting list control condition. By the end of therapy, those in the hypnosis condition were more improved on measures including video assessments of their specific symptoms and self-report quality of life. These gains were maintained up to their 6-month follow-up assessment. In an interesting alternative approach, Ataoglu et al. (2003) used paradoxical intention (see Chapter 5) to encourage participants diagnosed with pseudoseizures to maintain or even exacerbate their symptoms. After 6 weeks of treatment, 14 of 15 patients who completed the psychological treatment showed some improvement; of 15 treated with diazepam, 9 showed improvement.

Conversion disorder is not generally treated using pharmacological interventions. However, one physical treatment may prove to be of benefit. Transcranial magnetic stimulation (TMS) involves increasing neuronal activity in targeted areas of the brain for brief periods of time while an electric coil is placed against the scalp. In a study involving four individuals, Schönfeldt-Lecuona et al. (2006) reported some improvements on measures of limb paralysis following this treatment; one patient was completely improved, two evidenced some degree of improvement, while one showed no improvement. The potential impact of the placebo effect in such studies suggests these findings should be considered with caution. Nevertheless, TMS may be of benefit in some cases of conversion disorder.

Alzheimer's disease

Alzheimer's disease is the most common form of dementia. It can start at any age, but risk for the disorder increases markedly with age. It has been estimated to affect 2–10 per cent of the population aged over 65 years, and at least 20 per cent of those aged over 80 (Yamada et al. 2001).

It is a progressive disease, involving a gradual loss of memory. Recent memories are lost before remote ones, which are thought to be more resistant to loss due to rehearsal over time. However, even these memories are forgotten as the condition progresses. Early forgetfulness becomes a pathologically poor memory for present events, daily routine, and even family members. Word-finding difficulties are common. In its final stages, Alzheimer's disease destroys the ability to communicate in any meaningful way. The APA identified four key characteristics in its progressed form:

- *Amnesia*: loss of memory.
- *Aphasia*: language disturbance.
- *Apraxia*: impaired ability to carry out motor activities despite intact motor function.
- *Agnosia*: failure to recognize or identify objects despite intact sensory function.

In addition, the individual experiences significant disturbances in executive functioning, and has marked difficulties in planning, organizing, and sequencing their activities.

In the early stages of Alzheimer's disease, levels of insight are high. However, as the disease progresses, insight is lost. Loss of memory can lead to confusion, suspicion, and paranoia. Affected individuals may not recognize their loss of ability, and become angry if they are prevented from driving or leaving the house alone. Confusion may be worse at night when cues that orient the individual in time and place are less obvious, and oxygen supply to the brain is at its lowest. This can lead to wandering, placing the individual at considerable risk of harm. Up to 60 per cent of people with dementia are thought to wander (Robinson et al., 2007), and around 40 per cent of these get lost outside the home. Although this can be managed if someone is living with the affected person, it may trigger the need for institutional care. The individual may experience spontaneous changes in mood, including anger and irritability, as well as restlessness and agitation. Over time, they will lose a sense of 'self', and become increasingly dependent on the care of others. Many old people, who may themselves be physically ill or frail, become responsible for the care of people with Alzheimer's within their own home. Many people with the disorder are also admitted into some form of long-term health or social care.

Up to 80 per cent of people who develop dementia experience emotional problems, including depression, anxiety, and sleep disturbances at some time (Lyketsos et al. 2002). As the condition progresses, the person may be unable to report specific symptoms, so diagnosis may be based on observation of symptoms including withdrawal, inactivity, fatigue, and loss of interest. Anxiety-related disorders may be evident through obvious worrying, tension, somatic symptoms, anger, irritability, and agitation. Anxious individuals may have a decreased tolerance of stimulation, and be fearful when experiencing things they no longer understand.

Biological explanations

Alzheimer's disease is the consequence of neurological degeneration. It typically begins in the entorhinal cortex before proceeding to the hippocampus, and then gradually spreading to other regions, particularly the cerebral cortex (Hedden and Gabrieli 2005). As the hippocampal neurons degenerate, short-term memory begins to fail, as does the ability to perform routine tasks. As the disease spreads through the cerebral cortex, it begins to take away language.

This degeneration involves destruction of the neurons by two processes. The first involves damage to amyloid precursor protein (APT), which lies within the neuron cell membranes. These proteins act as a barrier, controlling which substances go in and out of the cells. Damage to APT results in the formation of beta amyloid fragments, which clump together to form amyloid plaques and cause neuronal death by forming tiny channels in neuron membranes through which uncontrolled amounts of calcium can flow. A second structural change in Alzheimer's disease involves the formation of neurofibrillary tangles: abnormal collections of twisted threads inside nerve cells. The chief component of these tangles is a protein called tau. In healthy brains, tau binds and stabilizes microtubules that carry nutrients and molecules from the bodies of the cells to the ends of their axon. In Alzheimer's disease, tau is changed chemically, twisting the microfilaments around each other to form tangles, resulting in failures of the transport system and neuronal death.

In addition to these structural changes, levels of the neurotransmitter acetylcholine, which contributes to memory formation and activity in the hippocampus and cerebral cortex, can fall by up to 90 per cent (Luque and Jaffe 2009). Serotonin and norepinephrine levels may also fall and contribute to sensory disturbances and aggressive behaviour (Zarros et al. 2005), as well as depression and anxiety.

Risk for these neurological changes appears to be influenced by genetic, physical, and behavioural factors. Genetic factors include alleles of the apoE gene, which influences the production of cholesterol within the body, as well as amyloid precursor protein (APP) gene, the presenilin 1 (PSEN1) gene, and the presenilin 2 (PSEN2) gene. Mutations in these genes, however, account for less than 5 per cent of the total number of cases. More modifiable risk factors include high blood pressure, diabetes, high cholesterol levels, being a smoker, and serious head injury (Schipper 2009). A common factor here appears to be factors that influence risk for arterial damage and the development of atheroma. Although the role of aluminium has been controversial for many years, there is an emerging consensus that significant exposure also appears to increase risk of Alzheimer's disease (Gupta et al. 2005).

Treatment

The most common medical treatment of Alzheimer's disease involves increasing levels of acetylcholine uptake in the synaptic cleft by preventing its breakdown by acetyl-cholinesterase. Unfortunately, acetyl-cholinesterase inhibitors, such as Aricept, delay rather than prevent cognitive decline. Only between 40 and 70 per cent of people benefit from cholinesterase inhibitor treatment, its effects may be relatively minor, and they generally last for only 6–12 months (Raina et al. 2008). Accordingly, while they may be of benefit to some people with more progressed disease, they are usually prescribed in the early to mid-stages.

Psychological interventions for people with Alzheimer's disease aim to enhance quality of life and functional ability: they are not seen as curative. One approach, reality orientation (Holden and Woods 1995), aims to maximize function and memory. It involves providing confused elderly people with relevant information to help them maintain an accurate understanding of the world. It has two forms. The first, known as 24-hour reality orientation, uses the environment to provide multiple cues to maximize memory and orientation in time and place: large clocks and calendars, reminders of the name of an institution or ward, the use of name badges, and so on. Interactions with people are used to provide relevant information: 'Hello, Mr Jones. It's Simon here... It's hot outside, like it usually is in July...'. Interactions are simple and specific, repeating information throughout the day and even within conversations. By contrast, classroom reality orientation involves structured meetings of small groups. Despite its rather formal name, these are informal and held in comfortable settings. They aim to maximize orientation and memory through the provision of information, discussion, and the use of multiple cues and modes of information involving, for example, discussion of newspaper clippings, photographs, and so on.

Current affairs

Reality orientation can present difficulties for those trying to implement it, particularly when it may be necessary to remind people of distressing information. Many people with Alzheimer's disease, for example, may forget about the death of a loved one, and in their confusion start looking for them or demanding they come and see them. Proper adherence to reality orientation involves a carer telling them that their loved one is dead. This can be devastating news and cause significant distress. Unfortunately, they may forget this information after a period of time and once more start looking for their loved one, requiring the carer to once more break the news of their loved one's death: a cycle that can be distressing for both the individual and carer. Is this fair and a reasonable way to treat people or, in this case, is ignorance really bliss?

In their review of the effectiveness of reality orientation, Spector et al. (2000) concluded it achieved small but significant benefits on measures of verbal orientation, but that any gains soon dissipated. This rather modest outcome led to the development of a less memory-specific intervention called cognitive stimulation (Woods et al. 2006), with the wider aim of maintaining or improving information processing. This shift is exemplified in questions around photographs of faces. In classroom reality orientation, participants would be asked 'Do you recognize these people?' In cognitive simulation groups, discussion centres around who looks the youngest, what the people may have in common, and so on. In their meta-analysis of 15 studies evaluating this approach, Woods et al. (2012) concluded that significant cognitive gains were achieved and maintained up to 3 months after the end of the groups. Improvements were also found on measures of self-reported quality of life and staff ratings of communication and social interaction.

Two further intervention approaches aim to facilitate emotional adjustment and deal with unresolved conflicts and difficulties the individual may have experienced during their life. Validation therapy involves listening to the individual's concerns and fears, taking time to fully understand and 'validate' them. Discussion is designed to elicit feelings of anger, separation, and loss. Through discussion and empathic responses, the individual is said to feel validated in their feelings and is more able to deal with any unresolved conflicts they may be experiencing. A second approach, reminiscence therapy, aims to facilitate the individual's review and contextualization of their life. McMahon and Rhudick (1964) devised three types of review: story-type reminiscence involving remembering factual memories for pleasure; life-review involving remembering and discussing memories, both good and bad, which come naturally to consciousness; and halo reminiscence involving the repeated recollection of a particular situation involving guilt or despair. These are thought to help resolve past conflicts. Evaluation of both types of therapy lacks a strong research base, and those studies that have been conducted (e.g. Tondi et al. 2007) report both successes and failures.

Psychological interventions for people with dementia who are depressed are necessarily different to those with people who have more intact cognitive function. They typically aim to help carers increase the number of pleasant events the cared for person experiences. This may not be easy for people who, themselves, are often very stressed. For this reason, this approach may be embedded with interventions designed to support carers and teach them skills to manage challenging behaviours and other problems they may encounter. In one such intervention, Teri et al. (1997) gave carers information about dementia, relevant communication skills, and realistic expectations and rationale for the behavioural treatment of dementia. They then focused on identifying, planning, and increasing pleasant events for the depressed individuals. Time was also spent working on strategies to manage behavioural disturbances that could have interfered with the individual engaging in such experiences. This involved an A-B-C model of change: identifying antecedents to the problem behaviours, the behaviour itself, and its consequences (see Chapter 5). Triggers to problem behaviours were changed, as were consequences that tended to reinforce them. Sixty per cent of the depressed individuals showed significant improvements following the programme, compared with 20 per cent of a no intervention control group. The A-B-C approach has also been used in the successful treatment of anxiety (Logsdon et al. 2005), reducing both distress in the person with dementia and carer burden.

A final intervention approach involves working at an environmental level. People with both sensory and memory loss may benefit significantly from care environments that are simplified and full of memory or other cues. One reason for incontinence on wards for elderly people, for example, is that they may forget where the toilets are and do not think to ask members of staff. A simple way to reduce this problem involves using the same brightly coloured doors on all toilets. This may be augmented by the use of appropriate pictures on the door instead of the usual abstract symbols or lines used to identify them. In addition, because people with dementia may not recognize the physical sensation of having a full bladder until it is too late, incontinence may be further reduced by regular prompts to go to the toilet. Environmental cues in the home may be equally important. Regular routines, having things in the same place all day every day, may help people cope with fading memory. One important and relatively recent innovation involves the use of alarm systems and tracking devices for people likely to wander. These new technologies allow individuals more freedom within and outside their home. Although some have questioned this from an ethical or civil liberties perspective, this approach appears acceptable to people in the early stages of dementia (Landau et al. 2010).

Caring for the carers

As has already been noted, Alzheimer's disease impacts not just on the individual with the disorder, but on those involved in their care. Many elderly people, mostly women, care for people with dementia in their own home. Caring often continues until the disease is far progressed. The carers may experience their loved one changing from a fully functioning, capable individual to one with all the problems of communication, odd or aggressive behaviours, and lack of motivation associated with dementia. It should not be surprising, therefore, that around a fifth of carers are clinically depressed (Molyneux et al. 2008) and may experience a form of bereavement: grieving for the existential loss of their partner. Levels of depression increase in line with the functional impairment of the person with Alzheimer's disease, and may combine with frustration to trigger inappropriate behaviour towards the cared for person. Cooper et al. (2009), for example, found that 34 per cent of carers reported partner abuse 'at least sometimes' over a 3-month period. Abuse was mainly verbal; only 1 per cent reported physical abuse.

Many carers benefit from some form of support and help. This is often provided by voluntary bodies such as the Alzheimer's Disease Society in the UK. Carers may also benefit from 'respite care': short periods during which the affected person stays in hospital to provide a break for the carer. They may also benefit from interventions to help them either manage the stress they experience or help them deal more effectively with difficult behaviours using the A-B-C approach described earlier in the chapter. In one interesting study designed to help people manage their own stress, Gallagher-Thompson and Steffen (1994) compared CBT and psychodynamic therapy in the treatment of depressed carers of elderly relatives. Both interventions proved equally effective, and by the end of the intervention 71 per cent of participants no longer met the criteria for depression. Their key finding, however, was that individuals who had been in the caring role for a relatively short time benefited most from dynamic therapy; those involved over a longer period gained most from the CBT. One explanation for these findings is that new carers benefited from exploration of their new role and its implications, while longer-term carers benefited from learning practical techniques to help them cope with their day-to-day stress. Overall, interventions designed to reduce individual stress through the use of CBT appear to both reduce carer burden and feelings of depression. In addition, teaching carers to manage difficult behaviours or their interactions with an individual with Alzheimer's disease may also be of benefit, particularly if this is done on a one-to-one basis and linked to long-term support on an ongoing basis (Parker et al. 2008).

Chapter summary

1. Somatic symptom disorder involves the long-term experience of physical sensations, often labelled as symptoms, with no physiological cause.
2. It may have a number of roots, including the labelling of emotional responses as physical symptoms, a biological sensitivity to physical sensations combined with perceptions of threat, and attentional bias towards them.
3. Treatment is difficult, but up to 60 per cent success rates have been reported in populations with non-clinical levels of the disorder.
4. Illness anxiety disorder has many characteristics of somatic symptom disorder. However, unlike somatic symptom disorder, people with illness anxiety disorder believe they have or will have an illness, either in the presence or absence of symptoms.
5. Cognitive explanations for the disorder suggest that the condition involves attention to physical experiences thought to be symptoms of disease, a rejection of disconfirmatory evidence, physiological changes that may be stress responses but are interpreted as evidence of disease, and a range of safety behaviours.
6. Treatment may involve CBT and acceptance and commitment therapy. Given the difficulties in changing cognitions, mindfulness-based interventions may prove to be the treatment of choice.
7. Body dysmorphic disorder is characterized by strong beliefs the individual has a significant physical defect.
8. It has many of the features of obsessive-compulsive disorder in that it comprises frequent intrusive and distressing thoughts that trigger a range of safety behaviours.
9. Treatment mirrors that of obsessive-compulsive disorder, and involves exposure plus response prevention. People with the disorder gradually expose the apparently defective body part in the absence of safety behaviours.
10. Conversion disorders are characterized by apparent neurological symptoms, including paralysis, pseudoseizures and blindness, in the absence of any neurological explanation.
11. It is thought to be the result of either deliberate dissimilation or higher neurological processes similar to those that occur in hypnotic suggestion.
12. A range of treatments have been used, ranging from education on psychosomatic disorders to transcranial magnetic stimulation. Good evidence of their relative effectiveness has yet to be determined.

13. Alzheimer's disease is a consequence of neural degeneration involving damage to amyloid precursor protein and tau within the neural neurons.
14. Medical treatment is designed to increase acetylcholine levels, but has relatively short-term results, and is best given to people with early dementia.
15. Psychological interventions include reality orientation, reminiscence therapy, and validation therapy. Cognitive behaviour therapy may be of value for affective disorders in early dementia, but behavioural interventions aimed at helping partners increase pleasurable events and reduce triggers to episodes of inappropriate behaviour are more appropriate as the disease progresses. These may also reduce some of the inherent stresses associated with being a carer.

Further reading

Abramowitz, J.S. and Braddock, A.E. (2012) *Hypochondriasis and Health Anxiety*. Cambridge, MA: Hogrefe.

James, I.A. (2011) *Understanding Behaviour in Dementia that Challenges: A guide to assessment and treatment*. London: Jessica Kinglsey.

NICE (2006) *Dementia: Supporting people with dementia and their carers in health and social care*. London: NICE.

Philips, K.A. (2005) *The Broken Mirror: Understanding and treating body dysmorphic disorder*. Oxford: Oxford University Press.

Stoke, G. (2010) *And Still the Music Plays: Stories of people with dementia*. London: Hawker Publications.

Woolfolk, R.L. and Allen, L.A. (2006) *Treating Somatization: A cognitive-behavioral approach*. New York: Guilford Press.

Glossary

Actualizing tendency: according to Rogers, an innate drive that pushes the person to fulfil his potentials.
Aetiology: explanation of the causes of mental health problems, whether psychosocial, biological, and so on.
Agonist: a drug that increases the action of a neurotransmitter.
Agranulocytosis: a condition in which the bone marrow fails to produce enough white blood cells called neutrophils; leaves the individual prone to infection.
Allele: an alternative form of a gene that is located at a specific position on a specific chromosome.
Alzheimer's disease: the most common cause of dementia in old age.
Aphonia: an inability to speak.
Atypical neuroleptics: drugs that increase serotonin and reduce dopamine levels in the treatment of schizophrenia.
Blood–brain barrier: protective barrier formed in blood vessels of the brain. Prevents some drugs from passing from the blood to the brain.
Casein: the main protein present in milk and (in coagulated form) in cheese.
Catatonic behaviour: behaviour found in one form of schizophrenia; includes posturing, or 'waxy flexibility', mutism, and stupor.
Challenging behaviour: behaviour of such intensity, frequency or duration that the physical safety of the person or others is placed in jeopardy.
Client: a term often used to denote an individual in therapy. In contrast to words such as patient or subject, it is used to indicate the helping, non-hierarchical nature of the therapeutic relationship between therapist and individual.
Command hallucinations: a state in which individuals experience hallucinations in the form of voices that demand they perform certain acts.
Community mental health team: a multidisciplinary team providing mental health care within the community. Usually includes psychiatrists, community psychiatric nurses, psychologists, and other therapists.
Co-morbidity: the presence of more than one mental health problem or physical disease.
Core beliefs: basic underlying beliefs linked to schemata; fundamental beliefs about the self, others, and the world.
Cortisol: a glucocorticoid produced by the adrenal cortex that mediates a range of metabolic processes. It has anti-inflammatory and immunosuppressive properties. Levels may be elevated in response to physical or psychological stress
Delusion: a strongly held inappropriate belief; usually a belief that is normally considered impossible.
Dementia: a group of degenerative brain disorders associated with loss of cognitive function; Alzheimer's disease is the best known form, but there are several others.

Depersonalization: loss of contact with one's own personal reality accompanied by feelings of unreality.
Derealization: a feeling that one's surroundings are not real.
Dysphoric: unhappy, but not sufficiently so to warrant a diagnosis of depression.
Dysthymia: a mild but chronic form of depression; symptoms usually last for at least 2 years.
Egocentricity: holding the view that the individual is the centre and object of all experience.
Endorphins: peptides that activate the body's opiate receptors, causing an analgesic effect.
Executive function: neurological coordination of a number of complex processes, including speech, motor coordination, and behavioural planning.
Flashback memories: sudden, powerful, re-experiencing of a past experience or its elements.
Flattened affect: lack of emotional response, either positive or negative, to events.
Functional magnetic resonance imaging (fMRI): a functional neuroimaging procedure using MRI technology to measure brain activity by detecting changes in blood flow.
Gluten: a mixture of two proteins present in cereal grains, especially wheat, which is responsible for the elastic texture of dough.
Habituation: a behavioural term, involving cessation of responding to a stimulus after repeated (non-rewarded) presentations.
Hallucination: the experience of touch, visions or sounds in the absence of external stimuli.
Hyperventilation: short rapid breaths that lead to low levels of carbon dioxide in the blood and physical sensations such as tingling in the arms, dizziness, and feelings of an inability to breathe.
Ideas of reference: the inappropriate belief that objects, events or people are of personal significance. For example, a person may think that a television programme he is watching is all about him. May reach sufficient intensity to constitute delusions.
Incidence: the frequency with which new cases of a condition arise within a given population.
Interpersonal psychotherapy: a form of therapy focusing exclusively on changing interpersonal problems that contribute to mental health problems.
Longitudinal study: a study that follows participants for a significant period of time. Such studies often determine which measures taken at the start of the study (baseline) predict subsequent outcomes.
Meta-analysis: a statistical method of combining the data from several studies using similar measures that allows a more powerful analysis of the effect of the intervention than that provided by single, relatively small studies.
Morbidity: the presence of mental health problems or physical disease (*note*: different to mortality, which involves death from disease).
Naso-gastric tube: a hollow plastic tube pushed through the nose, past the throat, and into the stomach. Liquid food can be passed down the tube in lieu of normal ingestion.
Negative symptoms (of schizophrenia): include absence of activation, together with apathy, lack of motivation or poverty of speech.
Neural network: interconnections between memories of events and their associated thoughts and emotions.
Neurosteroid: a brain steroid such as cortisone, progesterone or testosterone.
Neurotic-type disorders: disorders characterized by long-term moderate levels of anxiety or other negative emotional states.

Opioids: peptides that bind at or otherwise influence opiate receptors, and influence outcomes such as pain relief, sedation, constipation, and respiratory depression.

Panic attack: experience of intense fear of sudden onset accompanied by a range of cognitive and physiological symptoms, including heart palpitations, dizziness, hyperventilation, and derealization.

Phenothiazine: a group of drugs with antipsychotic actions that block dopamine transmission.

Placebo: inactive treatments (either pharmacological or psychological) against which active treatment trials are often evaluated. These allow the assessment of the general effects of receiving some form of attention or 'treatment'. Differences in outcomes between placebo conditions and active interventions are considered to show the specific effects of the therapy against which the placebo is compared.

Positive symptoms (of schizophrenia): include hallucinations, delusions, disorganized speech, and positive thought disorder.

Poverty of speech: minimal verbal communication, usually requiring prompts to evoke.

Prevalence: the frequency with which a particular condition is found within the population at any one time.

Pro-inflammatory cytokines: one of several regulatory proteins, such as the interleukins and lymphokines, that are released by cells of the immune system and act as intercellular mediators in the generation of an immune response.

Pseudophobia: a fear of imagination and fantasy.

Pseudoseizures: physical manifestation of an emotional disturbance. They resemble epileptic seizures, but are not caused by electrical disruptions in the brain.

Psychosis: a symptom or feature of mental disorder involving changes in personality, impaired functioning, and a distorted sense of objective reality.

Schizophrenia: a psychotic disorder marked by severely impaired cognition, emotion, and behaviour.

Self-harm: an action that involves actual or potential risk to the individual; can include actions such as taking drugs, driving fast, overdosing on drugs or cutting the skin.

Suicidal ideation: thoughts of committing suicide.

Thought alienation: a feature of psychosis in which the individual feels their thoughts are not under their own control.

Thought-stopping: a technique involving interrupting ongoing thought processes by replacing them with the word 'stop!!!' (which initially may be cried out loud, but eventually becomes internalized).

Ventricles (brain): a system of fluid-filled open spaces in the brain; they are filled with cerebral spinal fluid (CSF).

Appendix: DSM-5 diagnostic criteria

This appendix provides a slightly abridged set of diagnostic criteria for the disorders introduced in the book. Note that with the exception of paedophilic disorder, the others require that the symptoms experienced cause distress or incapacity in day-to-day life.

Attention-deficit/hyperactivity disorder (ADHD)

Six or more of each of the following groups of symptoms persisting for at least 6 months to a degree incompatible with developmental level:

- *Inattention*: often fails to give close attention to details or makes careless mistakes, has difficulties in sustaining attention in task or play, does not seem to listen when spoken to directly, does not follow through on instructions or fails to finish tasks, has difficulty organizing tasks and activities, avoids, dislikes or is reluctant to engage in tasks that require sustained mental effort, loses things necessary for tasks or activities, easily distracted by extraneous stimuli, forgetful in daily activities.
- *Hyperactivity and impulsivity*: often fidgets, taps hands or squirms, leaves seat in situations when remaining seated is expected, runs or climbs in inappropriate situations, unable to play quietly, 'on the go' or acting as 'driven by a motor', talks excessively, blurts out answer before question is completed, has difficulty waiting in turn, interrupts or intrudes on others.

Several inattentive or hyperactive-impulsive symptoms evident before age 12 years, and in two or more settings.

Alzheimer's disease (major neurocognitive disorder due to Alzheimer's disease)

All three of the following:

- Clear evidence of a decline in memory or learning and at least one other domain.
- Steadily progressive, gradual decline in cognition, without extended plateaux.
- No evidence of a mixed aetiology (e.g. other potential causes such as systemic or cerebrovascular disease).

Probable AD diagnosed if clear evidence of genetic risk for the disorder. Possible AD diagnosed if this is absent.

Anorexia nervosa

- Restriction of energy intake relative to requirements, leading to significantly low body weight in relation to age, sex, and developmental trajectory.
- Intense fear of gaining weight or of becoming fat, or persistent behaviour that interferes with weight gain even though at significantly low weight.
- Disturbances in the way body weight or shape is experienced due to undue influence of body weight or shape on self-evaluation; persistent lack of recognition of the seriousness of low body weight.

Restricting type: no binge eating or purging during last 3 months.
Binge-eating/purging: recurrent episodes of bingeing/purging during last 3 months.

Mild:	BMI > 16.99
Moderate:	BMI $= 16–16.99$
Severe:	BMI $= 15–15.99$
Extreme:	BMI < 15.

Antisocial personality disorder

Pervasive pattern of disregard for and violation of the rights of others from the age of 15 years, as indicated by three or more of the following:

- Failure to conform to social norms or respect lawful behaviours.
- Deceitfulness: repeated lying, use of aliases, conning others.
- Impulsivity or failure to plan ahead.
- Irritability and aggressiveness: repeated physical fights or assaults.
- Reckless disregard for safety of self and others.
- Consistent irresponsibility: repeated failure to sustain consistent work or honour financial obligations.
- Lack of remorse: indifferent to or rationalizing having hurt, mistreated or stolen from someone.

Individual must be at least 18 years old.
No evidence of conduct disorder before 15 years.

Autism spectrum disorder

Persistent deficits in social communication and interaction across multiple contexts, including:

- Deficits in social-emotional reciprocity, e.g. failure to initiate social interactions.
- Deficits in non-verbal communication, e.g. poorly integrated verbal/non-verbal communication, abnormalities in eye contact, lack of facial expression.
- Deficits in maintaining and understanding relationships.

Restricted, repetitive patterns of behaviour, interests or activities evidenced by at least two of the following:

- Stereotyped or repetitive motor movements.
- Insistence of sameness, inflexible adherence to routines, ritualized patterns of verbal or non-verbal behaviour.
- Highly restricted fixated interests that are abnormal in intensity or focus.
- Hyper- or hypo-reactivity to sensory input or unusual interest in sensory aspects of environment, e.g. indifference to pain/temperature, excessive smelling or touching of objects.

Symptoms must be present in early developmental period.

Bipolar disorder

Manic episode

Distinct period of persistently elevated, expansive or irritable mood and increased goal-directed activity or energy lasting at least one week and present most of the day or nearly every day. During this period, three or more of the following (four if mood is only irritable):

- Increased self-esteem or grandiosity.
- Decreased need for sleep.
- More talkative than usual or pressure to keep talking.
- Flight of ideas or subjective experience that thoughts are racing.
- Distractibility: attention easily drawn to unimportant external stimuli.
- Increase in goal-directed activity (social, work, sexual) or psychomotor agitation.
- Excessive involvement in activities that have high potential for painful consequences (e.g. sexual indiscretions, foolish business investments).

At least one lifetime manic episode is required for a diagnosis of type I bipolar disorder.

Major depressive episode

Five or more of the following present for a 2-week period:

- Depressed mood for most of the day, nearly every day.
- Markedly diminished interest in pleasure in all or almost all activities.
- Significant weight loss when not dieting, or weight gain.
- Insomnia or hypersomnia.
- Psychomotor agitation or retardation.
- Fatigue or loss of energy nearly every day.
- Feelings of worthlessness or excessive or inappropriate guilt.
- Diminished activity to think or concentrate, or indecisiveness.
- Recurrent thoughts of death, recurrent suicidal ideation with or without a specific plan.

Major depressive episodes common in type I bipolar disorder, but not required for diagnosis of type II.

Body dysmorphic disorder

- Preoccupation with one or more perceived deficits or flaws in physical appearance that are not observable or appear slight.
- At some point, the individual has performed repetitive behaviours (e.g. seeking reassurance, mirror checking) or mental acts (e.g. comparing self with others) in response to appearance concerns.

Borderline personality disorder

A pervasive pattern of instability of interpersonal relationships, self-image, affect, and marked impulsivity. Diagnosis requires five or more of the following:

- Frantic efforts to avoid real or imagined abandonment.
- Pattern of unstable and intense interpersonal relationships characterized by alternation between extremes of idealization and devaluation.
- Identity disturbance: markedly and persistently unstable self-image or sense of self.
- Impulsivity in at least two areas that are potentially self-damaging (e.g. sex, binge eating).
- Recurrent suicidal behaviour: gestures, threats or self-mutilating behaviour.
- Affective instability due to marked reactivity of mood (e.g. intense episodic dysphoria, anxiety).
- Chronic feelings of emptiness.
- Inappropriate intense anger or difficulty controlling anger.
- Transient stress-related paranoid ideation or severe dissociative symptoms.

Bulimia nervosa

- Eating in a discrete time (e.g. 2 hours) an amount of food greater than most people would eat in a similar period.
- A sense of lack of control over eating during the episode.
- Recurrent inappropriate compensatory behaviours in order to prevent weight gain, including self-induced vomiting, misuse of laxatives, excessive exercise.
- Episodes occur at least once a week for 3 months.
- Self-evaluation is unduly influenced by body weight and shape

Mild:	average of 1–3 episodes per week
Moderate:	average of 4–7 episodes per week
Severe:	average of 8–13 episodes per week
Extreme:	> 14 episodes per week.

Conduct disorder

A repetitive and persistent pattern of behaviour in which the rights of others or age-appropriate social norms are violated. Three of the following 15 behaviours present over the past 12 months, with at least one evident for 6 months:

- *Aggression to people and animals*: often bullies, threatens or intimidates, often initiates physical fights; used a weapon that could cause physical harm; physically cruel to people; been physically cruel to animals; stolen while confronting victim; forced someone into sexual activity.
- *Destruction of property*: deliberately engaged in fire setting; deliberately destroyed other people's property.
- *Deceitfulness or theft*: broken into someone's house or car; lies to obtain goods or favours, or to avoid obligations; stolen items of non-trivial value without confronting victim.
- *Serious violations of rules*: stays out at night despite parental prohibitions; has run away from home over night at least twice or once without returning for lengthy period; frequent truant from school beginning before age 13 years.

Specify if with limited pro-social emotions.

Conversion disorder (functional neurological symptom disorder)

- One or more symptoms of altered voluntary motor or sensory functions.
- Clinical findings provide evidence of incompatibility between the symptoms and recognized neurological or medical conditions.

Depression (major depressive disorder)

See criteria for depressive episode in bipolar disorder.

Dissociative identity disorder

- Disruption of identity characterized by two or more distinct personality states. This involves marked discontinuity in sense of self and sense of agency, accompanied by related alterations in affect, behaviour, consciousness, perception, memory, cognition, and/or sensory-motor function.
- Recurrent gaps in recall of everyday events, important personal information, and/or traumatic events inconsistent with ordinary forgetting.
- The disturbance is not a normal part of a broadly accepted cultural or religious practice.

Drug (alcohol/cannabis/heroin) use disorder

Problematic pattern of drug use with at least two of following within 12-month period:

- Drug taken in larger amounts or over longer period than intended.
- Persistent desire or unsuccessful attempts to cut down or control use.
- A great deal of time is spent in activities necessary to obtain the drug or recover from its effects.
- Craving or a strong desire or urge to use the drug.
- Failure to fulfil major role obligations.
- Continued drug use despite persistent or recurrent social or interpersonal problems exacerbated by drug use.
- Important alternative activities given up or reduced because of drug use.
- Recurrent drug use in situations where use is physically hazardous.
- Use continues despite knowledge of having persistent physical or psychological problems caused or exacerbated by the drug.
- Tolerance evident by either:
  - a need for markedly more drug to achieve its desired effects, or
  - a markedly diminished effect for same amount of drug.
- Withdrawal if use of the drug is stopped.

Gambling disorder

Persistent and recurrent problematic gambling over a 12-month period evidenced through four or more of following:

- Need to gamble with increasing amounts of money to achieve desired effect.
- Restless or irritable when attempting to cut down or stop gambling.
- Repeated unsuccessful efforts to control, cut back or stop gambling.
- Often preoccupied with gambling.
- Often gambles when feeling distressed.
- After losing money, often returns following day to get even ('chasing' the losses).
- Lies to conceal extent of gambling.
- Jeopardized or lost (for example) significant relationship/job because of gambling.
- Relies on others to provide money to relieve desperate financial consequences of gambling.

Gender dysphoria (in adults)

Marked incongruence between one's experienced/expressed gender and primary and/or secondary sex characteristics lasting at least 6 months. Strong desire:

- to be rid of one's primary and/or secondary sex characteristics;
- for the primary/secondary sex characteristics of the other gender;
- to be the other gender;

- to be treated as someone of the other gender;
- that one has the typical feelings and reactions of the other gender.

Generalized anxiety disorder

- Excessive anxiety and worry about a number of events or activities, occurring on more days than not, and observed over a period of at least 6 months.
- Difficulty in controlling the worry.
- One additional symptom for a diagnosis in children, three in adults from: being easily fatigued, finding it difficult to concentrate, irritability, build up of tension in muscles, disturbed sleep.

Illness anxiety disorder

- Preoccupation with having or acquiring a serious illness.
- Somatic symptoms are not present or only mild in intensity.
- There is a high level of anxiety about health, and individual is easily alarmed about their health status.
- Individual performs excessive health-checking behaviours (e.g. checking for signs of disease) or adopts maladaptive avoidance (e.g. avoids doctors).
- Illness preoccupation has to be present for at least 6 months, but the feared illness may change over this period.

Panic disorder

Recurrent unexpected panic attacks, involving four or more of the following symptoms:

- palpitations or 'pounding heart'; sweating; trembling or shaking; shortness of breath or feeling 'smothered'; feelings of choking; chest pain or discomfort; nausea or abdominal distress; feeling dizzy, unsteady, light-headed or faint; chills or heat sensations; numbing or tingling; derealization or depersonalization; feeling loss of control or 'going crazy'; fear of dying.

At least one attack followed by one month or more of the following:

- Persistent concern or worry abut additional panic attacks or their consequences.
- Significant maladaptive change in behaviour, including avoidance of exercise or unfamiliar situations.

Separation anxiety disorder

Developmentally inappropriate and excessive fear or anxiety regarding separation from the person to whom the individual feels attached. Three of the following are required:

- Recurrent excessive distress when anticipating or experiencing separation from home or major attachment figure.
- Persistent and excessive worry about losing major attachment figure or possible harm to them.
- Persistent and excessive worry about experiencing an untoward event (e.g. kidnap, getting lost) that causes separation from major attachment figure.
- Persistent reluctance or refusal to go away from home because of fear of separation.
- Persistent reluctance or refusal to sleep away from home or go to sleep away from major attachment figure.
- Repeated nightmares involving theme of separation.
- Repeated complaints of physical symptoms (e.g. headaches, nausea) when separation occurs or is anticipated.

Fear or avoidance lasts at least 4 weeks.

Schizophrenia

Two or more of the following present for significant portion of time during a one-month period. At least one must be 1, 2, or 3:

1. Delusions
2. Hallucinations
3. Disorganized speech
4. Grossly disorganized or catatonic behaviour
5. Negative symptoms, including diminished emotional expression or avolition.

Marked reduction in level of functioning in major areas such as work or interpersonal relationships

Continuous signs of the disturbance persist for at least 6 months, which must include one month of above symptoms.

Somatic symptom disorder

- One or more somatic symptoms that are distressing and result in significant disruption of daily life.
- Excessive thoughts, feelings or behaviours related to somatic symptoms or associated health concerns, evidenced by:
  - disproportionate and persistent thoughts about the seriousness of one's symptoms;
  - persistently high level of anxiety about health or symptoms;
  - excessive time and energy devoted to these symptoms or health concerns.

Specific phobia

- Marked fear or anxiety about a specific object or situation. In children, crying, tantrums, freezing or clinging may be used to express the anxiety.
- The phobic object or situation almost always provokes immediate fear or anxiety.
- The object or situation is actively avoided or endured with intense fear or anxiety.
- The fear or anxiety is out of proportion to the actual danger posed.
- The fear, anxiety or avoidance is persistent, typically lasting 6 months or more.

Obsessive compulsive disorder

Obsessions are characterized by:

- Recurrent and persistent thoughts, urges or images that are intrusive and unwanted, and generally cause marked anxiety or distress.
- The individual attempts to ignore or suppress such thoughts, urges or images or to neutralize them through thought or action.

Compulsions are characterized by:

- Repetitive behaviours or mental acts the individual feels driven to perform in response to an obsession or according to rules that must be applied with rigidity.
- Behaviours or acts aimed at preventing or reducing anxiety or distress, in an unrealistic way.

Obsessions or compulsions are time-consuming (e.g. take more than one hour per day) or cause significant distress.

Paedophilic disorder

- Over a period of at least 6 months, recurrent, intense sexually arousing fantasies, sexual urges, or behaviours involving sexual activity with a prepubescent child or children (usually 13 years or younger).
- The individual has acted on these sexual urges or they cause interpersonal distress.
- The individual is at least 16 years of age and 5 years older than the other involved child.

Post-traumatic stress disorder (adults and children over 6 years)

Exposure to actual or threatened death, serious injury or sexual violence in one or more of the following ways:

- Direct experience
- Witness events occurring to others

- Learning of traumatic events to emotionally close individual
- Experiencing repeated or extreme exposure to aversive details of traumatic events.

Presence of one or more of the following:

- Recurrent, involuntary and intrusive distressing memories of events.
- Recurrent distressing dreams of events.
- Dissociative reactions (e.g. flashbacks) that make it feel the event is reoccurring.
- Intense or prolonged psychological distress at exposure to internal or external cues that resemble the traumatic events.
- Marked physiological reactions to such cues.

Persistent avoidance of stimuli associated with traumatic events:

- Avoidance or efforts to avoid distressing memories, thoughts or feelings associated with the trauma.
- Avoidance or efforts to avoid external reminders of events.

Negative alterations in cognitions and mood associated with traumatic events, evidenced by two of the following:

- Inability to remember important aspects of traumatic events.
- Persistent and exaggerated negative beliefs or expectations about oneself, others, and the world.
- Persistent, distorted cognitions about the cause or consequences of the traumatic event.
- Persistent negative emotional state, including fear, horror, blaming self or others.
- Feeling of detachment or estrangement from others.
- Persistent inability to experience positive emotions.

Marked alterations in arousal and reactivity associated with traumatic events, evidenced by two of the following:

- Irritable behaviour and angry outbursts
- Reckless or self-destructive behaviour
- Hypervigilance
- Exaggerated startle response
- Problems concentrating
- Sleep disturbance.

Problems must persist for at least one month.

Transvestic disorder

- Over 6-month period, recurrent and intense sexual arousal from cross-dressing, as manifested in fantasies, urges or behaviours.
- These cause clinically significant distress or impairment.

References

Abela, J. and D'Allesandro, D. (2002) Beck's cognitive theory of depression: the diathesis-stress and causal mediation components, *British Journal of Clinical Psychology*, 41: 111–28.

Abramson, L., Seligman, M. and Teasdale, J. (1978) Learned helplessness in humans: critique and reformulation, *Journal of Abnormal Psychology*, 87: 49–74.

Agoston, A. and Rudolph, K. (2011) Transactional associations between youths' responses to peer stress and depression: the moderating roles of sex and stress exposure, *Journal of Abnormal Child Psychology*, 39: 159–71.

Agüera, Z., Riesco, N., Jiménez-Murcia, S. et al. (2013) Cognitive behaviour therapy response and dropout rate across purging and nonpurging bulimia nervosa and binge eating disorder: DSM-5 implications, *BMC Psychiatry*, 13: 285.

Ahmad, F., Quinn, T., Dawson, J. et al. (2008) A link between lunar phase and medically unexplained stroke symptoms: an unearthly influence?, *Journal of Psychosomatic Research*, 65: 131–3.

Ahnquist, J. and Wamala, S. (2011) Economic hardships in adulthood and mental health in Sweden: the Swedish National Public Health Survey 2009, *BMC Public Health*, 11: 788.

Ainsworth, M. and Bowlby, J. (1991) An ethological approach to personality development, *American Psychologist*, 46: 331–41.

Al-Modallal, H. (2012) Psychological partner violence and women's vulnerability to depression, stress and anxiety, *International Journal of Mental Health Nursing*, 21: 560–6.

Allan, A., Roberts, M., Allan, M. et al. (2001) Intoxication, criminal offences and suicide attempts in a group of South African problem drinkers, *South African Medical Journal*, 91: 145–50.

Amer, M. and Hovey, J. (2007) Socio-demographic differences in acculturation and mental health for a sample of 2nd generation/early immigrant Arab Americans, *Journal of Immigrant Minority Health*, 9: 335–47.

American Psychiatric Association (APA) (1987) *Diagnostic and Statistical Manual of Mental Disorders: DSM-111-R*. Washington, DC: APA.

American Psychiatric Association (APA) (2000) *Diagnostic and Statistical Manual of Mental Disorders: DSM-IV-TR*. Washington, DC: APA.

American Psychiatric Association (APA) (2013) *Diagnostic and Statistical Manual of Mental Disorders* (5th edn.). Washington, DC: APA.

Andersen, I., Thielen, K., Nygaard, E. et al. (2009) Social inequality in the prevalence of depressive disorders, *Journal of Epidemiology and Community Health*, 63: 575–81.

Anderson, R.N. and Smith, B.L. (2003) Deaths: leading causes for 2001, *National Vital Statistics Report*, 52: 1–86.

Angarne-Lindberg, T. and Wadsby, M. (2012) Psychiatric and somatic health in relation to experience of parental divorce in childhood, *International Journal of Social Psychiatry*, 58: 16–25.

Angold, A., Costello, E., Erkanli, A. et al. (1999) Pubertal changes in hormone levels and depression in girls, *Psychology of Medicine*, 29: 1043–53.

Antonuccio, D., Thomas, M. and Danton, W. (1997) A cost-effectiveness analysis of cognitive behaviour therapy and fluoxetine (Prozac) in the treatment of depression, *Behavioural Therapy*, 28: 187–210.

Arntz, A., Klokman, J. and Sieswerda, S. (2005) An experimental test of the schema mode model of borderline personality disorder, *Journal of Behavior Therapy and Experimental Psychiatry*, 36: 226–39.

Aro, S., Aro, H. and Kesimäki, I. (1995) Socio-economic mobility among patients with schizophrenia or major affective disorder: a 17-year retrospective follow-up, *British Journal of Psychiatry*, 166: 759–67.

Ascher-Svanum, H., Zhu, B., Faries, D. et al. (2006) A prospective study of risk factors for nonadherence with antipsychotic medication in the treatment of schizophrenia, *Journal of Clinical Psychiatry*, 67: 1114–23.

Asnaani, A., Richey, J., Dimaite, R. et al. (2010) A cross-ethnic comparison of lifetime prevalence rates of anxiety disorders, *Journal of Nervous Mental Disease*, 198: 551–5.

Ataoglu, A., Ozcetin, A., Icmeli, C. et al. (2003) Paradoxical therapy in conversion reaction, *Journal of Korean Medical Science*, 18: 581–4.

Attard, A. and Taylor, D. (2012) Comparative effectiveness of atypical antipsychotics in schizophrenia: what have real-world trials taught us?, *CNS Drugs*, 26: 491–508.

Babiak, P. and Hare, R. (2007) *Snakes in Suits: When psychopaths go to work*. New York: HarperCollins.

Baddeley, A. (2007) *Working Memory, Thought and Action*. Oxford: Oxford University Press.

Bahali, K., Tahiroglu A., Avci, A. et al. (2011) Parental psychological symptoms and familial risk factors of children and adolescents who exhibit school refusal, *East Asian Archives of Psychiatry*, 21: 164–9.

Bandelow, B., Krause, J., Wedekind, D. et al. (2005) Early traumatic life events, parental attitudes, family history, and birth risk factors in patients with borderline personality disorder and healthy controls, *Psychiatry Research*, 134: 169–79.

Bandura, A. (1977) *Social Learning Theory*. Englewood Cliffs, NJ: Prentice-Hall.

Barbaree, H. and Marshall, W. (1989) Erectile responses among heterosexual child molesters, father–daughter incest offenders and matched nonoffenders: five distinct age preference profiles, *Canadian Journal of Behavioural Science*, 21: 70–82.

Bargagli, A., Hickman, M., Davoli, M. et al. (2006) Drug-related mortality and its impact on adult mortality in eight European countries, *European Journal of Public Health*, 16: 198–202.

Barkhofa, E., Meijera, C., De Sonnevilleb, L. et al. (2012) Interventions to improve adherence to antipsychotic medication in patients with schizophrenia: a review of the past decade, *European Psychiatry*, 27: 9–18.

Barkley, R.A. (2005) *ADHD and the Nature of Self-control*. New York: Guilford Press.

Barlow, D.H., Gorman, J.M., Shear, M.K. et al. (2000) Cognitive-behavioural therapy, imipramine, or their combination for panic disorder: a randomized controlled trial, *Journal of the American Medical Association*, 283: 2529–36.

Barnes, A. (2007) Race and hospital diagnoses of schizophrenia and mood disorders, *Social Work*, 53: 77–83.

Baron-Cohen, S., Leslie, L. and Frith, U. (1985) Does the autistic child have a theory of mind?, *Cognition*, 21: 37–46.

Bartholomew, K. and Horowitz, L. (1991) Attachment styles among young adults: a test of a four-category model, *Journal of Personality and Social Psychology*, 61: 226–44.

Basso, M., Nasrallah, H., Olson, S. et al. (1998) Neuropsychological correlates of negative, disorganized and psychotic symptoms in schizophrenia, *Schizophrenia Research*, 25: 99–111.

Bateson, G., Jackson, D., Haley, J. et al. (1956) Toward a theory of schizophrenia, *Behavioural Science*, 1: 251–64.

Beck, A. (1977) *Cognitive Therapy of Depression*. New York: Guilford Press.

Beck, A. (1997) Cognitive therapy: reflections, in J. Zeig (ed.) *The Evolution of Psychotherapy: The third conference*. New York: Brunner/Mazel.

Beck, A., Freeman, A. and Associates (1990) *Cognitive Therapy of Personality Disorders*. New York: Guilford Press.

Beck, A., Wright, F., Newman, C. et al. (1993) *Cognitive Therapy of Substance Abuse*. New York: Guilford Press.

Bennetto, L., Pennington, B. and Rogers, S. (1996) Intact and impaired memory functions in autism, *Child Development*, 67: 1816–35.

Bentall, R. (1993) Deconstructing the concept of schizophrenia, *Journal of Mental Health*, 2: 223–38.

Bentall, R. and Fernyhough, C. (2008) Social predictors of psychotic experiences: specificity and psychological mechanisms, *Schizophrenia Bulletin*, 34: 1012–20.

Bentall, R., Corcoran, R., Howard, R. et al. (2001) Persecutory delusions: a review and theoretical integration, *Clinical Psychology Review*, 21: 1143–92.

Bettelheim, B. (1967) *The Empty Fortress*. New York: Free Press.

Biederman, J., Petty, C., Faraone, S.V. et al. (2005) Childhood antecedents to panic disorder in referred and nonreferred adults, *Journal of Child and Adolescent Psychopharmacology*, 15: 549–61.

Birbaumer, N., Veit, R., Lotze, M. et al. (2005) Deficient fear conditioning in psychopathy: a functional magnetic resonance imaging study, *Archives of General Psychiatry*, 62: 799–805.

Birmaher, B., Ryan, N., Williamson, D. et al. (1996) Childhood and adolescent depression: a review of the past 10 years, *Journal of the American Academy of Child and Adolescent Psychiatry*, 35: 1427–39.

Bishop, S., Dalgleish, T. and Yule, W. (2004) Memory for emotional stories in high and low depressed children, *Memory*, 12: 214–30.

Bisson, J. and Andrew, M. (2009) Psychological treatment of post-traumatic stress disorder (PTSD), *Cochrane Database Systematic Reviews*, 3: CD003388.

Bisson, J., Ehlers, A., Matthews, R. et al. (2007) Psychological treatments for chronic post-traumatic stress disorder: systematic review and meta-analysis, *British Journal of Psychiatry*, 190: 97–104.

Black, M., Papas, M., Hussey, J. et al. (2002) Behaviour and development of preschool children born to adolescent mothers: risk and 3-generation households, *Pediatrics*, 109: 573–80.

Bleich-Cohen, M., Strous, R., Even, R. et al. (2009) Diminished neural sensitivity to irregular facial expression in first-episode schizophrenia, *Human Brain Mapping*, 30: 2606–16.

Boesky, D. (1990) The psychoanalytic process and its components, *Psychoanalytic Quarterly*, 59: 550–84.

Bohne, A., Keuthen, N.J., Wilhelm, S. et al. (2002) Prevalence of symptoms of body dysmorphic disorder and its correlates: a cross-cultural comparison, *Psychosomatics*, 43: 486–90.

Boileau, I., Dagher, A., Leyton, M. et al. (2007) Conditioned dopamine release in humans: a positron emission tomographly [^{11}C] reclopride study with amphetamine, *Journal of Neuroscience*, 27: 3998–4003.

Bonanno, R. and Hymel, S. (2013) Cyber bullying and internalizing difficulties: above and beyond the impact of traditional forms of bullying, *Journal of Youth and Adolescence*, 42: 685–97.

Bonne, O., Vythilingam, M., Inagaki, M. et al. (2008) Reduced posterior hippocampal in posttraumatic stress disorder, *Journal of Clinical Psychiatry*, 69: 1087–91.

Bora, E. and Pantelis, C. (2013) Theory of mind impairments in first-episode psychosis, individuals at ultra-high risk for psychosis and in first-degree relatives of schizophrenia: systematic review and meta-analysis, *Schizophrenia Research*, 144: 31–6.

Borduin, C., Mann, B., Cone, L. et al. (1995) Multisystemic treatment of serious juvenile offenders: long-term prevention of criminality and violence, *Journal of Consulting and Clinical Psychology*, 63: 569–78.

Bornovalova, M., Hicks, B., Iacono, W.G. et al. (2010) Familial transmission and heritability of childhood disruptive disorders, *American Journal of Psychiatry*, 167: 1066–74.

Bowirrat, A. and Oscar-Berman, M. (2005) Relationship between dopaminergic neurotransmission, alcoholism, and reward deficiency syndrome, *American Journal of Medical Genetics B: Neuropsychiatric Genetics*, 5: 29–37.

Bowlby, J. (1969) *Attachment and Loss, Vol. 1: Attachment*. London: Hogarth Press.

Bowlby, J. (1973) *Attachment and Loss, Vol. 2: Separation: anxiety and anger*. London: Hogarth Press.

Boyd, R., Joe, S., Michalopoulos, L. et al. (2011) Prevalence of mood disorders and service use among US mothers by race and ethnicity: results from the National Survey of American Life, *Journal of Clinical Psychiatry*, 72: 1538–45.

Boysen, G. and VanBergen, A. (2013) A review of published research on adult dissociative identity disorder: 2000–2010, *Journal of Nervous and Mental Disease*, 201: 5–11.

Breslau, J., Miller, E., Jin, R. et al. (2011) A multinational study of mental disorders, marriage, and divorce, *Acta Psychiatrica Scandinavica*, 124: 474–86.

Brewerton, T. (2012) Antipsychotic agents in the treatment of anorexia nervosa: neuropsychopharmacologic rationale and evidence from controlled trials, *Current Psychiatry Report*, 14: 398–405.

Brewin, C. (2001) A cognitive neuroscience account of posttraumatic stress disorder and its treatment, *Behaviour Research and Therapy*, 39: 373–93.

Brown, A.S., Begg, M., Gravenstein, A. et al. (2004) Serologic evidence for prenatal influenza in the etiology of schizophrenia, *Archives of General Psychiatry*, 61: 774–80.

Brown, G., Ten Have, T., Henriques, G. et al. (2005) Cognitive therapy for the prevention of suicide attempts: a randomized controlled trial, *Journal of the American Medical Association*, 294: 563–70.

Brown, M. and Barraclough, B. (1997) Epidemiology of suicide pacts in England and Wales, 1988–92, *British Medical Journal*, 315: 286–7.

Brüne, M., Ozgürdal, S., Ansorge, N. et al. (2011) An fMRI study of 'theory of mind' in at-risk states of psychosis: comparison with manifest schizophrenia and healthy controls, *NeuroImage*, 55: 329–37.

Budney, A., Roffman, R., Stephens, R. et al. (2007) Marijuana dependence and its treatment, *Addiction Science and Clinical Practice*, 4: 4–16.

Bulloch, A. and Patten, S. (2010) Non-adherence with psychotropic medications in the general population, *Social Psychiatry and Psychiatric Epidemiology*, 45: 47–56.

Burneo, J., Martin, R., Powell, T. et al. (2003) Teddy bears: an observational finding in patients with nonepileptic events, *Neurology*, 61: 714–15.

Burt, S., McGue, M. and Iacono, W. (2009) Nonshared environmental mediation of the association between deviant peer affiliation and adolescent externalizing behaviours over time: results from a cross-lagged monozygotic twin differences design, *Developmental Psychology*, 45: 1752–60.

Butler, G., Fennel, M., Robson, P. et al. (1991) Comparison of behavior therapy and cognitive behavior therapy in the treatment of generalized anxiety disorder, *Journal of Consulting and Clinical Psychology*, 59: 167–75.

Carter, J.C., McFarlane, T.L., Bewell, C. et al. (2009) Maintenance treatment for anorexia nervosa: a comparison of cognitive behavior therapy and treatment as usual, *International Journal of Eating Disorders*, 42: 202–7.

Carthy, T., Horesh, N., Apter, A. et al. (2010) Emotional reactivity and cognitive regulation in anxious children, *Behavioural Research and Therapy*, 48: 384–93.

Caspi, A., Moffitt, T., Cannon, M. et al. (2005) Moderation of the effect of adolescent-onset cannabis use on adult psychosis by a functional polymorphism in the catechol-O-methyltransferase gene: longitudinal evidence of a gene × environment interaction, *Biological Psychiatry*, 15: 1117–27.

Cheasty, M., Clare, A. and Collins, C. (1998) Relation between sexual abuse in childhood and adult depression: case-control study, *British Medical Journal*, 17: 198–201.

Chenu, F. and Bourin, M. (2006) Potentiation of antidepressant-like activity with lithium: mechanism involved, *Current Drug Targets*, 7: 159–63.

Cherland, E. and Fitzpatrick, R. (1999) Psychotic side effects of psychostimulants: a 5-year review, *Canadian Journal of Psychiatry*, 44: 811–13.

Children's Society (2013) *The Good Childhood Report 2013* [http://www.childrenssociety.org.uk/good-childhood-report-2013-online/index.html].

Chou, K. (2012) Perceived discrimination and depression among new migrants to Hong Kong: the moderating role of social support and neighbourhood collective efficacy, *Journal of Affective Disorders*, 138: 63–70.

Christian, C., Lencz, T., Robinson, D. et al. (2008) Gray matter structural alterations in obsessive-compulsive disorder: relationship to neuropsychological functions, *Psychiatry Research*, 164: 123–31.

Chugani, D. (2004) Serotonin in autism and pediatric epilepsies, *Mental Retardation and Developmental Disabilities Research Reviews*, 10: 112–16.

Chung, M., Pressler, S., Dunbar, S. et al. (2010) Predictors of depressive symptoms in caregivers of patients with heart failure, *Journal of Cardiovascular Nursing*, 25: 411–19.

Clark, D. (1986) A cognitive approach to panic disorder, *Behaviour Research and Therapy*, 24: 461–70.

Clark, D., Salkovskis, P., Gelder, M. et al. (1988) Tests of a cognitive model of panic, in I. Hand and U. Wittchen (eds.) *Panic and Phobias* (Vol. 2). Berlin: Springer.

Clark, D., Salkovskis, P., Hackmann, A. et al. (1994) A comparison of cognitive therapy, applied relaxation and imipramine in the treatment of panic disorder, *British Journal of Psychiatry*, 164: 759–69.

Clark, D., Salkovskis, P., Hackmann, A. et al. (1998) Two psychological treatments for hypochondriasis: a randomised controlled trial, *British Journal of Psychiatry*, 173: 218–25.

Clarke, D.M., Piterman, L., Byrne, C. et al. (2008) Somatic symptoms, hypochondriasis and psychological distress: a study of somatisation in Australian general practice, *Medical Journal of Australia*, 189: 560–4.

Cleckley, H. (1941) *The Mask of Sanity: An attempt to clarify some issues about the so-called psychopathic personality*. St. Louis, MO: C.V. Mosby.

Cloutier, S., Martin, S. and Poole, C. (2002) Sexual assault among North Carolina women: prevalence and health risk factors, *Journal of Epidemiology and Community Health*, 56: 265–71.

Coelho, H., Canter, P. and Ernst, E. (2007) Mindfulness-based cognitive therapy: evaluating current evidence and informing future research, *Journal of Consulting and Clinical Psychology*, 75: 1000–5.

Coghill, D. and Banaschewski, T. (2009) The genetics of attention-deficit/hyperactivity disorder, *Expert Review of Neurotherapeutics*, 9: 1547–65.

Cohen, J., Mannarino, A. and Iyengar, S. (2011) Community treatment of posttraumatic stress disorder for children exposed to intimate partner violence: a randomized controlled trial, *Archives of Pediatric and Adolescent Medicine*, 165: 16–21.

Cohen, L., McGeoch, P., Gans, S. et al. (2002) Childhood sexual history of 20 male pedophiles vs. 24 male healthy control subjects, *Journal of Nervous and Mental Diseases*, 190: 757–66.

Coid, J., Petruckevitch, A., Chung, W. et al. (2003) Abusive experiences and psychiatric morbidity in women primary care attenders, *British Journal of Psychiatry*, 183: 332–9.

Coid, J., Ullrich, S., Keers, R. et al. (2013) Gang membership, violence, and psychiatric morbidity, *American Journal of Psychiatry*, 170: 985–93.

Cole, S., Kemeny, M., Taylor, S. et al. (1996) Elevated physical health risk among gay men who conceal their homosexual identity, *Health Psychology*, 15: 243–51.

Comings, D.E., Gade-Andavolu, R., Gonzalez, N. et al. (2001) The additive effect of neurotransmitter genes in pathological gambling, *Clinical Genetics*, 60: 107–16.

Compas, B., Forehand, R., Thigpen, J. et al. (2011) Family group cognitive-behavioural preventive intervention for families of depressed parents: 18 and 24 month outcomes, *Journal of Consulting and Clinical Psychology*, 79: 488–99.

Cook, A., Blaustein, M., Spinazzola, J. et al. (2003) *Complex Trauma in Children and Adolescents: White paper from the National Child Traumatic Stress Network Complex Trauma Task Force*. Los Angeles, CA: National Center for Child Traumatic Stress.

Cooper, C., Bebbington, P., Meltzer, H. et al. (2008) Depression and common mental disorders in lone parents: results of the 2000 National Psychiatric Morbidity Survey, *Psychology of Medicine*, 38: 335–42.

Cooper, C., Selwood, A., Blanchard, M. et al. (2009) Abuse of people with dementia by family carers: representative cross sectional survey, *British Medical Journal*, 338: b155.

Corcoran, C., Perrin, M., Harlap, S. et al. (2009) Effect of socioeconomic status and parents' education at birth on risk of schizophrenia in offspring, *Society of Psychiatry and Psychiatric Epidemiology*, 44: 265–71.

Cosgrove, V. and Suppes, T. (2013) Informing DSM-5: biological boundaries between bipolar I disorder, schizoaffective disorder, and schizophrenia, *BMC Medicine*, 11: 127.

Cowlishaw, S., Merkouris, S., Dowling, N. et al. (2012) Psychological therapies for pathological and problem gambling, *Cochrane Database Systematic Reviews*, 11: CD008937.

Craig, T., Bialas, I., Hodson, S. et al. (2004) Intergenerational transmission of somatization behaviour. 2. Observations of joint attention and bids for attention, *Psychological Medicine*, 34: 199–209.

Crawford, L., Holloway, K. and Domjan, M. (1993) The nature of sexual reinforcement, *Journal of Experimental Analysis of Behaviour*, 60: 55–66.

Creed, F. and Barsky, A. (2004) Systematic review of the epidemiology of somatisation disorder and hypochondriasis, *Journal of Psychosomatic Research*, 56: 391–408.

Crosby, A., Han, B., Ortega, L. et al. (2011) Suicidal thoughts and behaviours among adults aged ≥18 years United States, 2008–2009, *Morbidity and Mortality Weekly Report: Surveillance Summaries*, 60 (SS13): 1–22.

Cross-Disorder Group of the Psychiatric Genomics Consortium (2013) Genetic relationship between five psychiatric disorders estimated from genome-wide SNPs, *Nature Genetics*, 45: 984–94.

Cuijpers, P., Sijbrandij, M., Koole, S. et al. (2014) Adding psychotherapy to antidepressant medication in depression and anxiety disorders: a meta-analysis, *World Psychiatry*, 13: 56–67.

Daeppen, J., Bertholet, N., Gaume, J. et al. (2011) Efficacy of brief motivational intervention in reducing binge drinking in young men: a randomized controlled trial, *Drug and Alcohol Dependency*, 113: 169–75.

Day, J., Bentall, R., Roberts, C. et al. (2005) Attitudes toward antipsychotic medication: the impact of clinical variables and relationships with health professionals, *Archives of General Psychiatry*, 62: 717–24.

Deblinger, E., Mannarino, A., Cohen, J. et al. (2006) A follow-up study of a multisite, randomized, controlled trial for children with sexual abuse-related PTSD symptoms, *Journal of the American Academy of Child and Adolescent Psychiatry*, 45: 1474–84.

Degenhardt, L., Day, C., Dietze, P. et al. (2005) Effects of a sustained heroin shortage in three Australian States, *Addiction*, 100: 908–20.

Delfabbro, P. and Thrupp, L. (2003) The social determinants of youth gambling in South Australian adolescents, *Journal of Adolescence*, 3: 313–30.

Demyttenaere, K., Van Ganse, E., Gregoirre, J. et al. (1998) Compliance in depressed patients treated with fluoxetine or amitriptyline: Belgian Compliance Study Group, *International Clinical Psychopharmacology*, 13: 11–17.

Dhawan, S. and Marshall, W. (1996) Sexual abuse histories of sexual offenders, *Sexual Abuse: A Journal of Research and Treatment*, 8: 7–15.

Didie, E., Menard, W., Stern, A. et al. (2008) Occupational functioning and impairment in adults with body dysmorphic disorder, *Comprehensive Psychiatry*, 49: 561–9.

Dienes, K.A., Hammen, C., Henry, R.M. et al. (2006) The stress sensitization hypothesis: understanding the course of bipolar disorder, *Journal of Affective Disorders*, 95: 43–9.

Diller, R.S. (2003) Panic disorder in children and adolescents, *Yonsei Medical Journal*, 44: 174–9.
Dimsdale, J. and Dantzer, R. (2007) A biological substrate for somatoform disorders: importance of pathophysiology, *Psychosomatic Medicine*, 69: 850–4.
Distel, M., Hottenga, J., Trull, T. et al. (2008) Chromosome 9: linkage for borderline personality disorder features, *Psychiatric Genetics*, 18: 302–7.
Docter, R. and Prince, V. (1997) Transvestism: a survey of 1032 crossdressers, *Archives of Sexual Behaviour*, 26: 589–605.
Dollard, J. and Miller, N. (1950) *Personality and Psychotherapy*. New York: McGraw-Hill.
Dong, X., Beck, T. and Simon, M. (2009) The associations of gender, depression and elder mistreatment in a community-dwelling Chinese population: the modifying effect of social support, *Archives of Gerontology and Geriatrics*, 57: 250–6.
Dove, D., Warren, Z., McPheeters, M. et al. (2012) Medications for adolescents and young adults with autism spectrum disorders: a systematic review, *Pediatrics*, 130: 717–26.
Drageset, J., Espehaug, B. and Kirkevold, M. (2012) The impact of depression and sense of coherence on emotional and social loneliness among nursing home residents without cognitive impairment: a questionnaire survey, *Journal of Clinical Nursing*, 21: 965–74.
Drury, V., Birchwood, M. and Cochrane, R. (2000) Cognitive therapy and recovery from acute psychosis: a controlled trial. 3: Five-year follow-up, *British Journal of Psychiatry*, 177: 8–14.
Dumaret, A., Coppel-Batsch, M. and Couraud, S. (1997) Adult outcome of children reared for long-term periods in foster families, *Child Abuse and Neglect*, 21: 911–27.
Dyck, M., Habel, U., Slodczyk, J. et al. (2009) Negative bias in fast emotion discrimination in borderline personality disorder, *Psychological Medicine*, 39: 855–64.
Eack, S.M., Bahorik, A., Newhill, C. et al. (2012) Interviewer-perceived honesty as a mediator of racial disparities in the diagnosis of schizophrenia, *Psychiatric Service*, 63: 875–80.
Eamon, M. and Mulder, C. (2005) Predicting antisocial behaviour among Latino young adolescents: an ecological systems analysis, *American Journal of Orthopsychiatry*, 75: 117–27.
Egger, H., Costello, E. and Angold, A. (2003) School refusal and psychiatric disorders: a community study, *Journal of the American Academy of Child and Adolescent Psychiatry*, 42: 797–807.
Eisen, A., Raleigh, H. and Neuhoff, C. (2008) The unique impact of parent training for separation anxiety disorder in children, *Behavioural Therapy*, 39: 195–206.
Elliott, M. (2000) Gender differences in the causes of depression, *Women and Health*, 33: 163–77.
Ellis, A. (1957) Rational psychotherapy and individual psychology, *Journal of Individual Psychology*, 13: 38–44.
Elzinga, B., Phaf, R., Ardon, A. et al. (2003) Directed forgetting between, but not within, dissociative personality states, *Journal of Abnormal Psychology*, 112: 237–43.
Enache, D., Winblad, B. and Aarsland, D. (2011) Depression in dementia: epidemiology, mechanisms and treatment, *Current Opinion in Psychiatry*, 24: 461–72.
Engels, R.C., Hermans, R., van Baaren, R.B. et al. (2009) Alcohol portrayal on television affects actual drinking behaviour, *Alcohol and Alcoholism*, 44: 244–9.
Erikson, E. (1980) *Growth and Crisis of the Healthy Personality: Identity and the life cycle*. New York: W.W. Norton.

Escobar, J., Gara, M., Diaz-Martinez, A. et al. (2007) Effectiveness of a time-limited cognitive behaviour therapy type intervention among primary care patients with medically unexplained symptoms, *Annals of Family Medicine*, 5: 328–35.

Essau, C., Conradt, J., Sasagawa, S. et al. (2012) Prevention of anxiety symptoms in children: results from a universal school-based trial, *Behavioural Therapy*, 43: 450–64.

European Monitoring Centre for Drugs and Drug Addiction (2012) *Prevalence of Daily Cannabis Use in the European Union and Norway*. Luxembourg: Publications Office of the European Union.

Exline, J., Prince-Paul, M., Root, B. et al. (2012) Forgiveness, depressive symptoms and communication at the end of life: a study with family members of hospice patients, *Journal of Palliative Medicine*, 15: 1113–19.

Fagan, P., Wise, T., Schmidt, C., Jr. et al. (2002) Pedophilia, *Journal of the American Medical Association*, 288: 2458–65.

Fairburn, C. (2008) *Cognitive Behavior Therapy and Eating Disorders*. New York: Guilford Press.

Fairburn, C., Norman, P. and Welch, S. (1995) A prospective study of outcome in bulimia nervosa and the long-term effects of three psychological treatments, *Archives of General Psychiatry*, 52: 304–12.

Fairchild, G., Passamonti, L., Hurford, G. et al. (2011) Brain structure abnormalities in early-onset and adolescent-onset conduct disorder, *American Journal of Psychiatry*, 68: 624–33.

Fallon, B.A., Petkova, E., Skritskaya, N. et al. (2008) A double-masked, placebo-controlled study of fluoxetine for hypochondriasis, *Journal of Clinical Psychopharmacology*, 28: 638–45.

Fallon, B.A., Qureshi, A., Schneier, F. et al. (2003) An open trial of fluvoxamine for hypochondriasis, *Psychosomatics*, 44: 298–303.

Falloon, I., Boyd, J., McGill, C. et al. (1982) Family management in the prevention of exacerbations of schizophrenia: a controlled study, *New England Journal of Medicine*, 306: 1437–40.

Farrell, L. and Barrett, P. (2006) Obsessive-compulsive disorder across developmental trajectory: cognitive processing of threat in children, adolescents and adults, *British Journal of Psychology*, 97: 95–114.

Farrington, D. (2000) Psychosocial predictors of adult antisocial personality and adult convictions, *Behavioural Sciences and the Law*, 18: 605–22.

Feliu, M., Edwards, C., Sudhakar, S. et al. (2008) Neuropsychological effects and attitudes in patients following electroconvulsive therapy, *Neuropsychiatric Disease and Treatment*, 4: 613–17.

Fergusson, D., Boden, J. and Horwood, L. (2007) Exposure to single parenthood in childhood and later mental health, educational, economic, and criminal behaviour outcomes, *Archives of General Psychiatry*, 64: 1089–95.

Ferrara, M., Langiano, E., Di Brango, T. et al. (2008) Prevalence of stress, anxiety and depression in Alzheimer caregivers, *Health Quality and Life Outcomes*, 6: 6–93.

Findling, R.L., Kowatch, R.A. and Post, R.M. (2003) *Pediatric Bipolar Disorder: A handbook for clinicians*. London: Martin Dunitz.

Fineberg, N., Hengartner, M., Bergbaum, C. et al. (2012) A prospective population-based cohort study of the prevalence, incidence and impact of obsessive-compulsive symptomatology, *International Journal of Psychiatry and Clinical Practice*, 17: 170–8.

Fink, P., Hansen, M. and Oxhoj, M. (2004) The prevalence of somatoform disorders among internal medical inpatients, *Journal of Psychosomatic Research*, 56: 413–18.

Finkelhor, D. (1984) *Child Sexual Abuse: New theory and research*. New York: Free Press.

Fisher, H., Moffitt, T., Houts, R. et al. (2012) Bullying victimisation and risk of self-harm in early adolescence: longitudinal cohort study, *British Medical Journal*, 344: e2683.

Foa, E. and Kozak, M. (1986) Emotional processing of fear: exposure to corrective information, *Psychological Bulletin*, 99: 20–35.

Fonagy, P. (2000) Attachment and borderline personality disorder, *Journal of the American Psychoanalytic Association*, 48: 1129–46.

Fonagy, P., Bateman, A. and Bateman, A. (2011) The widening scope of mentalizing: a discussion, *Psychology and Psychotherapy*, 84: 98–110.

Forman, E., Shaw, J., Goetter, E. et al. (2012) Long-term follow-up of a randomized controlled trial comparing acceptance and commitment therapy and standard cognitive behaviour therapy for anxiety and depression, *Behavoiural Therapy*, 43: 801–11.

Freeman, D., Garety, P.A., Kuipers, E. et al. (2002) A cognitive model of persecutory delusions, *British Journal of Clinical Psychology*, 41: 331–47.

Freud, S. (1900) *The Interpretation of Dreams*. New York: Wiley.

Freud, S. ([1914] 1957) On narcissism: an introduction, in J. Strachey (ed. and trans.) *The Standard Edition of Complete Psychological Works* (Vol. 14). London: Hogarth Press.

Freud, S. ([1917] 1957) Mourning and melancholia, in J. Strachey (ed. and trans.) *The Standard Edition of Complete Psychological Works* (Vol. 14). London: Hogarth Press.

Freud, S. ([1920] 1990) *Beyond the Pleasure Principle*. New York: W.W. Norton.

Freud, S. (1922) *Introductory Lectures on Psychoanalysis*. London: George Allen & Unwin.

Freud, S. and Breuer, J. (2004) *Studies in Hysteria*. New York: Penguin.

Friedel, R. (2004) Dopamine dysfunction in borderline personality disorder: a hypothesis, *Neuropsychopharmacology*, 29: 1029–39.

Frith, C. and Corcoran, R. (1996) Exploring 'theory of mind' in people with schizophrenia, *Psychological Medicine*, 26: 521–30.

Frith, U. and Frith, C. (2003) Development and neurophysiology of mentalizing, *Philosophical Transactions of the Royal Society of London B*, 358: 459–73.

Frith, U. and Happe, F. (1994) Autism: beyond theory of mind, *Cognition*, 50: 115–32.

Fromm-Reichman, F. (1948) Notes on the development of treatment of schizophrenia by psycho-analytic psychotherapy, *Psychiatry*, 11: 263–73.

Fruzzetti, A.E., Shenk, C. and Hoffman, P.D. (2005) Family interaction and the development of borderline personality disorder: a transactional model, *Development and Psychopathology*, 17: 1007–30.

Gaebel, W. and Riesbeck, M. (2007) Revisiting the relapse predictive validity of prodromal symptoms in schizophrenia, *Schizophrenia Research*, 95: 19–29.

Gaebel, W., Janner, M., Frommann, N. et al. (2002) First vs. multiple episode schizophrenia: two-year outcome of intermittent and maintenance medication strategies, *Schizophrenia Research*, 53: 145–59.

Gallagher, D., Savva, G., Kenny, R. et al. (2013) What predicts persistent depression in older adults across Europe? Utility of clinical and neuropsychological predictors from the SHARE study, *Journal of Affective Disorder*, 147: 192–7.

Gallagher-Thompson, D. and Steffen, A. (1994) Comparative effects of cognitive behavioural and brief psychodynamic psychotherapies for depressed family caregivers, *Journal of Consulting and Clinical Psychology*, 62: 543–9.

Galves, A. and Walker, D. (2012) Debunking the science behind attention-deficit/hyperactivity disorder as a 'brain disorder', *Ethical Human Psychology and Psychiatry*, 14: 27–40.

Garnefski, N., Rieffe, C., Jellesma, F. et al. (2007) Cognitive emotion regulation strategies and emotional problems in 9–11-year-old children: the development of an instrument, *European Child and Adolescent Psychiatry*, 16: 1–9.

Geller, D. (2007) Obsessive-compulsive and spectrum disorders in children and adolescents, *Journal of Developmental and Behavioural Pediatrics*, 28: 225–33.

Gibbon, S., Duggan, C., Stoffers, J. et al. (2010) Psychological interventions for antisocial personality disorder, *Cochrane Database Systematic Reviews*, 6: CD007668.

Gilbert, P. (2010) *The Compassionate Mind*. London: Constable & Robinson.

Gilman, S., Kawachi, I., Fitzmaurice, G. et al. (2003) Family disruption in childhood and risk of adult depression, *American Journal of Psychiatry*, 160: 939–46.

Ginsburg, G., Kendall, P., Sakolsky, D. et al. (2011) Remission after acute treatment in children and adolescents with anxiety disorders: findings from the CAMS, *Journal of Consulting and Clinical Psychology*, 79: 806–13.

Glassman, L., Weierich, M., Hooley, J. et al. (2007) Child maltreatment, non-suicidal self-injury, and the mediating role of self-criticism, *Behaviour Research and Therapy*, 45: 2483–90.

Gleaves, D. (1996) The sociocognitive model of dissociative identity disorder: a reexamination of the evidence, *Psychological Bulletin*, 120: 42–59.

Goddard, A., Mason, G., Almai, A. et al. (2001) Reductions in occipital cortex GABA levels in panic disorder detected with 1H-magnetic resonance spectroscopy, *Archives of General Psychiatry*, 58: 556–61.

Goldacre, B. (2012) *Bad Pharma: How medicine is broken and how we can fix it*. London: Fourth Estate.

Grant, B., Chou, S., Goldstein, R. et al. (2008) Prevalence, correlates, disability, and comorbidity of DSM-IV borderline personality disorder: results from the Wave 2 National Epidemiologic Survey on Alcohol and Related Conditions, *Journal of Clinical Psychiatry*, 69: 533–45.

Grant, B., Stinson, F., Hasin, D. et al. (2005) Prevalence, correlates, and comorbidity of bipolar I disorder and axis I and II disorders: results from the National Epidemiologic Survey on Alcohol and Related Conditions, *Journal of Clinical Psychiatry*, 66: 1205–15.

Gray, J. (1991) The neurophysiology of temperament, in J. Strelau and A. Angleitner (eds.) *Explorations in Temperament: International perspectives on theory and measurement*, New York: Plenum.

Greeven, A., Van Balkom, A., Van der Leeden, R. et al. (2009) Cognitive behavioural therapy versus paroxetine in the treatment of hypochondriasis: an 18-month naturalistic follow-up, *Journal of Behavioural Therapy and Experimental Psychiatry*, 40: 487–96.

Grenier, S., Schuurmans, J., Goldfarb, M. et al. (2011) Scientific committee of the ESA study: the epidemiology of specific phobia and subthreshold fear subtypes in a community-based sample of older adults, *Depression and Anxiety*, 28: 456–63.

Grilo, C., Pagano, M., Skodol, A. et al. (2007) Natural course of bulimia nervosa and of eating disorder not otherwise specified: 5-year prospective study of remissions, relapses, and the effects of personality disorder psychopathology, *Journal of Clinical Psychiatry*, 68: 738–46.

Grinspoon, L. and Bakalar, J. (1986) Can drugs be used to enhance the psychotherapeutic process, *American Journal of Psychotherapy*, 40: 393–404.

Gruber, K., Chutuape, M. and Stitzer, M. (2000) Reinforcement-based intensive outpatient treatment for inner city opiate abusers: a short-term evaluation, *Drug and Alcohol Dependence*, 57: 211–23.

Grzywacz, J., Almeida, D., Neupert, S. et al. (2004) Socioeconomic status and health: a micro-level analysis of exposure and vulnerability to daily stressors, *Journal of Health and Social Behaviour*, 45: 1–16.

Guastella, A., Carson, D., Dadds, M. et al. (2008) Does oxytocin influence the early detection of angry and happy faces?, *Psychoneuroendocrinology*, 34: 220–5.

Guéguen, N., Jacob, C., Le Guellec, H. et al. (2008) Sound level of environmental music and drinking behaviour: a field experiment with beer drinkers, *Alcoholism: Clinical and Experimental Research*, 10: 1795–8.

Guiao, I. and Thompson, E. (2004) Ethnicity and problem behaviours among adolescent females in the United States, *Health Care for Women International*, 25: 296–310.

Gunn, J., Robertson, G., Dell, S. et al. (1978) *Psychiatric Aspects of Imprisonment*. London: Academic Press.

Gupta, V., Anitha, S., Hegde, M. et al. (2005) Aluminium in Alzheimer's disease: are we still at a crossroad?, *Cellular and Molecular Life Sciences*, 62: 143–58.

Guthrie, E. (1996) Psychotherapy for somatisation disorders, *Current Opinion in Psychiatry*, 9: 182–7.

Gyani, A., Shafran, R., Layard, R. et al. (2013) Enhancing recovery rates: lessons from year one of IAPT, *Behaviour Research and Therapy*, 51: 597–606.

Halligan, P., Athwal, B., Oakley, D. et al. (2000) Imaging hypnotic paralysis: implications for conversion hysteria, *Lancet*, 355: 986–7.

Halmi, K., Sunday, S., Strober, M. et al. (2000) Perfectionism in anorexia nervosa: variation by clinical subtype, obsessionality, and pathological eating behaviour, *American Journal of Psychiatry*, 157: 1799–1805.

Hammond, W., Gillen, M. and Yen, I. (2010) Workplace discrimination and depressive symptoms: a study of multi-ethnic hospital employees, *Race and Social Problems*, 2: 19–30.

Hane, A., Cheah, C., Rubin, K. et al. (2008) The role of maternal behaviour in the relation between shyness and social withdrawal in early childhood and social withdrawal in middle childhood, *Social Development*, 17: 795–811.

Hanrahan, F., Field, A., Jones, F. et al. (2013) A meta-analysis of cognitive therapy for worry in generalized anxiety disorder, *Clinical Psychology Review*, 33: 120–32.

Hare, R. (2002) Psychopathy and risk for recidivism and violence, in N. Gray, J. Laing and L. Noaks (eds.) *Criminal Justice, Mental Health, and the Politics of Risk*. London: Cavendish.

Hare, R., Clark, D., Grann, M. et al. (2000) Psychopathy and the predictive utility of the PCL-R: an international perspective, *Behavioural Sciences and the Law*, 18: 623–45.

Harrington, M., Robinson, J., Bolton, S. et al. (2011) A longitudinal study of risk factors for incident drug use in adults: findings from a representative sample of the US population, *Canadian Journal of Psychiatry*, 56: 686–95.

Harrington, R., Whittaker, J. and Shoebridge, P. (1998) Psychological treatment of depression in children and adolescents: a review of treatment research, *British Journal of Psychiatry*, 173: 291–8.

Harvey, A., Watkins, E., Mansell, W. and Shafran, R. (2004) *Cognitive Behavioural Processes across Psychological Disorders: A transtheoretical approach to research and treatment.* Oxford: Oxford University Press.

Haworth-Hoeppner, S. (2000) The critical shapes of body image: the role of culture and family in the production of eating disorders, *Journal of Marriage and the Family*, 62: 212–27.

Hayes, S., Luoma, J., Bond, F. et al. (2006) Acceptance and commitment therapy: model, processes and outcomes, *Behaviour Research and Therapy*, 44: 1-25.

Hazell, P. (2004) Depression in children and adolescents, *Clinical Evidence*, 12: 427–42.

Hazell, P., Kohn, M., Dickson, R. et al. (2011) Core ADHD symptom improvement with atomoxetine versus methylphenidate: a direct comparison meta-analysis, *Journal of Attention Disorders*, 15: 674–83.

Hedden, T. and Gabrieli, J. (2005) Healthy and pathological processes in adult development: new evidence from neuroimaging of the aging brain, *Current Opinion in Neurology*, 18: 740–7.

Hellstrom, K., Fellenius, J. and Öst, L. (1996) One versus five sessions of applied tension in the treatment of blood phobia, *Behaviour Research and Therapy*, 34: 101–12.

Hemsley, D. (1996) Schizophrenia: a cognitive model and its implications for psychological intervention, *Behaviour Modification*, 20: 139–69.

Hendin, H. (1992) The psychodynamics of suicide, *International Review of Psychiatry*, 4: 157–67.

Henquet, C., Murray, R., Linszen, D. et al. (2005) The environment and schizophrenia: the role of cannabis use, *Schizophrenia Bulletin*, 31: 608–12.

Henry, D., Tolan, P. and Gorman Smith, D. (2001) Longitudinal family and peer group effects on violence and nonviolent delinquency, *Journal of Clinical Child Psychology*, 30: 172–86.

Heylens, G., De Cuypere, G., Zucker, K. et al. (2012) Gender identity disorder in twins: a review of the case report literature, *Journal of Sexual Medicine*, 9: 751–7.

Hirshfeld-Becker, D., Biederman, J., Henin, A. et al. (2006) Behavioural inhibition in preschool children at risk is a specific predictor of middle childhood social anxiety: a five-year follow-up, *Psychiatric Clinics of North America*, 290: 353–70.

Hirshfeld-Becker, D., Masek, B., Henin, A. et al. (2010) Cognitive behavioural therapy for 4- to 7-year-old children with anxiety disorders: a randomized controlled trial, *Journal of Consulting and Clinical Psychology*, 78: 495–510.

Hodgins, D., Stea, J. and Grant, J. (2011) Gambling disorders, *Lancet*, 378: 1874–84.

Hoeve, M., Dubas, J., Eichelsheim, V. et al. (2009) The relationship between parenting and delinquency: a meta-analysis, *Journal of Abnormal Child Psychology*, 37: 749–75.

Hofmann, W., Rauch, R. and Gawronski, B. (2007) And deplete is not into temptation: automatic attitudes, dietary restraint, and self-regulatory resources as determinants of eating behaviour, *Journal of Experimental Social Psychology*, 43: 497–504.

Holden, U. and Woods, R. (1995) *Reality Orientation: Psychological approaches to the confused elderly.* Oxford: Churchill Livingstone.

Holen-Hoeksema, S. (1990) *Sex Difference in Depression*. Stanford, CA: Stanford University Press.

Hollon, S., DeRubeis, R., Shelton, R. et al. (2005) Prevention of relapse following cognitive therapy vs. medications in moderate to severe depression, *Archives of General Psychiatry*, 62: 417–22.

Honjo, S., Nishide, T., Niwa, S. et al. (2001) School refusal and depression with school nonattendance in children and adolescents: comparative assessment between the children's depression inventory and somatic complaints, *Psychiatry and Clinical Neurosciences*, 55: 629–34.

Horowitz, M. (1986) Stress-response syndromes: a review of posttraumatic and adjustment disorders, *Hospital and Community Psychiatry*, 37: 241–9.

Hotopf, M., Chidgey, J., Addington-Hall, J. et al. (2002) Depression in advanced disease: a systematic review. Part 1. Prevalence and case finding, *Palliative Medicine*, 16: 81–97.

Hovarth, A.O. and Symonds, B.D. (1991) Relation between working alliance and outcome in psychotherapy: a meta-analysis, *Journal of Counselling Psychology*, 38: 139–49.

Hrdy, S. (2009) *Mothers and Others: The evolutionary origins of mutual understanding*. Cambridge, MA: Belknap/Harvard.

Hugdahl, K., Nygård, M., Falkenberg, L. et al. (2013) Failure of attention focus and cognitive control in schizophrenia patients with auditory verbal hallucinations: evidence from dichotic listening, *Schizophrenia Research*, 147: 301–9.

Hunot, V., Churchill, R., Silva de Lima, M. et al. (2007) Psychological therapies for generalised anxiety disorder, *Cochrane Database Systematic Reviews*, 1: CD001848.

Hurwitz, R., Blackmore, R., Hazell, P. et al. (2012) Tricyclic antidepressants for autism spectrum disorders (ASD) in children and adolescents, *Cochrane Database Systematic Reviews*, 3: CD008372.

In-Albon, T. and Schneider, S. (2012) Does the vigilance-avoidance gazing behaviour of children with separation anxiety disorder change after cognitive-behavioural therapy?, *Journal of Abnormal Child Psychology*, 40: 1149–56.

In-Albon, T., Kossowsky, J. and Schneider, S. (2010) Vigilance and avoidance of threat in the eye movements of children with separation anxiety disorder, *Journal of Abnormal Child Psychology*, 38: 225–35.

Ipser, J., Seedat, S. and Stein, D. (2006) Pharmacotherapy for post-traumatic stress disorder: a systematic review and meta-analysis, *South Africa Medical Journal*, 96: 1088–96.

Ishihara, K. and Sasa, M. (1999) Mechanism underlying the therapeutic effects of electroconvulsive therapy (ECT) on depression, *Japanese Journal of Pharmacology*, 80: 185–9.

Janiak-Baluch, B. and Lehmkuhl, G. (2013) [Psychological disorders and somatoform symptoms in the outpatient pediatric practice], *Prax Kinderpsychologie und Kinderpsychiatrie*, 62: 654–69.

Jenike, M.A. (1998) Neurosurgical treatment of obsessive-compulsive disorder, *British Medical Journal*, 163 (suppl. 35): 75–90.

Jick, S., Dean, A. and Jick, H. (1995) Antidepressants and suicide, *British Medical Journal*, 310: 215–18.

Jimerson, D., Lesem, M., Kaye, W. et al. (1992) Low serotonin and dopamine metabolite concentrations in cerebrospinal fluid from bulimic patients with frequent bulimic episodes, *Archives of General Psychiatry*, 49: 132–8.

Jirapramukpitak, T., Harpham, T. and Prince, M. (2011) Family violence and its 'adversity package': a community survey of family violence and adverse mental outcomes among young people, *Social Psychiatry and Psychiatric Epidemiology*, 46: 825–31.

Johnson, L., Lundström, O., Aberg-Wistedt, A. et al. (2003) Social support in bipolar disorder: its relevance to remission and relapse, *Bipolar Disorder*, 5: 129–37.

Jokela, M., Batty, G. and Kivimäki, M. (2013) Ageing and the prevalence and treatment of mental health problems, *Psychology of Medicine*, 16: 1–9.

Jones, C., Cormac, I., Mota, J. et al. (2000) Cognitive behaviour therapy for schizophrenia, *Cochrane Database Systematic Reviews*, 2: CD000524.

Jones, L. (2005) Cognitive style in bipolar disorder, *British Journal of Psychiatry*, 187: 431–7.

Kabat-Zinn, J. (1990) *The Full Catastrophe Living: Using the wisdom of your body and mind to face stress, pain, and illness*. New York: Delacorte.

Kaplan, G., Casoy, J. and Zummo, J. (2013) Impact of long-acting injectable antipsychotics on medication adherence and clinical, functional, and economic outcomes of schizophrenia, *Patient Preference and Adherence*, 7: 1171–80.

Kaye, W. (2008) Neurobiology of anorexia and bulimia nervosa, *Physiology and Behaviour*, 94: 121–35.

Kaye, W., Frank, G., Bailer, U. et al. (2005) Serotonin alterations in anorexia and bulimia nervosa: insights from imaging studies, *Physiology and Behaviour*, 85: 73–81.

Kaye, W.H., Gwirtsman, H.E., Brewerton, T.D. et al. (1988) Bingeing behaviour and plasma amino acids: a possible involvement of brain serotonin in bulimia nervosa, *Psychiatry Research*, 23: 31–43.

Kearney, C. (2001) *School Refusal Behavior in Youth: A functional approach to assessment and treatment*, Washington, DC: American Psychological Association.

Kearney, C. and Albano, A. (2004) The functional profiles of school refusal behavior: diagnostic aspects, *Behavior Modification*, 28: 147–61.

Kellett, S. (2005) The treatment of dissociative identity disorder with cognitive analytic therapy: experimental evidence of sudden gains, *Journal of Trauma Dissociation*, 6: 55–81.

Kellogg, S. and Young, J. (2006) Schema therapy for borderline personality disorder, *Journal of Clinical Psychology*, 62: 445–58.

Kéri, S. and Kelemen, O. (2009) The role of attention and immediate memory in vulnerability to interpersonal criticism during family transactions in schizophrenia, *British Journal of Clinical Psychology*, 48: 21–9.

Kessler, R., Chiu, W., Demler, O. et al. (2005) Prevalence, severity, and comorbidity of twelve-month DSM-IV disorders in the National Comorbidity Survey Replication (NCS-R), *Archives of General Psychiatry*, 62: 617–27.

Kety, S. (1988) Schizophrenic illness in the families of schizophrenic adoptees: findings from the Danish national sample, *Schizophrenia Bulletin*, 14: 217–22.

Khanna, M. and Kendall, P. (2010) Computer-assisted cognitive behavioural therapy for child anxiety: result of a randomized clinical trial, *Journal of Consulting and Clinical Psychology*, 78: 737–45.

Khashan, A., Abel, K., McNamee, R. et al. (2008) Higher risk of offspring schizophrenia following antenatal maternal exposure to severe adverse life events, *Archives of General Psychiatry*, 65: 146–52.

Kiehl, K., Smith, A., Hare, R. et al. (2001) Limbic abnormalities in affective processing by criminal psychopaths as revealed by functional magnetic resonance imaging, *Biological Psychiatry*, 50: 677–84.

Kihlstrom, J. (2005) Dissociative disorders, *Annual Review of Clinical Psychology*, 1: 227–53.

King, M., Semlyen, J., Tai, S. et al. (2008) A systematic review of mental disorder, suicide, and deliberate self-harm in lesbian, gay and bisexual people, *BMC Psychiatry*, 8: 70.

King, N.J. and Bernstein, G.A. (2001) School refusal in children and adolescents: a review of the past 10 years, *Journal of the Academy of Child and Adolescent Psychiatry*, 40: 197–205.

King, S., Waschbusch, D.A., Pelham, W.E. et al. (2009) Social information processing in elementary-school aged children with ADHD: medication effects and comparisons with typical children, *Journal of Abnormal Child Psychology*, 37: 579–89.

Kirkbride, J., Errazuriz, A., Croudace, T. et al. (2012) Incidence of schizophrenia and other psychoses in England, 1950–2009: a systematic review and meta-analyses, *PLoS One*, 7: 31660.

Kirsch, I. (2009) *The Emperor's New Drugs: Exploding the antidepressant myth*. London: Bodley Head.

Klauke, B., Deckert, J., Reif, A. et al. (2010) Life events in panic disorder: an update on candidate stressors, *Depression and Anxiety*, 27: 716–30.

Klein, M. (1927) The psychological principles of infant analysis, *International Journal of Psychoanalysis*, 8: 25–37.

Koegel, R. and Koegel, L. (2012) *The PRT Pocket Guide: Pivotal response treatment for autism spectrum disorders*. Baltimore, MD: Brookes Publishing.

Kråkvik, B., Stiles, T. and Hugdahl, K. (2013) Experiencing malevolent voices is associated with attentional dysfunction in psychotic patients, *Scandinavian Journal of Psychology*, 54: 72–7.

Krampe, H., Stawicki, S., Wagner, T. et al. (2006) Follow-up of 180 alcoholic patients for up to 7 years after outpatient treatment: impact of alcohol deterrents on outcome, *Alcoholism: Clinical and Experimental Research*, 30: 86–95.

Krantz, G. and Lundberg, U. (2006) Workload, work stress, and sickness absence in Swedish male and female white-collar employees, *Scandinavian Journal of Public Health*, 34: 238–46.

Kripke, D.F., Nievergelt, C.M., Joo, E. et al. (2009) Circadian polymorphisms associated with affective disorders, *Journal of Circadian Rhythms*, 7: 2.

Kruijver, F., Zhou, J., Pool, C. et al. (2000) Male-to-female transsexuals have female neuron numbers in a limbic nucleus, *Journal of Clinical Endocrinology and Metabolism*, 85: 2034–41.

Ladouceur, R., Sylvain, C., Boutin, C. et al. (2003) Group therapy for pathological gamblers: a cognitive approach, *Behavioural Research and Therapy*, 41: 87–96.

Lam, D., Hayward, P., Watkins, E. et al. (2005). Relapse prevention in patients with bipolar disorder: cognitive therapy outcome after 2 years, *American Journal of Psychiatry*, 162: 324–9.

Landau, R., Werner, S., Auslander, G. et al. (2010) What do cognitively intact older people think about the use of electronic tracking devices for people with dementia? A preliminary analysis, *International Psychogeriatrics*, 22: 1301–9.

Langstrom, N. and Zucker, K. (2005) Transvestic fetishism in the general population: prevalence and correlates, *Journal of Sexual and Marital Therapy*, 31: 87–95.

Larochelle, S., Diguer, L., Laverdière, O. et al. (2011) Predictors of psychological treatment noncompletion among sexual offenders, *Clinical Psychology Review*, 31: 554–62.

Larson, J. and Lochman, J. (2002) *Helping Schoolchildren Cope with Anger: A cognitive-behavioural intervention*. New York: Guilford Press.

Laws, D. and Marshall, W. (2003) A brief history of behavioural and cognitive behavioural approaches to sex offenders: Part 1. Early developments, *Sexual Abuse: A Journal of Research and Treatment*, 15: 75–92.

Leff, J. and Vaughn, C. (1985) *Expressed Emotions in Families: Its significance for mental illness*. New York: Guilford Press.

Leonard, W., Pitts, M., Mitchell, A. et al. (2012) *Private Lives 2: The second national survey of the health and wellbeing of GLBT Australians*. Melbourne, VIC: Australian Research Centre in Sex, Health and Society, La Trobe University.

Leskin, G.A., Kaloupek, D.G. and Keane, T.M. (1998) Treatment for traumatic memories: review and recommendations, *Clinical Psychology Review*, 18: 983–1002.

Lessard, M., Marchand, A., Pelland, M. et al. (2012) Comparing two brief psychological interventions to usual care in panic disorder patients presenting to the emergency department with chest pain, *Behavioural Cognitive Psychotherapy*, 40: 129–47.

Lewinsohn, P., Youngren, M. and Grosscup, S. (1979) Reinforcement and depression, in A. Depue (ed.) *The Psychobiology of the Depressive Disorders*. New York: Academic Press.

Lewis-Morrarty, E., Degnan, K., Chronis-Tuscano, A. et al. (2012) Maternal over-control moderates the association between early childhood behavioural inhibition and adolescent social anxiety symptoms, *Journal of Abnormal Child Psychology*, 40: 1363–73.

Lewy, A.J., Bauer, V.K. and Cutler, N.L. (1998) Morning vs. evening light treatment of patients with winter depression, *Archives of General Psychiatry*, 55: 890–6.

Liau, A., Barriga, A. and Gibbs, J. (1998) Relations between self-serving cognitive distortions and overt vs. covert antisocial behaviour in adolescents, *Aggressive Behaviour*, 24: 335–46.

Lidbeck, J. (2003) Group therapy for somatization disorders in primary care: maintenance of treatment goals of short cognitive-behavioural treatment one-and-a-half year follow-up, *Acta Psychiatrica Scandinavica*, 107: 449–56.

Lieberman, J., Kinon, B. and Loebel, A. (1990) Dopaminergic mechanisms in idiopathic and drug-induced psychoses, *Schizophrenia Bulletin*, 16: 97–109.

Lindert, J., Ehrenstein, O., Priebe, S. et al. (2009) Depression and anxiety in labour migrants and refugees: a systematic review and meta-analysis, *Social Science and Medicine*, 69: 246–57.

Lindström, M. (2008) Social capital, anticipated ethnic discrimination and self-reported psychological health: a population-based study, *Social Science and Medicine*, 66: 1–13.

Linehan, M. (1993) *Cognitive Behavioural Treatment of Borderline Personality Disorder*. New York: Guilford Press.

Linehan, M., McDavid, J., Brown, M. et al. (2008) Olanzapine plus dialectical behaviour therapy for women with high irritability who meet criteria for borderline personality disorder: a double-blind, placebo-controlled pilot study, *Journal of Clinical Psychiatry*, 69: 999–1005.

Lingjaerde, O., Ahlfors, U., Bech, P. et al. (1987) The UKU side effect rating scale: a new comprehensive rating scale for psychotropic drugs and a cross-sectional study of side effects in neuroleptic-treated patients, *Acta Psychiatrica Scandinavica*, 334: 1–100.

Liotti, G. and Gilbert P. (2011) Mentalizing, motivation, and social mentalities: theoretical considerations and implications for psychotherapy, *Psychology and Psychotherapy*, 84: 9–25.

Liu, W., Lee, G., Goldweber, A. et al. (2012) Impulsivity trajectories and gambling in adolescence among urban male youth, *Addiction*, 108: 780–8.

Loebel, J., Loebel, J., Dager, S. et al. (1991) Anticipation of nursing home placement may be a precipitant of suicide among the elderly, *Journal of the American Geriatrics Society*, 39: 407–8.

Loewe, B., Zipfel, S., Buchholz, C. et al. (2001) Long-term outcome of anorexia nervosa in a prospective 21-year follow-up study, *Psychological Medicine*, 31: 881–90.

Logsdon, R., McCurry, S. and Teri, L. (2005) STAR-Caregivers: a community-based approach for teaching family caregivers to use behavioural strategies to reduce affective disturbances in persons with dementia, *Alzheimer's Care Quarterly*, 6: 146–53.

Loh, C., Teo, Y. and Lim, L. (2013) Deliberate self-harm in adolescent psychiatric outpatients in Singapore: prevalence and associated risk factors, *Singapore Medical Journal*, 54: 491–5.

Lokuge, S., Frey, B., Foster, J. et al. (2011) Depression in women: windows of vulnerability and new insights into the link between estrogen and serotonin, *Journal of Clinical Psychiatry*, 72: 1563–9.

Lopez, V. and Emmer, E. (2002) Influences of beliefs and values on male adolescents' decision to commit violent offenses, *Psychology of Men and Masculinity*, 3: 28–40.

Lösel, F. and Schmucker, M. (2005) The effectiveness of treatment for sexual offenders: a comprehensive meta-analysis, *Journal of Experimental Criminology*, 1: 117–46.

Lovaas, O.I. (1987) Behavioural treatment and normal educational and intellectual functioning in young autistic children, *Journal of Consulting and Clinical Psychology*, 55: 3–9.

Loy, J., Merry, S., Hetrick, S. et al. (2012) Atypical antipsychotics for disruptive behaviour disorders in children and youths, *Cochrane Database Systematic Reviews*, 9: CD008559.

Luque, F. and Jaffe, S. (2009) The molecular and cellular pathogenesis of dementia of the Alzheimer's type: an overview, *International Review of Neurobiology*, 84: 151–65.

Lyketsos, C., Lopez, O., Jones, B. et al. (2002) Prevalence of neuropsychiatric symptoms in dementia and mild cognitive impairment, *Journal of the American Medical Association*, 288: 1475–83.

Lyon, H., Startup, M. and Bentall, R. (1999) Social cognition and the manic defense: attributions, selective attention, and self-schema in bipolar affective disorder, *Journal of Abnormal Psychology*, 108: 273–82.

Magnusson, A. and Partonen, T. (2005) The diagnosis, symptomatology, and epidemiology of seasonal affective disorder, *CNS Spectrums*, 10: 625–34.

Mahmood, T. and Silverstone, T. (2001) Serotonin and bipolar disorder, *Journal of Affective Disorders*, 66: 1–11.

Mahoney, R., Regan, C., Katona, C. et al. (2005) Anxiety and depression in family caregivers of people with Alzheimer disease: the LASER-AD study, *American Journal of Geriatric Psychiatry*, 13: 795–801.

Malaspina, C., Corcoran, K., Kleinhaus, M. et al. (2008) Acute maternal stress in pregnancy and schizophrenia in offspring: a cohort prospective study, *BMC Psychiatry*, 8: 71.

Malberg, J., Eisch, A., Nestler, E. et al. (2000) Chronic antidepressant treatment increases neurogenesis in adult rat hippocampus, *Journal of Neuroscience*, 20: 9104–10.

Malizia, A. (2000) Neurosurgery for psychiatric disorders, in M. Gelder, J. Lopez-Ibor, Jr. and N. Andreasen (eds.) *New Oxford Textbook of Psychiatry*. Oxford: Oxford University Press.

Manassis, K., Mendlowitz, S., Scapillato, D. et al. (2002) Group and individual cognitive-behavioural therapy for childhood anxiety disorders: a randomized trial, *Journal of the American Academy of Child and Adolescent Psychiatry*, 41: 1423–30.

Mannuzza, S. and Klein, R.G. (2000) Long-term prognosis in attention-deficit/hyperactivity disorder, *Child and Adolescent Psychiatric Clinics of North America*, 9: 711–26.

March, J., Silva, S., Petrycki, S. et al. (2004) Fluoxetine, cognitive-behavioral therapy, and their combination for adolescents with depression: Treatment for Adolescents with Depression Study (TADS) randomized controlled trial, *Journal of the American Medical Association*, 292: 807–20.

Marcus, D., Gurley, J., Marchi, M. et al. (2006) Cognitive and perceptual variables in hypochondriasis and health anxiety: a systematic review, *Clinical Psychology Review*, 27: 127–39.

Marks, I., Lovell, K., Noshirvani, H. et al. (1996) Treatment of post-traumatic stress disorder by exposure and/or cognition restructuring, *Archives of General Psychiatry*, 55: 317–25.

Mari-Bauset, S., Zazpe, I., Mari-Sanchis, A. et al. (2014) Evidence of the gluten-free and casein-free diet in autism spectrum disorders: a systematic review, *Journal of Child Neurology*, 29: 1718–27.

Maric, M., Heyne, D.A., de Heus, P. et al. (2012) The role of cognition in school refusal: an investigation of automatic thoughts and cognitive errors, *Behavioural and Cognitive Psychotherapy*, 40: 255–69.

Marjoram, D., Tansley, H., Miller, P. et al. (2005) A Theory of Mind investigation into the appreciation of visual jokes in schizophrenia, *BMC Psychiatry*, 5: 12.

Marshall, J., Halligan, P., Fink, G. et al. (1997) The functional anatomy of a hysterical paralysis, *Cognition*, 64: 1–8.

Matthews, F., Arthur, A., Barnes, L. et al. (2013) A two-decade comparison of prevalence of dementia in individuals aged 65 years and older from three geographical areas of England: results of the Cognitive Function and Ageing Study I and II, *Lancet*, 382: 1405–12.

Matthews, K., Räikkönen, K., Gallo, L. et al. (2008) Association between socioeconomic status and metabolic syndrome in women: testing the reserve capacity model, *Health Psychology*, 27: 576–83.

Maughan, B., Rowe, R., Messer, J. et al. (2004) Conduct disorder and oppositional defiant disorder in a national sample: developmental epidemiology, *Journal of Child Psychology and Psychiatry*, 45: 609–21.

Mauramo, E., Lallukka, T., Laaksonen, M. et al. (2012) Past and present socioeconomic circumstances and psychotropic medication: a register-linkage study, *Journal of Epidemiology and Community Health*, 66: 1143–51.

Mazzotti, E., Sebastiani, C., Antonini Cappellini, G. et al. (2013) Predictors of mood disorders in cancer patients' caregivers, *Supportive Care in Cancer*, 21: 643–7.

McCabe, K., Lucchini, S., Hough, R. et al. (2005) The relation between violence exposure and conduct problems among adolescents: a prospective study, *American Journal of Orthopsychiatry*, 75: 575–84.

McCabe, R., Leudar, I. and Antaki, C. (2004) Do people with schizophrenia display theory of mind deficits in clinical interactions?, *Psychological Medicine*, 34: 401–12.

McCann, J., James, A., Wilson, S. et al. (1996) Prevalence of psychiatric disorders in young people in the care system, *British Medical Journal*, 313: 1529–30.

McCarthy, S., Wilton, L., Murray, M. et al. (2012) The epidemiology of pharmacologically treated attention deficit hyperactivity disorder (ADHD) in children, adolescents and adults in UK primary care, *BMC Pediatrics*, 12: 78.

McGorry, P.D., Yung, A.R., Phillips, L.J. et al. (2002) Randomized controlled trial of interventions designed to reduce the risk of progression to first-episode psychosis in a clinical sample with subthreshold symptoms, *Archives of General Psychiatry*, 59: 921–8.

McIntosh, V.W., Jordan, J., Carter, F. et al. (2005) Three psychotherapies for anorexia nervosa: a randomized controlled trial, *American Journal of Psychiatry*, 162: 741–7.

McLaughlin, K., Kubzansky, L., Dunn, E. et al. (2010) Childhood social environment, emotional reactivity to stress, and mood and anxiety disorders across the life course, *Depression and Anxiety*, 27: 1087–94.

McLean, C., Asnaani, A., Litz, B.T. et al. (2011) Gender differences in anxiety disorders: prevalence, course of illness, comorbidity and burden of illness, *Journal of Psychiatric Research*, 45: 1027–35.

McLeod, B., Weisz, J. and Wood, J. (2007) Examining the association between parenting and childhood depression: a meta-analysis, *Clinical Psychology Review*, 27: 986–1003.

McMahon, A. and Rhudick, P. (1964) Reminiscing, *Archives of General Psychiatry*, 10: 292–8.

McManus, F., Surawy, C., Muse, K. et al. (2012) A randomized clinical trial of mindfulness-based cognitive therapy versus unrestricted services for health anxiety (hypochondriasis), *Journal of Consulting and Clinical Psychology*, 80: 817–28.

Meichenbaum, D. (1985) *Stress Inoculation Training*. New York: Pergamon Press.

Melchior, M., Moffitt, T., Milne, B. et al. (2007) Why do children from socioeconomically disadvantaged families suffer from poor health when they reach adulthood? A life-course study, *American Journal of Epidemiology*, 166: 966–74.

Meltzer, H., Gatward, R., Goodman, R. and Ford, T. (2000) *The Mental Health of Children and Adolescents in Great Britain*. London: The Stationery Office.

Merikangas, K.R., He, J.P., Burstein, M. et al. (2010) Lifetime prevalence of mental disorders in U.S. adolescents: results from the National Comorbidity Survey Replication – Adolescent Supplement (NCS-A), *Journal of the American Academy of Child and Adolescent Psychiatry*, 49: 980–9.

Merry, S., Stasiak, K., Shepherd, M. et al. (2012) The effectiveness of SPARX, a computerised self-help intervention for adolescents seeking help for depression: randomised controlled non-inferiority trial, *British Medical Journal*, 344: 2598.

Meyer, R. (1995) Biology of psychoactive substance dependence disorders: opiates, cocaine, ethanol, in A. Schatzberg and C. Nemeroff (eds.) *The American Psychiatric Press Handbook of Psychopharmacology*. Washington, DC: American Psychiatric Press.

Meyer-Bahlburg, H. (2002) Gender identity disorder in young boys: a parent- and peer-based treatment protocol, *Clinical Child Psychology and Psychiatry*, 7: 360–76.

Micali, N., Heyman, I., Perez, M. et al. (2010) Long-term outcomes of obsessive-compulsive disorder: follow-up of 142 children and adolescents, *British Journal of Psychiatry*, 197: 128–34.

Michaliszyn, D., Marchand, A., Bouchard, S. et al. (2010) A randomized, controlled clinical trial of *in vitro* and *in vivo* exposure for spider phobia, *Cyberpsychology, Behaviour and Social Networking*, 13: 689–95.

Mikami, A., Griggs, M., Lerner, M. et al. (2013) A randomized trial of a classroom intervention to increase peers' social inclusion of children with attention-deficit/hyperactivity disorder, *Journal of Consulting and Clinical Psychology*, 81: 100–12.

Miklowitz, D. (2004) The role of family systems in severe and recurrent psychiatric disorders: a developmental psychopathology view, *Developmental Psychopathology*, 16: 667–88.

Miklowitz, D., Simponeau, T., George, E. et al. (2003) Family-focused treatment of bipolar disorder: 1-year effects of a psychoeducational program in conjunction with pharmacotherapy, *Biological Psychiatry*, 48: 582–92.

Millar, J., Wilson-Annan, J., Anderson, S. et al. (2000) Disruption of two novel genes by a translocation co-segregating with schizophrenia, *Human Molecular Genetics*, 9: 1415–23.

Miller, W.R. and Rollnick, S. (2002) *Motivational Interviewing: Preparing people to change*. New York: Guilford Press.

Mineka, S. and Ohman, A. (2002) Phobias and preparedness: the selective, automatic, and encapsulated nature of fear, *Biological Psychiatry*, 52: 927–37.

Minuchin, S., Rosman, B. and Baker, L. (1978) *Psychosomatic Families: Anorexia nervosa in context*. Cambridge, MA: Harvard University Press.

Miranda, A., Presentación, M.J. and Soriano, M. (2002) Effectiveness of a school-based multicomponent program for the treatment of children with ADHD, *Journal of Learning Disabilities*, 36: 546–62.

Moene, F., Spinhoven, P., Hoogduin, K. et al. (2003) A randomized controlled clinical trial of a hypnosis-based treatment for patients with conversion disorder, motor type, *International Journal of Clinical and Experimental Hypnosis*, 51: 29–50.

Moffitt, T. and Caspi, A. (2001) Childhood predictors differentiate life-course persistent and adolescence-limited antisocial pathways among males and females, *Development and Psychopathology*, 8: 355–75.

Moffitt, T. and Lynam, D., Jr. (1994) The neuropsychology of conduct disorder and delinquency: implications for understanding antisocial behavior, in D.C. Fowles, P. Sutker and S.H. Goodman (eds.) *Progress in Experimental Personality and Psychopathology Research* (Vol. 17). New York: Springer.

Molnar, B., Buka, S. and Kessler R. (2001) Child sexual abuse and subsequent psychopathology: results from the National Comorbidity Survey, *American Journal of Public Health*, 91: 753–60.

Molyneux, G., McCarthy, G., McEniff, S. et al. (2008) Prevalence and predictors of carer burden and depression in carers of patients referred to an old age psychiatric service, *International Psychogeriatrics*, 20: 1193–1202.

Monti, P., Colby, S., Barnett, N. et al. (1999) Brief intervention for harm reduction with alcohol-positive older adolescents in a hospital emergency department, *Journal of Consulting and Clinical Psychology*, 67: 989–94.

Montoya, E., Terburg, D., Bos, P. et al. (2012) Testosterone, cortisol, and serotonin as key regulators of social aggression: a review and theoretical perspective, *Motivation and Emotion*, 36: 65–73.

Monzani, B., Rijsdijk, F., Iervolino, A. et al. (2012) Evidence for a genetic overlap between body dysmorphic concerns and obsessive-compulsive symptoms in an adult female community twin sample, *American Journal of Medical Genetics B: Neuropsychiatric Genetics*, 159: 376–82.

Moreno, S., Gili, M., Magallón, R. et al. (2013) Effectiveness of group versus individual cognitive-behavioural therapy in patients with abridged somatization disorder: a randomized controlled trial, *Psychosomatic Medicine*, 75: 600–8.

Morken, G., Widen, J. and Grawe, R. (2008) Non-adherence to antipsychotic medication, relapse and rehospitalisation in recent-onset schizophrenia, *BMC Psychiatry*, 8: 32.

Morrissey, T. (2009) Multiple child-care arrangements and young children's behavioural outcomes, *Child Development*, 80: 59–76.

Morrison, A., French, P., Parker, S. et al. (2007) Three-year follow-up of a randomized controlled trial of cognitive therapy for the prevention of psychosis in people with ultrahigh risk, *Schizophrenia Bulletin*, 33: 682–7.

Morrison, A., Hutton, P., Shiers, D. et al. (2012) Antipsychotics: is it time to introduce patient choice?, *British Journal of Psychiatry*, 201: 83–4.

Mowrer, O. (1947) On the dual nature of learning: a reinterpretation of conditioning and problem-solving, *Harvard Educational Review*, 17: 102–48.

Murad, M., Elamin, M., Garcia, M. et al. (2009) Hormonal therapy and sex reassignment: a systematic review and meta-analysis of quality of life and psychosocial outcomes, *Clinical Endocrinology*, 72: 214–31.

Muris, P., Merckelbach, H. and Damsma, E. (2000) Threat perception bias in nonreferred, socially anxious children, *Journal of Clinical Child Psychology*, 29: 348–59.

Mustonen, U., Huurre, T., Kiviruusu, O. et al. (2011) Long-term impact of parental divorce on intimate relationship quality in adulthood and the mediating role of psychosocial resources, *Journal of Family Psychology*, 25: 615–19.

Muzik, M., Bocknek, E., Broderick, A. et al. (2012) Mother–infant bonding impairment across the first 6 months postpartum: the primacy of psychopathology in women with childhood abuse and neglect histories, *Archives of Women's Mental Health*, 16: 29–38.

Myin-Gerneys, I., Krabbendam, L. and van Os, J. (2003) Continuity of psychotic symptoms in the community, *Current Opinion in Psychiatry*, 16: 443–9.

Nash, J., Sargent, P., Rabiner, E. et al. (2008) Serotonin 5-HT1A receptor binding in people with panic disorder: positron emission tomography study, *British Journal of Psychiatry*, 193: 229–34.

National Center for Health Statistics (2013) *Suicide and Self-inflicted Injury* [http://www.cdc.gov/nchs/fastats/suicide.htm].

National Collaborating Centre (2013) *Antisocial Behaviour and Conduct Disorders in Children and Young People: The NICE guideline on recognition, intervention and management*. London: Royal College of Psychiatry.

National Institutes of Mental Health (2001) *Blueprint for Change: Research on child and adolescent mental health*. Report of the National Advisory Mental Health Council's Workgroup on Child and Adolescent Mental Health Intervention, Prevention and Deployment Bethesda, MD: NIMH.

New, A., Buchsbaum, M., Hazlett, E. et al. (2004) Fluoxetine increases relative metabolic rate in prefrontal cortex in impulsive aggression, *Psychopharmacology (Berlin)*, 176: 451–8.

Newcomb, M. (1985) The role of perceived relative parent personality in the development of heterosexuals, homosexuals, and transvestites, *Archives of Sexual Behaviour*, 14: 147–64.

NIH Consensus Development Panel on Effective Treatment of Opiate Addiction (1998) Effective medical treatment of opiate addiction, *Journal of the American Medical Association*, 280: 1936–43.

Nixon, R., Sterk, J. and Pearce A. (2012) A randomized trial of cognitive behaviour therapy and cognitive therapy for children with posttraumatic stress disorder following single-incident trauma, *Journal of Abnormal Child Psychology*, 40: 327–37.

Norman, R. and Malla, A. (1994) A prospective study of daily stressors and symptomatology in schizophrenic patients, *Social Psychiatry and Psychiatric Epidemiology*, 29: 244–9.

Nutt, D. and Law, F. (2000) Pharmacological and psychological aspects of drugs of abuse, in M. Gelder, J. Lopez-Ibor, Jr. and N. Andreasen (eds.) *New Oxford Textbook of Psychiatry*. Oxford: Oxford University Press.

O'Donnell, M., Lowe, R., Brotherton, H. et al. (2014) Heterosexual men's ratings of sexual attractiveness of pubescent girls: effects of labeling the target as under or over the age of sexual consent, *Archives of Sexual Behaviour*, 43: 267–71.

O'Kearney, R. (2007) Benefits of cognitive-behavioural therapy for children and youth with obsessive-compulsive disorder: re-examination of the evidence, *Australia and New Zealand Journal of Psychiatry*, 41: 199–212.

O'Malley, S., Garbutt, J., Gastfriend, D. et al. (2007) Efficacy of extended-release naltrexone in alcohol-dependent patients who are abstinent before treatment, *Journal of Clinical Psychopharmacology*, 27: 507–12.

Oades, R., Lasky-Su, J., Christiansen, H. et al. (2008) The influence of serotonin and other genes on impulsive behavioural aggression and cognitive impulsivity in children with attention-deficit/hyperactivity disorder (ADHD): findings from a family-based association test (FBAT) analysis, *Behavioural and Brain Functions*, 4: 48.

Oakley, D. (1999) Hypnosis and conversion hysteria: a unifying model, in P. Halligan and A. David (eds.) *Conversion Hysteria: Towards a Neuropsychological Account*. Hove: Psychology Press.

Olatunji, B.O., Davis, M.L., Powers, M.B. et al. (2013) Cognitive-behavioral therapy for obsessive-compulsive disorder: a meta-analysis of treatment outcome and moderators, *Journal of Psychiatric Research*, 47: 33–41.

Olivera, J., Benabarre, S., Lorente, T. et al. (2011) Detecting psychogeriatric problems in primary care: factors related to psychiatric symptoms in older community patients, *Mental Health and Family Medicine*, 8: 11–19.

Ormel, J., Oldehinkel, A. and Brilman, E. (2001) The interplay and etiological continuity of neuroticism, difficulties, and life events in the etiology of major and subsyndromal, first and recurrent depressive episodes in later life, *American Journal of Psychiatry*, 158: 885–91.

Overbeek, G., Vollebergh, W., De Graaf, R. et al. (2006) Longitudinal associations of marital quality and marital dissolution with the incidence of DSM-III-R disorders, *Journal of Family Psychology*, 20: 284–91.

Ovesey, L. and Person, E. (1973) Gender identity and sexual pathology in men: a psychodynamic analysis of heterosexuality, transsexualism, and transvestism, *Journal of the American Academy of Psychoanalysis*, 1: 53–72.

Oviedo-Joekes, E., Brissette, S., Marsh, D. et al. (2009) Diacetylmorphine versus methadone for the treatment of opioid addiction, *New England Journal of Medicine*, 361: 777–86.

Pagano, M.E., Skodol, A.E., Stout, R.L. et al. (2004) Stressful life events as predictors of functioning: findings from the collaborative longitudinal personality disorders study, *Acta Psychiatrica Scandinavica*, 110: 421–9.

Pally, R. (2002) The neurobiology of borderline personality disorder: the synergy of nature and nurture, *Journal of Psychiatric Practice*, 8: 133–42.

Palosaari, U., Aro, H. and Laippala, P. (1996) Parental divorce and depression in young adulthood: adolescents' closeness to parents and self-esteem as a mediating factor, *Acta Psychiatrica Scandinavica*, 93: 20–6.

Parker, D., Mills, S. and Abbey, J. (2008) Effectiveness of interventions that assist caregivers to support people with dementia living in the community: a systematic review, *International Journal of Evidenced Based Healthcare*, 6: 137–72.

Partonen, T. and Lonnqvist, J. (1998) Seasonal affective disorder, *Lancet*, 352: 1369–74.

Patterson, G. and Bank, L. (1989) Some amplifying mechanisms for pathological processes in families, in M. Gunnar and E. Thelen (eds.) *Systems and Development*. Minnesota Symposia on Child Psychology (Vol. 22). Hillsdale, NJ: Lawrence Erlbaum Associates.

Pearce, J. and Pezzot-Pearce, T. (2007) *Psychotherapy of Abused and Neglected Children*. New York: Guilford Press.

Pediatric OCD Treatment Study (POTS) Team (2004) Cognitive-behavior therapy, sertraline, and their combination for children and adolescents with obsessive-compulsive disorder: the Pediatric OCD Treatment Study (POTS) randomized controlled trial, *Journal of the American Medical Association*, 292: 1969–76.

Perich, T., Manicavasagar, V., Mitchell, P. et al. (2013) The association between meditation practice and treatment outcome in mindfulness-based cognitive therapy for bipolar disorder, *Behaviour Research and Therapy*, 51: 338–43.

Perkin, G. (1989) An analysis of 7936 successive new outpatient referrals, *Journal of Neurology, Neurosurgery and Psychiatry*, 52: 44–78.

Petras, H., Kellam, S., Brown, C. et al. (2008) Developmental epidemiological courses leading to antisocial personality disorder and violent and criminal behaviour: effects by young adulthood of a universal preventive intervention in first- and second-grade classrooms, *Drug and Alcohol Dependence*, 95: 45–59.

Pharoah, F., Mari, J., Rathbone, J. et al. (2010) Family intervention for schizophrenia, *Cochrane Database Systematic Review*, 12: CD000088.

Phillips, K. (1991) Body dysmorphic disorder: the distress of imagined ugliness, *American Journal of Psychiatry*, 148: 1138–49.

Phillips, K. (1996) *The Broken Mirror*. New York: Oxford University Press.

Phillips, K., Menard, W. and Fay, C. (2006) Gender similarities and differences in 200 individuals with body dysmorphic disorder, *Comprehensive Psychiatry*, 47: 77–87.

Phillips, K., Pinto, A., Menard, W. et al. (2007) Obsessive-compulsive disorder versus body dysmorphic disorder: a comparison study of two possibly related disorders, *Depression and Anxiety*, 24: 399–409.

Phillips, K., Quinn, G. and Stout, R. (2008) Functional impairment in body dysmorphic disorder: a prospective, follow-up study, *Journal of Psychiatric Research*, 42: 701–7.

Phillips, L., Francey, S., Edwards, J. et al. (2007) Stress and psychosis: towards the development of new models of investigation, *Clinical Psychology Review*, 27: 307–17.

Pier, C., Austin, D., Klein, B. et al. (2008) A controlled trial of internet-based cognitive-behavioural therapy for panic disorder with face-to-face support from a general practitioner or email support from a psychologist, *Mental Health and Family Medicine*, 5: 29–39.

Pike, K., Hilbert, A., Wilfley, D. et al. (2008) Toward an understanding of risk factors for anorexia nervosa: a case-control study, *Psychological Medicine*, 38: 1443–53.

Pirkola, S., Isometsä, E., Aro, H. et al. (2005) Childhood adversities as risk factors for adult mental disorders: results from the health 2000 study, *Social Psychiatry and Psychiatric Epidemiology*, 40: 769–77.

Pithers, W. (1990) Relapse prevention with sexual aggressors: a method for maintaining therapeutic gain and enhancing external supervision, in W. Marshall, D. Laws and H. Barbaree (eds.) *Handbook of Sexual Assault: Issues, theories, and treatment of the offender*. New York: Plenum Press.

Pjerk, E., Konstaninidis, A., Assem-Hilger, E. et al. (2009) Therapeutic effects of escitalopram and reboxetine in seasonal affective disorder: a pooled analysis, *Journal of Psychiatric Research*, 43: 792–7.

Pjerk, E., Winkler, D. and Kasper, S. (2005) Pharmacotherapy of seasonal affective disorder. *CNS Spectrums*, 10: 664–9.

Pjerk, E., Winkler, D., Statsny, J. et al. (2004) Bright light therapy in seasonal affective disorder: does it suffice?, *European Neuropsychopharmacology*, 14: 347–51.

Place, M., Hulsmeier, J., Davis, S. et al. (2002) The coping mechanisms of children with school refusal, *Journal of Research in Special Education Needs*, 2: 2.

Pomerantz, E. (2001) Parent × child socialization: implications for development of depressive syndromes, *Journal of Family Psychology*, 15: 510–25.

Portegijs, P., Jeuken, F., Van der Horst, F. et al. (1996) A troubled youth: relations with somatization, depression and anxiety in adulthood, *Family Practice*, 13: 1–11.

Powell, N., Lochman, J. and Boxmeyer, C. (2007) The prevention of conduct problems, *International Review of Psychiatry*, 19: 597–605.

Power, T., Mautone, J., Soffer, S. et al. (2012) A family–school intervention for children with ADHD: results of a randomized clinical trial, *Journal of Consulting and Clinical Psychology*, 80: 611–23.

Prasko, J., Ociskova, M., Kamaradova, D. et al. (2013) Bipolar affective disorder and psychoeducation, *Neuroendocrinology Letters*, 34: 83–96.

Prazeres, A., Nascimento, A. and Fontenelle, L. (2013) Cognitive-behavioural therapy for body dysmorphic disorder: a review of its efficacy, *Neuropsychiatric Disorders and Treatment*, 9: 307–16.

Proudfoot, J., Doran, J., Manicavasagar, V. et al. (2010) The precipitants of manic/hypomanic episodes in the context of bipolar disorder: a review, *Journal of Affective Disorders*, 133: 381–7.

Pruessner, J.C., Champagne, F., Meaney, M.J. et al. (2004) Dopamine release in response to a psychological stress in humans and its relationship to early life maternal care: a positron emission tomography study using [11C]raclopride, *Journal of Neuroscience*, 24: 2825–31.

Pumariega, A., Rothe, E. and Pumariega, J. (2005) Mental health of immigrants and refugees, *Community Mental Health Journal*, 41: 581–97.

Raina, P., O'Donnell, M., Rosenbaum, P. et al. (2005) The health and well-being of caregivers of children with cerebral palsy, *Pediatrics*, 5: 626–36.

Raina, P., Santaguida, P. and Ismaila, A. (2008) Effectiveness of cholinesterase inhibitors and memantine for treating dementia: evidence review for a clinical practice guideline, *Annals of Internal Medicine*, 148: 379–97.

Raine, A., Reynolds, C. and Venables, P.H. (1998) Fearlessness, stimulation seeking, and large body size at 3 years as early predispositions to childhood aggression at age 11 years, *Archives of General Psychiatry*, 55: 745–51.

Rajagopal, S. (2004) Suicide pacts and the internet, *British Medical Journal*, 329: 1298–9.

Read, J., Fosse, R., Moskowitz, A. and Perry, B. (2014) The traumagenic neurodevelopmental model of psychosis revisited, *Neuropsychiatry*, 4: 65–79.

Regier, D., Rae, D., Narrow, W. et al. (1998) Prevalence of anxiety disorders and their comorbidity with mood and addictive disorders, *British Journal of Psychiatry*, 173: 24–6.

Reichelt, K., Knivsberg, A., Lind, G. et al. (1991) Probable etiology and possible treatment of childhood autism, *Brain Dysfunction*, 4: 308–19.

Reinders, A., Willemsen, A., Vos, H. et al. (2012) Fact or factitious? A psychobiological study of authentic and simulated dissociative identity states, *PLoS One*, 7: 39279.

Reinhold, J., Mandos, L., Rickels, K. et al. (2011) Pharmacological treatment of generalized anxiety disorder, *Expert Opinion on Pharmacotherapy*, 12: 2457–67.

Rhode, D. (2011) *The Beauty Bias: The injustice of appearance in life and law*. New York: Oxford University Press.

Rhule, D., McMahon, R. and Spieker, S. (2004) Relation of adolescent mothers' history of antisocial behaviour to child conduct problems and social competence, *Journal of Clinical Child and Adolescent Psychology*, 33: 524–35.

Rice, M., Harris, G. and Cormier, C. (1992) An evaluation of a maximum security therapeutic community for psychopaths and other mentally disordered offenders, *Law and Human Behaviour*, 16: 399–412.

Richards, M., Hardy, R. and Wadsworth, M. (1997) The effects of divorce and separation on mental health in a national UK birth cohort, *Psychology and Medicine*, 27: 1121–8.

Rief, W. and Barsky, A. (2005) Psychobiological perspectives on somatoform disorders, *Psychoneuroendocrinology*, 30: 996–1002.

Rinne, T., Van den Brink, W., Wouters, L. et al. (2002) SSRI treatment of borderline personality disorder: a randomized, placebo-controlled clinical trial for female patients with borderline personality disorder, *American Journal of Psychiatry*, 159: 2048–54.

Ritsher, J., Warner, V., Johnson, J. et al. (2001) Inter-generation longitudinal study of social class and depression: a test of social causation and social selection models, *British Journal of Psychiatry*, 178: 84–90.

Robinson, D., Woerner, M., McMeniman, M. et al. (2004) Symptomatic and functional recovery from a first episode of schizophrenia or schizoaffective disorder, *American Journal of Psychiatry*, 161: 473–9.

Robinson, L., Hutchings, D., Dickinson, H. et al. (2007) Effectiveness and acceptability of non-pharmacologica interventions to reduce wandering in dementia: a systematic review, *International Journal of Geriatric Psychiatry*, 22: 9–22.

Rodnick, E., Goldstein, M., Lewis, J. et al. (1984) Parental communication style, affect, and role as precursors of offspring schizophrenia-spectrum disorders, in N. Watt, E. Anthony, L. Wynne et al. (eds.) *Children at Risk of Schizophrenia*. Cambridge: Cambridge University Press.

Rogers, C. (1957) The necessary and sufficient conditions of therapeutic personality change, *Journal of Consulting and Clinical Psychology*, 21: 95–103.

Rogers, C. (1961) *On Becoming a Person*. Boston, MA: Houghton Mifflin.

Romme, M. and Escher, S. (2000) *Making Sense of Voices*. London: Mind Publications.

Rose, S., Bisson, J., Churchill, R. et al. (2002) Psychological debriefing for preventing post traumatic stress disorder (PTSD), *Cochrane Database Systematic Reviews*, 2: CD000560.

Rosen, J. (1996) Body dysmorphic disorder: assessment and treatment, in J. Thompson (ed.) *Body Image, Eating Disorders and Obesity*. Washington, DC: American Psychological Association.

Rosen, J.C., Reiter, J. and Orosan, P. (1995) Cognitive-behavioral body image therapy for body dysmorphic disorder, *Journal of Consulting and Clinical Psychology*, 63: 263–9.

Rosenthal, N.E., Sack, D.A., Gillin, J.C. et al. (1984) Seasonal affective disorder: a description of the syndrome and preliminary findings with light therapy, *Archives of General Psychiatry*, 41: 72–80.

Rösler, A. and Witztum, E. (1998) Treatment of men with paraphilia with a long-acting analogue of gonatropin-releasing hormone, *New England Journal of Medicine*, 338, 416–22.

Ross, C., Miller, S., Reagor, P. et al. (1991) Structured interview data on 102 cases of multiple personality disorder from four centres, *American Journal of Psychiatry*, 147: 596–600.

Rossell, S. and Boundy, C. (2005) Are auditory-verbal hallucinations associated with auditory affective processing deficits?, *Schizophrenia Research*, 78: 95–106.

Rudd, M. (2000) The suicidal mode: a cognitive-behavioural model of suicidality, *Suicide and Life Threatening Behaviour*, 30: 18–33.

Rutledge, K., Van den Bo, W., McClure, S. et al. (2012) Training cognition in ADHD: current findings, borrowed concepts, and future directions, *Neurotherapeutics*, 9: 542–58.

Rutter, M., Andersen-Wood, L., Beckett, C. et al. (1999) Quasi-autistic patterns following severe early global privation, *Journal of Child Psychology and Psychiatry*, 40: 537–49.

Saavedra, L., Silverman, W., Morgan-Lopez, A. et al. (2010) Cognitive behavioural treatment for childhood anxiety disorders: long-term effects on anxiety and secondary disorders in young adulthood, *Journal of Child Psychology and Psychiatry*, 51: 924–34.

Sagvolden, T., Johansen, E., Aase, H. (2005) A dynamic developmental theory of attention-deficit hyperactivity disorder (ADHD) predominantly hyperactive/compulsive and combined subtypes, *Behavioural and Brain Sciences*, 28: 397–468.

Salkovskis, P. and Kirk, J. (1997) Obsessive-compulsive disorder, in D. Clark and C. Fairburn (eds.) *Science and Practice of Cognitive Behaviour Therapy*. Oxford: Oxford University Press.

Salokangas, R.K. and McGlashan, T.H. (2008) Early detection and intervention of psychosis: a review, *Nordic Journal of Psychiatry*, 62: 92–105.

Sanders, A., Duan, J., Levinson, D. et al. (2008) No significant association of 14 candidate genes with schizophrenia in a large European ancestry sample: implications for psychiatric genetics, *American Journal of Psychiatry*, 165: 497–506.

Santucci, L. and Ehrenreich-May, J. (2012) A randomized controlled trial of the Child Anxiety Multi-Day Program (CAMP) for separation anxiety disorder, *Child Psychiatry and Human Development*, 44: 439–51.

Saunders, L. and Broad, B. (1997) *The Health Needs of Young People Leaving Care*. Leicester: De Montfort University.

Sayette, M. (1999) Does drinking reduce stress?, *Alcohol Research and Health*, 23: 250–5.

Scaini, S., Ogliari, Q., Eley, T. et al. (2012) Genetic and environmental contributions to separation anxiety: a meta-analytic approach to twin data, *Depression and Anxiety*, 29: 754–61.

Schaie, K. (2005) *Developmental Influences on Adult Intelligence: The Seattle longitudinal study*. New York: Oxford University Press.

Scheeringa, M., Weems, C., Cohen, J. et al. (2011) Trauma-focused cognitive behavioural therapy for posttraumatic stress disorder in three- through six-year-old children: a randomized clinical trial, *Child Psychology and Psychiatry*, 52: 853–60.

Scherbaum, N., Kluwig, J., Specka, M. et al. (2005) Group psychotherapy for opiate addicts in methadone maintenance treatment: a controlled trial, *European Addiction Research*, 11: 163–71.

Schilling, E., Aseltine, R., Jr. and Gore, S. (2007) Adverse childhood experiences and mental health in young adults: a longitudinal survey, *BMC Public Health*, 7: 30.

Schipper, H. (2009) Apolipoprotein E: implications for AD neurobiology, epidemiology and risk assessment, *Neurobiology of Aging*, 32: 778–90.

Schönfeldt-Lecuona, C., Connemann, B., Viviani, R. et al. (2006) Transcranial magnetic stimulation in motor conversion disorder: a short case series, *Journal of Clinical Neurophysiology*, 23: 472–5.

Schreibman, L., Stahmer, A. and Suhrheinrich, J. (2008) Enhancing generalization of treatment effects via pivotal response training and the individualization of treatment protocols, in C. Whalen (ed.) *Real Life, Real Progress for Children with Autism Spectrum Disorders: Strategies for successful generalization*. Baltimore, MD: Paul H. Brookes.

Schreier, A., Wolke, D., Thomas, K. et al. (2009) Prospective study of peer victimization in childhood and psychotic symptoms in a nonclinical population at age 12 years, *Archives of General Psychiatry*, 66: 527–36.

Schulz, S., Zanarini, M., Bateman, A. et al. (2008) Olanzapine for the treatment of borderline personality disorder: variable dose 12-week randomised double-blind placebo-controlled study, *British Journal of Psychiatry*, 193: 485–92.

Schulze-Rauschenbach, S., Harms, U., Schlaepfer, T. et al. (2005) Distinctive neurocognitive effects of repetitive transcranial magnetic stimulation and electroconvulsive therapy in major depression, *British Journal of Psychiatry*, 186: 410–16.

Schwitzer, A., Rodriguez, L., Thomas, C. et al. (2001) The eating disorders NOS diagnostic profile among college women, *Journal of the American College of Health*, 49: 157–66.

Seal, K., Mansell, W. and Mannion, H. (2008) What lies between hypomania and bipolar disorder? A qualitative analysis of 12 non-treatment-seeking people with a history of hypomanic experiences and no history of major depression, *Psychology and Psychotherapy*, 81: 33–53.

Seligman, M. (1971) Phobias and preparedness, *Behaviour Therapy*, 2: 307–20.

Seligman, M.E.P. (1975) *Helplessness*. San Francisco, CA: Freeman.

Semiz, U., Basoglu, C., Oner, O. et al. (2008) Effects of diagnostic comorbidity and dimensional symptoms of attention-deficit-hyperactivity disorder in men with antisocial personality disorder, *Australian and New Zealand Journal of Psychiatry*, 42: 405–13.

Semrud-Clikeman, M., Nielsen, K., Clinton, A. (1999) An intervention approach for children with teacher- and parent-identified attentional difficulties, *Journal of Learning Disabilities*, 32: 581–90.

Seto, M. (2004) Paedophilia and sexual offenses against children, *Annual Review of Sex Research*, 15: 321–31.

Shaffer, H.J. (2005) From disabling to enabling the public interest: natural transitions from gambling exposure to adaptation and self-regulation, *Addiction*, 100: 1227–30.

Shahmanesh, M., Wayal, S., Cowan, F. et al. (2009) Suicidal behaviour among female sex workers in Goa, India: the silent epidemic, *American Journal of Public Health*, 99: 1239–46.

Shapiro, F. (1995) *Eye Movement Desensitisation and Reprocessing: Basic principles*. New York: Guilford Press.

Sharpe, L. (2002) A reformulated cognitive-behavioural model of problem gambling: a biopsychosocial perspective, *Clinical Psychology Review*, 22: 1–25.

Shear, K., Jin, R., Ruscio, A. et al. (2006) Prevalence and correlates of estimated DSM-IV child and adult separation anxiety disorder in the National Comorbidity Survey Replication, *American Journal of Psychiatry*, 163: 1074–83.

Sheffield, J.M., Williams, L.E., Woodward, N.D. et al. (2013) Reduced gray matter volume in psychotic disorder patients with a history of childhood sexual abuse, *Schizophrenia Research*, 143: 185–91.

Sher, L. (2001) Genetic studies of seasonal affective disorder and seasonality, *Comprehensive Psychiatry*, 42: 105–10.

Simpson, H., Foa, E., Liebowitz, M. et al. (2008) A randomized, controlled trial of cognitive behavioral therapy for augmenting pharmacotherapy in obsessive-compulsive disorder, *American Journal of Psychiatry*, 165: 621–30.

Smink, F., Van Hoeken, D. and Hoek, H. (2012) Epidemiology of eating disorders: incidence, prevalence and mortality rates, *Current Psychiatry Reports*, 14: 406–14.

Smith, M., Glass, G. and Miller, T. (1980) *The Benefits of Psychotherapy*. Baltimore, MD: Johns Hopkins University Press.

Smith, T., Buch, G. and Gamby, T. (2000) Parent-directed, intensive early intervention for children with pervasive developmental disorder, *Research in Developmental Disabilities*, 21: 297–309.

Smith, Y., Van Goozen, S. and Cohen-Kettenis, P. (2001) Adolescents with gender identity disorder who were accepted or rejected for sex reassignment surgery: a prospective follow-up study, *Journal of the Academy of Child and Adolescent Psychiatry*, 40: 472–81.

Sobanski, E. and Schmidt, M. (2000) Everybody looks at my pubic bone: a case report of an adolescent patient with body dysmorphic disorder, *Acta Psychiatrica Scandinavica*, 101: 80–2.

Social Exclusion Unit (1998) *Truancy and School Exclusion: Report*. London: The Stationery Office.

Solowij, N., Stephens, R., Roffman, R. et al. (2002) Marijuana Treatment Project Research Group: cognitive functioning of long-term heavy cannabis users seeking treatment, *Journal of the American Medical Association*, 287: 1123–31.

Somashekar, B., Jainer, A. and Wuntakal, B. (2013) Psychopharmacotherapy of somatic symptoms disorders, *International Review of Psychiatry*, 25: 107–15.

Soo-Jin, K., Bung-Nyun, K., Soo-Churl, C. et al (2010) The prevalence of specific phobias and associated co-morbid features in children and adolescents, *Journal of Anxiety Disorder*, 24: 629–34.

Sourander, A., Ronning, J., Brunstein-Klomek, A. et al. (2009) Childhood bullying behaviour and later psychiatric hospital and psychopharmacologic treatment, *Archives of General Psychiatry*, 66: 1005–12.

Spanos, N. (1994) Multiple identity enactments and multiple personality disorder: a sociocognitive perspective, *Psychological Bulletin*, 116: 143–65.

Spanos, N., Weekes, J. and Bertrand, L. (1985) Multiple personality: a social psychological perspective, *Journal of Abnormal Psychology*, 94: 362–76.

Spataro, J., Mullen, P., Burgess, P. et al. (2004) Impact of child sexual abuse on mental health: prospective study in males and females, *British Journal of Psychiatry*, 184: 416–21.

Spector, A., Davies, S., Woods, B. et al. (2000) Reality orientation for dementia: a systematic review of the evidence of effectiveness from randomized controlled trials, *Gerontologist*, 40: 206–12.

Spiegel, D. (1993) Multiple post-traumatic personality disorder, in R. Kluft and C. Fine (eds.) *Clinical Perspectives on Multiple Personality Disorder*. Washington, DC: American Psychiatric Press.

Spiegel, D. and Barlow, D. (2000) Generalized anxiety disorders, in M. Gelder, J. López-Ibor, Jr. and N.C Andreasen (eds.) *New Oxford Textbook of Psychiatry*. Oxford: Oxford University Press.

Spinhoven, P., Elzinga, B., Hovens, J. et al. (2010) The specificity of childhood adversities and negative life events across the life span to anxiety and depressive disorders, *Journal of Affective Disorders*, 126: 103–12.

Spitzer, C., Barnow, S., Gau, K. et al. (2008) Childhood maltreatment in patients with somatization disorder, *Australian and New Zealand Journal of Psychiatry*, 42: 335–41.

Stafford, M., Jackson, H., Mayo-Wilson, E. et al. (2013) Early interventions to prevent psychosis: systematic review and meta-analysis, *British Medical Journal*, 346: f185.

Steptoe, A. and Noll, A. (1997) The perception of bodily sensations with special reference to hypochondriasis, *Behaviour Research and Therapy*, 35: 901–10.

Stoffers, J., Völlm, B., Rücker, G. et al. (2012) Psychological therapies for people with borderline personality disorder, *Cochrane Database Systematic Reviews*, 8: CD005652.

Stoller, R. (1968) *Sex and Gender: Vol. 1. The development of masculinity and femininity*. New York: Jason Aronson.

Storebo, O.J., Darling Rasmussen, P. and Simonsen, E. (2013) Association between insecure attachment and ADHD: environmental mediating factors, *Journal of Attention Disorders* [DOI: 10.1177/1087054713501079].

Striegal-Moore, R. and Smolak, L. (2000) The influence of ethnicity on eating disorders in women, in R. Esler and M. Hersen (eds.) *Handbook of Gender, Culture, and Health*. Mahwah, NJ: Erlbaum.

Strong, R.E., Marchant, B.K., Reimherr, F.W. et al. (2009) Narrow-band blue-light treatment of seasonal affective disorder in adults and the influence of additional nonseasonal symptoms, *Depression and Anxiety*, 26: 273–8.

Strosahl, K., Hayes, S., Wilson, K. et al. (2004) An ACT primer: core therapy processes, intervention strategies and therapist competencies, in S. Hayes and K. Strosahl (eds.) *A Practical Guide to Acceptance and Commitment Therapy.* New York: Springer.

Stuart, S. and Noyes, R. (1999) Attachment and interpersonal communication in somatization, *Psychosomatics*, 40: 34–43.

Sumaya, I., Rienzi, B.M., Deegan, J.F., II et al. (2001) Bright light treatment decreases depression in institutionalized older adults: a placebo-controlled crossover study, *Journal of Gerontology*, 56A: M356–60.

Suppes, T., Baldessarini, R., Faedda, G. et al. (1991) Risk of recurrence following discontinuation of lithium treatment in bipolar disorder, *Archives of General Psychiatry*, 48: 1082–8.

Swannell, S., Martin, G., Page, A. et al. (2012) Child maltreatment, subsequent non-suicidal self-injury and the mediating roles of dissociation, alexithymia and self-blame, *Child Abuse and Neglect*, 36: 572–84.

Swift, W., Hall, W. and Teeson, M. (2001) Cannabis use and dependence among Australian adults: results from the National Survey of Health and Wellbeing, *Addiction*, 96: 737–48.

Szabo, S., Machado-Vieira, R., Yuan, P. et al. (2009) Glutamate receptors as targets of protein kinase C in the pathophysiology and treatment of animal models of mania, *Neuropharmacology*, 56: 47–55.

Tager-Flusberg, H. (2007) Evaluating the theory-of-mind hypothesis of autism, *Current Directions in Psychological Science*, 16: 311–15.

Tarrier, N., Kinney, C., McCarthy, E. et al. (2000) Two-year follow-up of cognitive–behavioral therapy and supportive counseling in the treatment of persistent symptoms in chronic schizophrenia, *Journal of Consulting and Clinical Psychology*, 68: 917–22.

Taylor, A., Chittleborough, C., Gill, T. et al. (2012) Relationship of social factors including trust, control over life decisions, problems with transport and safety, to psychological distress in the community, *Social Psychiatry and Psychiatric Epidemiology*, 47: 465–73.

Teri, L., Logsdon, R., Uomoto, J. et al. (1997) Behavioural treatment of depression in dementia patients: a controlled clinical trial, *Journals of Gerontology B: Psychological Sciences and Social Sciences*, 52: 159–66.

Terman, M. (1988) On the question of mechanism in phototherapy for seasonal affective disorder: considerations of clinical efficacy and epidemiology, *Journal of Biological Rhythms*, 3: 155–72.

Thompson, C., Raheja, S.K. and King, E.A. (1995) A follow-up study of seasonal affective disorder, *British Journal of Psychiatry*, 167: 380–4.

Tienari, P., Wynne, L., Moring, J. et al. (2000) Finnish adoptive family study: sample selection and adoptee DSM-III-R diagnoses, *Acta Psychiatrica Scandinavica*, 101: 433–43.

Timko, C., Moos, R., Finney, J. et al. (2000) Long-term outcomes of alcohol use disorders: comparing untreated individuals with those in Alcoholics Anonymous and formal treatment, *Journal of Studies in Alcohol*, 61: 529–40.

Tobias, M., Kokaua, J., Gerritsen, S. et al. (2010) The health of children in sole-parent families in New Zealand: results of a population-based cross-sectional survey, *Australian and New Zealand Journal of Public Health*, 34: 274–80.

Tolin, D., Maltby, N., Diefenbach, G. et al. (2004) Cognitive behavioral therapy for medication nonresponders with obsessive-compulsive disorder: a wait-list-controlled open trial, *Journal of Clinical Psychiatry*, 65: 922–31.

Tondi, L., Ribani, L., Bottazzi, M. et al. (2007) Validation therapy (VT) in nursing home: a case-control study, *Archives of Gerontology and Geriatrics*, 44 (suppl. 1): 407–11.

Trapp, G.S., Allen, K., O'Sullivan, T. et al. (2014) Energy drink consumption is associated with anxiety in Australian young males, *Depression and Anxiety*, 31: 420–8.

Trower, P., Birchwood, M., Meaden, A. et al. (2004) Cognitive therapy for command hallucinations: randomised controlled trial, *British Journal of Psychiatry*, 184: 312–20.

Tsai, Y., Yeh, S. and Tsai, H. (2005) Prevalence and risk factors for depressive symptoms among community-dwelling elders in Taiwan, *International Journal of Geriatric Psychiatry*, 20: 1097–1102.

Twohig, M., Hayes, S., Plumb, J. et al. (2010) A randomized clinical trial of acceptance and commitment therapy versus progressive relaxation training for obsessive compulsive disorder, *Journal of Consulting and Clinical Psychology*, 78: 705–16.

Valenstein, M., Kavanagh, J., Lee, T. et al. (2011) Using a pharmacy-based intervention to improve antipsychotic adherence among patients with serious mental illness, *Schizophrenia Bulletin*, 37: 727–36.

Van der Kolk, B. (2005) Developmental trauma disorder: toward a rational diagnosis for children with complex trauma histories, *Psychiatric Annals*, 35: 401–8.

Van Dijke, A. (2012) Dysfunctional affect regulation in borderline personality disorder and in somatoform disorder, *European Journal of Psychotraumatology*, 3 [DOI: 10.3402/ejpt.v3i0.19566.].

Varela, R., Sanchez Sosa, J., Biggs, B. et al. (2009) Parenting strategies and socio-cultural influences in childhood anxiety: Mexican, Latin American descent, and European American families, *Journal of Anxiety Disorder*, 23: 609–16.

Vaughn, C. and Leff, J. (1976) The influence of family and social factors on the course of psychiatric patients, *British Journal of Psychiatry*, 129: 125–37.

Vivanti, G., Barbaro, J., Hudry, K. et al. (2013) Intellectual development in autism spectrum disorders: new insights from longitudinal studies, *Frontiers in Human Neuroscience*, 7: 354.

Voisey, J., Swagell, C.D., Hughes, I.P. et al. (2009) The DRD2 gene 957C>T polymorphism is associated with posttraumatic stress disorder in war veterans, *Depression and Anxiety*, 26: 28–33.

Volkmar, F. (2002) Conduct disorders and associated antisocial behaviour: recognition, intervention and management of conduct disorders and associated antisocial behaviour in children and young people: considering disruptive behaviors, *American Journal of Psychiatry*, 159: 349–50.

Vuilleumier, P., Chicherio, C. and Assal, F. (2001) Functional neuroanatomical correlates of hysterical sensorimotor loss, *Brain*, 124: 1077–90.

Wade, T., Veldhuizen, S. and Cairney, J. (2011) Prevalence of psychiatric disorder in lone fathers and mothers: examining the intersection of gender and family structure on mental health, *Canadian Journal of Psychiatry*, 6: 567–73.

Wagner, A., Aizenstein, H., Venkatraman, V. et al. (2007) Altered reward processing in women recovered from anorexia nervosa, *American Journal of Psychiatry*, 164: 1842–9.

Wahlberg, K., Jackson, D., Haley, H. et al. (2000) Gene–environment interaction in vulnerability to schizophrenia: findings from the Finnish adoptive family study of schizophrenia, *American Journal of Psychiatry*, 154: 355–62.

Wakefield, A., Murch, S., Anthony, A. et al. (1998) Ileal-lymphoid-nodular hyperplasia, non-specific colitis and pervasive developmental disorder in children, *Lancet*, 351: 637–41.

Waldron, H., Miller, W. and Tonigan, J. (2001) Client anger as a predictor of differential response to treatment, in R. Longabaugh and P. Wirtz (eds.) *Project MATCH Hypotheses: Results and causal chain analyses*. Project MATCH Monograph Series (Vol. 8). Bethesda, MD: National Institute on Alcohol Abuse and Alcoholism.

Wallien, M. and Cohen-Kettenis, P. (2008) Psychosexual outcome of gender-dysphoric children, *Journal of the American Academy of Child and Adolescent Psychiatry*, 47: 1413–23.

Walsh, F. (1998) *Strengthening Family Resilience*. New York: Guilford Press.

Wang, L. and Crane, D. (2001) The relationship between marital satisfaction, marital stability, nuclear family triangulation and childhood depression, *American Journal of Family Therapy*, 2: 337–47.

Ward, T. and Siegert, R. (2002) Toward a comprehensive theory of child sexual abuse: a theory knitting perspective, *Psychology, Crime and Law*, 9: 319–51.

Ward, T., Louden, K., Hudson, S. et al. (1995) A descriptive model of the offense chain for child molesters, *Journal of Interpersonal Violence*, 10: 452–72.

Warwick, H. and Salkovskis, P. (1990) Hypochondriasis, *Behaviour Research and Therapy*, 28: 105–17.

Watanabe, Y., Someya. T., Nawa, H. et al. (2010) Cytokine hypothesis of schizophrenia pathogenesis: evidence from human studies and animal models, *Psychiatry and Clinical Neuroscience*, 64: 217–30.

Waters, A., Craske, M., Bergman, R. et al. (2008) Threat interpretation bias as a vulnerability factor in childhood anxiety disorders, *Behaviour Research and Therapy*, 47: 39–47.

Watson, J. and Rayner, R. (1920) Conditioned emotional reaction, *Journal of Experimental Psychology*, 3: 1–14.

Watzlawick, P., Weakland, J. and Fisch, R. (1974) *Change: Principles of problem formulation and problem resolution*. New York: W.W. Norton.

Weatherly, J., Sauter, J. and King, B. (2004) The big win and resistance to extinction when gambling, *Journal of Psychology*, 138: 495–504.

Webster-Stratton, C., Reid, J. and Beauchaine, T. (2013) One-year follow-up of combined parent and child intervention for young children with ADHD, *Journal of Clinical Child and Adolescent Psychology*, 42: 251–61.

Weich, S., Sloggett, A. and Lewis, G. (1998) Social roles and gender difference in the prevalence of common mental disorders, *British Journal of Psychiatry*, 173: 489–93.

Weiner, I. and Lubow, R. (2010) *Latent Inhibition: Cognition, neuroscience and applications to schizophrenia*. Cambridge: Cambridge University Press.

Wells, A. (1995) Meta-cognition and worry: a cognitive model of generalized anxiety disorder, *Behavioural and Cognitive Psychotherapy*, 23: 301–20.

Wells, A. (2000) *Emotional Disorders and Metacognition: Innovative cognitive therapy*. Chichester: Wiley.

Weyers, S., Elaut, E., De Sutter, P. et al. (2009) Long-term assessment of the physical, mental, and sexual health among transsexual women, *Journal of Sexual Medicine*, 6: 752–60.

Whitaker-Azmitia, P. (2005) Behavioural and cellular consequences of increasing serotonergic activity during brain development: a role in autism?, *International Journal of Developmental Neuroscience*, 23: 75–83.

Wickrama, K. and Noh, S. (2010) Long arm of community: the influence of childhood community contexts across the early life course, *Journal of Youth and Adolescence*, 39: 894–910.

Wileman, S.M., Eagles, J.M., Andrew, J.E. et al. (2001) Light therapy for seasonal affective disorder in primary care, *British Journal of Psychiatry*, 178: 311–16.

Williams, D., González, H., Neighbors, H. et al. (2007) Prevalence and distribution of major depressive disorder in African Americans, Caribbean blacks, and non-Hispanic whites: results from the national survey of American life, *Archives of General Psychiatry*, 64: 305–15.

Wilson, K., Mottram, P. and Sixsmith, A. (2007) Depressive symptoms in the very old living alone: prevalence, incidence and risk factors, *International Journal of Geriatric Psychiatry*, 22: 361–6.

Winters, K. and Neale, J. (1985) Mania and low self-esteem, *Journal of Abnormal Psychology*, 94: 282–90.

Wolke, D., Schreier, A., Zanarini, M. et al. (2012) Bullied by peers in childhood and borderline personality symptoms at 11 years of age: a prospective study, *Journal of Child Psychology and Psychiatry and Allied Disciplines*, 53: 846–55.

Won, H., Myung, W., Song, G. et al. (2013) Predicting national suicide numbers with social media data, *PLoS One*, 8: 61809.

Wong, S. and Hare, R. (2002) *Program Guidelines for the Institutional Treatment of Violent Psychopathic Offenders*. Toronto: Multi-Health Systems.

Wood, J., McLeod, B., Sigman, M. et al. (2003) Parenting and childhood anxiety: theory, empirical findings and future directions, *Journal of Child Psychology and Psychiatry*, 44: 134–51.

Woods, B., Aguirre, E., Spector, A. et al. (2012) Cognitive stimulation to improve cognitive functioning in people with dementia, *Cochrane Database Scientific Reviews*, 2: CD005562.

Woods, B., Thorgrimsen, L., Spector, A. et al. (2006) Improved quality of life and cognitive stimulation therapy in dementia, *Aging and Mental Health*, 10: 219–26.

Woodside, D., Bulik, C., Halmi, K. et al. (2002) Personality, perfectionism, and attitudes toward eating in parents of individuals with eating disorders, *International Journal of Eating Disorders*, 31: 290–9.

Woodward, T., Buchy, L., Moritz, S. et al. (2007) A bias against disconfirmatory evidence is associated with delusion proneness in a nonclinical sample, *Schizophrenia Bulletin*, 33: 1023–8.

Wootton, J., Frick, P., Shelton, K. et al. (1997) Ineffective parenting and childhood conduct problems: the moderating role of callous unemotional traits, *Journal of Consulting and Clinical Psychology*, 65: 301–8.

World Health Organization (WHO) (2014) *Child Maltreatment*. Factsheet No. 150. Geneva: WHO [http://www.who.int/mediacentre/factsheets/fs150/en/].

World Health Organization (WHO) (undated) *Gender Disparities in Mental Health* [http://www.who.int/mental_health/media/en/242.pdf].

Xiu-Ying, H., Qian, C., Xiao-Dong, P. et al. (2012) Arrangements and risk for late life depression: a meta-analysis of published literature, *International Journal of Psychiatry and Medicine*, 43: 19–34.

Yamada, T., Hattori, H., Miura, A. et al. (2001) Prevalence of Alzheimer's disease, vascular dementia and dementia with Lewy bodies in a Japanese population, *Psychiatry and Clinical Neurosciences*, 55: 21–5.
Yang, L., Phillips, M., Licht, D. et al. (2004) Causal attributions about schizophrenia in families in China: expressed emotion and patient relapse, *Journal of Abnormal Psychology*, 113: 592–602.
Yau, Y.H., Pilver, C.E., Steinberg, M.A. et al. (2014) Relationships between problematic Internet use and problem-gambling severity: findings from a high-school survey, *Addictive Behaviors*, 39: 13–21.
Young, J. (1999) *Cognitive Therapy for Personality Disorders: A schema-focused approach*. Sarasota, FL: Professional Resources Press.
Young, J. and Lindemann, M. (1992) An integrative schema-focused model for personality disorders, *Journal of Cognitive Psychotherapy*, 6: 11–23.
Zanarini, M., Frankenburg, F., Hennen, J. et al. (2005) The McLean Study of Adult Development (MSAD): overview and implications of the first six years of prospective follow-up, *Journal of Personality Disorders*, 19: 505–23.
Zarros, A., Kalopita, K. and Tsakiris, S. (2005) Serotoninergic impairment and aggressive behaviour in Alzheimer's disease, *Acta Neurobiologiae Experimentalis*, 65: 277–86.
Zimmerman, J. and Grosz, H. (1966) 'Visual' performance of a functionally blind person, *Behaviour Research and Therapy*, 4: 119–34.
Zivin, K., Campbell, D., Lanto, A. et al. (2012) Relationships between mood and employment over time among depressed VA primary care patients, *General Hospital Psychiatry*, 34: 468–77.
Zlomke, K. and Davis, T. (2008) One-session treatment of specific phobias: a detailed description and review of treatment efficacy, *Behaviour Therapy*, 39: 207–23.
Zucker, K. and Bradley, S. (1995) *Gender Identity Disorder and Psychosexual Problems in Children and Adolescents*. New York: Guilford Press.
Zucker, K., Green, R., Garofano, C. et al. (1994) Prenatal gender preference of mothers of feminine and masculine boys: relation to sibling sex composition and birth order, *Journal of Abnormal Child Psychology*, 22: 1–13.
Zwi, M., Jones, H., Thorgaard, C. et al. (2011) Parent training interventions for attention deficit hyperactivity disorder (ADHD) in children aged 5 to 18 years, *Cochrane Database Scientific Reviews*, 3: CD003018.

Index

Note: Glossary terms are in **bold** type.

ABA *see* applied behaviour analysis
absolutistic thinking 10
abuse *see* child sexual abuse
acceptance and commitment therapy (ACT) 72–3
acetylcholine 50
ACT *see* acceptance and commitment therapy
actualizing tendency 12
addiction
    alcohol 180–3
    cannabis dependence 183–5
    drug use 179–80
    gambling disorder 187–8
    heroin 185–7
    pathways 180
    'reward system' 180
    risk factors 180
    working with 188–9
ADHD *see* attention-deficit/hyperactivity disorder
adherence to drug treatments 54–5
aetiology 49
agonists 103
agranulocytosis 54
alcohol, childhood mental health 30
alcohol addiction 180–3
    Alcoholics Anonymous (AA) 182–3
    antidipstrotrophic drugs 182
    biological explanations 181
    cognitive behaviour therapy (CBT) 183
    DSM-5 diagnostic criteria 227
    Minnesota (treatment) model 182–3
    motivational enhancement therapy (MET) 183
    motivational interviewing 183
    naltrexone 182
    opioid agonists 182
    psychosocial explanations 181–2
    treatment 182–3
Alcoholics Anonymous (AA) 182–3
alleles 16
Alzheimer's disease 47, 212–17
    biological explanations 213–14
    carers 216–17
    characteristics 212
    DSM-5 diagnostic criteria 222
    incidence 212
    prevalence 212
    reality orientation 214–15
    reminiscence therapy 215
    risk factors 213–14
    treatment 214
    validation therapy 215
anal stage, developmental stage 2
anorexia nervosa 26, 92–9
    biological explanations 94–5
    vs. bulimia nervosa 94
    DSM-5 diagnostic criteria 223
    psychosocial explanations 95–6
    treatment 96–7
antidipstrotrophic drugs, alcohol addiction 182
antipsychotic medication 172–3
antisocial personality and psychopathy 111–15
    biological explanations 112–13
    DSM-5 diagnostic criteria 223
    psychosocial explanations 113
    treatment 113–15
anxiety
    behaviour therapy 65–7
    behavioural explanations 65–6
    cognitive behaviour therapy (CBT) 70–1
    defence mechanisms 4–5
    parental/family influences 24, 25–6
    treating 53
    types 4–5
anxiety disorders 117–36
    childhood origins 119–21
    generalized anxiety disorder (GAD) 125–7
    neurological factors 117–18
    obsessive-compulsive disorder (OCD) 129–36
    panic disorder 127–9
    separation anxiety disorder (SAD) 121–2
    specific phobias 122–5
    trans-diagnostic model of anxiety 118–19
    treatment consequences 120–1

anxious-ambivalent, attachment pattern 7
anxious-avoidant, attachment pattern 7
aphonia 211
applied behaviour analysis (ABA) 77–9
arbitrary inference 10
ASD *see* autistic spectrum disorder
attachment theory 6–8
attention-deficit/hyperactivity disorder (ADHD) 82–6
   biological explanations 83
   DSM-5 diagnostic criteria 222
   psychosocial explanations 84–5
   trauma 84
   treatment 85–6
atypical neuroleptics 54
autistic spectrum disorder (ASD) 101–5
   biological explanations 103–4
   DSM-5 diagnostic criteria 223–4
   naltrexone 104
   opioid agonists 104
   psychosocial explanations 102–3
   treatment 104–5
autonomic nervous system 49–50
avoidance, dysfunctional schemata and behaviour 11

Beck, A. 10–11
behaviour, planning of 47
behaviour therapy
   see also cognitive behaviour therapy (CBT)
   anxiety 65–7
   applied behaviour analysis (ABA) 77–9
behavioural explanations, anxiety 65–6
benzodiazepines 53
biopsychosocial model, childhood mental health 22–3
bipolar disorder 148–50
   biological explanations 148
   DSM-5 diagnostic criteria 224–5
   lithium 150
   natural histories 148
   psychological strategies 150
   psychosocial explanations 149
   treatment 149–50
blood–brain barrier 104
body dysmorphic disorder 207–9
   biological explanations 208
   DSM-5 diagnostic criteria 225
   psychosocial explanations 208
   treatment 208–9

borderline personality disorder (BPD) 106–11
   biological explanations 108
   DSM-5 diagnostic criteria 225
   psychosocial explanations 107–8
   treatment 109–11
Bowlby, John 6–7
BPD *see* borderline personality disorder
brain areas 46–7
bulimia nervosa 92–9
   vs. anorexia nervosa 94
   biological explanations 94–5
   DSM-5 diagnostic criteria 225
   psychosocial explanations 95–6
   treatment 97–8
bullying, childhood mental health 29–30

cannabis dependence 183–5
   biological explanations 184
   DSM-5 diagnostic criteria 227
   psychosis 184
   treatment 184–5
caring
   care-eliciting and attachment mentality 8
   care-giving mentality 8
   carers, Alzheimer's disease 216–17
   family influences 40–1
casein 103
catatonic behaviour 167
CBT *see* cognitive behaviour therapy
challenging behaviours 105
child sexual abuse 26–7, 157
childhood mental health
   alcohol 30
   biopsychosocial model 22–3
   bullying 29–30
   child sexual abuse 26–7, 157
   dissociative identity disorder (DID) 161–4
   emotions 20–1
   genetic influences 21–2
   looked-after children 30–1
   parental/family influences 23–8
   peer influences 29–30
   post-traumatic stress disorder (PTSD) 157, 158–9
   risky behaviours 30
   single-parent families 27
   socio-economic factors 29
childhood origins, anxiety disorders 119–21
client 62
cognitive behaviour therapy (CBT) 55–6, 67–71, 73

alcohol addiction 183
anxiety 70–1
depression 142–4
gambling disorder 188
mood disorders 67–70
post-traumatic stress disorder (PTSD) 157–9
schizophrenia 174–6, 177
trauma-focused exposure CBT 157–9
cognitive functioning, old age 42
cognitive models 9–11
depression 140–1
command hallucinations 175–6
community mental health team 177
co-morbidity 81–2
competitive mentality 9
completion tendency, post-traumatic stress disorder (PTSD) 156
conduct disorder 86–90
biological explanations 87
DSM-5 diagnostic criteria 226
psychosocial explanations 88
treatment 88–90
conversion, defence mechanism 4
conversion disorder 209–12
biological explanations 210–11
DSM-5 diagnostic criteria 226
hypnosis 211–12
hysteria 209, 210
prevalence 209
psychosocial explanations 210
transcranial magnetic stimulation (TMS) 212
treatment 211–12
cooperative mentality 8
core beliefs 197
cortisol 87
cost-effectiveness
medication 55–6
cross-dressing *see* transvestic disorder

defence mechanisms, anxiety 4–5
delusions 14
explaining 169–71
dementia 42
denial, defence mechanism 4
depersonalization 157
depression 138–45
biological explanations 139–40
cognitive behaviour therapy (CBT) 142–4
cognitive model 140–1
DSM-5 diagnostic criteria 226
fluoxetine 143

Increasing Access to Psychological Therapies (IAPT) programme 143
prevalence 138–9, 142
psychological explanations 140–1
psychosocial explanations 141–2
treating 51–3
treatment 142–4
derealization 157
DID *see* dissociative identity disorder
discrimination influence, adult mental health 37
disorganized/disoriented, attachment pattern 7
displacement, defence mechanism 4, 5
dissociative identity disorder (DID) 161–4
DSM-5 diagnostic criteria 226
psychosocial explanations 162–4
treatment 164
divorce 27–8
dopamine 14–17, 49
Down syndrome 22
dream interpretation 62
drug abuse, defining 180
drug dependence, defining 180
drug use disorder
addiction 179–87
DSM-5 diagnostic criteria 227
DSM-5 diagnostic criteria 222–31
dysphoric 35
dysthymia 39–40

eating disorders
anorexia nervosa 26, 92–9
bulimia nervosa 92–9
strategic approach 98–9
structural approach 98
echolalia
autistic spectrum disorder (ASD) 102
ECT *see* electroconvulsive therapy
ego 2
ego-based anxiety 4–5
egocentricity 112
Electra complex 3
electroconvulsive therapy (ECT) 57–8
EMDR *see* eye movement desensitization and reprocessing
emotions
childhood mental health 20–1
developing 20–1
regulation 20–1
empathy, self-actualization 13
end of life 42
endorphins 103

epinephrine 50
ethnicity influence
   adult mental health 36–8
   schizophrenia 36–7
executive functions 47
eye movement desensitization and reprocessing (EMDR) 159–60

family
   single-parent families 27, 39
   strategic family therapy 76–7
   structural family therapy 74–6
family influences
   see also parental/family influences
   adult mental health 39–41
   caring 40–1
   living alone 39–40
   schizophrenia 39
family interventions, schizophrenia 174
flashback memories 26
flattened affect 167
fluoxetine 143
Fragile X syndrome 22
free association 62
Freud, Sigmund 1–6, 62–3
functional analysis 78–9
functional magnetic resonance imaging (fMRI) 15

GABA *see* gamma-aminobutyric acid
GAD *see* generalized anxiety disorder
gambling disorder 187–8
   biological explanations 187
   cognitive behaviour therapy (CBT) 188
   DSM-5 diagnostic criteria 227
   psychosocial explanations 187
   treatment 188
gamma-aminobutyric acid (GABA) 50
gender dysphoria 191–3
   see also transvestic disorder
   biological explanations 192
   DSM-5 diagnostic criteria 227–8
   psychosocial explanations 192
   treatment 192–3
gender influence, adult mental health 35–6
generalized anxiety disorder (GAD) 125–7
   biological explanations 125–6
   DSM-5 diagnostic criteria 228
   psychosocial explanations 126–7
   treatment 127

genetic influences, childhood mental health 21–2
genital stage, developmental stage 3–4
genuineness, self-actualization 13
Gilbert, P. 8–9
gluten 103

habituation 66
hallucinations 14
   explaining 169–71
heroin dependence/addiction 185–7
   biological explanations 185
   DSM-5 diagnostic criteria 227
   methadone 186
   naltrexone 186
   opioid agonists 186
   psychosocial explanations 185–6
   treatment 186–7
humanistic approach 11–13
humanistic therapy 63–5
hyperventilation 121
hypnosis
   conversion disorder 211–12
hypochondriasis *see* illness anxiety disorder
hysteria 209, 210
   see also conversion disorder

IAPT *see* Increasing Access to Psychological Therapies programme
id 2
ideas of reference 167
illness anxiety disorder 205–7
   DSM-5 diagnostic criteria 228
   prevalence 205
   psychosocial explanations 205–6
   treatment 206–7
immigration influence, adult mental health 37–8
incidence 15
   Alzheimer's disease 212
Increasing Access to Psychological Therapies (IAPT) programme 143
interpersonal psychotherapy 97

Jung, Carl 5–6

latency stage, developmental stage 3
lithium 150
living alone 39–40
longitudinal study 27
looked-after children
   childhood mental health 30–1

MAOIs *see* monoamine oxidase inhibitors
mating mentality 8
mentalities, social 8–9
MET *see* motivational enhancement therapy
meta-analysis 23
methadone, heroin dependence/addiction 186
Minnesota (treatment) model, alcohol addiction 182–3
minority status influence, adult mental health 36–8
monoamine oxidase inhibitors (MAOIs) 51
mood disorders, cognitive behaviour therapy (CBT) 67–70
moral anxiety 4
morbidity 40
motivational enhancement therapy (MET), alcohol addiction 183
motivational interviewing, alcohol addiction 183

naltrexone
   alcohol addiction 182
   autistic spectrum disorder (ASD) 104
   heroin dependence/addiction 186
naso-gastric tube 96
NATS *see* negative automatic thoughts
NEE *see* negative expressed emotion
negative automatic thoughts (NATS) 10, 68–9
negative expressed emotion (NEE) 168–9
negative symptoms 14
neural network 155
neurochemical model 13–17
neurological treatments 57–9
neurons 48–50
neurosteroid 35
neurotic anxiety 4
neurotic-type disorders 35
neurotransmitters 48–50
   see also pharmacotherapy
norepinephrine 49, 50

obsessive-compulsive disorder (OCD) 129–36
   see also body dysmorphic disorder
   biological explanations 131
   DSM-5 diagnostic criteria 230
   psychosocial explanations 131–2
   treatment 134
   working with 135–6
Oedipal conflict 3
old age 41–2
opioid agonists
   alcohol addiction 182
   autistic spectrum disorder (ASD) 104
   heroin dependence/addiction 186
opioids 103
oral stage, developmental stage 2
over-generalization 10

paedophilic disorder 193–7
   conditions 195
   DSM-5 diagnostic criteria 230
   pathways 195–6
   psychosocial explanations 195–6
   treatment 196–7
panic attacks 121
panic disorder 127–9
   biological explanations 128
   DSM-5 diagnostic criteria 228
   psychosocial explanations 128–9
   treatment 129
parental/family influences
   see also family influences
   anxiety 24, 25–6
   childhood mental health 23–8
   single-parent families 27, 39
peer influences, childhood mental health 29–30
personality disorders 105–15
   antisocial personality and psychopathy 111–15
   borderline personality disorder (BPD) 106–11
phallic stage, developmental stage 3
pharmacotherapy 50–4
phenothiazines 14, 53–4
phobias, specific *see specific phobias*
placebo 56–7
planning of behaviour 47
positive symptoms 14, 54
post-traumatic stress disorder (PTSD) 154–61
   biological explanations 155
   childhood mental health 157, 158–9
   completion tendency 156
   drug treatment 160
   DSM-5 diagnostic criteria 230–1
   eye movement desensitization and reprocessing (EMDR) 159–60
   psychosocial explanations 155–7
   situationally accessible memories (SAMs) 156–7
   trauma-focused exposure CBT 157–9
   treatment 157–60
   verbally accessible memories (VAMs) 156–7

poverty of speech 14
prevalence 26
pro-inflammatory cytokines 16
projection, defence mechanism 4
pronoun reversal, autistic spectrum disorder (ASD) 102
pseudophobia 91
pseudoseizures 157
psychoanalysis 62–3
psychoanalytic approach 1–6
psychosis 29, 166–77
  see also schizophrenia
  cannabis dependence 184
psychosurgery 58–9
PTSD *see* post-traumatic stress disorder

reaction formation, defence mechanism 4
reality orientation
  Alzheimer's disease 214–15
reminiscence therapy
  Alzheimer's disease 215
repression, defence mechanism 4, 5
risky behaviours, childhood mental health 30
Rogers, Carl 12–13, 63–5

SAD *see* seasonal affective disorder; separation anxiety disorder
SAMs *see* situationally accessible memories
schema compensation, dysfunctional schemata and behaviour 11
schema maintenance, dysfunctional schemata and behaviour 11
schema models 10–11
schizophrenia 9, 13–17
  see also psychosis
  antipsychotic medication 172–3
  cognitive behaviour therapy (CBT) 174–6, 177
  command hallucinations 175–6
  delusions 169–71
  diagnosing 166–8
  DSM-5 diagnostic criteria 229
  early signs 173–4
  ethnicity influence 36–7
  family influences 39
  family interventions 174
  hallucinations 169–71
  negative expressed emotion (NEE) 168–9
  psychosocial explanations 168–9
  risk 22–3
  risk factors 168–9
  symptoms 166–7
  trauma model 16–17
  treating 53–4
  treatment 172–6
school refusal 90–2
  psychosocial explanations 91
  treatment 92
seasonal affective disorder (SAD) 150–2
  biological explanations 151–2
  treatment 151–2
secure, attachment pattern 7
selective serotonin re-uptake inhibitors (SSRIs) 52–3
self-harm 24, 27, 29
separation anxiety disorder (SAD) 121–2
  DSM-5 diagnostic criteria 228–9
  psychosocial explanations 122
  treatment 122
serotonin 49
serotonin–norepinephrine re-uptake inhibitors (SNRIs) 52–3
sexual abuse, child 26–7, 157
sexuality influence, adult mental health 38
single-parent families
  adult mental health 39
  childhood mental health 27
situationally accessible memories (SAMs) 156–7
SNRIs *see* serotonin–norepinephrine re-uptake inhibitors
social mentalities 8–9
socio-economic factors, childhood mental health 29
socio-economic status influence, adult mental health 33–4
somatic symptom disorder 200–5
  DSM-5 diagnostic criteria 229
  prevalence 201
  psychosocial explanations 202–3
  treatment 203
  working with 204–5
specific phobias 122–5
  biological explanations 123
  DSM-5 diagnostic criteria 230
  psychosocial explanations 123–4
  treatment 124–5
SSRIs *see* selective serotonin re-uptake inhibitors
strategic family therapy 76–7
structural family therapy 74–6
sublimation, defence mechanism 4
suicidal ideation 24, 146
suicide 145–7

assisted suicide 147
prevalence 146
psychosocial explanations 146–7
suicide pacts 146
treatment 147
triggers 146
superego 2

thought alienation 167
thought-stopping 147
TMS *see* transcranial magnetic stimulation
token economy 79
transcranial magnetic stimulation (TMS) 58, 212
transference 62
transvestic disorder 189–91
　see also gender dysphoria
　DSM-5 diagnostic criteria 231
　psychosocial explanations 190–1
　treatment 191

trauma 154–65
　attention-deficit/hyperactivity disorder (ADHD) 84
　dissociative identity disorder (DID) 161–4
　post-traumatic stress disorder (PTSD) 154–61
trauma model
　schizophrenia 16–17
trauma-focused exposure CBT 157–9
tricyclics 52–3

unconditional positive regard, self-actualization 13
undoing, defence mechanism 4

validation therapy, Alzheimer's disease 215
VAMs *see* verbally accessible memories
ventricles (brain) 14
verbally accessible memories (VAMs) 156–7

ABNORMAL AND CLINICAL PSYCHOLOGY
An Introductory Textbook
Third Edition

Paul Bennett

9780335237463 (Paperback)
March 2011

eBook also available

Extensively updated, this popular textbook includes the latest research and therapeutic approaches, including CBT, as well as developments in clinical practice. The book introduces and evaluates the conceptual models of mental health problems and their treatment, and provides valuable analyses of various disorders, such as schizophrenia and paedophilia.

Key features:

- Provides new case formulations to illustrate discussion of clinical work
- Includes new chapter on cognitive theory and therapies
- Lists further reading extended with web links

www.openup.co.uk

OPEN UNIVERSITY PRESS
McGraw - Hill Education